D1084478

Philosophy, History, and the Sciences

By the same author

The Problem of Historical Knowledge: An Answer to Relativism
Philosophy, Science, and Sense Perception: Historical and Critical Studies
The Phenomenology of Moral Experience
History, Man, and Reason: A Study in Nineteenth-Century Thought
The Anatomy of Historical Knowledge

Maurice Mandelbaum

Philosophy, History, and the Sciences

Selected Critical Essays

The Johns Hopkins University Press
Baltimore and London

The Johns Hopkins University Press, Baltimore, Maryland 21218
The Johns Hopkins Press Ltd., London

Library of Congress Cataloging in Publication Data

Mandelbaum, Maurice.
  Philosophy, history, and the sciences.

  Includes index.
  1. Philosophy—Addresses, essays. lectures.
2. History—Philosophy—Addresses, essays, lectures.
3. Science—Philosophy—Addresses, essays, lectures.
I. Title.
B53.M334 1984   100   83-18721
ISBN 0-8018-3112-1

Contents

Preface   *vii*

I Some Problems in the Theory of Knowledge

1   On Doubting and Believing   *3*
2   Definiteness and Coherence in Sense-Perception   *23*
3   Subjective, Objective, and Conceptual Relativisms   *36*
4   Some Instances of the Self-excepting Fallacy   *60*
5   A Note on Emergence   *64*

II Methodology in Historical Studies

6   The Philosophy of History: Some Neglected Philosophic
     Problems Regarding History   *73*
7   Historical Explanation: The Problem of Covering
     Laws   *84*
8   The Presuppositions of Hayden White's *Metahistory*   *97*
9   A Note on Thomas S. Kuhn's *Structure of Scientific
     Revolutions*   *112*
10   The History of Philosophy: Some Methodological
     Issues   *120*
11   Some Forms and Uses of Comparative History   *131*

III Methodology in Psychology and the Social Sciences

12   A Note on "Anthropomorphism" in Psychology   *147*
13   Professor Ryle and Psychology   *150*
14   To What Does the Term *Psychology* Refer?   *158*
15   Societal Facts   *171*
16   Societal Laws   *184*
17   Psychology and Societal Facts   *195*
18   Functionalism in Social Anthropology   *213*
19   A Note on Homans's Functionalism   *241*
20   G. A. Cohen's Defense of Functional Explanation   *247*

IV   **Historical Interpretations**

21   The Distinguishable and the Separable:
     A Note on Hume and Causation   *253*
22   On Interpreting Mill's *Utilitarianism*   *259*
23   Two Moot Issues in Mill's *Utilitarianism*   *272*
24   The Scientific Background of Evolutionary
     Theory in Biology   *289*
25   Darwin's Religious Views   *307*

Name Index   *322*

Preface

The reader of the following essays will note that at several points I refer to the distinction that C. D. Broad drew between critical and speculative philosophy. While such a distinction is not without its difficulties, and while Broad's own characterizations of these two forms of philosophy need not be accepted, the distinction itself is not without use. Each of the following essays belongs within the tradition of critical philosophy.

That tradition, however, has recently come to be more narrowly conceived than it formerly was. At present, there is a tendency to equate it with what is loosely called "analytic philosophy," and "analytic philosophy," in turn, has come to be identified with those forms of thought which evolved out of the aims and methods of Logical Positivism, or else with those usually denominated as Ordinary Language Philosophy. When, however, one recalls the work of Broad himself, and that of Russell, or when one takes account of a number of American philosophers such as Ralph Barton Perry, Morris R. Cohen, or C. J. Ducasse, one will recognize that the two streams of thought currently identified with "analytic philosophy" do not include all that was once properly designated as critical philosophy.

A major difference between most earlier and most later forms of critical philosophy concerns the relationship between philosophy and the sciences. There was a time, not long ago, when philosophers not only were interested in examining the presuppositions, methods, and basic concepts of the sciences but also regarded the results of scientific inquiries as directly relevant to the solution of philosophic issues. This was especially true with respect to the relations between philosophy and psychology. While psychologists qua psychologists might not themselves pose the problems that philosophers were likely to pose, the ongoing investigations psychologists made were widely regarded as relevant to basic philosophic issues, especially in epistemology and ethics. This tradition gradually became attenuated. With the rise of Logical Positivism, the concern of philosophers with the sciences tended to focus more and more on the formal characteristics of scientific inquiry, rather than on the implications of the various sciences for the analysis of traditional philosophic issues. Thus, even within Logical Positivism, there was a tendency to separate empirical problems from philosophic problems. An even sharper line of demarcation was drawn by Ordinary Language Philosophers, who regarded the task of philosophy as being that of conceptual analysis and who distinguished conceptual analysis from any form of empirical inquiry. I regard such attempted distinctions as artificial and untenable, and there are many points in the following essays at which I have deliberately disregarded them.

This disregard is perhaps most apparent in the first two articles, which deal with the data of sense-perception in the context of some problems relevant to the theory of knowledge. The approach in these two articles is, in a broad sense, phenomenological. It belongs to that type of phenomenological analysis (sometimes represented by Scheler, and more often by Moritz Geiger) in which an attempt is made to describe some aspect of direct experience, unprejudiced by antecedently held theories, in order to see what implications such a description might have for some traditional philosophic problem or problems. When tracing these implications, one finds that psychological theories are often extremely relevant, and in these essays, as well as in the essays on Ryle and on Hume, it will be apparent that the point of view I am inclined to accept is the type of Gestalt psychology represented by Wolfgang Köhler's analyses of perception.

While the analysis of sense-perception has always constituted one important aspect of the theory of knowledge, it by no means exhausts the field. Another area in which I have long been interested, and which is the focus of attention in the third and fourth essays, is the view that our claims to knowledge are not to be regarded as true or false in themselves, but are in all cases relative to the standpoint from which they are put forward.

The last of the articles in Part 1 introduces questions concerning the methodology of the sciences, and it, like the articles concerned with relativism, affords a transition to some of the issues with which the essays in Parts 2 and 3 are concerned.

In other places, I have dealt extensively with problems relating to the methodology of historical studies, and I have therefore included in Part 2 only those essays that there were special reasons to include. The first of these essays is an attempt to characterize the basic nature of alternative forms of the philosophy of history. It also serves to suggest the relevance for historical studies of those problems in sociological theory which are raised in some of the articles in Part 3. The second, third, and fourth essays in Part 2 involve critical discussions of the views of others, discussions that are not to be found or are not adequately developed in my other published works. The last two essays in Part 2 are ones that, for me, broke new ground, and they are included for that reason.

More needs to be said, however, concerning the essays in Part 3. They fall into three classes: essays concerned with the nature of psychology as a discipline; essays attempting to show that sociological facts and processes are not to be explained in exclusively psychological terms; and essays concerning the concept of functional explanation as it has been applied in social theory. What especially calls for comment concerning these essays is whether they are descriptive of actual practices or whether their aim is to prescribe what such practices ought to be. In my opinion, the attempt to draw this distinction is frequently apt to be more misleading than helpful, and in the present instance I hold this to be the case. To be sure, if one can adequately explain sociological facts in terms of psychological processes or adequately explain facts concerning society in functional terms, and if no equally adequate alternative explanations can be given, the issue of competing methodologies will be foreclosed. But this has not occurred. As long as it has not occurred, it is useful for methodologists (whether they be labeled "philosophers," or whether they bear any other name) to point out any reasons why it is or is not likely to occur at some future time. The strength of the reasons offered may serve as an effective guide for the direction in which it would be most fruitful for research to move. This is not to prescribe how the social scientist *must* proceed; on the other hand, it is not simply to describe how many or most social scientists *do* proceed. It attempts to expose faults in some programs, in order to suggest that other modes of procedure are more likely to be effective. By their nature, such methodological analyses are neither exclusively descriptive nor arbitrarily prescriptive, but proceed along both lines at once.

The five essays in Part 4 represent attempts to effect an accurate recovery of important aspects of past thought. In such studies my aim has always been to understand the past in its own terms and its own context, rather than viewing it in relation to present beliefs or modes of thought. Unfortunately, this has not recently been the most widely diffused practice among Anglo-American philosophers when dealing with major figures in our philosophic past. Their practice has represented—sometimes explicitly, but more often only implicitly—a special form of historical relativism in which what is taken to be important in the past is only that which has significance for ongoing work in the present. It is of course true that only some present interest will generate inquiry into the past, and that interest may well be a concern with some current philosophic issue. This has in fact been the case in my various discussions of Hume, one of which is included here. On the other hand, such an interest may be purely historical, and it was this that led me to undertake a study of Darwin's religious thought, as well as to inquire into the extent to which the state of the sciences at the time provided a background for the reception of his theory. Alternatively, a historical inquiry may originate out of more than one concern, as did my essays on Mill. Having studied his associationism and various aspects of his thought in other contexts, I became convinced that Mill could not have been as philosophically obtuse as many criticisms of his ethical theory implied that he was. I therefore set about reviewing *Utilitarianism* in the light of his psychological assumptions and in relation to various formative influences on his thought. Thus, while the originating motive for some study of the past may be of various kinds, in no case is it proper to judge its accuracy in terms of its original motivation. In fact, in my own inquiries—and especially in a study I once made of Locke's theory of knowledge—there have been times when what I set out to show proved to be false, and the results I reached were far different from those I had anticipated. Thus, my own practice has fortified the belief, which runs through several of these essays, that relativistic attacks on the objectivity of historical knowledge are in large measure misguided.

I have taken the liberty of prefixing a brief paragraph regarding the origin of each essay to the notes accompanying that essay. This will, I hope, help to indicate connections among the various essays and will in addition suggest some of the relations they bear to my other work.

I

Some Problems in the Theory of Knowledge

1

On Doubting and Believing

"Seeing is believing" is a phrase with which we are all familiar. On the other hand, near the beginning of a well-known book entitled *Perception* one finds the statement, "When I see a tomato there is much that I can doubt."[1] This essay is concerned with believing and doubting, and I shall begin where these two remarks would lead you to expect me to begin: with a discussion of doubt and belief as they occur with respect to the testimony of our senses. What I hope to establish in considering such cases will then lead me to formulate some tentative suggestions regarding the bases of belief in other, wider contexts as well. Although my approach to these problems is in large measure both phenomenologically and psychologically oriented, diverging therein from most recent philosophic discussions of belief, the claim that I shall initially advance concerning the relations of doubt and belief is by no means unprecedented, having also been pressed in different ways by Peirce and by Wittgenstein. I shall be claiming that doubt is always parasitic on belief, that belief precedes doubt, not only temporally, but also in the logical sense that every act of doubting presupposes a full acceptance of one or more other beliefs, such that if these beliefs were themselves to be doubted no reason would remain for the doubt that was initially entertained. Peirce put his view of the matter succinctly in one of his many criticisms of Descartes' method of doubt when he said, "We cannot begin with complete doubt. . . . A person may, it is true, in the course of his studies, find reason to doubt what he began by believing; but in that case he doubts because he has a positive reason for it."[2] This, as I shall now show, is a justified claim with respect to each of the stages through which Descartes' doubt proceeded in his *Meditations.*

In the *Meditations,* as you may recall, Descartes began his methodological doubt with doubts concerning sense-perception, because he found that in some instances his senses had deceived him. It was his contention that even though his senses might not always deceive him, the fact that they were sometimes deceptive was a sufficient reason for distrusting them. As he said, "It is wiser not to trust entirely to any thing by which we have once been deceived." Let us, however, look at one case to which Descartes himself alludes in his sixth *Meditation.* There he refers to a tower that appears to be round when seen from a distance, but is later seen to be square when viewed from closer at hand. In such a case, in order to characterize our earlier

3

experience as having been deceptive, three assumptions must be made. First, we must hold that this particular tower, which we are now seeing, is not in fact round; second, we must assume that what we saw from a distance is the same tower which we are now seeing; and, third, we must assume that towers, unlike some objects, such as hedgehogs, do not change shape as we approach them. In the absence of any one of these assumptions, it could not be claimed that our senses had deceived us. Yet, the sole basis on which each of these assumptions rests is to be found in sense-experience. Thus, it is only because we accept some of the testimony of our senses as trustworthy that we are in a position to reject other experiences as illusory. On what basis we grant precedence to some forms of sense-experience rather than to others will later occupy me. First, however, I must proceed to a second argument which Descartes offered for doubting what was presented to him in sense-experience: the fact that in dreams he often supposed himself to have been in familiar surroundings when in fact he had been asleep.

This argument, too, is directed against the trustworthiness of sense-experience, and it, too, rests on assumptions that contradict the general thesis it is designed to prove. In this case, however, the contradiction is less immediately obvious, and we must examine the presuppositions of the argument more closely. In this connection, we must first note that Descartes could not seek to undermine our reliance on sense-experience through appealing to dreams if he did not from the outset assume that a distinction of some kind is to be drawn between actually seeing, hearing, and touching objects and whatever is occurring in dreams. At this point Descartes noted that our waking experiences are clearer and more distinct than our dreams, but he rejected that difference as capable of authenticating waking experience. As he said, "There are no certain indications by which we may distinguish wakefulness from sleep."[3] Nevertheless, one finds that he did in fact assign precedence to waking experience, for why else should he have said in *Recherche de la verité,* "How can you be certain that your life is not a perpetual dream and all that you imagine you learn by means of your senses is not as false now as it is when you sleep?"[4] Yet, had Descartes really assumed that both types of experience are equally convincing, why view as *false* that which occurs in dreams? Bernard Williams has suggested one basis for doing so: the fact that following a dream we awaken in our own room, in our own bed.[5] On awakening, we reject what we have dreamt, no matter how convincing it was at the time, because we cannot have been where we dreamt we were, nor could we have done the things we had dreamt we had done, unless we believe—contrary to all our other experience—that where we are at one moment, and how we then act, is discontinuous with the situations in which we find ourselves at the next moment. Thus, in order to characterize dreams as false, Descartes must have accepted the truth of a particular set of sense-experiences: those which occurred on his awakening. But on what must that acceptance have been based? If Descartes was indeed serious in denying that we can distinguish between dreams and waking experience in terms of how clearly we apprehend what is present in each, he must have relied on some other criterion. Near the end of the sixth *Meditation* he suggests what that criterion was: the coherence of waking experience as contrasted with dreams.[6] Thus, his willingness to characterize dreams as illusory rested on a blief that the regularities among natural events with which he was acquainted in waking experience provided evidence that those events were not illusory. Thus, the dream argument fails to avoid the charge that I have levelled against Descartes: in this case, too, his doubt could only arise insofar as he had antecedently accepted another set of beliefs as true.

It was not, however, by appealing to specific illusions in sense-experience, nor by introducing his argument from dreams, that Descartes ultimately sought to undermine all faith in the senses. For that purpose he feigned the hypothesis that a malignant demon might be deceiving him, implanting in him thoughts that led him to believe that his sense-experience informed him of objects existing in an external, independent world, even though no such objects did in fact exist. I shall now try to show that in this hypothesis Descartes again relied on assumptions that were incompatible with the doubts he wished to instill.[7]

Why, we may ask, did Descartes hold that his thoughts were deceptive if they had in fact been implanted in him by the demon? It could only be because his direct experience carried no hint that there was a demon causing him to see, hear, touch, taste, or smell what he was perceiving; on the contrary, his experience seemed to depend directly on the existence of a world of objects which appeared to be independent of him. To be sure, not all of our ideas have this characteristic: we distinguish, for example, between *seeing* something and remembering or imagining it. As Descartes suggested near the end of the *Meditations*, our ideas of sense are livelier, clearer, and in a way more distinct than are those of memory or imagination. Furthermore, they differ with respect to the fact that we have a lesser degree of control over them. As he says, "I found by experience that these ideas presented themselves to me without my consent being requisite, so that I could not perceive any object, however desirous I might be, unless it were present to the organs of sense; and it was not in my power not to perceive it, when it was present."[8] Here Descartes obviously presupposed a causal theory of perception, in which what we perceive depends upon the functioning of our sense-organs, and this is in fact the test that he cannot, in the end, avoid using. He could not simply appeal to liveliness, clarity, and distinctness in order to distinguish between perceiving and, say, remembering, because some memory-images possess these characteristics in a very high degree. For example, the memory of a faux pas one has just committed may displace any clear awareness of what one is presently seeing, hearing, or tasting. Nor is it merely the involuntariness of our sense-perception which distinguishes perceiving from remembering or imagining, because there are many occasions on which our thoughts and our memories come to us unsought and seem to be as little under our control as are our sense-perceptions. Thus, it is the role of the senses in perception which Descartes must stress, and even though he does not develop his causal theory of perception until the sixth *Meditation,* that theory was presupposed by him all along. Had he not assumed it, he could not have claimed that if his ideas had been implanted in him by the demon they would not, like a dream, be false. In short, he could only use the demon hypothesis to cast doubt on our sense-perceptions because it contradicted another theory that he did not doubt: the causal theory of perception which he had developed in his earlier work, particularly in the first chapter of *Le Monde* and the sixth *Discourse* of his *Optics.* That Descartes claimed that only an appeal to God's existence provided an escape from doubt should not be allowed to obscure the point that at every stage in his methodological doubt, including his use of the demon hypothesis, his argument presupposed the truth of a causal theory of perception. In fact, even in terms of his own argument, Descartes was saved from skepticism regarding the senses only because God's veracity guarantees that our perceptions are in fact caused by the existence of an independent, external world.[9]

I

Using the *Meditations* as an example, I have argued that the phenomenon of doubt only arises on the basis of one or more antecedently accepted beliefs.[10] But on what does the phenomenon of belief itself depend? Unfortunately, this is not a point on which our philosophical literature is particularly rich. One type of theory was Descartes', which held that belief is a function not of the intellect but of the will. Theories of this type rest on the fact that our understanding of a particular proposition does not, of itself, seem to determine how we respond to it. Among our various possible responses, however, only two are directly relevant to the concept of belief; these are affirmation or denial (or their derivatives). Because it appears possible for a person who understands a proposition to either affirm or deny it, it would seem that something more than the understanding is involved in belief. This additional element Descartes identified as an act of will.

For a variety of reasons, which we need not here disentangle, both Hobbes and Spinoza rejected Descartes' attempt to separate the understanding from the will. Spinoza's theory was explicitly developed in his *Treatise on the Improvement of the Understanding* and later served as basis for his theory of the emotions. He held that every idea had its own inherent force, or *conatus,* and that the movement of thought, like the movement of material bodies, continues unchecked until some other force opposes it. Thus, he maintained that any idea is believed insofar as it occupies the mind and will continue to be believed until some incompatible idea arises to oppose it. In order to accommodate those cases in which belief is suspended—for example, when we entertain fictions, or regard something as possible without believing it—he held that a balance of forces may be present to our minds, and when this occurs neither idea carries conviction. Thus, Spinoza held that even such cases should not lead us to accept the Cartesian theory that belief involves a separate act of will. For him, as for Hegel, ideas carry their own conviction.

A different view of belief, but one equally opposed to that of Descartes, was held by Hume.[11] Like Spinoza, he denied that belief involves any special act of the mind, but he differed from Spinoza in regarding belief as a feeling that attaches to some of our ideas but not to others. He attempted to explain the conditions responsible for this feeling. Unfortunately, however, his analysis did not clearly explicate the foundation on which it rested. As I now propose to show, once its real basis is recognized, one can see that he had in fact left the crucial issue where it was when he started.

From the very outset, Hume had distinguished between impressions and ideas; impressions are more forceful and vivacious than ideas and come to us via the senses. Ideas, on the other hand, arise through memory or through the imagination and are always based on prior impressions. In discussing belief, that with which Hume was concerned was not our impressions: he took it for granted that these invariably carry conviction. On the other hand, he held that only some of our ideas are accompanied by belief. What he sought to explain was why belief attaches to what we remember and to some of the ideas for which he held the imagination accountable. His explanation rested on an appeal to a bond of association which connected the idea of something we are not directly experiencing with some vivacious present impression. It was from the vivacity of the present impression that the idea received its own vivacity, eliciting belief. Whether or not this is a plausible account is not my concern. I merely wish to point out that in Hume's explanation of why belief attaches to *some* of our ideas he depends upon the assumption that it attaches to *all* of our impressions. However, he did not raise the question as to why these impressions evoke belief. Therefore, he cannot be credited with having propounded a comprehensive account of the conditions on which, in all cases, belief depends.

Of course, it may be impossible to push this question beyond the point at which Hume left it. It might conceivably be futile to try to discover anything concerning our impressions which accounts for the fact that they are accompanied by belief. Perhaps, in Samuel Alexander's phrase, we must simply accept this fact "with natural piety." This Hume apparently did. In most cases he spoke as if the force and vivacity of our impressions was enough to account for the feeling of belief. Also, as we have noted, in explaining why belief attaches to some ideas, he relied on the force and vivacity with which a present impression imbues those ideas. Thus, Hume wished to hold that in all cases it is force and vivacity which are responsible for belief. Yet, as we have already noted in discussing Descartes, in some cases an *idea*, such as the memory-image of a faux pas, can eclipse our present impressions because of its greater force and vivacity. Hume himself admitted the existence of similar cases when, in the first paragraph of the *Treatise,* he mentioned the delusions that may accompany a fever or arise when a person is otherwise deranged. In such cases, Hume could not appeal solely to force and vivacity as providing the basis for belief. Instead, like Descartes, he appealed to the fact that our *impressions* depend on how our sense-organs are being affected, whereas our *ideas* do not.[12] The question therefore arises whether Hume should have relied on force and vivacity alone to account for belief in our impressions or whether he should have added that what we regard as impressions *always* involve the operation of our sense-organs. Unfortunately, his initial acceptance of a phenomenalistic approach prevented him from attempting to solve the problem the latter way. In what follows, this is the approach I shall take.

Let us start from the point that the first section of this paper attempted to establish: that belief is prior to doubt. This entails that we believe that which we directly experience, unless some other experience awakens our doubt.[13] But what is to be meant by "direct experience"? (In characterizing it, let me say that I wish to remain within the realm of direct experience itself, regardless of any traditional philosophic problems associated with the terms I use.) Perhaps the first thing to say in characterizing direct experience is that whatever we experience is experienced as being "somewhere": in some portion of the surrounding space in which we find ourselves, in our bodies, or among the thoughts we are experiencing in our minds. So far as immediate experience is concerned, the attitude that we characterize as belief is typically connected with what we experience as existing outside ourselves. It is a state of acceptance of what is presented to us. Though we are also directly aware of states of our own bodies and are aware of our thoughts, we are not apt to describe them as objects in which we *believe.*[14] They are present to us, but not *presented* to us. Alternatively, we may say that while the objects we see, feel, or hear are present *for* us, they are not present *to* us in the same sense as are our bodily states or our ideas. Thus, I wish to draw an initial phenomenological distinction between experiences that refer to objects outside us and the experience we have of our own inner states and of our ideas. Insofar as "vivacity" alone is concerned, no distinction need be drawn between these types of experience, nor can it in all cases be drawn. There is, however, a decided difference with respect to *where* that which we experience appears. Objects, as distinct from our ideas and from our inner sensations, are experienced as outside us, at some more or less definite location in the space around us.[15] While we are not aware of precisely how such experience is related to the activity of our sense-organs, our behavior testifies to the fact that we recognize a direct connection between these organs and our ability to experience the presence of objects. To see an object, we know we must look at it; to feel it, we much touch it; and we also recognize that when we hear, smell, or taste something, what we hear, smell, or taste comes through the channels of our senses. To be sure, in the latter cases, in which the localization of our percepts is less precise than it is in the case of sight (or in most cases of touch), we may be puzzled as to whether we are really hearing, smelling, or tasting what we think we are: in Hume's phrase, we are not certain whether what we are experiencing is an impression or an idea. To distinguish between impressions and ideas in such cases, we are indeed apt to appeal to Hume's criterion of force and vivacity. It is also to be noted that even when we do not have to rely on this criterion to distinguish between impressions and ideas, a difference of the same sort usually exists. It is only rarely that an idea has the force and vivacity that my impressions have when I directly attend to objects in the surrounding world. Thus, even though force and vivacity, when taken alone, fail to provide an adequate criterion for distinguishing between impressions and ideas, one can see why Hume's original account had the degree of plausibility it did.

When I say that unless some other experience contradicts it, we believe whatever is directly presented to us, it may be thought that I have not advanced the problem of belief beyond the point at which Hume left it. Apparently, like Hume, I simply accept the brute fact that belief is an attitude that characterizes some forms of our experience and not others.[16] Yet, there is a fundamental difference between these approaches. Hume's account stressed only the subjective pole of the experience—the force and vivacity with which impressions strike us—whereas in my account, as we shall now see, it is not the force and vivacity of our experience which are primary in evoking belief; rather, belief naturally attaches to our experience of objects in which certain characteristics are present.[17]

What are these characteristics? In the first place, as I have noted, objects of direct experience which evoke belief appear as external to us, and this carries with it a sense that they are independent of us.[18] It is not, however, merely to these features that we must look for the force and vivacity to which Hume appealed in distinguishing between impressions and ideas; there are, in addition, two other features that characterize our experience of external, independent objects, features that are lacking when our experience is confined to the realm of "ideas." These characteristics I have elsewhere termed *definiteness* and *coherence*.[19]

By *definiteness* I refer to our experience of perceived objects in which the object as perceived is clearly set off from its background, and in which those of its qualities which are perceived to be present are themselves clearly perceived.[20] In speaking of *coherence,* I shall be referring to coherence among various perceptions of one and the same object (whether through the same or different sense-modalities), and not to coherence in any broader sense of that term, such as whether what is perceived fits coherently into a theory or fits with what we otherwise believe. Thus, the coherence with which I am concerned is the coherence of the various aspects of an object, and not necessarily its coherence with other accepted facts. Let me now briefly illustrate my view that definiteness is a characteristic of our perception of external objects.

I shall first direct attention to our visual experience of objects, because vision is the easiest form of sensory experience to describe. One of its ubiquitous characteristics is the figure-ground relationship: whatever we perceive as an object is set off against a background and is seen as distinct from that background. When it is not, its object-character disappears. We can point to an object and say, "It is there"; and if someone does not see it, we trace its outline for him, setting it off from its background.[21] Although we can also indicate the general location of inner sensations, such as a pain, these objects of awareness to not have equally sharp contours that differentiate them from the background of whatever other sensations accompany them. Furthermore, we cannot separately inspect, one by one, the individual features of what we experience as our inner states, though this is one important factor that contributes to definiteness in our visual perception of objects.[22]

Not only do inner sensations lack these attributes of definiteness, but memory-images and thoughts, such as desires, hopes, and plans, do so as well. In the first place, these sensations are not experienced as having a specific location—except "in our thoughts." Furthermore, inner sensations lack the more or less precise contours that, because of the figure-ground relationship, seen objects possess. Instead, they either tend to occupy the whole field of our attention, for the moment excluding definite awareness of anything else or they are experienced as part of a flow of thought in which no sharp boundaries are present. Thus, even though we can in many cases summon up clear and detailed memory-images, neither they nor our other thoughts stand out against their backgrounds as do objects actually seen. To this extent memory-images or thoughts are less definite, and consequently strike us as less firm and vivid and usually as less forceful, than what is seen.

What has been said with special reference to vision can also be said, though with less assurance, with respect to our other sense-modalities. That the various phenomena to which I have been referring are less prominent in other forms of perception should not occasion surprise. While touch in many instances approximates vision with respect to these characteristics, what comes to us via our other sense-modalities usually does not. For example, it is through vision and touch, rather than through sound, odor, or taste, that we most sharply and precisely locate objects as existing independently of us in an external world. Furthermore, the figure-ground relationship is more prominent in vision than it is in any other form of perception, even touch. Also, in the case of forms of perception other than vision, it is difficult for most people to hold clearly before their minds the distinctive characteristics of that which they are perceiving.[23] Nevertheless, the force and vivacity that Hume attributed to our impressions, as compared to our ideas, seems also to hold with respect to these other forms of perception. This, I think, may be accounted for by the heightened role that is played by our sense-organs in these experiences. In vision, we are not immediately aware of the fact that our eyes are being affected by that which we see: we only know that we must look in order to see. In touch, on the contrary, we are immediately aware of being directly affected by that which we are touching: the greater the firmness or resistance we feel, the greater is our assurance that what we are touching is real—in Hume's phrase, that it is an impression and not merely an idea. Such experiences are aptly described by speaking of force and vivacity, calling attention to the fact that we recognize them as impinging directly upon us. This characteristic is sufficient to lend a degree of definiteness to these sensations of touch, for they stand out in awareness, leading us to focus attention on them. The same connection between the qualities of objects and our responses to them seems to hold with respect to taste and to smell, and even with respect to what we hear. In the case of hearing, for example, loud or strident noises call attention to themselves and are forceful in a way that the softest of sounds are not. In such cases, therefore, we feel more certain that we are actually hearing, and not merely imagining, that which we take ourselves to be hearing. Thus, in many cases, the particular qualities of that which we are perceiving are responsible for the force and vivacity of our impressions, and it is this force and vivacity that lend them the definiteness that, as I have argued, is the hallmark we implicitly use in distinguishing between perceiving objects and merely thinking about them.

Let us now turn to the characteristic of *coherence* in perception. When we take ourselves to be seeing some object, we expect to be able to touch it and find that what we feel does not contradict what we see. For example, we expect that a stick that looks straight will feel straight, or that an object that looks smooth will feel smooth.[24] Similarly, when it is solely a question of sight, we expect that if we view the same object from a continuous series of changing perspectives, there will be acceptable transitions, rather than radical discrepancies, between what we see from any two successive perspectives. Such continuities in experience are not, I submit, generally present in our dream life, which is why even the most vivid dream-states do not, when we recall them, have the same mark of authenticity as attaches to our experience of objects in the external world. This holds true not only with respect to dreams but also with respect to processes of thought. We do not find it contradictory or even unexpected to think of one thing at one moment and in the next instant to think of something else. When, however, the flow of our perceptual experience is characterized by similar discontinuities, it engenders doubt. Thus, while definiteness leads to an initial and unquestioning acceptance of what is being experienced, any lack of coherence among our impressions of an object challenges that acceptance, and belief gives way to doubt. This, of course, is what Spinoza held, but the test of coherence with which he was concerned was broader than that which I am presently using. For Spinoza, nothing short of the total network of beliefs was ultimately needed in order to distinguish between that which is fictional or merely possible and that which is true. So far, however, it is solely with coherence as it applies to the various aspects of perceived objects that I have been concerned.

While it may seem self-stultifying to have restricted the problem in this way, it has, I believe, one advantage: it helps us to understand why, in specific instances, we trust one particular sense-impression rather than another.

This is a problem with which I have dealt elsewhere: there I attempted to show that definiteness and coherence provide the reasons why we in some cases trust touch rather than sight, whereas in others we trust sight rather than touch. In the course of my treatment of that issue, light was also cast on some facts that have frequently arisen in epistemological discussions: for example, that we differentiate between the "real" qualities that objects possess when they are seen under so-called normal conditions, and the qualities they merely *seem* to possess when they are seen under other conditions.[25] Of greater importance, however, was the thesis that, in some cases at least, the distinction we draw between reliable and unreliable observations is a distinction found within experience itself. This is a point not generally recognized; on the contrary, it is commonly believed that the acceptance of what is observed in one case rather than in another always depends on at least a tacit appeal to some theory, rather than being decided in terms of the characteristics of the objects observed. Assuming for the moment that my view is plausible, I now wish to suggest that it can be extended by analogy to another problem not generally discussed. That problem concerns scientific inquiry; it may briefly be put in the form of a question, Why is it that some hypotheses are accepted with great assurance after only a limited number of trials, whereas in other cases we demand a vast array of data before we take the hypothesis to be reasonably well confirmed?[26]

II

This raises the issue of how observation and theory are related within the context of scientific inquiry. I take it as being now universally accepted that, in science, observation does not proceed independently of theory.[27] Nevertheless, any scientific theory must always, at some point, appeal to observation for its validation. To be sure, no theory—and, indeed, not even a severely limited hypothesis—is justified by any single observation, nor by any set of repeated observations, taken alone. In testing even limited hypotheses, not only must observations be repeated, but they must be repeated under varying conditions, and in testing a general theory a wide variety of observations must usually be brought into play. When the question is raised as to what range of observations is likely to be adequate in supporting either a hypothesis or a theory, it is generally assumed that the better a hypothesis or theory coheres with already accepted hypotheses or theories, the less additional observational evidence is needed to give it support. Yet, were nothing more to be said about the matter, it would be difficult to account for some revolutionary changes that have occurred in the sciences when new observations and new hypotheses have subverted previously accepted, well-entrenched beliefs. In such cases there may be a valid reason, other than the coherence of a hypothesis with other hypotheses, which justifies our acceptance of it. Such a reason would be the apparent conclusiveness of the evidence in its favor. What I now wish to suggest is that criteria similar to those we use in sifting our perceptual experience also apply to the relation between a hypothesis and the evidence in favor of it. In examining this issue, I shall restrict my attention to questions concerning the acceptance of hypotheses of limited scope, because the most readily applicable criterion that is used in validating general theories or even broadly applicable hypotheses is the range over which they have explanatory power. With respect to more limited hypotheses, the question of range does not arise; instead, I shall argue, we find analogues to the definiteness and coherence on the basis of which our sense-perceptions are assessed.[28]

Let us first consider in what sense an analogue to definiteness can be said to be applicable to the relation between a hypothesis and its evidence.

It will be recalled that when applied to perceptual experience, the concept of definiteness referred to two aspects of that which is perceived: its distinctness from other objects in the perceived environment and the clarity with which its individual parts were themselves perceived. Insofar as we are concerned with limited hypotheses only, there is an analogue to the first aspect in the self-limiting nature of the hypothesis: it is formulated to apply only to some verifiable relationships that occur in the entities with which it deals. Consequently, as confirmatory evidence accumulates in favor of that hypothesis, one can have greater confidence in its adequacy than would be the case if a broader set of data was assumed to be directly relevant to it. To be sure, the restricted and relatively closed nature of a limited hypothesis has disadvantages, because its range of explanatory power will itself be limited by the range of materials to which it is intended to apply. In extreme cases, the limitations placed on a hypothesis may trivialize it: it may apply to so few cases, and they may be so similar, that it will do little more than codify observations already made. Recognizing this fact, I am not arguing that the formulation and testing of very limited hypotheses provides a model as to how science should proceed; I am merely calling attention to the fact that in the case of such hypotheses we have greater assurance of their accuracy than we have with respect to hypotheses broader in scope.

To be sure, if this were all that definiteness meant when applied to limited hypotheses, our assurance would have been purchased at too high a price. Definiteness, however, has a second aspect: the elements that are recognized can themselves be attended to individually, and can be clearly perceived. The analogue of this aspect of perceptual definiteness is the fact that a limited hypothesis receives its confirmation through a series of independent observations and experiments that bear directly on it. Unlike broad hypotheses and general theories, in which the relevant evidence consists in more or less widely scattered facts, the evidence for a limited hypothesis can be more readily inspected, and its bearing on the truth of the hypothesis more directly ascertained.

The aspect of definiteness, as thus defined, would not account for the degree of assurance which may be accorded a limited hypothesis: in addition, that assurance depends on the internal coherence through which such a hypothesis is related to its evidence taken as a whole. In very broad hypotheses and in general theories, facts cited as evidence are likely to be extremely varied, often bearing little relationship to one another except that each is held to be related to the hypothesis or theory it helps to confirm. In limited hypotheses, however, links can be seen between the various fragments of evidence, so that they form a closely knit structure supporting the hypothesis that they confirm. When each observation and each experiment provides a different but related view of the same process, the evidence in favor of the hypothesis appears as a coherent whole. Therefore, unless the accuracy of some of the observations or experiments is challenged, or unless it can be shown that they are not to be interpreted as proving what they are thought to prove, a limited hypothesis would seem to be invulnerable to doubt: its truth would seem to be thoroughly perspicuous — that is, *evident* — so that we feel no need to appeal to further experience in order to take it as confirmed.[29] In such cases, we are likely to feel forced to accept the hypothesis even if we cannot see how it is to be assimilated into other, previously accepted beliefs. Thus, a single, limited hypothesis may sometimes cast doubt on even the most deeply entrenched beliefs, causing us to modify, reformulate, or abandon them.

Such cases attest to an asymmetry between the probative value of what we take to be established by observation or experiment and the networks of theory through which these are interpreted.[30] It is not the case, as has sometimes been suggested, that one can always legitimately discount an observed fact through appealing to a theory, rather than discounting the theory because of an observed fact.[31] To be sure, scientists will sometimes retain hypotheses even when not all relevant observations appear to be in conformity with them, but this is regarded as a temporary and transitional stage in inquiry which remains to be resolved. Even initially, some facts resist reinterpretative dismissals more tenaciously than do others, and negative experimental findings are not in all cases readily dismissed. In my view, such differences are not to be explained solely in terms of pragmatic considerations, but are based on the solidity of our faith in the adequacy of a given observation and on the degree of conviction which particular experiments carry. These — if I am correct — depend in no small measure on the factors of definiteness and coherence with which I have been concerned.[32]

This view, however inadequately it has been sketched, has parallels when applied beyond sense-perception and beyond scientific inquiry to wider issues of philosophic and religious belief. In these areas, one is dealing with interpretive theories more comprehensive than any scientific theory can be, because they always presuppose one or another attitude toward science itself. I would hold that in such theories, no less than in scientific theories, there may be an asymmetry between the strength of conviction that attaches to some particular experience or belief and the assurance accorded the theory as a whole. In such cases, these experiences or beliefs constitute, so to speak, nodal points in the total web of belief. When these beliefs seem unassailable in themselves, the fact that a particular philosophic system or religious *Weltanschauung* cannot comfortably assimilate other ranges of fact will not immediately lead its adherents to change it. Rather, an attempt will be made to reinterpret the obtrusive facts in a way that accommodates them to the theory, or the hope will be held out that such will ultimately prove to be the case. Alternatively, the theory itself may be partially reinterpreted, with some of its aspects no longer regarded as essential to it. One does not initially surrender whatever experience or belief originally evoked a feeling of deep commitment. In short, as Walter Bagehot contended, there is an "emotion of conviction" attaching to some experiences or beliefs which is not only resistant to change, but is itself capable of shutting off the consideration of alternative interpretations.[33] Both the critics of religion and its most fervent supporters will acknowledge the existence and strength of such religious experiences and beliefs. For the believer, the emotion is an appropriate one, because the experiences that have aroused it are of the highest worth. On the other hand, people who are hostile to a specific religion (or, perhaps, to all religions) do not acknowledge the value of these experiences, and they therefore contend that it is nothing but the emotion of conviction which has rendered the believers blind to argument. Parallel situations must be acknowledged to arise in philosophy. In many cases, the defenders of a philosophic system are unwilling, under any circumstances, to relinquish the beliefs that constitute the foundations of their system, and their opponents are unwilling to acknowledge the primacy (or, perhaps, even the truth) of these beliefs. When such situations arise in either religion or philosophy, the opponents of a system are more apt to denounce the phenomenon than to understand it; they are likely to fail to see that what is at stake need not be blind adherence to a system, as a system, but the depth of conviction attaching to some particular experience or belief. Such tenacity is not in all cases to be deprecated. As we noted in the case of scientific inquiry, it is sometimes fortunate that we stubbornly adhere to what appears to be unassailably important or true, even though it does not conform to a theory that would otherwise be acceptable. Such stubbornness helps to forestall our frequent willingness to neglect recalcitrant facts. To be sure, if the emotion of conviction attaching to some experiences or beliefs were wholly immune to criticism, it would be impossible—even in principle—to adjudicate the claims of conflicting systems of philosophic or religious thought. It is therefore important to see what can effectively raise doubts concerning such systems.

If we cast our minds back to the model of doubt provided by Descartes, we will recall that he followed the method of doubt because he wished to reject any beliefs which might possibly be false. This not only was the stance he adopted with respect to questions concerning the veracity of sense-perception but was the reason why he attempted to reject all of his former beliefs and make an absolutely new philosophic beginning. While his account of this process in his *Discourse on method* is notoriously inaccurate, one point that it repeatedly stressed need not be rejected: Descartes' doubt proceeded from his dissatisfaction with the conflicts he found in the opinions of others. If we may place any trust whatsoever in his account, he was clearly unwilling to accept any of the alternative views with which he was familiar, and this would seem to imply—contrary to what I have argued —that, in his case at least, doubt did not presuppose belief. Yet, when we view the path he chose as a means of escaping from doubt, rebuilding his own philosophic system, we find that he did employ a criterion of truth which he did not doubt; this criterion, exemplified in mathematics, was the clarity and distinctness of the ideas and the propositions that his mind apprehended.[34] Thus, I would contend that in his case, as in others, doubt always presupposes the acceptance of some more fundamental belief.

I find this case illuminating with respect to the problem of how it is possible effectively to criticize a philosophic theory. One cannot, I submit, do so simply by finding points at which that theory is either unclear or internally inconsistent, unless these points are integrally related to the basic tenets of that theory. Such basic tenets may be found either in its presuppositions or in its necessary consequences. The fact that the acceptability of a theory will rest on the acceptability of its presuppositions is, I should suppose, obvious. It is no less certain, however, that its acceptability also rests on its consequences, whether these be intellectual or moral. To appeal to the consequences of a theory in testing its truth does not necessarily entail the acceptance of a pragmatic theory of truth, nor does an appeal to its moral as well as its intellectual consequences necessarily lead one to accept William James's position regarding the relevance of moral concerns to the solution of intellectual problems. The extent to which it is appropriate to appeal to presuppositions rather than to consequences and to appeal primarily to intellectual or to moral consequences will vary from system to system. When one considers the system of Descartes, for example, one's dissatisfaction is far less likely to be focussed on any intellectual or moral consequences it may have than on its presuppositions and especially on its presuppositions regarding method. On the other hand, it is probably true that more critics of the Kantian system have been dissatisfied with its intellectual consequences, and more critics of materialism dissatisfied with its moral consequences, than they have been with the presuppositions of either of these systems. Be this as it may, the presuppositions and the consequences of a philosophic system constitute the points at which these systems must be criticized, if they are to be effectively criticized at all. So long as neither is effectively challenged, the web of belief can remain intact, needing only internal adjustments. On the other hand, when we regard either the presuppositions or consequences of a system as having been falsified, the system itself will no longer carry conviction. Therefore, I now wish very briefly to consider the basis on which either the presuppositions or the consequences of a philosophic system can be effectively criticized.

What must first be said is that it is not effective to criticize the presuppositions of a system from a point of view based on a different set of presuppositions. To undermine a system's own presuppositions one must bring to bear some facts that those accepting these presuppositions cannot explain in terms of their own system. One must, in short, cut through the claims and counterclaims of alternative systems, appealing to identifiable phenomena that await interpretation, rather than appealing to one's preference regarding how these phenomena may be interpreted. For example, if we consider Descartes' view that the clear and distinct ideas that are to be found in the axioms of geometry and in other necessary truths provide us with an unassailable criterion of truth, we can see that this presupposition must be abandoned, because *some* truths can be shown to be necessary merely because they are analytic propositions. To be sure, this does not prove that *all* necessary truths are analytic, but it does subvert the claim that clarity and distinctness constitute an adequate criterion of truth when we seek to deal with matters of fact. Similarly, if one is to confute Descartes' other presuppositions, such as his axiom of substance,[35] one must find instances in which they prove to be unacceptable even to those who would in other cases be willing to accept them. This, of course, is more easily said than done, insofar as convincing the actual proponents of a system is concerned. Nevertheless, it is a method that can carry conviction to people who would otherwise be sympathetic to a given system, or who, in search of some set of beliefs which will be philosophically adequate, are willing to examine the system before being inclined to commit themselves to it. Persons who recognize the strength of the emotion of conviction should not be inclined to insist that an argument's failure to overcome belief is to be taken as proof that the argument was fallacious or even that it was weak.

The same may be said with respect to arguments based on the consequences of a system. Insofar as intellectual consequences are concerned, one may of course attempt to show that the system engenders an inconsistent set of necessary consequences, as has often been claimed with respect to Kant's attempt to solve the antinomy between determinism and free-will. In most cases, however, such apparent inconsistencies will already have been foreseen by those who develop the system, and will have been interpreted in a way that is claimed to obviate any genuine inconsistency. That, of course, was Kant's view regarding his reconciliation of determinism and free-will. Such a defense can only be countered if one can show that there is some precisely definable set of facts which is incompatible with at least one of the system's consequences. To be effective, such an argument cannot rest on a prior acceptance of an alternative theory, but must constitute an appeal to facts which the proponent of the system will be able neither to deny nor adequately to explain in terms of his own system.

If this is difficult with respect to the intellectual consequences of a philosophic system—as I readily grant that it is—it becomes even more difficult with respect to its moral consequences. One need not accept either moral relativism or moral skepticism to acknowledge that different individuals possess different ideals of life, and this is probably no less true of philosophers than of others. Such ideals are not to be thought of as free-floating systems or as the necessary consequences of one or another intellectual conviction; in general, they are rooted in some particular form or forms of experience which the individual holds to be of primary worth. To change such convictions through argument is difficult; some would hold it to be impossible. Whatever may be the truth in this matter, it is surely no easier, and probably much harder, to criticize a philosophic system adequately in terms of its moral consequences than it is to criticize it in any other way, because the emotion of conviction seems to be particularly strong with respect to fundamental moral beliefs. Though intellectual argument can sometimes dispel this conviction, it is more usual that only further experience will change it. The necessary forms of experience are often connected with changes in the conditions of one's own life, or with a growth in awareness of the customs and ideals of others with whom one had formerly failed to have understanding contact. In either case, it is experience that provides a basis for change. What James thought held in all cases assuredly holds here:

> Our requirements in the way of reality terminate in our own acts and emotions, our own pleasures and pains. These are the ultimate fixities from which . . .
> the whole chain of our beliefs depends, object hanging to object, as the bees, in swarming, hang to each other until, *de proche en proche*, the supporting branch, the Self, is reached and held.[36]

And since systems of religious thought are apt to depend even more than philosophic systems on ultimate moral beliefs, it is small wonder that in them the emotion of conviction is an especially powerful opponent of doubt. Yet, religions, too, change over time, and if what I have argued is true, they change not because any general skepticism has set in, but because the doubts that arise are doubts engendered by what appear to be other, better-founded beliefs.

Notes

This paper was delivered as a lecture at the University of Rochester in 1982 as one of a series sponsored by the Matchette Foundation in honor of Lewis White Beck. Its criticism of Descartes, on doubt, and of Hume, on belief, are independent of the suggestions offered concerning belief. As will be apparent, those suggestions rely on the phenomenological analyses contained in the article that follows. In addition, in the final section, some tentative suggestions are offered as to how this analysis may be relevant in contexts other than sense-perception.

1. H. H. Price, *Perception* (New York: McBride & Co., 1933), p. 3.
2. *Collected Papers* (Cambridge: Harvard University Press, 1934), vol. 5, no. 265, pp. 156-57.
3. It was only later, in the sixth *Meditation*, that he used the coherence of waking experience to distinguish it from dreams; yet, as we shall see, this also fails to provide a criterion sufficient to distinguish wakefulness from sleep.

4. *Philosophical Works,* Haldane and Ross translation (Cambridge: University Press, 1911-12), 1, 314.

5. Bernard Williams, *Descartes: The Project of Pure Inquiry* (Sussex: Harvester Press, 1978), p. 57.

A further reason, suggested by Williams's more extended discussion of doubts based on the hypothesis of a malignant demon (pp. 57-59), is that Descartes throughout assumed a causal theory of perception. On the basis of that theory, dreams must be accorded a different status from that assigned to sense-experience. I shall deal with this point below.

6. There is, however, a difference between the way in which Descartes used the criterion of coherence and the way in which I am using it here. His test was the lack of coherence among his various dreams, when contrasted with the coherence of his experiences in waking life. My argument, on the other hand, rests on the discontinuity (and therefore the lack of coherence) between the content of any particular dream and the experiences that follow upon it.

I might also add (as will later become clear) that I do not agree that there are no differences between what is present to us when we are dreaming and the characteristics of experience in our waking lives. In fact, Descartes must himself have been aware of there being such a difference, because he would not otherwise have been in a position to sort out dreams from waking experience, comparing them with respect to the coherence present in each. (Cf. my article, "Definiteness and Coherence in Sense-Perception," reprinted below [ch. 2])

7. In what follows, I shall be proceeding along lines different from those which have been followed in recent attempts to refute Descartes' use of the demon hypothesis. In a searching and perceptive article, "Can I know that I am not Dreaming?" (in Michael Hooker, ed., *Descartes: Critical and Interpretive Essays* [Baltimore: Johns Hopkins University Press, 1978], David and Jean Beer Blumenfeld have criticized these attempts; however, they did not consider one aspect of Bernard Williams's view, which my own view resembles. (Cf. note 5 above.)

8. *Philosophical Works,* Haldane and Ross translation, 1, 188.

9. In a chapter entitled "On Scepticism regarding the Senses," in *Philosophy, Science, and Sense Perception* (Baltimore: Johns Hopkins Press, 1964), I discussed Hume's arguments for subjectivism, attempting to show: first, that his use of contradictions within sense-perception did not justify subjectivism; second, that his argument from an analysis of the perceptual process presupposed a realistic, rather than a subjectivistic, interpretation of our sensing organs. Thus, in his case, too, doubts concerning the truth of realism only arose in conjunction with prior, implicit, realistic assumptions.

10. To be sure, the form of argument I have employed is not one that could be used to rebut a complete skepticism in any case in which the skeptic refuses to offer reasons for doubting that which he doubts. While I know of no argument capable of doing so, I suspect that no one—either philosopher or layman—has ever espoused skepticism without having *some* reason for doubting what others believe.

11. With respect to Hume's theory of belief, and for a contrast of it with the Cartesian theory, cf. H. H. Price, *Belief* (London: Allen & Unwin, 1969), pp. 157-86 and 221-40. Unfortunately, Price casts only a perfunctory glance at the type of theory held by Spinoza, discussing it primarily with reference to an essay by Bagehot, whose separation of the "intellectual" from the "emotional" aspects of belief would have been rejected by Spinoza.

Price, however, did discuss Cardinal Newman's position at considerable length. That position rested on the view that our apprehension of the relations between particulars, which Newman termed *real apprehension,* is to be distinguished from *notional apprehension,* which consists of an apprehension of propositions using abstract terms. According to Newman, all *real apprehension* involves assent, and to that extent (but to that extent only) his theory was similar to Spinoza's.

12. For a more extended discussion of this point, cf. my *Science, Philosophy, and Sense Perception,* pp. 157-64.

13. In what immediately follows, my account is close to that which William James gave at the beginning of Chapter 21, "The Perception of Reality," in his *Principles of Psychology.*

14. The concept of belief is, of course, not only applicable within the realm of immediate experience, but is used to refer to our attitude toward various propositions, such as "God

exists," or "It is true that smoking increases the chance of developing lung cancer." Therefore, when I hold that it is inapproapriate to speak of belief with respect to our *thoughts,* I am not referring to propositions. When a proposition is understood, affirmed, denied, doubted, or the like, an act of thought is involved, but the proposition itself is not a "thought" in the same sense as are memory-images, daydreams, hopes, plans, or the like.

On the other hand, I wish to make it clear that I am presently dealing only with belief as it pertains to perceptual situations. Later, I shall extend that treatment by analogy. At no point, however, shall I be attempting to deal with the phenomenon of belief when it arises in connection with our acceptance of the *validity* of an inductive or a deductive inference.

15. In speaking of objects, I am not to be understood as referring only to tangible, solid objects, such as stones or chairs. Though in ordinary speech we are not apt to refer to a cloud or a beam of light in the darkness as "an object," these are nonetheless presented to us in direct experience, are seen as being outside us, and appear as existing independently of us. To be sure, there is a difference between what is sometimes called the "reality character" of such objects and those which look solid. If I am not mistaken, this difference relates in large measure to the difference between surface colors (such as characterize objects that appear solid) and volume or film colors. (Cf. David Katz, *The World of Colour* [London: Kegan Paul, Trench, Trubner, 1935]). This difference, in turn, seems in large part to depend upon definiteness of contour, with which I shall later be concerned.

16. John Stuart Mill also accepted as brute fact the difference between belief and mere imagination: see his notes to his father's *Analysis of the Phenomena of the Human Mind* (London: Longmans, Green, Reader, and Dyer, 1869), 2, 411-13.

17. At one point, in an addition to the *Treatise,* Hume implicitly introduced characteristics of the objects of belief and the relation they bear to our experience. In that passage he spoke of the *solidity, firmness,* and *steadiness* of impressions as terms equivalent to *force* and *liveliness.* Unlike *force* and *liveliness,* these terms do not carry the suggestion that the character of what is being experienced is without bearing on whether or not belief is elicited. (For this passage, cf. Hume's Appendix, supplementing book 1, part 3, sect. 7, p. 629 in the Selby-Bigge edition of the *Treatise on Human Nature.*)

18. I believe it can be shown that externality and apparent independence are phenomenologically connected (cf. note 22, below); but I do not regard it as essential for my present purposes to attempt to establish that fact.

19. For my previous, more extended discussion of these two characteristics, cf. my "Definiteness and Coherence in Sense-Perception," referred to in note 6, above.

20. These two characteristics, as the reader will note, are identical with the two characteristics that Descartes used to describe what he referred to as "distinctness." For his differentiation between the clear and the distinct and his characterization of them, cf. his *Principles of Philosophy,* part 1, Props. 45 and 46.

It is to be noted that Descartes denied that any perceptual experiences can be distinct; for that reason, and because I find it descriptively more accurate, I prefer to use the term *definiteness,* rather than *distinctness.*

21. To camouflage an object is to color it in a way that breaks up its contour as a single, identifiable object.

If a question arises concerning objects such as clouds, which frequently do not have clearly defined contours, we can only point to their general location in space. Because even such objects appear as set off against a background, the figure-ground relation holds of them as well.

22. For this reason, when we see a sudden flash of light or hear a fleeting sound, we cannot be sure that we have really seen or heard something that existed independently of us. Thus, at least a minimal degree of persistence in what we are experiencing seems to be a factor contributing to the belief that an object that appears as external to us is also independent of us.

23. In these respects, however, attending to music—as distinct from hearing ordinary sounds—may be compared with vision. In the case of the blind, the same may also be said with respect to touch.

24. The assumption that the same quality can be directly experienced through different sense-modalities has frequently been challenged, but any familiarity with the evidence produced

by Gestalt psychologists concerning this question should be sufficient to dispel the challenge.

25. In offering an explanation of such cases in terms of coherence, I do not imply that coherence is the factor that underlies so-called constancy phenomena. Brightness constancy, size constancy, etc., have in many cases been adequately explained in psychophysical terms. Here I refer only to cases in which two distinct and incompatible experiences are compared, and we judge that one truly represents the object, while the other does not.

In treating these distinct issues, William James failed to distinguish between them: he did not differentiate between the reasons why, in a given case, we see an object as square even though its retinal image, due to perspective, is not square, and why, on the other hand, when an object appears on different occasions to have different shades of color, we regard one as its true color. In both types of case, James appealed to "the mind's selection." In explaining this selectivity, he cited a variety of factors, but only concluded that "the mind chooses to suit itself" (*Principles of Psychology* [in *The Works of William James*, Cambridge: Harvard University Press, 1981], 1, 274-75). In the cases of size (2, 815-18) and of shape (2, 869-72), he offered a more precise list of the factors responsible for our assigning reality to one particular view of an object rather than another. In these cases his appeal was to "aesthetic and practical advantages," referring to various factors that presumably afford us the most accurate view of the object. He failed, however, to take into account either the characteristics of the objects or their relations to the background; these, however, are the factors that play a major role in contemporary explanations of constancy phenomena.

26. Just as I would not claim that we in all cases decide which is the more adequate view of an object on the basis of perceptual characteristics alone, independently of any theory, so I do not claim that the difference in the amount of evidence needed to justify an experimental conclusion is *in all cases* independent of a network of theory. In most cases it is not. Nevertheless, it is important to recognize the existence of these exceptional cases; as I shall suggest, it is they that often lead to basic revisions in previously accepted theories.

27. However, the present tendency to assume that the same situation holds with respect to all perceptual experience and that observation is always theory-laden, seems to me not only dubious, but false.

28. In speaking of a *limited hypothesis,* I am using a vague term, but it is clear that a hypothesis of law that is formulated so as to apply only to some relatively restricted and homogeneous class of phenomena, such as a particular species of plant, is more limited than a hypothesis or law that is claimed to be applicable to a much wider class, such as all plants or all living things. While no sharp line of demarcation can be drawn between more and less limited hypotheses or laws, *theories* are, I believe, to be distinguished from hypotheses, and even from those well-confirmed hypotheses which we commonly refer to as *laws* (cf. my *Anatomy of Historical Knowledge* [Baltimore: Johns Hopkins University Press, 1977], pp. 156-57). So far as the general structure of confirmation is concerned, I find no difference between theories and wide-ranging hypotheses. That to which I wish to call attention is the fact that with respect to more limited hypotheses a different, independent criterion is often initially applied.

29. In this, it resembles those intellectual truths which Descartes, in his *Rules for the Direction of the Mind,* characterized as examples of "true and evident cognition."

30. Cf. James, *Principles of Psychology,* 2, 929-30.

31. The view that were it not for pragmatic reasons one could as easily proceed in one direction as in the other is at least suggested in the conclusion of Quine's "Two Dogmas of Empiricism," reprinted in his *From a Logical Point of View,* 2nd ed., (Cambridge: Harvard University Press, 1980). Cf., especially, pp. 43-44.

32. At this point it may be useful to indicate the difference between my view and the pragmatic theory of belief developed by Bain in *The Emotions and the Will,* and by Peirce. In my view, the basis of belief is not to be sought in the consequences of thought; rather, I take some forms of experience to be directly belief-evoking. Then, if no countervailing force exists, belief leads directly to action. As James said:

What characterizes both consent and belief is the cessation of theoretic agitation, through the advent of an idea which is inwardly stable, and fills the mind solidly to the exclusion of contradictory ideas. When this is the case, motor effects are apt to follow. Hence the states of consent and belief, characterized by repose on the purely intellectual side, are both intimately connected with practical activity (*Principles of Psychology*, 2, 913-14).

Whatever consequences later follow may reinforce the belief, may leave it untouched, or may lead to its modification or extirpation. However, neither the actual consequences of a belief nor its foreseen consequences account for its origin.

Because both Bain and Peirce were concerned to have a theory of belief which could be extended to analogous phenomena in animal behavior (cf. Murray Murphy, *The Development of Peirce's Philosophy* [Cambridge: Harvard University Press, 1961], pp. 162-63), it is of interest to see whether the view I have sketched can meet the same test. I submit that it can. Substituting *perception* for what James referred to as "the intellectual side" of the situation, one is in a position to explain what is comparable to belief in animal behavior. In contrast to an explanation that depends solely upon habits formed through trial and error, patterns of action which have not been inherited will be understood as arising out of an initial reaction to a given type of situation, then becoming fixed through the favorable consequences they engender.

33. "The Emotion of Conviction," *Literary Studies*, 2nd ed. (London: Longmans, Green, 1879), 2, 412-21.

James, citing Bagehot, also discusses the relation of emotion to belief; cf. *Principles of Psychology*, 2, 935-39.

34. Although Descartes speaks only of the clarity and distinctness of *ideas*, according to his usage, the term *ideas* includes both specific ideas and how they are related in propositions.

In saying that he did not doubt the criterion of clarity and distinctness and that this criterion was exemplified for him in mathematics, I am not unmindful of the fact that when he advanced the hypothesis of a malignant demon in his *Meditations*, Descartes proposed that one might even doubt mathematical truths, if one did not first know that God exists and is no deceiver. How to interpret this aspect of his hyperbolic doubt poses a serious problem for Descartes scholarship, but I know of no interpretation of the passage which holds that it involves a retreat from the position that in forming judgments on which we can absolutely rely, the criterion to be used is clarity and distinctness.

35. "It is very manifest by the natural light which is in our souls, that no qualities or properties pertain to nothing; and that where some are perceived there must necessarily be some thing or substance on which they depend" (*Principles of Philosophy*, part 1, Prop. 11, in *Philosophical Works*, Haldane and Ross translation, 1, 223.

36. *Principles of Psychology*, 2, 939.

2

Definiteness and Coherence
in Sense-Perception

      In the present paper I shall be dealing in a preliminary and exploratory way with the epistemological significance of certain aspects of our perceptual experience. I shall attempt to show that there are two principles of which we often make use when, in everyday life, we estimate the reliability of particular instances of sense-perception. Assuming that this can be established, one would expect that the epistemological theories advanced by philosophers would, at some points, reflect their own everyday use of such principles. And this, as I shall suggest, has to some extent occurred. However, most philosophers have focused their attention on more general problems than the reasons why, in specific cases, we reject one instance of sense-perception in favor of another; therefore the topics with which I am here concerned have not received the attention I believe they deserve.

      The two principles with which I shall deal—a principle of definiteness and a principle of coherence—are to be construed as tacitly accepted rather than explicitly formulated. They should therefore not be expected to operate as premises for arguments; rather they represent psychological factors that serve as determinants when we assess the reliability of particular instances of perception. The discovery that there are such factors would not prejudge any issues concerning the reliability of sense-perception in general, as compared with other possible sources of knowledge. Nor would a formulation of these principles necessarily suggest the ways in which we can most effectively analyze perception and the status of that which is perceived. Furthermore, questions concerning the evidence which perception provides for our beliefs in the existence and nature of an independent physical world would not be answered through uncovering the modes of operation of the principles with which I am here concerned. Thus, I am not dealing with the issues that have been standard in philosophic discussions of sense-perception.

      My present concern is limited to questions concerning factors that are present *within* perceptual experience. I am concerned with the fact that whatever may be our ultimate assessment of perceiving as a way of knowing, in everyday life each of us sifts and sorts our perceptual experience in terms

Reprinted by permission from *Nous* 1 (1967):123-38.

of its trustworthiness. If I am not mistaken, these evaluations are not based on some complex apparatus of theory which we bring to bear (consciously or not) on the particular experiences that we accept or reject.[1] Nor do we wait upon the solution of philosophic controversies to make such assessments. Yet, it would be surprising if there were no general principles that effectively guide us in this process; it will be my aim to isolate and characterize two of them. I do not claim that these are the only such principles, and I shall deliberately avoid discussing how, if at all, they are related to one another. What I shall do is delineate the nature of each, and suggest ways in which they are related to some familiar discussions of more standard epistemological issues. At the end, I shall also suggest that the operative presence of such principles in our experience may have wider implications than might originally be thought.

I

In order to start from concrete instances, let me point out that there are cases in which we accept the testimony of one sense-modality (e.g., touch) as being more accurate than another (e.g., vision); yet there are other cases in which our reliance is reversed (e.g., we accept vision rather than touch). As an example of such a reversal consider the following pair of cases. When I look at a large photographic reproduction of a low-relief, the figures on it may appear to be raised, but if I touch it and it feels two-dimensional, I acknowledge it to *be* two-dimensional. On the other hand, if I am blindfolded and feel one point of stimulation on the back of my hand, and if I am then permitted to look and I see two caliper points touching my skin, I will accept what I see in preference to what I feel. Thus, the decisive factor is not exclusively a question of which sense-modality is involved.

In such cases it is likely that all will agree as to which of the conflicting experiences is to be taken as authoritative, and because of this agreement the problem with which I am concerned has often been overlooked by philosophers. However, the fact that there is agreement does not inform us on what such agreement may be based, and it is precisely that question I here wish to raise. Insofar as this topic has been discussed by other philosophers, an answer to it has usually been given in terms of various "external" criteria; for example, it has sometimes been held that familiarity is responsible for our taking one view of an object as more reliable than another, or that our choices are based on what has proved to be the most reliable predictive indicator in the past. While not wishing to deny that these criteria may be of importance in assessing what we take to be the truth-value of particular perceptual experiences, it is not with them that I shall here be concerned. What I am interested in establishing is that there are features of perceptual experience itself which incline us to take some experiences as reliable and accurate, and the absence of which leads us to doubt the reliability of others. To be sure, our convictions of reliability or of unreliability may be altered by the use of external criteria, e.g., by explicit comparisons with what we remember as having occurred in the past. Furthermore, I believe that what appears to us as being unquestionably reliable may sometimes legitimately be challenged on the basis of theories that are the products of scientific inquiry rather than being directly suggested by perceptual experience itself.[2] Nonetheless, I think it can be shown that, independently of any external factors, we do in fact distinguish within our experience between perceptions that bear the mark of trustworthiness and those that do not;. and it is with this phenomenological fact (or, if one prefers, with this psychological fact) that I am here concerned. I will aim to isolate two features of perceptual experience which seem to be basic in these discriminations of trustworthiness and untrustworthiness. The first of them I shall term "definiteness."

To grasp what is meant by definiteness, it will be helpful if the reader recalls Descartes' discussion of the clarity and the distinctness of ideas. By a *clear* idea Descartes meant an idea that was present and manifest to an attentive mind; in giving an example of such ideas he drew upon our visual perception of objects.[3] On the other hand, he rejected the possibility that vision could provide examples of *distinct* ideas; he held that distinct ideas were only to be found in the realm of intellectual judgments. However, each of the characteristics that, together, constituted Descartes' criterion for distinctness assuredly has an analogue in sense-perception.[4] It is to these analogues that I shall refer in speaking of the criterion of definiteness. I shall ascribe definiteness to a perception when what is perceived is precisely distinguishable from its background and from other perceived entities, and when, in addition, each of its presented features is manifest to the perceiver.[5] I shall take these two characteristics as constituting the dimensions of definiteness. What we shall find is that they are frequently, although not invariably, linked in sense-perception. And it will be my contention that when they are so linked they provide us with the standard that we actually use in discriminating between better and worse in perception. In other words, those instances which we take to be paradigm cases of an accurate and adequate perception of objects are precisely those cases in which there is a combination of two characteristics: distinctness of that object from other things, and clarity of its individual features.[6]

To illustrate the point, I shall cite a familiar but often neglected aesthetic phenomenon: that apart from certain special types of painting, there seems to be one proper distance from which to look at any particular painting. Applying the criterion of definiteness to this phenomenon, one would expect that what is taken as a proper distance will be one from which we are able to see the picture as a whole (i.e., as a particular isolable object, distinct from its background), and yet from which we can also distinguish its parts, attending to them individually. To be sure, the question of what are the "parts" of a painting raises important aesthetic and perceptual issues which cannot here be discussed. However, apart from this issue. the example should prove to be a happy one, for it illustrates how a specifically perceptual criterion may lead to results quite different from those which are relevant to particular interests and purposes. For example, if one is particularly interested in a painter's technique, one may wish to examine a painting from very close by, or even use a magnifying glass in doing so; yet no one, I take it, would claim that such would be the proper manner in which to view the painting for its aesthetic effect as a painting. Similarly, from the point of view of interior decoration a painting may be treated as an interesting and arresting touch of color on a particular wall; however, to view it merely as a decorative item in the room as a whole is not to see it as a particular work of art. In order to see a painting properly, one must be able to view it as a whole and at the same time be able to discern as clearly as possible each of the elements of which (as a painting) it is composed.

Even if it be granted that my point has been made with respect to certain types of case, such as how we view paintings, the reader may be disposed to challenge the relevance of this point to other, more standard instances of perceiving. To such a challenge I would answer that when we discriminate between *normal* perception and instances that deviate from the normal, we are making the same sort of discrimination that the foregoing aesthetic example involves. While it is of course true that there are many cases in which we designate a particular instance of perception as normal on the basis of external criteria derived from past experience, the foregoing example should serve to suggest that this is perhaps not always the case. And it is this point that I shall now attempt to make plausible by showing that the criterion of definiteness can in fact serve to explain some of the most usual cases in which we take one instance of perception as the standard against which others are judged.

Consider, for example, the fact that when persons are challenged to say what the real color of an object is, they tend to appeal to the color that it is seen as having "in ordinary daylight;" that is, when the light is not too strong, as it is in the full glare of the sun, and not too weak, as it becomes toward dusk. On this basis, it might be suggested that what is meant by *ordinary* daylight is simply the central range of illumination under which we most frequently see objects; its familiarity would then be regarded as the explanation of why we take it as our standard. However, I believe it more plausible to hold that the particular range that is taken as a norm (in the normative sense of that term) is whatever degree of illumination permits us to distinguish with maximum clarity the color at which we are looking. What constitutes this range may vary with variations in distance, with the particular hue or saturation of the color, or with the size of the object, etc. In short, I do not suppose that there is a single norm of illumination which is the same in all cases of color-vision; I am only contending that, within one context or another, what appears to a particular person to be the proper illumination of an object's color is that illumination which he experiences as providing him the best discrimination.[7] And what is taken to be the best discrimination of a color is itself an example of definiteness of perception; not only must we be able to discriminate this patch of color as distinct from other shades of the same color if we are to claim that we see it *well*, but we must also be able to discern the particular characteristics of its surface, noting, for example, whether the surface is mottled, or streaky, or is smoothly colored overall.

Now, it is to be noted that precisely the same sorts of discriminations are present when we view objects under conditions of artificial illumination. Under incandescent or fluorescent lighting, we distinguish between better and worse discriminations no less than we do when we inspect objects in daylight. To be sure, the color that an object appears to us to have under each of these forms of illumination will be different; but in each case, if I am correct, the criterion of definiteness will be used. If we then compare these colors and ask what is the *true* color of the object (as we sometimes do),[8] we shall doubtless take what constitutes its most definite daylight color as our standard. Why we should choose daylight as providing this standard is not my present concern. What concerns me is that, within the range of daytime vision, we take one particular manifestation of an object as presenting its true color, and that this manifestation is that in which its color has the greatest degree of definiteness for us. In other words, and speaking more generally, what I wish to make clear is that definiteness is a criterion that we use in testing the whole range of our visual perceptions, and what constitutes the best illumination of an object is simply that illumination under which we feel entitled to say that, whatever we are looking at, we see it best.[9]

Should such observations sound like mere mystification, I should like to call to the reader's attention what transpires when an ophthalmologist tests one's vision. Throughout such an examination we are called upon to make judgments of when we see *best* ("Is this better or worse?" he asks as he fits a new lens, or adjusts the axis of that lens). What we take to be "best" is, I submit, whatever affords us what we are apt to call the "clearest" view of what we are seeing, and here we mean by the clearest the most definite: the clearest view of a letter, or pattern, or object is one in which what we view stands out most distinctly from its background and in which each of its parts is most sharply defined.[10] And should it still be thought that the norms that we accept are determined solely by past experience, I should like the reader to note that when we have for a very long time been using lenses that under-correct for a defect in vision, and when we then have our prescription altered, we suddenly find ourselves seeing *better*, and not merely seeing differently.

Cases in which we make normative comparisons of these sorts are not confined to vision. In auditory experiences, and in tactile experience, and even in questions of taste and of odor, similar criteria of "normality" are applied. (To be sure, our acuity of perception is less marked with respect to many phenomena related to these sense-modalities, and our criteria are therefore in many instances also less precise.) If sounds are confused by the intrusion of noise, or muffled by reverberations, we say that we are unable to hear what there is to be heard. Also, the conditions of our sense-organs — such as the aftertaste of strong food, or the effect of a head cold — may "mask", we say, the taste or the odor that we regard as being really there. And in such cases, too, the standard cases against which other instances are to be judged are those cases in which we discriminate "best."

If I may now take this briefly characterized phenomenological fact for granted, I think that I shall be able to suggest that the difference between perceiving, on the one hand, and states such as imagining, remembering, or dreaming, on the other, may be characterized in terms of it. If one examines what one takes to be a case of remembering or of imagining, one cannot, I think, claim that one can really *see* what one remembers or imagines — say, a particular face — as standing out from its background: no matter how clearly one envisions the features of the face, the background against which it exists remains a shadowy, ill-defined, and featureless "ground" as compared with the backgrounds against which one actually sees a face when one is perceiving it, rather than remembering it or imagining it. If I am not mistaken, the same situation holds in the case of dreams — although usually in a more extreme form. In dreams, it is not merely the background that remains featureless, but many of the details of that which is dreamt also seem to be left blank, that is, they cannot be inspected one by one.[11]

If this phenomenological characterization of one of the differences between *perceiving* and states such as imagining, remembering, and dreaming is accepted, we may perhaps interpret this as the phenomenon that Hume sought to indicate when he spoke of the liveliness and vivacity of our *impressions* as contrasted with our *ideas*.[12] I say "sought to indicate" because liveliness, taken by itself, is surely not sufficient as a means of distinguishing between impressions and ideas: the thought of a faux pas that I have committed, may — in any usual sense of "lively" — be far livelier than the sights and sounds that surround me as I leave the scene of my embarrassment; yet the memory-image of that faux pas is not taken to be an instance of perceiving. According to my suggestion, one reason that it is not so taken is because it is not sharply defined against its own background: it swims in a space, so to speak, which is not the space of my present surroundings, and it is not sharply defined in a space of its own.[13]

Once again it might be charged that this attempt to distinguish between perceiving, on the one hand, and imagining, remembering, or dreaming, on the other, rests upon phenomenological facts that are vague, and that an appeal to these supposed facts leads merely to obfuscation. Might it not be better, one could presumably argue, to draw the distinction by means of a contrast between the *coherence* of our waking states with one another, and the lack of coherence which characterizes our various dreams? Could not this difference then be fortified by appealing to inconsistencies between the content of our waking states and that of our dreams, and could it not be further buttressed by the coherence of the waking states of different persons and the lack of coherence among their individual dreams; etc., etc.? Unfortunately there is a fatal flaw in this type of suggestion, familiar as such suggestions have become. The flaw may be indicated in the following way. (1) While it *is* true that there is greater coherence within our waking experience from day to day and week to week than there is among our various dreams, and while it is also true that dreams not only fail to cohere with one another, but are inconsistent with what we know through our waking states; (2) it must be recognized that *prior* to establishing these differences in the coherence of our waking and our dreaming states, we must be able to pick out *which* of our experiences are to be denominated as dreams. In other words, the contrast with respect to coherence presupposes that there is an independent criterion of perceiving; it cannot of itself give us that criterion.

If the foregoing observations are correct, then the distinction that we draw between perceiving and, say, remembering or dreaming, depends in the first instance upon some features inherent in perception and lacking in memory or dreams.[14] I trust that I have now made it plausible to hold that one such criterion may well be what I have called definiteness.

II

It would, however, be quite wrong to suppose that the only criterion for the reliability of a perceptual judgment lies in the definiteness of what we experience. I wish now to consider a second such factor, which I shall call "the coherence of aspects." It will be my contention that one of the tests that serves as a criterion for veridical perception is coherence among the aspects of an object as we inspect it from varying points of view, or under varying conditions, or by means of different sense-modalities.

As a first attempt to make this criterion clear, let us return to the case of the photograph of the low-relief, in which the figures looked as if they were raised but what we felt was smooth and flat to the touch. In that case, of course, we relied upon touch and not upon sight. Our present concern is with the basis for that reliance. I do not wish to deny that an acquaintance with photographs, as well as past experience with similar deceptions, may play an important role in such cases; and these factors, of course, are included within the usual test of coherence. However, one need not always appeal to theoretical knowledge or to knowledge drawn from earlier experience: within the context of our present experience we often sift and sort what appear to be inconsistencies. For example, we often find ourselves shifting the position from which we view an object, observing whether its appearance alters as we do so. In this particular case, of course, the apparently raised figures appear to flatten out as we move to view the object more obliquely; and when we stand so as to view it from a very oblique angle, the photograph will be seen as two-dimensional. Thus, what we see comes to cohere with what we have felt, and not with what we at first saw. It is our demand for this sort of coherence among the various impressions of what we take to be a single and stable object which forces us to reject our original visual impression. And such, I take it, would be the case even for persons who had no prior knowledge of photographs and no theories to guide them as to how two-dimensional surfaces may come to appear as characterized by depth.

Similarly, in the case of the calipers: although we only feel one source of stimulation on the back of our hand when the calipers are at rest and in direct contact with our skin, if they are then rocked back and forth we can feel two discrete stimuli. While our first criterion—that of definiteness—seems better satisfied in this experience, that criterion is not likely to be prominent enough, or unequivocal enough, to convince us that our second judgment is to be taken as more reliable than the first. What is needed is likely to be a further exploration of the object under varying conditions of perception. Vision, of course, offers a test that we consider decisive in this particular case. However, in the absence of visual checks, further tactile impressions suffice to afford us an equal degree of assurance. For example, if we are permitted to feel the calipers with our other hand, we find that they terminate in two points rather than one. While it is surely true that in each of these further experiences a higher degree of definiteness is present, definiteness alone is not responsible for our conviction of trustworthiness: it is also important that when *two* points are felt this experience conforms to our visual experience and to our subsequent tactile experiences, whereas our original, somewhat vaguer impression of a single, undifferentiated object does not.

As these illustrations suggest, what has usually been termed "the converging testimony of the senses" is one type of instance in which we make use of the principle of the coherence of the aspects of an object. However, the same principle applies equally when only one sense-modality is involved. There are, for example, cases in which we resolve an apparent conflict in our experience solely through an appeal to successive visual experiences. If, for instance, we look at a remote object, and if what we see from one position seems quite different and incompatible with what is seen from another place, we attempt to bring the two views of the object into congruence by slowly shifting our position, keeping the object in sight. If in so doing, we get a continuous and coherent series of views, this series can serve to integrate the two views which originally struck us as so different that we regarded them as inconsistent. Thus, even when only one sense-modality is involved, we resolve apparent contradictions through successive trials or "experiments", using as a criterion for trustworthy perception the mutual consistency and coherence of the various perceptual aspects of objects.

I should not expect anyone to challenge the contention that we do in fact use such a test in estimating the trustworthiness of particular instances of sense-experience. However, most philosophers have been inclined to hold that the consistency to which we appeal is not merely a consistency and coherence of the various aspects of objects as those objects are presented in sense-perception; instead, they regard it as inevitable that interpretative schema—whether explicitly formulated or not—provide a framework within which various characteristics are judged to be compatible or incompatible. Usually, views of this type seek to break down our ordinary distinctions between observation and interpretation, fact and theory. In opposition to those who adopt such a position, I wish to suggest that the coherence or lack of coherence which we discover among the various aspects of the objects with which we are acquainted through sense-experience is a discovery made within the framework of that experience itself. This seems to me to be a natural implication of the specific cases which I have cited: in none of these cases would it have been plausible to hold that our judgment of reliability was theory-dependent. However, in order to defend my view with respect to this issue it will be important to examine—even though briefly—two closely related problems.

The first of these concerns the basis on which we actually do hold that two specific impressions of an object are either compatible or incompatible. (Or, if one preferred to phrase the issue in a non-psychological way, the basis on which we would seek to justify our beliefs in their compatibility or incompatibility.) While it might initially be thought that such judgments rest on a logical consistency or inconsistency between the characteristics in question, such is not usually the case. For example, there would be no logical contradiction in holding that objects that *look* flat might yield tactile impressions entirely different from those which they presently do; nor would it be logically contradictory if objects that *feel* flat were to look quite different from the way in which we now expect them to look. Our conviction that objects which feel "flat" should also look "flat" is a conviction that depends upon experience: the connection is contingent, and not logically necessary. Such, of course, was the position maintained by Berkeley and by Hume. And it was also an essential feature of their positions to hold that sense-experience itself (and not any presupposed theory, or any set of explanatory concepts) leads us to regard some characteristics as mutually compatible, and others as not. In my view, as in theirs, it is only through connections established within sense-experience, and not on logical considerations or on theoretical explanations, that our judgments of the reliability or unreliability of specific instances of perception must rest.

However, it must be noted that this fact does not, of itself, determine the precise way in which experience enables us to discover the connections that obtain among various qualities. It might be the case, as Berkeley and as Hume actually held, that we relate one perceptible characteristic to another solely on the basis of our past experience and the expectations that that experience has aroused. On the other hand, there may be cases in which the relationships that we find among particular characteristics are—in part at least—attributable to the presence of directly experienced similarities in what is presented through different sense-modalities. (The existence of the latter possibility, and of related possibilities, has of course been stressed by Gestalt psychologists.) Fortunately, we need not decide between these alternatives; for our present purposes it is only important to note that, in *either* case, the consistency or inconsistency which we find among the various characteristics of objects rests upon what we derive from sense-experience itself.

The second problem that is relevant to this issue concerns the basis on which two impressions are taken as revealing two aspects of a single object, rather than as being independent, unconnected existences.[15] Once again two alternative types of psychological theory present themselves by way of explanation. On the one hand, the empiristic theories of Berkeley, Hume, or Mill would lead us to regard our conception of an object as a product of repeated conjunctions of sensations. On the other hand, it is possible to argue that various relational characteristics, such as the figure-ground relationship, serve to define what we take to be an object; on the basis of this assumption, our conception of the relations between an object and its specific qualities would not be what empiristic theories claim them to be. While I regard the second of these general types of psychological theory to be overwhelmingly more plausible than the first, it is not with that issue that I am here concerned. On *either* hypothesis, it would be in and through sense-experience itself that our conception of particular objects is formed; thus the criterion of the coherence of the aspects of an object does not rest upon prior commitments to particular networks of theory or so-called conceptual schemes.

The importance of these points for what I here wish to argue may be summarily stated in the following way. I have endeavored to show that we do in fact use a criterion of coherence as a test of the trustworthiness of particular observations; however, our use of such a test might be supposed to prove that one could not establish the trustworthiness of any particular observation without presupposing, or explicitly invoking, a network of *theory* to which the trustworthiness of particular observations would be relative. While I should not wish to deny that there may be some instances in which this is true, it has been my aim to establish the fact that it is surely not always true: many of our judgments of perceptual reliability are not theory-dependent. To recall merely one example, I have attempted to show that when we appeal to criteria such as the converging testimony of our senses, we are appealing to a coherence that is validated for us within perceptual experience itself.

III

In this paper I have attempted to uncover two very general criteria that we do in fact use in distinguishing between instances of sense-perception which are reliable and those which we regard as either less reliable or unreliable. If my analyses have been correct, our initial judgments of reliability are not based upon networks of theory or upon interpretative, explanatory schema. To be sure, we may raise further and more ultimate questions as to the place—within the realm of human knowledge—which one can properly assign to even the most accurate and reliable instances of sense-perception. As I have said, it has not been the aim of the present paper to deal with such wider issues: I have been concerned only with the particular criteria that we use within the field of sense-experience itself. However, if I have been successful in uncovering the presence of such criteria, they may be of importance with respect to estimating various claims regarding more comprehensive and more traditional epistemological issues.

In the first place, a recognition of the fact that we do not believe all instances of sense-experience to be equally reliable should put us on our guard against any general theory of knowledge which bases its claims regarding sense-perception on some narrowly selected group of instances. This is equally true whether such selected instances are those in which we place least trust or whether they are those which appear to be wholly trustworthy. An exclusive emphasis on the former would suggest that *no* instances of sense-perception are really reliable; an exclusive emphasis on the latter has led some contemporary philosophers to minimize the epistemological significance of various forms of delusive sense-experience.

In the second place, if we recognize that we do in fact use criteria of reliability which are not derived from a prior acceptance of networks of theory, but are indigenous to perceptual experience itself, it may again be possible to take seriously a distinction which was once generally accepted but is so no longer: that, in some cases, there is a difference worth noting between the so-called hard facts of experience and the theoretical interpretation of these facts. By and large, this traditional distinction withstood the attacks of Anglo-American idealism, only to succumb to recent pragmatic tendencies in the theory of knowledge and the philosophy of science. However, if my analyses have been correct, and if we do in many cases distinguish reliable from unreliable observations independently of networks of theory, the purported equivalence between adjusting fact to theory, or theory to fact, may have to be re-examined. Thus, it might once again become permissible to reaffirm (though doubtless more cautiously) one of the traditional dogmas of empiricism, distinguishing between the hard facts of experience and the various alternative ways in which those facts are to be interpreted.

Notes

Unsatisfied by the position of Duhem, Quine, and others on the respective roles of observation and theory in the sciences, I was led to consider the question of what criteria we actually use to distinguish between those observations in which we naturally place most trust and those which we are more willing to doubt. In this phe-

nomenologically oriented paper, I attempt to identify two characteristics that are present within sense-experience, independently of theory, on the basis of which we take some of these experiences to more trustworthy than others.

1. I am aware of various ways in which such a statement might be challenged, but I ask the reader to suspend judgment on this issue until concrete examples are given.

2. I have attempted to justify this opinion in the concluding chapter of my book, *Philosophy, Science, and Sense Perception* (Baltimore, 1964).

3. For the Cartesian definitions of clarity and distinctness, cf. *Principles of Philosophy*, Part I, Prop. 45, and also Prop. 46. Unfortunately, the Haldane and Ross translation of these passages is not in strict accord with the standard version given in the Adam and Tannery edition of Descartes' works. However, the slight differences between them are not of consequence in the present context.

4. These two characteristics may be designated as (a) distinctness from other things, and (b) clarity (in Descartes' sense) of its individual parts. Descartes' own definition of that which is distinct reads as follows: "celle qui est tellement precise & differente de toutes les autres, qu'elle ne comprend en soy que ce qui paroit manifestement a celuy qui la considere comme il faut" (Descartes, *Principles of Philosophy*, Prop. 45).

5. In the present context it is worth noting that Descartes, at one point in the sixth *Meditation*, admitted that sense-perception might *almost* be said to yield distinct ideas, as compared with those ideas which depend upon memory or which can be framed through an act of the imagination. The passage reads, in translation:

> And because the ideas which I received through the senses were much more lively, more clear, and even, in their own way, more distinct than any which I could of myself frame in meditation, or than those I found impressed on my memory. . . (Haldane and Ross: *Philosophical Works of Descartes*, 1, 188. Cf. Adam and Tannery edition of the *Oeuvres*, 9, 60).

As I shall later endeavor to point out, the characteristic of distinctness may itself provide a basis for discriminating between what we perceive and what we merely remember or imagine.

6. This does not preclude the fact that, for certain specific purposes, we may select one of these characteristics as more important to us than the other, altering the perceptual situation so that the distinctness of our perception is maximized at the expense of clarity in its individual features, or vice versa. And we may, of course, regard the most accurate conception of an object as one that involves piecing together two or more such independent experiences. However, this remains a *conception* of the object, and I am here concerned with direct perception only.

To avoid misunderstandings it should also be noted that the criterion of definiteness is wholly applicable even in those cases in which the features of what we perceive are "indefinite." For example, there is a striking difference between the definiteness of the specific features of a painting by Mondrian and those of a painting by Delacroix; similarly, one might think of the features of Michelangelo's *Pietà* as "indefinite" when compared with those of his *David.* Nevertheless, so far as our *perceiving* what the features of an object may be, it does not matter whether these features themselves are "definite" or are "indefinite."

7. Naturally, what constitutes the best illumination for the perception of color may not constitute the best illumination for the perception of contour or of texture. For example, in some cases very intense illumination falling obliquely on an object best permits us to see its contours and discriminate the texture of its surface, but no one would hold these to be ideal conditions under which to discern its color. Thus, what one regards as the best illumination under which to inspect an object may vary with what one most wishes to see. However, this does not alter the fact with which I am here concerned: with respect to the perception of any particular aspect of an object, we use the criterion of definiteness as our norm.

8. It will be recalled that Austin challenged some instances of this sort of claim; also, he challenged the notion that there is one "real" shape of any particular cat (cf. *Sense and Sensibilia*, pp. 65-67). With respect to some of the instances he cites, I would be wholly in agreement; for example, I would challenge the view that every object must be taken as having *a* true color. (Cf.

my discussion of the color of mountains in *Philosophy, Science, and Sense Perception*, pp. 183-186). Nevertheless, such examples do not alter the fact that there are many other instances in which we *do* regard objects such as books, or neckties, or dresses, as having a specific color that is sometimes distorted by the illumination or that is not seen because of a lack of illumination.

9. It is to be noted that when we are looking at an object without artificial illumination and the colors we see are very indefinite, we feel no hesitation in using artificial illumination to see *better*. It is only when the norm of definiteness is attained in both cases that we give preference to colors seen under conditions of ordinary daylight.

10. To be sure, insofar as the test patterns used consist in simple block letters, only definiteness of contour, and not definiteness of individual features, comes into question; in more complex visual patterns, however, the latter are of fundamental importance in our comparative judgments.

11. It appears to me that there also are other distinguishing criteria on the basis of which waking experience and dreams are distinguished, and that some of these have to do with kinaesthetic sensations, particularly relating to our sense organs. However, for my present purposes such additional factors can be neglected.

12. Furthermore, in the passage from the *Meditations* which I cited in note 5, above, Descartes seems to me to be making use of the same phenomenon; and Hobbes's description of memory and imagination as "decaying sense" is presumably also related to it. One may also note that both Leibniz and Berkeley introduced the criterion of vividness, no less than relying on coherence, in drawing their distinctions between ideas of perception and other ideas: cf. Leibniz's *Philosophic Papers and Letters*, ed. Leroy Loemker, 2, 603, and Berkeley's *Principles of Human Knowledge*, part 1, sect. 36.

13. In the *Analysis of Sensation*, ch. 1, sect. 11, Ernst Mach cited the same phenomenon with respect to what Hume had called an idea, as distinct from an impression. As he said with respect to such an idea: " . . . and what is of especial note, it plainly appears in a different domain."

14. In *Sense and Sensibilia* (p. 48f.), Austin has made a related point, arguing that dreams may be said to have a dreamlike quality.

15. This is obviously a more fundamental problem than the one just discussed, for unless two impressions are taken to be impressions of one and the same object, the question of their consistency or inconsistency would not arise.

3

Subjective, Objective,
and Conceptual Relativisms

Frequently, throughout the history of modern philosophy, it has been held that although claims to knowledge can be adequately defended against relativistic arguments, judgments of value cannot. Positions of this type were widely accepted in Anglo-American philosophy during the last half-century. To be sure, some philosophers have at all times attacked such a dichotomy, holding that arguments similar to those that justify a rejection of relativism are mistaken in both spheres. Recently, however, there has been an attack on the same dichotomy from the opposite direction. An increasing number of philosophers have accepted positions that lead to a relativization of judgments of fact as well as of judgments of value. This tendency has many independent roots, and those who accept it in one form or another may hold antithetical positions on a variety of other issues. I shall therefore not attempt to disentangle the presuppositions that underlie contemporary relativistic theories of knowledge, though I shall indicate some of them in passing; rather, I shall confine myself to showing that an acceptance of relativism in the theory of knowledge frequently—and perhaps always—involves a prior commitment to nonrelativistic interpretations of at least *some* judgments concerning matters of fact. Consequently, whatever may be the case with respect to judgments of value, epistemological relativism may be said to be self-limiting.[1]

I

In order to proceed with the argument, it will be necessary to identify what various forms of "relativism" have in common. The most basic common denominator appears to be the contention that assertions cannot be judged true or false in themselves, but must be so judged with reference to one or more aspects of the total situation in which they have been made. The aspects of a particular assertion's context with respect to which it is treated as relative may be of various types; I shall single out three such types for discussion. The first holds that any assertion must be viewed in relation to the beliefs and attitudes of the particular individual making the assertion. As a consequence, one cannot speak of the truth or falsity of an assertion

Reprinted by permission from the *Monist*, 62 (1979):403-28.

simpliciter: what should be understood is that the assertion is "true (or false) for him or for her." A relativism of this type may best be described as *subjective relativism*, the truth being relative to the characteristics of the person making the assertion. Though a relativism of this sort has sometimes been accepted with respect to judgments of value (as uses of the *de gustibus* maxim remind us), it has rarely been applied in a wholesale manner when the truth or falsity of judgments of fact is at issue.

A second type of relativism is that which has been characterized as *objective relativism*. It takes as its point of departure the undoubted fact that whenever a person makes an assertion there is some reason for his making that assertion; further, it appeals to the fact that whenever an assertion is made, the person making that assertion occupies some particular position, or point of view, with reference to that with which his assertion is concerned; finally, it points out that any assertion refers only to some and not other aspects of that with which it is concerned. These three components in the knowledge relationship are not likely to be wholly independent of one another. A person's purposes will often determine with which aspects of an object he is concerned, and his purposes frequently depend upon the specific relationship in which he stands to that particular object. Consequently (the objective relativist argues), the truth of what is asserted cannot be judged independently of the context in which the assertion is made: all assertions are relative to the purposes of whoever makes the assertion, the point of view from which his judgment is made, and the aspect of the object with which he is concerned. While this leads an objective relativist to deny that assertions are either true or false *simpliciter*, his position is not identical with that of a subjective relativist. Unlike the subjective relativist, he would deny that what is taken to be true or false is primarily a function of the beliefs and attitudes of the particular person making the assertion: rather, it is relative to the nature of the total context in which the assertion is made. Also, unlike the subjective relativist, an objective relativist claims that such judgments will be concurred in by others who are similarly placed and share the same concerns. Thus, he claims that knowledge can be said to be objective in spite of its being relative to a particular context.

A third general form of relativism is that which I shall term *conceptual relativism*. Like objective relativism, it holds that judgments concerning matters of fact are to be interpreted with reference to the context in which they are made, not with reference to the individual who makes them. That which is relevant for a conceptual relativist is not, however, the individual's purposes or interests, nor the particular relationship in which he stands to the objects with which his judgments are concerned; rather, what is relevant is taken to be the intellectual or conceptual background that the individual brings to his problems from the cultural milieu to which he belongs. A relativism of this type has been brought to the forefront of attention by aspects of Wittgenstein's later work, by Benjamin Lee Whorf, by T. S. Kuhn, and more recently by Richard Rorty, among others. I shall attempt to show that in its appeal to what may be termed culture-bound interpretations of matters of fact, this type of relativism must rely on data that are not to be interpreted as themselves being culture-bound. In this case as in the others, I shall argue that those who attempt to establish relativism make claims that involve what I have elsewhere termed "the self-excepting fallacy," that is, the fallacy of stating a generalization that purports to hold of all persons but which, inconsistently, is not then applied to oneself.[2]

Let us first take the case of subjective relativism and consider it briefly. A subjective relativist puts forward the claim that the judgments of fact which are made by others are always relative to their own interests, attitudes, and biases as these are reflected in antecedently held commitments or beliefs. Not only does he make this claim, but he attempts to support it by evidence. Yet, in order to do so, he must assume that he himself actually knows the interests, attitudes, and biases of others and that, in addition, he knows that their assertions would have been significantly different had it not been for these particular interests, attitudes, and biases. Thus, when a historical relativist such as Charles A. Beard offers evidence in favor of his relativism by analyzing the role of bias in the historical writings of others, he fails to take seriously the fact that if his thesis were universally true it would also apply to his own analysis, thus destroying the evidence on which it was based.

To be sure, evidence *can* be gathered to show that there are many cases in which one can only understand why a person asserted what he did—and why he presumably took his assertion to be true—by understanding that his assertion was related to his own particular interests, attitudes, and biases. What must not be overlooked, however, is that evidence of this sort is only convincing so long as it is not itself interpreted relativistically, as a consistent subjective relativist would be forced to interpret it. Nor could a subjective relativist escape this criticism by appealing to some general Protagorean or Carneadean thesis instead of actual instances in which an individual's judgments are distorted: such general theses are only convincing insofar as they are assumed to follow from psychological or ontological premises. Such premises, however, must be taken to be true in a sense other than the only sense which the subjective relativist ascribes to the concept of truth.

II

It is a less simple matter to single out the difficulties in objective relativism, but such difficulties nonetheless exist. I shall discuss them under three heads: first, with respect to the role of interest or purpose in judgments concerning matters of fact; second, with respect to the influence of the standpoint of the observer on the judgments he makes; and, third, with respect to the consequences that follow from the fact that any judgment is selective, dealing only with particular features or aspects of the object or situation judged. While there is in each case an element of truth in the contentions of the objective relativist, the conclusions that are claimed to follow from these facts will not successfully withstand scrutiny.

The term *objective relativism* was coined by Arthur E. Murphy in 1927, in an article entitled "Objective Relativism in Dewey and Whitehead."[3] As one notes in that article, what was most characteristic of the position was a belief that events and relationships, not objects, are the ultimate constituents of what there is. However, as the term suggests, it was on the epistemological consequences held to follow from this ontological position that attention was primarily focused.[4] It is with these epistemological consequences that I shall here be concerned.[5]

No one, I take it, would be likely to deny that every judgment concerning a matter of fact issues from a situation in which the person making that judgment has an interest or a purpose related to that with which his judgment is concerned. One should, however, distinguish two ways in which such interests can presumably come into play. On the one hand, whatever is an object of knowledge may interest a person because it is instrumentally connected with some state of affairs which he would like to bring about or avoid; in such cases his present interest in the object depends upon a further purpose that is of interest to him. On the other hand, a person may presumably be interested in an object for no reason other than that it does in fact interest him. In that case his activity with respect to that object need not be said to be lacking in purpose; the purpose, however, will be one of appreciating, or exploring, or understanding, or explaining the particular object or state of affairs in which he is interested. Of course, these two basic types of interest need not be mutually exclusive: an individual's purposes in any situation may be of both types, and both may be simultaneously present. What the objective relativist underemphasizes, overlooks, or sometimes even denies, is that there are these two possible relations between an individual's interests and that with which his judgments are concerned; in the account of knowledge most characteristic of objective relativists, only the instrumental relationship, and not an interest in the object for its own sake, is stressed.[6]

In the case of Dewey at least, the objective relativist's stress on this aspect of judgments can be accounted for in terms of his acceptance of an instrumental view of mind. It is clear, however, that anyone holding such a view does so with the intention of claiming that this view is true independently of his own interests and purposes. Pushing this contention a step further, it may plausibly be argued that one reason why Dewey accepted an instrumental theory of mind was that he believed it to be demanded by evolutionary theory. As his famous essay on the influence of Darwinism on philosophy makes clear, Dewey derived great support for his own philosophic views from that which was revolutionary in Darwin's thought. At the same time, it was only because he regarded Darwin's theory as true, independently of the use to which he could put it, that Dewey could in fact use it in this way. In fact, in order to accept Darwin's theory as true, the only instrumental function that had to be attributed to it was that it had permitted Darwin and others to understand and explain a wide variety of facts with which biologists, paleontologists, philosophers, and theologians were concerned. Thus, it is my contention that the view of the knowledge relationship stressed by objective relativists such as Dewey, ultimately depends on regarding *some* assertions concerning matters of fact as true or false independently of any further uses to which those assertions can be put.

I now turn to consider the second aspect of the objective relativist's thesis: that judgments of matters of fact are always relative to the standpoint of the person judging. Here the notion of "a standpoint" can be conceived in either of two ways: temporally or spatially. Those objective relativists who have been primarily concerned with historical knowledge, rather than with sense-perception, have emphasized the relativity of our judgments with respect to *when* they are made, whereas those who have been primarily concerned with sense-perception, or with analogues to it, have frequently placed greater emphasis on the fact that different observers, looking at the same object, do so from different points of view. Yet, no sharp line is to be drawn between these two approaches. Objective relativists are also apt to use the concept of "a point of view" in at least a metaphorical sense when dealing with historical knowledge; similarly, temporal factors may be taken into account in discussions of sense-perception when, for example, objective relativists refer to the epistemological implications of the Doppler effect or to those entailed by the finite velocity of light. Regardless of whether they emphasize the implications of temporal or spatial relations, objective relativists hold that differences in standpoints are objective facts and that they influence every judgment that it is possible for anyone to make. Whether this claim is consistent with an acceptance of relativism, as I have defined it, is what I propose to examine.

With respect to the influence of the temporal factor on judgments of the past, those objective relativists who are concerned with historical knowledge may stress either of two ways in which such influences are brought to bear. Each, however, depends on the fact that selection and interpretations are essential to the writing of history. The first and less radical of these arguments consists in the claim that what dominates the selection and interpretation of the past by those writing history in the present is to be found in present interests, *and* that those events on which interest will be focused are events that the historian sees as in some way continuous with his present. Consequently, as the present changes, so will interpretations of the past.[7] This argument is flawed. It fails to take into account the basis on which historians are led to accept, reject, or modify the work of other historians. Even if one were to accept the fundamental premise of the argument—that historians are only interested in the past insofar as they see it as continuous with their present—it would be inconsistent with the ways in which historians actually assess the accounts of both their contemporaries and their predecessors. For example, historical accounts are criticized for claiming continuities among events which evidence fails to substantiate; furthermore, they are even more severely criticized for having neglected those aspects of the past which are discontinuous with what is characteristic of the historian's present. In short, it is in relation to accumulated evidence deriving from many sources, and not in relation to the historian's own present, that the works of past and present historians are actually judged. That this is so should not be surprising: the very notion of taking something as *evidence* involves treating it as not being self-referential, but as pointing beyond itself. Thus, even a historian who may be exceptionally immersed in present concerns, treats the evidence on which his account is based as referring not to his own situation but to something that occurred in the past. When later historians subsequently assess the reliability of his account, it is in relation to all the evidence at their disposal, and not merely in terms of whatever evidence his own situation led him to use. Thus, if an objective relativist is to take seriously criticism as it is practiced in the historical profession, he will have to enlarge his theory, allowing some assertions to be true or false with reference to accumulated evidence rather than in relation to the particular historical conditions out of which they arose. Because objective relativists such as Dewey and Randall do not in their own historical writings seem to deny that one interpretation of the past is better warranted than another, their actual critical practice is not consistent with the form of relativism they espouse.[8]

The second and more radical argument that objective relativists derive from the purported influence of a temporal factor on historical judgments rests on the claim that in fact the past itself undergoes significant change through what later develops. This thesis rests on the contention that what is incipient in any event cannot be recognized until the future unrolls, and the connections between that event and its consequences become apparent. As Randall said, "the history the historian will write, and the principle of selection he will employ, will be undergoing continual change, because the histories things themselves possess are continually changing, always being cumulatively added to. With the occurrence of fresh events, the meaning and significance of past events is always changing."[9] Therefore, a historian who attempts to write contemporary history is not likely to hit upon an adequate interpretation of the events with which he deals, since he will be too close in time to those events to grasp their actual outcomes. Nor will the work of later historians prove to be more acceptable, because ever new consequences of the past will continue to appear in the future.[10] Therefore, contrary to fact, each historical inquiry will have to be evaluated with reference to its own standpoint only; as Randall said, "Knowledge is 'objective' only *for* some determinate context: it is always knowledge of *the* structure and relations essential *for* that context. In historical knowledge, the context is always a teleological and functional one, pointing to a structure of means and ends, of 'means *for*' or 'relative *to*' ends and eventuations."[11]

Once again we must ask whether these assertions are to be applied to the contentions of the objective relativist himself. What obviously underlay Randall's thesis was a set of metaphysical assumptions which can be described as a modernized form of Aristotelianism. Randall, however, does not ask whether one is to view his acceptance of these assumptions as relative to his own historical situation. In that case, what would follow from them would presumably have to undergo change as the historical situation in philosophy changes. Yet, Randall defines metaphysics as "the investigation of existence as existence, an inquiry distinguished from other inquiries by a subject-matter of its own, the general characters and the ultimate distinctions illustrated and exhibited in each specific and determinate kind of existence and existential subject-matter."[12] Given that definition, one has a right to expect that such inquiries uncover a set of categories which are objective, not only in the sense that they are nonarbitrary, but also as denominating the pervasive features of whatever exists. Randall himself assuredly believed that his metaphysical categories were, in principle, capable of doing this, since it was only because of his insistence that process is the ultimate metaphysical category, and that the world involves a pluralism of processes, that (like Dewey and Whitehead) he initially accepted objective relativism. Yet, if objective relativism were to be applied to this metaphysical position it would undercut that position's claim to being true in any nonrelative sense. Once again, then, it should be apparent that even though it is always possible to show that *some* assertions are indeed relative to the interests, purposes, and historically conditioned circumstances of those who assert them, not all assertions can consistently be interpreted in this way.

At this point an objective relativist might abandon a temporalistic interpretation of what constitutes the standpoint to which judgments are relative (except perhaps in the case of historical judgments), and might instead appeal to the analogy of spatial location to indicate that to which every judgment is relative. He might then hold that just as objects appear to be of different shapes when viewed from different perspectives, or of different sizes when viewed from different distances, so the truth of any factual judgment is relative to the point of view from which that object is seen. In metaphysical propositions, for example, one philosopher might stress mobility and change whereas another might stress relative permanence, and both might be correct if that which is judged does in fact have both aspects: each judgment would then be true relative to those features of the object to which the judgment had reference. As McGilvary said in the opening sentences of his Carus Lectures. "Every philosophy is the universe as it appears in the perspective of a philosopher. It is a *Welt angeschaut* and not *die Welt an und für sich.*"[13] This statement, taken alone, may appear as a relatively innocuous truism, but its consequences, as McGilvary developed them, were radical; and it was with these consequences that his book as a whole was concerned. In his case as in the case of Randall, one finds that underlying his perspectival relativity there was a fundamental metaphysical thesis. He stated this thesis as follows:

> Every particular in the world is a member of a context of particulars and is what
> it is only because of its context; and every character any member has, it has only
> by virtue of its relations to other members of that context. (P. 17)

He then interpreted this as implying that

> In a world of nature any 'thing' at any time is, and is nothing but, the totality of
> the relational characters, experienced or not experienced, that the 'thing' has
> at that time in whatever relations it has at that time to other 'things.' (P. 30)

From this it followed as a corollary that

> Every character which any thing has at any time it has only as it is a term of
> some relation in which at that time it stands to some other thing. (P. 36)

I do not believe that these metaphysical doctrines can be rendered harmless
by turning McGilvary's own perspectival theory against them; unlike Randall's temporalistic version of objective relativism, McGilvary's perspectivism does not undercut his own metaphysical claims. Nevertheless, there are
important difficulties in his theory which must be brought to light.

One such difficulty is that to which Lovejoy continually referred in his
attack on objective relativism: that the doctrine dissolves the object (whatever
it is) into a set of perspectival views. Therefore, two persons standing in different relations to what is ostensibly one and the same object will not be en-
countering the same object at all. Where that is the case, their views could
not be said to be contradictory, and the question of whether any of these
diverse views is more correct than any other is not a question that should
arise. To this McGilvary would presumably have answered through appealing to his basic realistic postulate: that we are living organisms and that
there is presented to us in sense experience a real world in which each of us
does and must live.[14] While an appeal of this type would not have satisfied
Lovejoy, who would have insisted (and rightly, I believe) that such a contention presupposes knowledge that is not restricted to the knower's own standpoint,[15] let us grant that McGilvary's realistic assumption provides an escape from the danger than when two people claim to know a particular
object, what they know is not in any sense the same object. Even so, a difficulty remains. Because the characters possessed by any object are in all
cases claimed to be dependent on its relations to other objects and because
these relations vary indefinitely, it will possess many characteristics that
will appear to be incompatible. The same railroad tracks will be parallel
and convergent, the surface of the same coin will be both circular and
elliptical, depending on the position in which a percipient organism stands
(or might stand) in relation to it. The same person may be kind or cruel, the
same object a piece of brass or a work of art, the same drug curative or
poisonous, depending on what experiences define the characteristics of the
object with which we are concerned. None of this need be troublesome so

long as we find ways to explain why it is that the same object can take on characteristics that appear to be antithetical. This, however, involves offering explanations that appeal to differences between the various relations in which that object stands to other objects. Such explanations could not be given were our knowledge limited to the relations directly existing between these objects and ourselves. We must also know how they affect other persons and how they affect other objects. This is the sort of knowledge which, for example, we acquire through physical and physiological optics; such knowledge is neutral with respect to any one perspective, and through it we are in a position to explain the differences in perception which depend upon perspectival differences. Similarly, the physics of acoustics serves to explain why a train's whistle sounds as it does when the train is approaching and sounds differently as it recedes. In these explanations of the Doppler effect, a standpoint is adopted which is free of these differing perspectival views, neither of which is adopted, though both are explained. Nor would one be entitled to take the perspective of the train's engineer as authoritative if one could not, through a knowledge of physics, reconcile what is given from his perspective with what is given from each of the other two points of view. Or, to choose an example of a different sort, it is necessary for us to gain nonperspectival knowledge of the characteristics of human beings in order to explain why some particular person may be kind to some and cruel to others, or kind under one set of circumstances and cruel under others. In order to make sense of his actions, we must somehow place ourselves within the perspective of that person himself, or we shall not understand how such contrary characteristics are elicited by different situations. The striving to justify this sort of transcendence of one's *own* perspective is evident even among some of the strongest defenders of perspectivism, as is evident both in Karl Mannheim's essay, "Wissenssoziologie,"[16] and in George Herbert Mead's paper, "The Objective Reality of Perspectives."[17] Both Mannheim and Mead in fact assumed that the theorist can escape the limitations of his own perspective, and this is but another example of what I have termed the self-excepting fallacy.

I come now to the third aspect of the objective relativist's position, the fact that every judgment is selective and does not fully mirror all that an observer viewing an object is actually in a position to see. Thus, the knowledge we have of any object is limited not only by the position we occupy with respect to that object, but it is also limited by the focus of our interest on one rather than another of its characteristics. It is on this basis that the objective relativist argues that the object as we know it is not knowledge of what it may be like independently of us, but only what it is like for and to us.

In order to draw this conclusion from the undoubted fact that our attention is always selective, the objective relativist must assume that if we could simultaneously discern all of the characteristics of any object, no one of them would be exactly like what we take it to be when viewed independently of the others. This is surely not always the case. I may, for example, be so situated that I at first can see only one surface of an object, but when, later, I am able to view it from other angles, my conception of that surface may not have had to undergo change. Nor is this sort of independence of one characteristic of an object from its other characteristics always confined to simple cases of this sort. In coming to know a person, for example, I may first be struck by some trait, such as his shyness, and may only later come to discover that he is also exceptionally bright. While the fact that I know him to be bright as well as being shy will round out my picture of the person and will provide additional insight into his character, this will not alter my view that he is in fact exceptionally shy, nor will my awareness of his shyness conceal the fact that he is exceptionally bright. To be sure, it is often the case that various characteristics possessed by a person, or by an object, are so related that if one were to attempt to describe one of these characteristics independently of its relations to the others that description might be not only inadequate but positively misleading. The existence of such cases does not, however, establish the objective relativist's thesis, because what they involve is a *correction* of the original judgment, not merely the substitution of one judgment for another. That which entitles one to view them as corrections is the fact that what has changed is not the relationship between the observer and that which he is observing; rather, it is the obserever's discernment of a previously unrecognized relationship *within* the object itself.

An objective relativist might be inclined to challenge such an answer, asking why one should hold that the discernment of this relationship can be said to have yielded a more adequate view of the object, rather than merely a different one. To this there is, I believe, an obvious answer. While all objective relativists hold that judgments are relative to a particular standpoint, they do not hold that all are equally worthy of credence. For example, although a judgment regarding the past is made with reference to the relationships between that past and the present, not all judgments that purport to refer to the past are taken to be equally reliable: only those that refer to what did actually exist in the past are to be accepted.[18] Thus, even though every judgment is made from some point of view and deals with only some aspects of an object that is seen from that point of view, it is not with reference to its point of view that we discriminate among judgments. Instead, we are forced to appeal to whatever judgments issue from a point of view that permits an observer to discern whatever qualities the object itself possesses. Thus, objective relativists, no less than those holding other epistemological positions, will have to appeal to tests that decide what characteristics particular objects do in fact possess. This involves an abandonment of the assumption that objects possess characteristics only insofar as they are seen from certain points of view and with respect to certain purposes.

III

We now turn to a consideration of the even more radical thesis of conceptual relativism.[19] While its background is complex, one can isolate three convergent streams of influence which have been of special importance in establishing the widespread acceptance it enjoys today. The first stems from developments within the philosophy of science; the second from problems of method in the *Geisteswissenschaften*; the third from the ways in which certain perceptual phenomena, and also date drawn from comparative linguistics, have often been interpreted. I shall briefly—and admittedly inadequately—identify each of these factors.

With respect to the first, since the last quarter of the nineteenth century it has increasingly come to be recognized that scientific explanations are not uniquely determined by the observations from which they may have been derived, nor from those which are used as confirmatory evidence for them. While this conviction was an essential feature in the otherwise divergent views of Mach, Poincaré, and Duhem, among others, it failed to forestall the acceptance of the epistemological foundationalism that was characteristic of logical positivism. The acceptance of that form of foundationalism was, however, shaken by Quine's "Two Dogmas of Empiricism," in which it was claimed that in conflicts between observations and a theory it is not necessarily the theory that must be abandoned. Instead, these conflicting observations may be reinterpreted in terms of an alternative theory. In addition, logical positivism had been committed to drawing a sharp distinction between observational terms and theoretical terms, but that distinction came under increasingly severe attack, which also served to undermine the foundationalism characteristic of the positivist's position.

With respect to the second of the influences, a cognate issue arose in connection with the interpretation of texts and also in connection with the interpretation of the character of a person or a historical period. Ast, Schleiermacher, and Dilthey identified this problem as "the hermeneutic circle."[20] The apparent circularity in interpretation arises because one can presumably only interpret any given portion of a text in terms of the whole of which it is a part, but one is only in a position to interpret that whole through experiencing its individual parts. Thus, the interplay of part and whole in all interpretations of texts, and in interpreting the character of persons or of historical periods, parallels the interplay of observation and theory in interpretations of nature. Here, too, the search for a rock-bottom and unassailable foundation of facts, on which interpretation is supposedly based, is lacking.

In addition to the problems ostensibly posed by the hermeneutic circle, the thought of those who were concerned with the methods of the *Geisteswissenschaften* was often deeply affected by subjective relativism, and sometimes by that form of objective relativism which stresses the role of ideological factors in determining the content of our systems of knowledge. In either case it was claimed that whatever individual facts could be objectively established would be insufficient to determine the account in which they were included. Instead, it was held that these facts were fitted into a structure that depended on the values that the inquirer himself had brought to the materials with which he sought to deal. Once again, this parallels the position of conceptual relativism when applied to the sciences: interpretations do not emerge directly from the facts in any given situation; rather, the facts cited are those which conform to some accepted interpretation.[21]

Turning now to the impact of psychology and comparative linguistics, we may note that conceptual relativism has been fostered by interpretations placed on our perception of reversible figures, such as the duck-rabbit figure made familiar through Wittgenstein's use of it; in addition, conceptual relativism has been fostered by the uses to which data derived from comparisons between Indo-European languages and native American languages have been put by Whorf and by others.

First, with respect to the question of the epistemological significance of reversible figures, one can see that if one takes such figures as paradigmatic of what occurs in all sense-perception, one would be tempted to accept conceptual relativism. It is, for example, natural to say when describing what one sees when one looks at the duck-rabbit figure that one sees it as a duck or else as a rabbit. Similarly, in the reversible cube figure, one can describe what one sees as a cube seen from above or as a cube seen from below. In such cases the same visual figure is seen in either of two ways, and each is no less legitimate than the other. Thus, what is directly presented to our sense organs does not uniquely determine in what ways we may describe it. When these cases are taken as paradigmatic for the analysis of perceptual experience (as they have been by such conceptual relativists as Hanson and Kuhn), attention is focused on the question of "seeing *as*," rather than on whatever is involved in the act of seeing itself. As a consequence, in many instances philosophic interest has been diverted from those traditional epistemological questions that had their roots in analyses of the specific conditions that are responsible for different persons (or for the same person at different times) attributing different properties to the same object. Many contemporary philosophers (unlike Locke, Berkeley, and Hume) would regard all such empirically oriented questions as lying wholly outside philosophical analysis. As a consequence, they are unlikely to ask in what ways reversible figures differ from nonreversible figures. However, unless it can be shown that there are no epistemologically relevant differences between reversible and nonreversible figures, it is odd to take the former as paradigmatic for analyses of perception generally.[22]

Furthermore, a blanket use of the concept "seeing as" conceals difficulties. It is perfectly normal to say that one sees the duck-rabbit figure first "as a duck" and then "as a rabbit." It is sometimes also perfectly normal to use the locution "seeing as" in cases in which one is not referring to reversible figures. For example, one can say that the astronomer looking at a photographic plate sees a point of light "as a star." However, there is no parallel between that case and what occurs with respect to reversible figures, except that the same locution has been used. In looking at the photographic plate, the astronomer can simultaneously recognize what he sees "as a point of light" and "as a star," but what he sees is not a reversible figure. Rather, that which is seen can be described in either of two ways, each of which is equally applicable *at the same time.*[23] In a reversible figure, on the contrary, what I see at any one time is *either* a rabbit or a duck, not both. I do not see a rabbit that I also recognize to be a duck, nor a duck that I can equally well describe as a rabbit. Given this difference in the two types of case, the mere fact that the same locution is used does not justify the analogy that N. R. Hanson, T. S. Kuhn, and others have drawn between reversible figures and the observational data used in the sciences.[24]

Having considered, and rejected, the ways in which reversible figures have recently been used in support of conceptual relativism, I now turn to a comparable argument that has its source in comparative linguistics. The most striking instance of epistemological conclusions being drawn from this source is Benjamin Lee Whorf's hypothesis that all natural languages include an implicit metaphysics and that how the world appears to those using a language reflects the metaphysics contained in its grammatical structure. To choose merely one example of his formulation of this point, I shall cite the following:

> The background linguistic system (in other words, the grammar) of each language is not merely a reproducing instrument for voicing ideas but rather is itself the shaper of ideas, the program and guide for the individual's mental activity, for his analysis of impressions, for his synthesis of his mental stock in trade. . . . The categories and types that we isolate from the world of phenomena we do not find there because they stare every observer in the face; on the contrary, the world is presented as a kaleidoscopic flux of impressions which has to be organized by our minds—and this means largely by the linguistic systems in our minds.[25]

Whorf's thesis was based on an analysis of differences in the grammatical structure of different languages, with reference, for example, to factors such as whether there are tenses representing past, present, and future in the language; or, to choose another example, whether or not sentences in the language are formed in terms of subject and predicate. That there are significant differrences of this sort in the structure of different languages cannot be questioned. What must not be overlooked, however, is that the illustrations used by Whorf show that, in spite of linguistic differences, users of different languages in many cases refer to precisely the same objects and activities. For example, his illustrations in "Science and Linguistics" show that persons using Shawnee and persons using English are equally able to refer to cleaning a gun with a ramrod. Similarly, as is evident in his paper, "Language and Logic," it is possible in both the English and Nootka languages to refer to inviting people to a feast, though the grammatical structure of the two sentences is wholly different.

Nor is this situation confined to cases in which two alternative languages refer to relatively isolable objects or activities. As Whorf's own translations indicate, precisely the same situation obtains in those cases in which he seeks to deny that it does—for example, in how the world of nature is viewed by those using different languages. Comparing the views of nature of the Apache with those which ostensibly depend on the structure of Indo-European languages, he said:

> The real question is: What do different languages do, not with artificially isolated objects but with the flowing fact of nature in its motion, color, and changing form; with clouds, beaches, and yonder flight of birds? For as goes our segmentation of the face of nature, so goes our physics of the cosmos.[26]

Then, speaking of the Apache, he continues:

> Such languages, which do not paint the separate-object picture of the universe to the same degree as do English and its sister tongues, point toward possible new types of logic and possible new cosmical pictures.

Yet, even though Whorf was brought up on Indo-European languages, with the logic of his thinking presumably dependent on the grammatical structure of these languages, he was able to understand how nature appeared to the Apache. In short, as a linguist, he was not bound by his own grammar, but stood outside both his own language and theirs. In doing so he was not only able to understand both languages, but was able, using English, to explicate the world-views implicit in other languages. It follows, then, that conceptual relativism, as represented by Whorf, is not universally applicable: at least he and other linguists are not entrapped within it.

And how, we may ask, does the linguist escape? It is, I submit, because he takes statements made in each language to be referential and in each case seeks to establish that to which they refer. If it were the case that every statement in a language received its meaning solely through other expressions used within that language, each language would be self-enclosed, and no equivalence of meaning between statements in any two languages could be established. Thus, contrary to fact, neither Whorf nor anyone else could effect even a rough translation from one language to another. What breaks the circle is a recognition of the intentionality inherent in all uses of language and of the possibility of offering ostensive definitions of the meanings of many words, phrases, and sentences that occur in a given language. It is on these foundations that any person must ultimately rely when learning a language. It is only later, after having acquired knowledge of two or more languages, that anyone is in a position to compare their lexicons, grammatical structures, and modes of expression. Such comparisons are of interest, and perhaps suggest that those who use a particular language will be likely to single out for attention aspects of the environment which may not so readily be noticed by those whose language possesses a very different form. Conceptual relativism, however, goes beyond a recognition that this may be the case. In its linguistic form, it holds that the influence of language on thought is so pervasive and so compelling that, insofar as it is a question of truth or falsity, one cannot legitimately compare statements made in one language with those made in another: the truth of each must be assessed within the framework provided by the conceptual system implicit in the structure of the language used. In short, paraphrasing Kuhn, one might say that the Whorfian hypothesis contends that different languages are incommensurable, for they serve to structure different worlds. It is *this* contention that must be rejected.

As we have seen, if the Whorfian thesis were accepted without limitation, Whorf himself would have been unable to draw the contrasts he drew between different languages: in order to draw them he initially had to assume that the same objects and activities were being referred to in both languages. Therefore, it cannot be the case that how the world appears to those who speak a particular language is in *all* respects determined by the language they speak. While varying grammatical forms may lead to varying ways of classifying objects and relating them to one another, languages presuppose a world of extralinguistic objects to which the speakers of a language refer. Because, however, it is possible to refer to the same aspects of this world when using radically different languages (as Whorf's own practice established that one can), it cannot be maintained that those whose thought is expressed in different languages do not share a common world.

As we shall now see, objections of a similar sort can be raised when Kuhn speaks of scientific theories that are based on different paradigms as being incommensurable because they structure different worlds. To be sure, his thesis is less all-embracing than was Whorf's, for he confined his attention to what occurs within science, thus excluding any discussion of the more general world pictures.[27] Furthermore, in speaking of scientific theories he explicitly acknowledged that historians of science *are* in a position to compare these theories (just as linguists are in a position to compare languages); he also held that scientists themselves are able to do so. Nevertheless, he held that merely being able to recognize the point of view from which another theory was formulated does not serve to establish true communication between those holding different theories.[28] Although he then outlined various stages in a process of persuasion which could lead from the acceptance of an old paradigm to the adoption of a new one, he nevertheless insisted that, in the end, it is only through a "gestalt-switch," that is, a "conversion," that the new comes to be established.

In this discussion, and throughout his analyses of scientific procedures, Kuhn was forced to assume that rival theories do in fact include reference to some of the same sets of facts, although placing different interpretations on them.[29] Were this not the case, there would be no conflict whatsoever between them: they would in so sense be *rival* theories, because each would pass the other by, without contact. That there is in fact rivalry concerning the proper interpretation of the same data was acknowledged by Kuhn when he said,

"Before the group accepts it, a new theory has been tested over time by the research of a number of men, some working within it, others within its traditional rival."[30] Nevertheless, he placed relatively little emphasis on this stage in scientific conflicts. While he would surely admit that particular conflicts are sometimes resolved by an appeal to further facts, as is the case when hypotheses of limited generality are tested, what he emphasized were those clashes in which differences between an old and a new interpretation of many of the same data rested on the use of basically different conceptual frameworks. To the question of how such differences can be adjudicated, Kuhn's answer is that they cannot be: one theory simply supplants the other. In this connection he quotes Planck's dictum: "A new scientific theory does not triumph by convincing its opponents and making them see the light, but rather because its opponents eventually die, and a new generation grows up that is familiar with it."[31]

It cannot be denied that there usually is a deep, ingrained conservatism in those who uphold an earlier theory, but it is nevertheless also necessary to account for the fact that those in the new generation convert to the new theory. As I have indicated, Kuhn uses terms such as "gestalt-switch" and "conversion" to indicate the change that occurs when a revolution has taken place, but this treatment of the mechanisms needed for such a change are not, I believe, adequately analyzed.[32] To be sure, he stresses the role of anomalies in the normal science of the preceding period, but such anomalies only arise because the world of nature does not in all respects conform to what the theory had originally anticipated. Consequently, if a new theory is able, without strain, to incorporate what were formerly regarded as anomalies, and especially if the new interpretation of them constitutes an important component within the new theory, that fact alone would explain much of its appeal. What this indicates, however, is that scientific theories are not to be considered as self-enclosed systems; rather, each claims to depict and explain features of the world which are what they are, independently of the theories. This point is not, of course, in any sense novel; it is perhaps for that reason that Kuhn failed to place any emphasis on it. Had he done so, however, his account of what is involved in scientific inquiry, and how scientific change occurs, would have been far less radical than it now appears to be.[33] As I shall next indicate, in his account of what makes one scientific theory more acceptable than another, Kuhn did in fact appeal to the way the world is, but because he failed to make such appeals clear and explicit, the most striking feature of his position is his claim that alternative scientific theories are incommensurable.

As examples of passages in which an appeal is made to the world as it is, independently of theory, consider the following. "Successive paradigms tell us different things about the population of the universe and about that population's behavior."[34] Also, Kuhn acknowledges that scientific theories "attach to nature" at various points.[35] Furthermore, in discussing prerevolutionary and postrevolutionary paradigms, he holds that even in the case of those who accept differing paradigms "both their everyday and most of their scientific world and language are shared."[36] To be sure, although each of these statements suggests that no scientific theory is wholly self-enclosed, in the same passages Kuhn immediately qualifies his statements in ways that stress the interpretive role played by an accepted theoretical framework. For example, the different things we learn from different theories reflect the structure of the theory, not merely what is found in nature; similarly, while all scientific theories "attach to nature" at some points, there may be large interstices between these points which can only be filled by theory, and will be differently filled by different theories; finally, while there may be much that is shared by those who accept differing theories, the acceptance of one rather than another way of interpreting what is experienced depends not on an appeal to nature but on how rival theories structure nature.[37]

Faced by what appear to be these conflicting strains in Kuhn's epistemology, I suggest that it is enlightening to turn to what he says concerning the criteria to be used in evaluating any scientific theory. In a previously unpublished lecture, now found in *The Essential Tension*, he lists five such criteria, which, as he says, "play a vital role when scientists must choose between an established theory and an upstart competitor. Together with others of much the same sort, they provide the shared basis for theory choice."[38] I shall quote his characterizations of these criteria, at least three of which—and perhaps all five—contain an implicit appeal to facts that are theory-independent. In order to direct attention to this aspect of these criteria, I shall italicize those phrases which I take to be most significant in this respect. Kuhn says:

> First, a theory should be accurate: within its domain, that is, consequences deducible from a theory should be in demonstrated *agreement with the results of existing experiments and observations.* Second, a theory should be consistent, not only internally or with itself, but also with currently accepted theories applicable to *related aspects of nature.* Third, it should have broad scope: in particular, a theory's consequences should extend far beyond the particular observations, laws, or subtheories it was initially designed to explain. Fourth, and closely related, it should be simple, bringing order to phenomena that in its absence would be individually isolated and, as a set, confused. Fifth, . . . a theory should be fruitful of new research findings; it should, that is, *disclose new phenomena or previously unnoticed relationships among those already known.*

Kuhn does not intend this list to be exhaustive, and he is insistent that it should not be interpreted as providing an algorithm capable of unambiguously determining which of two theories is to be granted precedence. In this connection he points out that these criteria are imprecise, and that individuals may differ as to how they apply them in particular cases; furthermore, in particular cases there may be conflict between them. Consequently, he does not regard them as *rules* to be followed, but rather as *values* that guide but do not dictate the choices scientists make.[39]

With this one can have no quarrel, but it is worth noting that there are a number of passages that show that Kuhn does not actually regard each of these criteria as equally fundamental.[40] For example, he frequently stresses *accuracy*. Yet, accuracy is a relational attribute: there must be something (presumably observations of one sort or another) with respect to which a theory is judged to be accurate or lacking in accuracy; yet Kuhn does not specify what this is. To pursue this point, we may note that among the passages that stress accuracy, some single out the importance of quantitative formulations;[41] others stress accuracy of prediction, which Kuhn characterizes as being "probably the most deeply held value."[42] In fact, he holds that if one subtracts "accuracy of fit to nature" from the list of criteria, "the enterprise may not resemble science at all, but perhaps philosophy instead."[43] With respect to accuracy we may also note that Kuhn claims that "with the passage of time, scientific theories taken as a group are obviously more and more articulated. In the process, they are matched to nature at an increasing number of points and with increasing precision."[44] Finally, it is important to recall that in discussing scientific change Kuhn emphasized the role of anomalies in preparing the way for paradigm shifts. An anomaly, however, only exists when observations are apparently at odds with what an otherwise entrenched theory would lead one to expect: in short, at such points the theory ceases to be accurate. If, however, a theory were to be treated as wholly self-enclosed, there actually would not be anything to designate as an anomaly.

It is at this point that one can see the tension, and indeed the vacillation, within Kuhn's epistemology. On the one hand, his criteria are, as he says, "all standard criteria for evaluating the adequacy of a theory;" otherwise, he tells us, he would have discussed them more fully in *The Structure of Scientific Revolutions*.[45] On the other hand, however, the standard interpretation of these criteria falls within what Kuhn called "the traditional epistemological paradigm," which emphasizes the fundamental character of observation in scientific procedures, whereas Kuhn himself argues that observation is *not* foundational since it is always theory-laden. This tension can be concretely illustrated in contrasting two possible interpretations of the criterion of accuracy, as Kuhn formulates it. As we have seen, he said that accuracy demands that "consequences deducible from a theory should be in demonstrated agreement with the results of existing experiments and observations." To interpret this passage one must, however, know what are to be taken as "the results" of an experiment or observation. If these "results" are how an experiment or observation is interpreted when seen from the point of view of an antecedently accepted theory, then they cannot serve as an adequate test of that theory. It is only if they are initially taken to be neutral with respect to alternative theories that they provide a test for those theories. According to Kuhn's epistemology, however, no observation or experiment is in fact theoretically neutral.

How is one to escape this dilemma? The answer, I suggest, lies in considering what led Kuhn into it. On the one hand, he did not wish to deny or fundamentally reinterpret the standard criteria actually used by scientists in theory-choice, and these criteria include, among other elements, a reliance on the role of observation and experiment in confirming a theory. On the other hand, he insisted that the foundationalist epistemology of the positivistic interpretation of scientific procedures failed to do justice to the ways in which theory-construction can alter the *significance* of the supposedly "hard data" that observation and experiment supply. However, these two theses are not, in themselves, incompatible. What led Kuhn so to regard them was his acceptance of the view that "observation" is never controlled by that which is observed, but depends upon the prior experience of the observer, and that, as a consequence, seeing is never merely *seeing*, but is always *seeing as.* . . . He derived this view from an unqualified acceptance of conclusions drawn from various psychological experiments that he mistakenly identified with Gestalt psychology[46] and from the faulty assumption that reversible figures furnish reliable clues to what occurs in perception generally. If, however, one were to abandon these psychological assumptions, a rejection of positivistic foundationalism would be entirely compatible with ascribing to observation and experiment a role no less important than that ascribed to them by the positivist tradition.

The path to this reconciliation lies in an acceptance of the now familiar view that in a scientific theory what is to be confirmed is the theory itself, not its individual components, taken individually. But how is one to test a theory taken as a whole? To attempt to match each of two theories, taken as wholes, with "the way the world is" would be futile if both theories were relatively comprehensive in what they included.[47] This was the sort of difficulty which Kuhn stressed: each scientific theory had its own way of organizing its data, and each differed from the other in how it did so. Nevertheless, one can test a theory as a whole in a way other than attempting to *test* it *as a whole.* Every theory includes observational elements and also holds that these elements are related to one another in certain definable ways: the theoretical aspect of a theory lies precisely in this—in the relations it ascribes to the observations and experiments included within it. Therefore, one can test the adequacy of a theory as a whole by attempting to show whether or not the ascribed connections among observables, as deducible from the theory, do or do not exist; and whether their relations have been accurately determined. In addition, of course, a theory is tested through seeking out new observational or experimental data which, if the theory were true, could be immediately absorbed by it, or which, alternatively, would call for adjustments in it. If absorption or adjustments were to fail, this would ultimately lead to abandonment of the theory.

Although crudely drawn, this picture, I submit, is consistent with what was fundamental in traditional views of theory-confirmation, but does not involve the foundationalism that Kuhn attributed to positivistic philosophies of science. In this respect it admits what Kuhn attempted to establish: that no set of observational or experimental data, taken individually, can either falsify or adequately confirm a scientific theory. Yet, unlike Kuhn's position with respect to that point, it does not commit one to the view that scientific theories can successfully resist the impact of new observational and experimental data. If a view such as that which I propose were to be accepted, it would follow that even the most comprehensive scientific theories are not to be construed as self-enclosed systems, with the acceptance of one rather than another resting solely—or even largely—on sociological and psychological factors. Instead, the chief factor inducing scientific change would be located in those further inquiries that uncover relationships in nature which previous inquiry had failed to reveal.

It is, then, my contention that what is generally taken to be Kuhn's position, and what he tends to emphasize in that position, is not ultimately tenable. As in the case of Whorf and others, the conceptual relativism that he apparently sought to establish was not established; like Whorf, he was forced to relate alternative conceptual systems to various points of contact with what lay outside those systems, and it was with respect to that which was thus "outside" that the systems themselves were interpreted and judged. If what I have briefly suggested concerning the role of observational and experimental data in confirming scientific theories is sound, that which was held in common by Mach, Poincaré, and Duhem with respect to the role played by theory in the sciences need not be taken as establishing conceptual relativism. What I have suggested concerning the relation of whole and part in confirmation procedures in the domain of science can, in my opinion, also be applied to the so-called hermeneutic circle. Consequently, I believe that issues concerning interpretation within the *Geisteswissenschaften* do not pose a unique sort of problem, but that is another question that I cannot here address.

Notes

This paper, written for an issue of The Monist *which had as its subject "Objectivity in Knowledge and Valuation," distinguishes three types of cognitive relativism. With respect to each I claim that it is self-limiting, because it presupposes a commitment to a non-relativistic interpretation of some judgments. Having frequently criticized the first form, subjective relativism, in other writings—especially in* The Problem of Historical Knowledge *(1938)—I here discuss it in cursory fashion only. When considering objective relativism I was surprised to discover the extent to which it permeated American philosophy in the 1920s and 1930s; I therefore undertook to examine it at greater length than has lately been usual. At present, the form of cognitive relativism which is most pervasive is conceptual relativism, and I examine it in terms of the views of Benjamin Lee Whorf and Thomas S. Kuhn, whom I take to be two of its most widely influential representatives.*

1. I attempted to establish a similar point with respect to skepticism regarding the senses in *Philosophy, Science, and Sense Perception* (Baltimore: Johns Hopkins Press, 1964), ch. 3.

2. "Some Instances of the Self-Excepting Fallacy," reprinted below (ch. 4).

3. *Philosophical Review*, 36 (1927):121-44. Reprinted, along with a further essay, "What Happened to Objective Relativism?" in *Reason and the Common Good* (Englewood Cliffs, N.J.: Prentice-Hall, 1963).

4. The same may be said with respect to E. B. McGilvary's Carus Lectures, *Toward a Perspective Realism* (La Salle, Ill.: Open Court Publishing Co., 1956). Murphy wrote an extended review of McGilvary's book in *Journal of Philosophy*, 54 (1959):149-65. He was sympathetic but critical and reiterated his belief that objective relativism is untenable.

5. As the example of C. D. Broad illustrates, one can accept the ontological thesis underlying objective relativism but not accept its supposed epistemological consequences.

6. This parallels a criticism made by Lovejoy with reference to the application of objective relativism to historical studies. (Cf. "Present Standpoints and Past History," *Journal of Philosophy*, 36 [1939]:477-89.)

For his more extended criticism of objective relativism, cf. *The Revolt against Dualism* (Chicago: Open Court Publishing Co., 1930), especially chs. 3 and 4.

7. For example, J. H. Randall says, "A 'history' thus always involves the relation between an outcome in a present, and the past of that present. It will have both a determinate 'focus' in a 'present,' and a past from which that focus selects what has a bearing on that particular history." (*Nature and Historical Experience* [New York: Columbia University Press, 1958], p. 36.)

8. In an essay on Hobbes, Dewey wrote:

> It is the object of this essay to place the political philosophy of Hobbes in its historical context. The history of thought is peculiarly exposed to an illusion of perspective. Earlier doctrines are always getting shoved, as it were, nearer our own day. (*Studies in the History of Ideas* [New York: Columbia University Press, 1918], 1, 236.)

Yet, in the *Journal of Philosophy* in 1938, he espoused what would appear to be a diametrically opposed position, which is reiterated in *Logic: The Theory of Inquiry* (New York: Henry Holt and Co., 1938), where he says, "historical inquiry . . . is controlled by the dominant problems and conceptions of the period in which it is written" (p. 236).

With respect to the relation between Randall's theory and his practice, one may note that in "Controlling Assumptions in the Practice of American Historians" (written with George Haines, IV), the position of objective relativism was stated as follows: "Knowledge can be objective only *for* a determinate context; it is always a knowledge of the relations essential for that context." However, only five sentences later we find the following: "It is the aim of this essay to illustrate [that thesis] in terms of the principles of selection and interpretation *actually employed* by certain of the major historians of the last two generations." (Social Science Research Council, *Theory and Practice in Historical Study*, Social Science Research Council, Bulletin 54, p. 23. Italics added.) In short, it was assumed possible to discover the controlling assumptions actually employed by other historians, not how such assumptions appear to later historians from the point of view of their own controlling assumptions. A few pages later we also find the following: "These salient facts of the institutional development of the historical profession in the United States have been emphasized, because they provide the framework indispensible for understanding the assumptions and principles of selection American historians have actually employed" (p. 27). Once again, Randall's own practice seems not to have been covered by the principle of objective relativism that he held to be universally true.

9. *Nature and Historical Experience*, p. 39. As is well known, the same point is stressed in G. H. Mead's *Philosophy of the Present* (Chicago: Open Court Publishing Co., 1932).

A similar view, though based on entirely different metaphysical presuppositions, is to be found in F. H. Bradley's essay, "What is the Real Julius Caesar?" in *Essays on Truth and Reality* (Oxford: Clarendon Press, 1914). We may also note that Bergson held that the future alters the past, as when he said:

Nothing hinders us today from associating the romanticism of the nineteenth century to that which was already romantic in the classicists. But the romantic aspect of classicism is only brought [about] through the retroactive effect of romanticism once it has appeared. If there had not been a Rousseau, a Chateaubriand, a Vigny, a Victor Hugo, not only should we never have perceived, but *there would never really have existed,* any romanticism in the earlier classical writers. (*The Creative Mind* [New York: Philosophical Library, 1946], p. 23)

10. Cf. Randall, *Nature and Historical Experience,* p. 42.

11. *Nature and Historical Experience,* pp. 60-61. Cf. p. 54. For another statement of the position held by objective realists, cf. *Theory and Practice in Historical Study: A Report of the Committee on Historiography,* Social Science Research Council Bulletin 54 (1946):22-23.

12. *Nature and Historical Experience,* p. 144.

13. *Toward a Perspective Realism,* p. 1.

14. Cf. *Toward a Perspective Realism,* p. 15. Though McGilvary did take note of Lovejoy's *Revolt against Dualism,* his only extended discussion of Lovejoy concerned the interpretation of Einstein's theory of relativity, not Lovejoy's criticism of objective relativism. (Cf. *Toward a Perspective Realism,* ch. 10.)

15. Cf. *Revolt against Dualism,* p. 120.

16. Reprinted as an appendix to *Ideology and Utopia* (New York: Harcourt, Brace, 1936). Especially relevant are pp. 270-72.

17. *Proceedings of the Sixth International Congress of Philosophy* (New York: Longmans Green, 1927), pp. 75-85.

18. In this connection we may quote Randall, adding italics to signal the points at which reference is made to the actual past, not its continuity with the present:

"Objective relativism" means concretely: The history of anything is *what has happened* and becomes relevant in the envisaged past of that thing. The understanding of that history consists in looking backward from a "focus," *tracing the continuities or persistences of materials to be found in that history, uncovering the operations of the various factors and processes that have in the past modified and reconstructed those materials,* and understanding those modifications in terms of the best scientific knowledge available today. (*Nature and Historical Experience,* p. 61)

19. I have been unable to determine when, and by whom, this term was first used, but one source that has doubtless contributed to the frequency of its recent occurrence is to be found in Donald Davidson's "On the Very Idea of the Conceptual Scheme," *American Philosophical Association, Proceedings and Addresses,* 47 (1973-74):5-20. In the various uses to which the term has been put, there have been some variations in its extension, but so far as I am aware it has in all cases been used to refer to positions that strongly resemble one another.

20. Cf. Richard E. Palmer, *Hermeneutics* (Evanston: Northwestern University Press, 1969).

21. For a recent example of this point of view in historiography, cf. Wolfgang J. Mommsen, "Social Conditioning and Social Relevance," *History and Theory,* vol. 17, no. 4 (Beiheft 17):22.

22. The oddity here does not depend on the fact that reversibility occurs less frequently than nonreversibility. Rather, one should note that reversibility as it occurs in vision does not occur in any of the other sense modalities; it is thus a doubtful example to use as a paradigm for what is involved in all cases of perceiving. One should also note that it is extremely difficult to construct reversible figures. Unless one comes upon them by chance, one must in fact understand the general principles underlying visual organization, *and be able to negate them,* in order to construct such figures. Finally we may note that those optical illusions which have in the past been regarded as most important for epistemology have *not* been reversible figures. This is readily intelligible. Epistemologically important illusions are always, at the time, experienced as veridical; we later find that they conflict with other perceptual experiences that were also regarded as veridical. In the case of reversible figures, however, no comparable conflict is engendered: we simply see that the figure *is* reversible, that it can be seen in either of two ways, neither of which

need be taken to be better justified than the other. If we are puzzled by such figures, we are only puzzled as to why they are in fact reversible. (For a similar point, cf. Israel Scheffler, "Vision and Revolution: A Postscript on Kuhn," *Philosophy of Science*, 39 [1972], 372.)

23. Similar situations obtain with respect to touch and to our other sense modalities. I can, for example, designate what I hold in my hand as being a solid, cylindrical object or as being my pen; I can say that I hear a train or that I hear a train's whistle, etc. Both descriptions are in these cases (as in the photograph of a star) applicable at the same time, and there is not the involuntary alteration in them which is to be found in reversible figures.

24. Cf. N. R. Hanson, *Patterns of Discovery* (Cambridge: The University Press, 1958), ch. 1, and T. S. Kuhn, *The Structure of Scientific Revolutions*, 2d. enlarged edition (*International Encyclopedia of Unified Science*, vol. 2, no. 2. [Chicago: University of Chicago Press, 1970]), pp. 85, 111, 126f.

25. Benjamin Lee Whorf, "Science and Linguistics," in *Language, Thought, and Reality*, ed. by J. B. Carroll (Cambridge: Technology Press of Massachusetts Institute of Technology, 1956), pp. 212-13.

It is perhaps worth noting that Whorf recognizes at least one possible exception to the view that it is language that structures experience. That exception is to be found in our experience of space. However, Whorf held that even in this case our *concepts* of space (Newtonian space, Euclidean space, etc.) are linked to other concepts that are language dependent. (Cf. "Relation of Habitual Thought and Behavior to Language," in Carroll, *Language, Thought, and Reality*, p. 158f.) Whether there are other aspects of experience not directly tied to linguistic structures remains an open question. My criticism of the Whorfian hypothesis suggests that there may be, but my argument will not presuppose that there are.

It is worth noting that Kuhn also accepts the assumption that the world is originally presented as being without structure, as being—in William James's phrase—"a bloomin', buzzin' confusion." (Kuhn, *Structure of Scientific Revolutions*, p. 113.)

26. "Languages and Logic," in Carroll, *Language, Thought, and Reality*, pp. 240-41.

27. Not all who have adopted Kuhnian concepts have been equally restrained. It is perhaps worth noting that Kuhn acknowledges having received early stimulation from Whorf's theory, but mentions no special indebtedness to him (*Structure of Scientific Revolutions*, p. vi). In Kuhn, *The Essential Tension* (Chicago and London: University of Chicago Press, 1977) Whorf is mentioned, but noncommittally (p. 258).

28. *Structure of Scientific Revolutions*, pp. 202-3.

29. Kuhn rejects this phraseology, which he associates with "the traditional epistemological paradigm." Instead of referring to what occurs in a scientific revolution as providing a new *interpretation* of some of the same facts that had been included within the theories of the previous period, he describes what happens as the opening up of a new world: a seeing of different things than had previously been seen. (Cf. *Structure of Scientific Revolutions*, pp. 120-23, 111, and 150.) Because, as Kuhn acknowledges (p. 150), he has not yet worked out the epistemological consequences of this position (which is formulated by him chiefly in metaphors), I shall continue to speak of facts and their interpretation. However, the argument that follows does not, I believe, rest on my use of this terminology.

The same rejection of any dichotomy between facts and their interpretation was stressed by N. R. Hanson in ch. 1 of *Patterns of Discovery*.

30. *Essential Tension*, p. 332.

31. *Structure of Scientific Revolutions*, p. 151. For Kuhn's comparable analysis, ibid., p. 203.

32. Cf. my "Note on T. S. Kuhn's *Structure of Scientific Revolutions*," reprinted below (ch. 9).

33. In fact, Kuhn acknowledged that no new and adequate epistemological paradigm has as yet developed; therefore, he found that he was unable wholly to give up the traditional one. On the other hand, he also found himself unable to accept it (*Structure of Scientific Revolutions*, p. 126). As I shall later suggest, his dilemma was not inescapable.

34. *Structure of Scientific Revolutions*, p. 103.

35. *Essential Tension*, p. 290.

36. *Structure of Scientific Revolutions*, p. 201.

37. In this connection Kuhn says, "There is, I think, no theory-independent way to reconstruct phrases like 'really there'; the notion of a match between the ontology of a theory and its 'real' counterpart in nature now seems to me illusive in principle" (*Structure of Scientific Revolutions*, p. 206).

38. From "Objectivity, Value Judgment, and Theory Choice," *Essential Tension*, p. 322.

39. *Essential Tension*, pp. 322-25 and 330-31. In *Structure of Scientific Revolutions* (pp. 184-86), he also spoke of the criteria used by scientists as "values." It is of interest that he held that criteria such as accuracy "do much to provide a sense of community to natural scientists as a whole," and he considered such criteria as being "relatively, though not entirely, stable from one time to another and from one member to another in a particular group" (p. 185).

40. In fact, at the end of the same essay, he adds a parenthetical remark concerning the application of the five criteria to problems of theory choice. He says, "Accuracy and fruitfulness are the most immediately applicable, perhaps followed by scope. Consistency and simplicity are far more problematic" (*Essential Tension*, p. 339).

41. For example, *Structure of Scientific Revolutions*, pp. 153f. and 185.

42. *Structure of Scientific Revolutions*, p. 185; cf. *Essential Tension*, pp. 222f. and 331f.

43. *Essential Tension*, p. 331. For another instance in which he uses the locution of a fit between a theory and facts, *Structure of Scientific Revolutions*, p. 147.

44. *Essential Tension*, p. 289. As is well known, Kuhn wrestled time and again with the problem of whether or not there is progress in science. The interpretation of his views on this matter is not of primary importance for the present discussion. It is to be noted, however, that he rather consistently holds that the theories of successive periods become "vastly more powerful and precise" than those of their predecessors (*Essential Tension*, p. 30; also, cf. pp. 288-89). What he *rejects* is that such growth is continuous, and that it is incrementally cumulative, suffering no losses when one paradigm is given up for another. What he does *not* reject is that changes over time represent long-term gains—not stasis, mere alteration, or retrogression.

45. *Essential Tension*, p. 322.

46. This is pointed out in my article on Kuhn cited in n. 32 above.

47. This point has already been stressed by Quine in his "Two Dogmas of Empiricism," where he signalized it in the following striking fashion:

Physical objects are . . . convenient intermediaries—not by definition in terms of experience, but simply as irreducible posits comparable, epistemologically, to the gods of Homer. For my part I do, qua lay physicist, believe in physical objects and not in Homer's gods; and I consider it a scientific error to believe otherwise. But in point of epistemological footing the physical objects and the gods differ only in degree and not in kind. (*From a Logical Point of View* [Cambridge: Harvard University Press, 1953], p. 44).

Kuhn acknowledges a debt to this essay (*Structure of Scientific Revolutions*, p. vi). For Quine's later statment of his position, which would appear to be less extreme, cf. *Word and Object* (Cambridge: MIT Press, 1960), ch. 1 (especially, sections 5 and 6) and ch. 2 (especially sections 7 and 10).

4

Some Instances of the
Self-excepting Fallacy

When we make an empirical generalization that purports to apply to all men, we must take it as applying to ourselves no less than to others. To fail to do so is to commit what I shall term the *self-excepting fallacy*.

There doubtless are many reasons why men slip into this fallacy and these reasons are likely to differ from case to case. At least some of them may well be of psychological interest and perhaps of psychological importance. However, it is not with causal questions that I shall here be concerned. Rather, I wish to examine some of the consequences that follow when a theoretical enquirer commits this fallacy, and when, therefore, he employs generalizations about others which he does not apply to his own activities as a theoretician.

1. Let us take as a first and easy example certain forms of relativism. Among theorists of historiography is has sometimes been claimed that every historical interpretation reflects the standpoint of the observer more accurately than it reflects what the observer claims to depict in his historical account. Such a claim is often put forward on the basis of comparisons between divergent interpretations of what occurred in the past, coupled with attempts to explain these divergences in terms of the influence of biographical and sociological factors upon their authors. However, to argue for historical relativism in this way is to commit the self-excepting fallacy, because the person conducting this argument must trust his own enquiries into these biographical and sociological conditions and must take literally his own interpretations of the influence of these conditions upon his predecessors. Were he not to do so, and were he to relativize his own accounts of the lives and times of his predecessors, he would not have a basis within the history of historiography upon which to ground the relativistic thesis.

The above example may be taken as a paradigmatic case, typical of many recent views concerning human knowledge. For example, Marxism may readily fall into a similar predicament; so, too, may interpretations of Freudian theory. In addition to Freudian theorists, there are others who also accept what may be called "the motivational thesis," claiming that perceiving and thinking are invariably affected by motivational factors

Reprinted by permission from *Psychologische Forschung*, 6 (1962):383-86. Copyright © by Springer-Verlag.

whose influence cannot be isolated and cannot, therefore, be discounted. Only the self-excepting fallacy has permitted those who accept such a thesis to believe that they themselves are free from the distorting effects of motivational factors when, in their studies, they construct theories to explain what they have observed. Were it not for this fallacy their own generalizations would not have an empirical basis upon which to rely. Thus, in this case no less than in the case of historical relativism, we encounter a doctrine that is self-refuting, once the theoretician is not permitted to make an exception of himself.

2. In the above type of case an actual contradiction existed between the grounds on which a position was held and the conclusion that such a position affirmed. However, not every instance of the self-excepting fallacy is of this sort. Another type of case is that in which there is no logical contradiction between premises and conclusion, but in which, instead, an empirical generalization can be seen to be implausible as soon as one uncovers the self-excepting fallacy that that generalization involves. A paradigmatic case of this sort is to be found in certain simplistic theories of value.

Owing to the impact of some interpretations of evolution, it has frequently been assumed that human values must be regarded as based upon those biological needs that men have in common with other animal species. Thus the underived, or primary, or basic needs of men have been taken to be biological in nature, relating to biological self-maintenance and the preservation of the species; all values not directly related to the satisfaction of these needs have therefore been interpreted as being derivative from them, and secondary or less important. However, for a social psychologist to argue in this way is only possible on the basis of the self-excepting fallacy; his own work and the value that he attaches to it are not readily interpretable in terms of the satisfaction of biological needs. Thus, the crudity of an empirical generalization concerning human beings is frequently concealed from sight simply because the question of whether it is adequate when applied to the theoretician's own behavior is not raised.

Other subtler cases of this sort may also be cited. Take, for example, John Stuart Mill's analysis of why men praise virtue, taking "virtue" to mean (as did Mill) certain types of action and certain dispositions that are actually prized and pursued for their own sakes, and are so pursued even when they do not directly promote the pleasure of the agent or of others. (Mill never specifies instances of these types of action or dispositions, but he would presumably count such virtues as "self-abnegation," or "fidelity," or "moral courage" among them. It is to the praise of such dispositions, or the actions that flow from them, that I am here referring.) Mill's account of such cases leans heavily upon his interpretation of the genesis of miserliness, and of how it is that men come to pursue power or fame. In all of these instances Mill's explanation involves what has come to be called *functional autonomy.* According to the hypothesis of functional autonomy what was originally only a means to an end (e.g., money, or power, or fame) comes to be valued as an end in itself, and it comes to be so valued solely because of its prior efficacy as means. Had Mill examined the question of whether he could account for his own high estimate of the various forms of virtue in terms of their contribution to pleasure in his life or in the lives of others, he might have been led to doubt whether the sole ground for the value of these actions and dispositions was explicable in terms of functional autonomy. In cases of this sort, the self-excepting fallacy readily fosters dubious genetic generalizations, for it is easier to interpret the behavior of others in terms of preconceived genetic explanations than it is to interpret our own direct experience in similar terms.

3. In addition to leading to a self-refuting position, and in addition to permitting us to overlook the questionable character of some empirical generalizations, the self-excepting fallacy may, in one of its forms, lead to a trivialization of science itself.

The form to which I here wish to call attention involves the failure to see that in pursuing science men do not become transformed from what they otherwise are. We are all familiar with popular conceptions in which scientists are regarded as possessing unique characteristics, either evil or good. However, scientists should not fall into an error of this type, assuming that they do not share whatever capabilities and whatever limitations are characteristic of other men. To be sure, the tools of science—both physical and methodological—have been developed to perform tasks more exacting than those which can be performed without them; nonetheless, the methods of science remain tools that are employed by scientists, that is, by individual men. The more technical science becomes, the easier it is to overlook this simple fact. Yet, when it is overlooked, there quickly follows a worship of some peculiarly austere and aseptic method, because it is supposedly through a rigid adherence to such a method that a scientist can transform himself into something he would not otherwise be. The moment this happens—and the history of psychology will show that it has sometimes happened—a whole series of knotty intellectual problems will be dismissed, simply because they cannot be solved by the method that the scientific purist feels himself obliged to use. It is in this way that the scientist's self-image, if based on the self-excepting fallacy, can lead to a trivialization of science.

The scientific problems that Wolfgang Köhler has set himself to solve have never undergone this trivialization; their instrinsic difficulty has never led him to set them aside in favor of pursuing a method for its own sake. For him science has not been a game, a livelihood, or a technique, but an essential means of satisfying men's intellectual needs. Such needs, he has seen, are not the needs of the scientist alone, nor are they disguised expressions of senseless and irrational forces; rather, he has taught us to see that the principles underlying human intellectual activity may be regarded not as isolated phenomena, divorced from feeling and from action, but as principles that are present throughout nature, and that therefore lie at the very center of man.

Note

This article appeared in an issue of Psychologische Forschung *published in honor of Wolfgang Köhler. Much that it contains reflects Köhler's influence on me, which began in 1936, when we first became colleagues and friends at Swarthmore, and which has affected my thought ever since.*

The manner in which I here interpret Mill on the nature of virtue rests on a misinterpretation, which my essay, "On Interpreting Mill's Utilitarianism,*" can serve to correct. This does not, however, affect my criticism of his appeal to functional autonomy as providing an account of our praise of specific virtues.*

5

A Note on Emergence

It is my purpose in this paper concerning the doctrine of emergence to formulate a theoretical position that has not previously been explicitly formulated.[1] A clear indication of the nature of this position may, I believe, be of some help in clarifying the substantive issues that are raised whenever the problem of emergence is discussed. In this belief lies the appropriateness of including this tentative paper in the present volume: whatever is written in the hope that it may lead to a clarification of fundamental philosophic issues may properly be dedicated to the lucid and inquiring spirit of Morris R. Cohen.

I

It will be useful to note at the outset the distinction that Lovejoy has drawn between existential and functional emergence.[2]

To believe in *existential emergence* is to believe that during the course of time there have come into existence qualities, objects, or events of a type not previously present in the world, and that knowledge concerning the specific nature of such novel types of existents could not have been derived from a knowledge, however complete, of the nature of what previously existed.

To believe in *functional emergence* is to believe that the modes of functioning exhibited by existents of different types are, in some cases, ultimately and irreducibly discontinuous, so that no single set of laws could be adequate to explain the characteristic functions of all types. Such functional discontinuities may be held to be due either to the emergence of novel types of existents or to the presence of "levels of organization" among existents, regardless of whether these levels are novel or were always present in the world.[3] Where temporal novelty is stressed, the doctrine of functional emergence consists in the belief that the behavior of new types of entities cannot be adequately described through special applications of those laws that were adequate to describe the functioning of previously existing entities; where levels of organization are stressed, the doctrine of functional emergence consists in the belief that each higher level of organization possesses modes

Reprinted with permission of the publisher from *Freedom and Reason: Essays in Honor of Morris R. Cohen*, edited by Salo V. Baron, Ernest Nagel, Koppel S. Pinson. Copyright © 1951 by the Free Press. Copyright renewed 1979.

of functioning which cannot be adequately described in terms of laws that are applicable to the functioning of entities on lower levels. In either case, a belief in functional emergence consists in the claim that there is an ultimate pluralism in the laws that are adequate to describe the functioning of different types of existents.

What the concepts of existential emergence and functional emergence have in common should now be clear: both claim the nondeducibility of that with which they are concerned. Existential emergence claims that the existence of novel types of quality, objects, or events would not have been deducible from a knowledge, however complete, of the previously manifested nature and properties of existing entities. This nondeducibility of novel existents is usually referred to as "unpredictability." Functional emergence, on the other hand, claims that the laws that are necessary to explain the characteristic modes of functioning of some existents are not deducible from the laws that are adequate to explain the modes of functioning of other types of entity. This nondeducibility of particular laws is most usefully designated as "irreducibility."[4]

Now, it is to be noted that while the doctrine of emergence usually involves the claim that reality presents examples of both existential and functional emergence, it is theoretically possible to hold that there are functional emergents but no existential emergents, or that there are existential emergents but no functional emergents. In the first case one would be denying that any genuinely novel existents arise in the course of time but would be claiming an irreducible pluralism in the types of law necessary to explain the functioning of existing types of entities. In the second case one would be admitting the existence of unpredictable novelty in the universe but would be claiming that the laws that explain the manner in which these novelties function, once they exist, are reducible to the laws that explain the manner in which all other existents function, being merely special applications of these more general laws. It is this second (apparently paradoxical) position that it is my aim to elucidate.

II

Let us now connect Broad's useful distinction between transordinal, intraordinal, and ordinally neutral laws with our present distinction between existential and functional emergence.[5] What Broad means by a transordinal law is a law stating a relationship between diverse types of existents, for example, between a novel property and the conditions that are always concomitant with its presence. By an intraordinal law Broad means a law that is not reducible to ordinally neutral law and that serves to explain the mode of functioning of a given type of existent in terms of its characteristic organizational (or "novel") properties. By ordinally neutral laws Broad means whatever laws apply to the modes of functioning of all existents without restriction as to type.

We may say that if *all* laws are ordinally neutral the theory of emergence is false so far as functional emergence is concerned. It would also be false in so far as existential emergence is concerned, unless the coming into being of novel entities or properties is subject to *no* law. The latter position, that emergents arise independently of all natural necessity, has sometimes been attributed to those who believe in emergence, but it is not in fact widely held, nor is it a position that possesses much to commend it. We may therefore safely say that if *all* laws are ordinally neutral the theory of emergence is false.

The theory of functional emergence holds that there are irreducible intraordinal laws, the existence of such laws being in fact the essential contention of this doctrine. It is to be noted, however, that the conception of intraordinal laws only refers to the question of what laws are adequate to explain the functioning of entities of a given type: to deny the existence of irreducible intraordinal laws is to deny functional, but not necessarily existential, emergence.

What Broad terms transordinal laws are, in essence, laws of existential emergence. It is their purpose to state a relationship between a given novel type of quality, object, or event and the conditions that are invariantly and necessarily correlated with its existence. To hold that there are such laws is not to deny that the phenomenon in question is novel: it remains unpredictable (i.e., nondeducible) on the basis of any knowledge afforded by the nature of what previously existed. What the belief in transordinal laws involves is the dual contention that novel existents of specific types arise only under certain specifiable conditions, *and* that the connection between these existents and their necessary conditions is a connection of "brute fact," the existence of the novel phenomenon not being deducible from the previously existing conditions by means of any ordinally neutral law. Therefore, the existence of a nondeducible transordinal law would prove existential emergence, but it would not, in itself, tell us whether the theory of functional emergence is also true.

III

Utilizing these distinctions I should now like to present two considerations concerning existential and functional emergence. These considerations are not, of course, sufficient to decide the substantive question as to whether the emergent doctrine in any of its forms is true: they may, however, be of use in lending some weight to the particular position that it is the aim of this paper to formulate.

It would seem to me that no philosophic theory can deny that in the course of time there have occurred in nature genuinely "augmentative or transmutative events."[6] To do so would be to deny what is known of the earth's history. If, for example, we examine the nature and characteristics of living things without a prejudice born of opposition to the supposed existence of intraordinal laws, we cannot, I believe, fail to admit that there have arisen objects with properties that previously existing objects did not possess.

Granting the existence of such properties, the so-called reductionist must, I believe, also grant that there are transordinal laws: to deny such laws would be to hold that these properties bear no necessary relation to the conditions with which they are invariably associated. This, as we have seen, would be precisely the position that he charges—usually unfairly—that the believer in emergence upholds.

But if one grants that there are transordinal laws that state a connection between a property not formerly present (or not present at all levels) and the conditions under which it appears, such a law would not be deducible from ordinally neutral laws. This follows necessarily from two facts: first, a law that aims to state such a relationship must contain the property in question as an inexpungeable term; second, such a property is, by definition, different from any property common to all existents, i.e., it itself is not ordinally neutral. Therefore, no transordinal law would be reducible to ordinally neutral laws.

It is this line of argumentation which leads me to conclude that existential emergence, as defined above, is a fact. Contained in this conclusion there is, so far as I can see, nothing that is not compatible with an unbridled acceptance of the ideals of scientific explanation.

On the other hand, it appears to me to be far from certain that there are any irreducible intraordinal laws. While it is doubtless possible to formulate specifically biological and psychological laws that are descriptive of organic and human modes of functioning, it is conceivable (as I shall later show) that these laws are but special applications of ordinally neutral laws. Whether or not this is the case is an empirical problem, and the empirical evidence that is available is inconclusive. However, there is one problem inherent in the assumption of irreducible intraordinal laws to which I should like to direct the reader's attention.

The doctrine of functional emergence, it will be recalled, holds that the modes of functioning exhibited by existents of different types are, in some cases at least, discontinuous, so that no single set of laws could be adequate to explain the modes of functioning of all existents. Intraordinal laws are formulated to explain those modes of functioning which are characteristic of novel types of existents or of specific levels of organization. But it is to be noted that in the traditional interpretations of the doctrine of emergence the number of such types or levels is limited, the discriminated number usually ranging between three and six. At the same time it is usually admitted that finer discriminations can be made.

This situation I find disturbing. It would appear that once we admit the existential emergence of novel properties or concentrate on the differences in the levels of organization represented by existing entities, we find that important discriminable differences are extremely numerous. To hold that there are as many irreducible intraordinal laws as there are novel emergents (or as there are differences in levels of organization among existing entities) would, I believe, be false: there appears to be far more unity in the ways in which entities function that one could then expect. But if, on the other hand, one seeks to limit the number of intraordinal laws to cover only broad bands of phenomena (e.g., matter, life, mind), the discriminable novel properties or levels of organization within each of these bands is left unexplained by the intraordinal laws, and presumably also by the ordinally neutral laws.

This difficulty concerning the possible number of irreducible intraordinal laws has been rather frequently noted, but it has not, I believe, been adequately solved by those who believe in functional emergence. The question is, of course, an empirical one, and if the theory of functional emergence were true no final answer could be forthcoming until all intraordinal laws had in fact been discovered. But the inconclusiveness of my argument with respect to the question of how many irreducible intraordinal laws there may be does not furnish an excuse for the failure of the theory of functional emergence to provide an answer to the other facet of the same problem: when one intraordinal law applies equally to two discriminable novelties, by means of what type of law can we explain the differences in their characteristic modes of functioning? For example, if (as Broad suggests) irreducible intraordinal laws are necessary to account for the organic function of reproduction, by what means other than postulating two different intraordinal laws can we account for the functional differences represented by asexual and sexual reproduction? In short, the upholder of functional emergence is caught in a dilemma: either he will introduce so many supposedly irreducible intraordinal laws that the degree of systematic unity which we find in nature will be inexplicable, or he will confine attention to relatively few types of irreducible modes of functioning and leave unexplained the observable differences within each of these modes. It is for this reason (buttressed by what I believe the recent history of the sciences to have illustrated) that I am doubtful as to the claims put forward on behalf of the theory of functional emergence.

IV

The position that I therefore propose as worthy of consideration is that there arise in the course of time entities possessing novel, emergent properties;[7] that the transordinal laws linking such properties to the conditions upon which they depend are not deducible from ordinally neutral laws; but that the latter are nonetheless adequate to explain the mode of functioning of all existent entities, intraordinal laws being but instances of them.

The apparent paradox contained in this position—viz., that there are genuinely novel properties, but that the behavior of entities possessing these properties is explicable in terms of the same laws that hold of all other entities—disappears when we consider the differences and the connections between transordinal and intraordinal laws.

A transordinal law takes a particular mode of functioning as a datum and correlates it with the occurrence of events that are invariantly copresent with it. But because the datum is, by definition, a novel element in existence, it differs in character from the events that are claimed to be invariantly connected with it. On the other hand, an intraordinal law attempts to explain a characteristic function through correlating one novel property with another: it is not concerned with the conditions underlying the existence of these novel properties, but with their functional interrelationships.

Now, each novel property is (theoretically) capable of being connected with events that are not novel by means of a transordinal law. And such non-novel types of events, it is generally admitted, are related to one another in ways describable through what are termed ordinally neutral laws. It is therefore conceivable that we could state every so-called intraordinal law as a special case of ordinally neutral laws, by "translating" the relationship between novel properties into a relationship between the conditions found to underlie each of them. In making such a translation we should not be guilty of any "reductionist" fallacy, for what is in question in an intraordinal law is not the existence of particular novel properties but the determination of relationships among them. I therefore believe it legitimate (in principle) to hold that the invariant connections that are formulated in so-called intraordinal laws may be but special cases of ordinally netural laws: when novel properties are expressed in terms of their invariant non-novel correlates, ordinally neutral laws would then state precisely those functional relationships which are to be found on the emergent level. In this sense intraordinal laws could be said to be deducible from ordinally neutral laws whenever we have an adequate knowledge of the relevant transordinal laws.

Applied to the field of organic and mental phenomena the position that I have suggested would mean: first, that in the course of time entities have arisen which possess properties such as cell-division and cognition which were not the properties of any previously existing entities; second, that such properties are correlated with specific physical-chemical constituents or forms of organization, such correlations being formulated in terms of transordinal laws; third, that we may formulate "intraordinal" (i.e., specifically biological or psychological) laws, stating relationships between one novel property and another; but, fourth, that while transordinal laws are not deducible from ordinally neutral laws (because they contain as data novel properties), the intraordinal laws are, in principle, thus deducible through the mediation of transordinal laws.

V

That the position thus stated is in fact correct cannot be claimed on the basis of empirical evidence: our knowledge of the transordinal laws connecting specific novel properties with underlying conditions is too limited to permit us to judge whether all intraordinal laws are expressions of the ordinally neutral laws that have been (or may be) discovered. But advances in biology seem to show that this position is not implausible, and there may be grounds for the belief that a similar development is also occurring in psychology.

Whether or not this position is correct (as I believe it to be) it deserves formulation as one possible answer to the problems posed by the concept of emergence.

Notes

Given Ernest Nagel's well-known treatment of reductionism and emergence in his Structure of Science *(1971), this paper— which was contributed to a Festschrift for Morris R. Cohen— will no longer seem to stake out a novel position. It was, however, written in 1949 without knowledge of Nagel's earlier treatment of reduction in the sciences, published in the same year in* Science and Civilization, *edited by Robert C. Stauffer. While there are obvious differences both in terminology and approach between my paper and Nagel's, the two positions are, in general, compatible.*

1. It is perhaps suggested in ch. 4 of Edel's *Theory and Practice of Philosophy* (New York: Harcourt, Brace, 1946) (taking p. 59f. and 61 conjointly), but it is not there developed as a single consistent position.

2. Cf. "The Discontinuities of Evolution," in *University of California Publications in Philosophy,* 5, especially p. 178f.; and "The Meaning of 'Emergence' and Its Modes," in *Journal of Philosophical Studies,* 2, especially p. 173ff.

It should be noted that my use of these terms is not wholly congruent with that of Lovejoy, but a discussion of the differences would not be in place here.

3. For an example of the rather widespread tendency to give a nontemporal definition of emergence, stressing the whole-part relationship, cf. Hempel and Oppenheim: *Studies in the Logic of Explanation* (*Philosophy of Science*, 15:146ff.). Cf. also the origin of the concept of emergence in Mill and Lewes, and Broad's definition— *The Mind and Its Place in Nature* (New York: Harcourt, Brace, 1925), p. 61 —which does not utilize any temporal terms.

4. In Henle's critique of the use of the concept of "unpredictability" in discussions of emergence (cf. *Journal of Philosophy,* 39:486-93) no distinction between existential and functional emergence is maintained. It appears to me that his argument would not be valid with respect to existential emergents, whatever may be the case with respect to functional emergence. What he terms the "logically unrelated" is, I believe, primarily a question of functional emergence, and I should prefer to use the term "irreducibility" in this connection.

5. Cf. *The Mind and Its Place in Nature,* p. 77ff.

6. This phrase is Lovejoy's: cf. "Meaning of 'Emergence' and Its Modes," p. 169.

7. For the sake of convenience in exposition I shall at this point assume that all existential emergents are temporally novel, neglecting the possibility that there were eternally existing differences in levels of organization.

II

Methodology
in Historical Studies

6

The Philosophy of History: Some Neglected
Philosophic Problems Regarding History

The following paper is primarily programmatic in character: I wish to call attention to some important theoretical problems which are, in my opinion, philosophical problems, but which are not often explicitly discussed by philosophers, and which are frequently not acknowledged to be philosophical problems by those who do discuss them. What these problems are will become clear as we proceed. I shall attempt to indicate their nature, and demonstrate their importance, through discussing the topic proposed for this symposium: What Is a Philosophy of History?

The Nature of Formal
and Material Philosophies of History

Just as the term *history* has come to have two fundamentally different meanings, the one referring to occurrences in the past and the other referring to the knowledge, or supposed knowledge, of these occurrences, so the term *the philosophy of history* has come to refer to two different types of philosophic inquiry. These two types of inquiry are usually, and most conveniently, designated as *formal* and *material* philosophies of history. Briefly stated, a formal philosophy of history represents a philosophic concern with the problem of historical knowledge, while a material philosophy of history represents an attempt to interpret the historical process itself. Each of these characterizations demands some elaboration.

1. The formal philosophy of history may be said to have three different branches. The first of these involves a consideration of the problem of the "objectivity" of historical knowledge; that is, it is concerned with what constitutes valid knowledge of the historical process, and with estimating whether we may be said ever to possess such knowledge. The second branch involves a consideration of the relations between historical knowledge and other forms of knowledge or of pseudo-knowledge; for example, it is concerned with the relations between history and memory, between history and folklore, and between history and scientific modes of generalization (and, more particularly, with the relations between history and the social sciences). These two branches cover the main areas of modern formal phi-

Reprinted by permission from *Journal of Philosophy*, 49 (1952):317-29.

losophies of history; they are not, of course, without their connections, and neither can be claimed to be more basic than the other. However, the third branch of the formal philosophy of history clearly presupposes both of them. It is concerned with the question of what may be said to be the practical, educational, or intellectual value of a study of the past. This third branch, which we may term the pragmatics of the discipline of history, is not much discussed by those philosophers who are today concerned with the formal philosophy of history, but it does properly belong within their field.

2. Let us now examine the nature of a material philosophy of history. Here we cannot simply point to the problems with which such interpretations of the historical process are concerned, because—as the examples of Saint Augustine, Comte, Hegel, and Spencer clearly show—the scope of these problems varies widely from one such philosophy of history to another. Nor is it possible to find a single characteristic method of procedure in all classic examples of material philosophies of history. What all have in common is, rather, the attempt to find what may be termed some *meaning* within the whole of man's historical experience; this meaning they all seek to establish through discovering an ultimate principle that is claimed to be the most basic factor operative within history.

This characterization of the material philosophy of history demands further elucidation.

It must first be noted that the ultimate principle, or basic factor, operative within history is not necessarily conceived in the same terms in all philosophies of history. It is, I believe, useful to distinguish between two fundamentally different forms that such a principle may take. On the one hand, and perhaps most commonly, it is conceived of as being a law of history, which serves as an explanation of the ultimate direction of historical change.[1] Such theories can conveniently be distinguished into linear and morphological subspecies, the linear considering the whole of the history of mankind as a single history, while the morphological type (as exemplified in Spengler or Toynbee) views the fundamental law of history as being exemplified in the growth and death of self-enclosed civilizations. Further differentiations can of course also be made (for example, in terms of the methods by which such laws of history are ostensibly established, or the metaphysical interpretations that are given these laws), but with these problems I shall not here be concerned. It only remains to point out concerning this general type of a material philosophy of history that the search for an ultimate law of history commits one to a survey of universal history. Whatever is taken to be a significant part of man's historical experience must be included within a philosophy of history which seeks to establish a law that can serve to explain the ultimate direction of historical change.[2]

The second form that an ultimate principle of historical interpretation may take is not committed to any such survey of the whole of the "significant" past. In this type of philosophy of history the ultimate principle, or basic factor, operative within all history is not conceived as a law of historical development. Substituted for such a law is some explanatory concept that is held to be applicable to each and every crucial event in the historical process and to be capable of affording a basis for grasping the meaning of the process. What may be termed a simple providential interpretation of history would serve as an example of this type of theory. Similarly, in Niebuhr's complex theological philosophy of history there is, substituted for the idea of a necessary pattern or law of history, the view that in every historically significant event there is a tension between opposing pulls in human nature, and that the meaning of history can only be discerned in terms of the theological doctrine that renders intelligible the omnipresence of this factor.

Whether a material philosophy of history finds its interpretative principle in a developmental law of history or in some other factor believed to be universally operative in the historical process, it is such a principle that is held to give the processes of history a *meaning*. It is to the elucidation of what constitutes *meaning*, when used in this sense, that we must now turn.

Meaning, as the term is here used, refers to the "significance" of the historical process, its import for man as a valuing being. The philosopher of history, like all other men, finds certain entities to be the proper object of attitudes such as hope, fear, admiration, reverence, resignation, or defiance. In thinking of events of the past, in contemplating the present, or in considering the possibilities of the future, he, like other men, is not left unmoved: some of these events or possibilities, and some of the persons or entities that are involved in them, seem to be proper objects of certain valuational attitudes. When the ultimate principle that is thought to be exemplified in the historical process is either the source of or is taken as a justification for these attitudes, the concrete phenomena of history take on a "meaning." In other words, meaning is found in history when actual events are interpreted in terms of an ultimate principle that is held to be capable not only of explaining what has occurred but also of indicating what attitude it is proper to adopt toward these events. Thus, every material philosophy of history possesses an ultimate principle of interpretation which serves as a connective link between a reading of the actual events of history and what is taken as a standard of evaluation for history.[3]

In summary let me say that every material philosophy of history involves the attempt to find a principle of explanation which is the most ultimate explanation that can be given of the particular events in history or of their sequences; it attempts to apply such a principle to all of history, either by tracing out the actual course of events which exemplifies this law of historical change or by showing that at each point in history what has occurred exemplifies the validity of this explanation; and, whichever form of explanation is used, it holds that this ultimate principle is morally significant in the sense that it is able to show what attitude men ought to adopt toward the events of the past or of their own time, or toward the possibilities that are open to them in the future. Thus, we may define a material philosophy of history as the attempt to discover within the facts of history some principle that is taken as the ultimate explanation of why these facts are as they are, and that, it is believed, ought to be determinative of our attitudes toward these facts.

What the methodological difficulties of such an enterprise may be, or even whether it is a legitimate enterprise, is not my concern in this paper. However, I wish now to examine what relations may be said to obtain between formal and material philosophies of history.

3. During the past half-century it was widely held that a formal philosophy of history is, in a methodological sense, more basic than a material philosophy of history and should serve as a necessary propaedeutic to it. The reason for this belief is not difficult to find. Because a material philosophy of history presupposes a grasp of the nature of historical events, anything that sheds light upon the adequacy or inadequacy of our historical knowledge will have important implications for the material philosophy of history.

To be sure, a formal philosophy of history is not generally claimed to be a necessary propaedeutic to a material philosophy of history in the sense that one cannot make an attempt to construct the latter without first investigating the former. Such a contention would be as untrue as it would be to hold that no historian can embark on an historical inquiry unless he has first reached a reasoned conclusion regarding the problems that arise in the formal philosophy of history. Like the historian, one who constructs a material philosophy of history makes certain assumptions regarding the objectivity of historical knowledge and regarding the relations of such knowledge to other forms of knowledge; it need not be his task to examine these assumptions. However, it is proper for the formal philosophy of history to examine them; and any justified conclusion that is reached regarding such assumptions will be relevant to the acceptance or rejection of the material philosophy of history in question. It is in this sense that the formal philosophy of history may be considered to be methodologically more basic than the material philosophy of history.

However, it is one of the most significant features of the recent revival of interest in the material philosophy of history that this conviction has been either disregarded or openly challenged. If I am not mistaken, there is even a tendency in some quarters to view a material philosophy of history as providing a means by which one can test the adequacy of a formal philosophy of history. However, I do not find that any of the arguments that have been offered to prove the autonomy of a material philosophy of history are successful, and I should personally conclude that the more usual contention regarding the methodological priority of a formal philosophy of history is warranted.

The real strength of recent attacks upon this contention comes from the fact that those who have concerned themselves with the problem of historical knowledge (and here I include my own work in the field) have overlooked the extent to which an adequately comprehensive formal philosophy of history must make assumptions regarding the nature and status of historical entities. Because material philosophies of history have been more cognizant of the importance of these problems and frequently have explicitly discussed them, there is some merit in the claim that formal philosophies of history, as presently developed, take for granted solutions to some of the problems that material philosophies of history critically discuss. However, as I shall attempt to show, the type of nonepistemological assumptions that a formal philosophy of history must make are not themselves adequately established within a material philosophy of history. Thus it will be my contention that there is need for an attempt to solve certain problems that appear in both formal and material philosophies of history, and it is my primary, or programmatic, purpose to call these neglected problems to your attention.

Nonepistemological Assumptions in the Formal Philosophy of History

As has been noted, the two most basic concerns of a formal philosophy of history are the attempt to assess the degree to which historical knowledge may be claimed to be "objective" and the attempt to define the place that such knowledge occupies in the total economy of knowledge. These problems are, as I have indicated, interconnected: we cannot adequately assess the objectivity of historical knowledge without having a view as to what such knowledge may be said to aim to achieve, and we cannot understand its relations to such other areas of human thought as myth or scientific generalizations without having some fairly definite views as to what warranted claims to objectivity may be made on its behalf. In attempting to reach a conclusion on these two interlocking problems we must, I submit, first consult the nature of actual historical works: we must critically examine the underlying assumptions and procedures of practicing historians. To be sure, these assumptions will, to some extent, differ from historian to historian, but it is not illegitimate to say that one can raise problems concerning the types of assumptions and the more general methods of procedure which are common to most, if not all, of those works that are by common consent designated as historical works. The types of assumptions and the methods of procedure which are characteristic of these works will then, in most cases, be found to be related to, if they are not identical with, the assumptions and procedures that are present in other works that, at the outset, we did not know whether we should include among the examples of historical inquiry.

Now it is, I believe, characteristic of those works that are universally acknowledged to be historical works that they are concerned to understand and depict the nature of, and the changes in, the life of specific societies. An event or a person is of importance to the historian insofar as that event or person is seen as being significant for the life of a society at any one time or for changes that have occurred in that society.[4] If this suggested definition of the subject matter of the historian is accepted, it becomes clear that it is a necessary, and not an accidental, feature of historical works that they should employ terms that refer to the various aspects of man's life in an organized society; that persons are characterized with respect to their institutionalized status; that events are estimated with respect to their political, economic, religious, literary, or other implications. No recognized historical work merely chronicles the actions of "unclassified" persons or traces a course of events without making reference to its place in the life of the society in which it transpired. The historian, in brief, views all of his subject matter in its societal context and in the light of its societal implications. For this reason every historical account necessarily proceeds on the basis of what is at least an implicit theory of the nature of a society.

Now, the historian himself may not be interested in making his assumptions concerning the nature of a society explicit; neither will he always be willing to generalize on the basis of them. He may in effect say that he has used societal terms in the manner that seemed best suited to the documents with which he worked and that it is the function of someone else (if anyone else should be interested) to trace the assumptions that he has made and to appraise their validity. Whether, for example, the implicit definition of "a nation" or of "literature" which might be extracted from his manner of treating a national history or a literary movement is or is not an adequate definition for all instances might not concern him; it is adequate for his purposes if it enables him to organize and render intelligible all of the documents with which he wishes (or finds himself forced) to deal.

Such a position is not uncommon, though it is far from universal. Whether it is ultimately tenable is not a problem that I shall here discuss. For the sake of the argument, let us grant that it may be upheld. What I should now like to point out is that although a practicing historian may make this agnostic plea, a person who is concerned with the formal philosophy of history cannot adopt the same attitude. If he is to estimate the objectivity or lack of objectivity of historical accounts, and if he is to find what relation obtains between historical accounts and, say, scientific generalizations, he must examine the nature and ontological status of those cultural entities to which the historian makes reference. Such an examination will not, in itself, answer the problems with which a formal philosophy of history is concerned, but it is an indispensable prerequisite to a comprehensive and thoroughly grounded answer. This can, I believe, be seen from the following considerations.

1. Some of the entities with which historians deal are the actions of individual persons, but many are such "collective entities" or "abstractions" as the United States, the Catholic Church, the Monroe Doctrine, the doctrine of the Divine Right of Kings, the guild system, the stock-market crash of 1929, or Deism. A formal philosophy of history cannot maintain neutrality concerning the general nature and ontological status of "collective entities"

or "abstractions" of this type (or of these types), because the extent to which a historian may be said to grasp their nature through the documents or protocols to which he has access will be determined in no small measure by the view that is taken on these issues. For example, if those entities or events were to be defined merely in terms of the behavior of all of the individuals whose activities entered into them, and if their history were, consequently, merely an aspect of the histories of each of these individuals, the histories of at least some of the above-mentioned entities could not plausibly be claimed to be knowable: the material for even a fairly adequate history of the United States or of the Catholic Church could never be collected, much less organized or written. In order that we may claim to know as inclusive and long-enduring an entity as the Catholic Church we must be in a position to single out for consideration the activities of those individuals who, by reason of their status, were important in the history of that institution; but to know what it means to have a particular status in an institution involves us in knowing the institution and is not reducible, without circularity, to how an individual influences the actions of other individuals. What institutions are and how we may know them, is therefore an important problem that anyone interested in the objectivity of historical knowledge must face if he is to justify the claim that an historian can attain adequate knowledge of that which has occurred.[5]

2. It is universally agreed that the historian must, in almost all cases, make a selection from among the data to which he has access. The question of the possibility of historical objectivity hinges upon the question of whether or not there are criteria that justify one selection rather than another. Now, the practicing historian does as a matter of fact select his materials (or think that he is selecting his materials) on the basis of which events are relevant to the political, economic, religious, or other aspects of the society with which he deals.[6] If the formal philosophy of history is to examine whether such accounts are governed by a criterion of selection which yields the possibility of "objectivity," it must inquire into the validity of grouping facts under these aspects and seek to ascertain in what sense, if any, what is called a political event is inherently connected with other political events of that time and place. In short, it must ask whether these classificatory categories are based upon characteristics that are grounded in the nature of societies, or whether they are categories that each historian may redefine at will in order to organize the data with which he happens—or wants—to deal.

3. The historian speaks of one event as causally related to one or more other historical events, and it is, of course, one of the major problems of a formal philosophy of history to assess what meaning, if any, can be attached to the notion of historical causation and how historical causes are related, if at all, to the formulation of sociological, psychological, economic, and other, laws. Now, it is possible to treat these problems in terms of a general or abstract philosophical theory of causation and law, and thus not raise any questions concerning the nature and status of the specific types of events

with which historians deal. However, the existence of conflicting theories concerning the applicability of the concepts of cause and law to historical events makes it incumbent upon one who is concerned with the problem of historical knowledge to examine whether or not a philosophic treatment of these problems as they arise in, say, the natural sciences, has any applicability to historical materials. This necessitates an examination of the nature of these materials.

These three considerations are, I believe, sufficient to show that a formal philosophy of history cannot reach an adequately grounded conclusion regarding its fundamental problems merely by examining the practice of historians and attempting to relate this practice to general epistemological discussions. It is my thesis that in every such attempt one can find that assumptions have been made concerning the nature and, I believe, the ontological status of some of the most important entities with which historians deal. A critical examination of the alternative assumptions that have been made and a tracing of their implications may, if one wishes, be included within the province of a formal philosophy of history. If so, then these are problems that have been almost entirely neglected in the literature of the field. However, because the implications of these problems, and, in fact, the empirical materials needed for their solution, are by no means confined to the province of history as a discipline, it would seem to me advisable to say that a formal philosophy of history must make assumptions drawn from what I shall call the problems of a critical social philosophy.

Critical Social Philosophy
and the Material Philosophy of History

Problems concerning the nature and ontological status of social entities are frequently discussed in material philosophies of history. When they are not explicitly discussed their presence may none the less be detected. Among the more obvious of such problems I would cite the following: first, what constitutes a nation or a civilization; second, what status is to be ascribed to social institutions, and how are they related to the activities of individuals (e.g., do they, in some sense, "have a life of their own"); third, what meaning can be ascribed to terms such as "the spirit of the age," and what status is to be ascribed to such a spirit?

Now, questions such as these belong, I have claimed, to what may be called a critical social philosophy. Although they are discussed by those concerned with the material philosophy of history, answers to them in fact function as assumptions for any material philosophy of history, rather than being propositions that a material philosophy of history can prove. This can be seen from the following considerations.

1. Those who attempt to establish that there is an ultimate law of historical development do not attempt to prove that this law is exemplified in every particular event that occurs at any place or time in the historical

process. Rather, certain types of event are chosen as the real "bearers of history." What these events are—whether they are nations or civilizations or strands of development within certain human institutions—is of decisive importance for both the formulation of the law and for the conditions under which it can be verified. However, the selection of what types of event are the real "bearers of history" raises precisely the questions of definition and ontological status with which we are concerned. He who sets up such a law of development has already selected the materials to which his law is to be applied on the basis of the assumptions he has made concerning these questions. Therefore, it is not the law that he sets up which establishes what the answers to these questions must be; it is the nature of his answers to them which will, in large measure, dictate the nature of the law that he applies to history. All that can be claimed for the relevance of such a law to the assumptions that are made is that anyone who finds this law to be an adequate interpretation of the ultimate principle of history will have reason to say that these assumptions are more fruitful, and presumably truer, than a contrary set of assumptions.

2. Those who construct a material philosophy of history on the basis of factors that they believe to be operative at every point in the historical process, and who do not seek to establish a law of historical development, must, I should claim, also make assumptions regarding the nature and status of the basic elements in man's social life. This may be most clearly seen if we ask the question of whether we should look to some factor in the nature of man's constitution (as does Niebuhr) or to some factor in the organization of life in society (e.g., technology) in order to find the ultimate explanation we seek. Once again we can see that it is not from the establishment of a universal principle that our definitions of social institutions and our views concerning their status will follow; it is our assumptions concerning these problems which will channelize our search for such a principle. And, once again, it is to be noted that a material philosophy of history only throws light on the validity of such assumptions indirectly: to the extent to which it is viewed as adequate it affords a presumption that these assumptions, rather than others, are true.

3. In constructing a material philosophy of history one must espouse some theory concerning the ways in which entities within the historical process are related to one another. Here the general metaphysical position of the philosopher of history plays an important, or even decisive, role. His views on the nature of causation, on teleology, and on kindred questions, are inescapably involved. However, such metaphysical assumptions do not operate in vacuo: the actual interpretation that he gives concerning the relations between historical entities is also in part determined by his conception of the nature of these entities and the ontological status that may be ascribed to them. Thus, in this perhaps most important of all aspects of a material philosophy of history, the type of assumption we have noted plays an important role.

Concerning a Critical Social Philosophy

What is usually designated as *social philosophy* is an agglomerate mass of empirical and normative questions, drawn from political theory, comparative government, "philosophical anthropology," and normative ethics. It is usually concerned to discuss problems involving the evaluation of social institutions. However important these problems may be, it is not with them that what I term a *critical social philosophy* is concerned. In fact, I think it may reasonably be held that a social philosophy of the traditional type can only successfully proceed if it is founded upon an adequate analysis of the nature of the entities that constitute a society and of the types of relations which obtain among these entities. It is my opinion that in this case, as in others, what Broad has termed the *critical* function of philosophy has important implications for the synthetic, or *speculative*, aspect of the philosophical enterprise.

The problems that a critical social philosophy must face are problems that are now coming to be recognized as important by those empirical social scientists who have sought to clarify the nature of their own methods and the relations that their respective disciplines bear to each other. Among these problems the one that has been most frequently raised is whether psychological concepts provide an adequate basis for an understanding of sociological phenomena.[7] As is well known, this problem was clearly and explicitly raised by Durkheim, and it is still an important subject of debate, as the theoretical writings of Kroeber, Malinowski, Radcliffe-Brown, Kardiner, Herskovits, and others testify. In the course of these debates it is abundantly clear that the problem of the nature and ontological status of social institutions, and the problem of whether there are emergent sociological laws, raise philosophical issues.[8] Similarly, in the examinations of the nature of sociological explanations which we find in Parsons, in Merton, and in Nadel there are numerous philosophical issues. All of these issues are, I submit, worthy of the same kind of attention which philosophers of science devote to the philosophical issues that are raised by the physical sciences. While any practicing scientist may (presumably) adopt a position of neutrality on all of the philosophical issues that his discipline raises, a philosopher of science cannot bracket ontological and epistemological problems. Similarly, the social sciences raise problems that transcend a mere discussion of actual methodologies and force a philosopher who is interested in these sciences to raise questions concerning the ontological status of the materials with which the empirical social scientist deals. The task of examining these questions and of relating our methodological considerations to them is, I submit, a task for a critical social philosophy. And if my foregoing argument concerning formal and material philosophies of history has been correct, the exploration of these questions is essential to the construction of any adequately grounded formal philosophy of history and will also provide one of the bases upon which we may examine the validity of the claims of any material philosophy of history.

Notes

This paper was presented in a symposium on the philosophy of history at the 1951 meeting of the Eastern Division of the American Philosophical Association. As the first of the papers, I chose to lay out what I took to be the essential problems in the field. In doing so, I followed Rickert's terminology, using the terms formal *and* material *philosophies of history; these terms have now generally been replaced by* critical *and* speculative.

In the latter parts of the paper I argue that some ontological and epistemological assumptions regarding societal facts are inescapable for both types of philosophy of history. Further discussion of questions related to this issue will be found in some of the essays in Part 3 below.

1. For a critique of the attempts to establish such laws, see my "Critique of Philosophies of History," *Journal of Philosophy*, 45 (1948):365ff. As I now see, my definition of a material philosophy of history in terms of this type only was inadequate. I wish to express my debt in this connection to Reinhold Niebuhr, whose *Faith and History* showed me the narrowness of the definition I had proposed.

2. The circularity of this is of course apparent: the law of history is used to render intelligible the significant portions of man's historical experience; what is significant is that which manifests the law. This circularity appears in both linear and morphological theories, as is easily seen in both Hegel and Toynbee.

3. To the extent that some sociologists believe that the laws of development (or the universal constants) which they seek to establish not only represent ultimate explanatory principles but also serve to indicate the proper standard of valuation for history, they may be—and usually have been—termed philosophers of history. Further, it might also be legitimate to say that he who would set up the universal proposition that there is *no* meaning in history and who would offer this proposition as a justification for his attitude toward specific events has a "philosophy of history." To say this, however, would be to use the term in an extended sense; such a philosophy of history would be far different from the classic constructive examples.

4. Cf. Mandelbaum, *The Problem of Historical Knowledge* (New York: Liveright, 1938), pp. 9ff.; Bernheim, *Lehrbuch der historischen Methode* (Leipzig: Duncker and Humblot, 1889), ch. 1, sect. 1; Barth, *Die Philosophie der Geschichte als Soziologie* (Leipzig: O. R. Reisland, 1922), ch. 1.

5. In this connection we may note that those who deny the objectivity of historical knowledge frequently base their contention upon the fact that no historian can ever attain knowledge of the activities of that vast host of individuals who participated in any historical event: in other words, because they assume that the "abstractions" or "collective entities" with which the historian deals are reducible without remainder to the actions of a sum of individuals, they deny the possibility of adequate historical knowledge.

6. Or, if his is a specialized study, to the events relevant to one of these.

7. A similar problem has been widely discussed by economic theorists.

8. The same issue is posed for political theory by works such as Lasswell and Kaplan's *Power and Society* (New Haven, Conn.: Yale University Press, 1966).

Historical Explanation:
The Problem of Covering Laws

In recent years the question of what constitutes an historical explanation has probably been more frequently discussed by English and American philosophers than has any other question concerning history. William Dray's interesting and influential book, *Laws and Explanation in History*, is perhaps the focal point for this discussion, and from that book I shall borrow the term *covering-law theorists*, using it (as does Dray) to refer to that group of theorists which includes Popper, Hempel, and Gardiner, among others. But because I shall need some term to denote those who have recently reacted against the views of these theorists, as have Professors Dray, Donagan, Nowell-Smith and Berlin, I shall (if I may) use the term *reactionists* to refer to them. I do so not in order to suggest that their works are merely reactions against the views of the covering-law theorists, but rather in order to distinguish them from another group of philosophers of history who also reject the covering law model of explanation, namely, the idealists.[1] To be sure, there are some points at which Professors Dray, Donagan, and Nowell-Smith seem to make common cause with idealists such as Croce or Collingwood or Oakeshott; and the example of W. H. Walsh shows how closely the two positions may seem to approach one another. However, what characterizes the starting point of the reactionists is their assumption that a proper analysis of historical explanation must conform to the statements that historians actually make when they are giving what they take to be explanations of particular occurrences. The idealists assuredly made no such assumption; nor would idealist accounts of what constitutes a historical explanation actually fit this criterion of adequacy. Furthermore, the reactionists do not accept the general arguments by means of which idealists have attacked nonidealist theories, and in their frequent discussions of Collingwood they have been apt to expunge or radically reinterpret his more general metaphysical and epistemological theses.[2] I therefore find it useful to distinguish between the idealists and the reactionists. The actual lineage of the reactionists seems to be quite different: each of them appears to stem from that newer branch of analytic philosophy which may be called ordinary usage analysis and which is to be distinguished from the science-oriented form of analysis which the covering-law theorists represented. In

Reprinted by permission from *History and Theory*, 1 (1961):229-42.

this case, as in a variety of other cases, ordinary usage analysts can be found as allies of philosophers of very different sorts, one common bond that unites them being the conviction that it is a mistake to hold that scientific explanation serves as the correct model for all forms of explanation.

I find myself in the position of wishing to defend those who regard scientific explanation as the model for all explanation, and yet I cannot do so without abandoning certain of the assumptions usually associated with that view. In other words, I share the general sort of conclusion which covering-law theorists maintain, although I do not find it possible to defend the assumptions that are used in reaching that conclusion. This is an embarrassing position because I am certain that covering-law theorists attach far more importance to the particular assumptions that I wish to abandon than they do to their interpretation of what constitutes a historical explanation. The assumptions on which I disagree with them concern the meaning of the term *cause*, the relation between the concepts of "cause" and of "law," and the supposed temporal priority of cause to effect.[3] Merely to mention my disagreement on these points is to suggest the extent of my embarrassment. Nonetheless, what I wish to do is to support the general position reached by covering-law theorists and to reject the position of the reactionists regarding the differences between historical and scientific explanation. In doing so, I shall first attack the covering-law theorists, but in a way different from that which characterizes the reactionists.

I

Viewing the matter in historical perspective, one should recall that covering-law theorists were in rebellion against a very widespread and influential movement in German thought which attempted to show that the methods of the historian were necessarily different from the methods employed in the natural sciences. The contrasts between "Naturwissenschaft" and "Geisteswissenschaft," between "erklären" and "verstehen," between "the repeatable" and "the unique," between nomothetic and ideographic disciplines, were the stock-in-trade of those against whom the covering-law theorists rebelled. This the reactionists have scarcely taken into account. Therefore, while the reactionists have been unsparing in their criticisms of covering-law theorists, they have not in fact noticed one point that should by now be abundantly clear: that these earlier distinctions between historical understanding and other forms of understanding were either falsely drawn or were badly overdrawn. For example, no historical event could even be described, much less could it be in any sense explained, if it were wholly unique. To have insisted upon this and allied points and to have done so effectively is something which we must surely place to the credit of the covering-law theorists.

Nonetheless, as Dray and the other reactionists have pointed out, there is something quite odd in viewing the task of the historian as that of explaining the events of history by showing that they follow deductively from a general law. What is odd is not that the covering-law theorists claim that there should be such laws, though they are of course often criticized for this by the idealists. What is odd is that we do not really have the laws which, according to the covering-law model, would serve to explain the particular events we wish to explain. As Dray has insisted, those general statements which might be claimed to serve as the grounds for acceptable explanations are too loose and too porous to serve as laws from which the particular events of history might be deduced. And, as Dray has also shown, when these laws are tightened and sealed, we find that they are not really general laws, but statements so particularized that we would not expect them to apply to any other instance in the world, save the one that they purportedly explain. All of this part of Dray's argument I accept, and in fact (as Dray would acknowledge) these difficulties were at least adumbrated by Gardiner, and even earlier by Hempel when the latter found himself forced to distinguish between an explanation and "an explanation sketch." But what, then, has gone wrong with the covering-law argument, that it should have shown that generalizations must be in some sense, or in some ways, present in historical explanation; and yet that it should have failed to offer an analysis which conforms to what historians actually do? On this point, it seems to me, the reactionists have not thrown any light.[4]

Taking Hempel's article, "The Function of General Laws in History," as the *locus classicus* for the covering-law theory, I think it is easy to see what has gone wrong. Hempel holds the position that historians are mistaken if they believe that it is their essential task to describe particular events. He holds this position because he apparently believes that it is only by doing so that he can assimilate the methods of historical explanation to the methods of scientific explanation. The mixture of these two theses can be seen in the opening two sentences of his article. He says:

> It is a rather widely held opinion that history, in contradistinction to the so-called physical sciences, is concerned with the description of particular events of the past rather than with the search for general laws which might govern those events. As a characterization of the type of problem in which some historians are mainly interested, this view probably can not be denied; as a statement of the theoretical function of general laws in scientific historical research, it is certainly unacceptable.

This is a brambly pair of sentences. Surely it should be clear that historians might be interested in particular events, and yet this might not distinguish them from natural scientists; natural scientists too might be interested in particular events, such as the formation of a particular geologic deposit, or the appearance of a new biological variety in a particular environment. It might also be the case that in order to describe, to understand, or to explain particular events of the past, historians must utilize general laws; however, it need not be the case that it either has been, or should be, their primary concern to discover such laws. As the next sentence of Hempel's article makes perfectly clear, the essential point that he wished to establish was that general laws have a necessary explanatory function in historical inquiry, and that historical explanation does not therefore utilize a different type of explanation from that which is to be found in the natural sciences.[5] And with this fundamental thesis, as I have said, I agree.

What has in my opinion led to an unnecessary confusion is the fact that in making his point Hempel has spoken as if the nature of scientific explanation were restricted to the formulation of laws. Now, no one will deny that scientists do formulate laws. However, as Hempel himself rightly insists, every law is a statement that connects one *type* of event with another *type* of event: no law is a statement that directly refers to a single event, nor does it cover every aspect of those events to which it can be applied.[6] To take an example from Hempel's own article, in explaining a particular event, such as the cracking of an automobile radiator on a cold night, we must be able to state a law concerning the relation between the type of event which constitutes a drop in temperature to another type of event which is water freezing, and we must also connect water freezing with an expansion of its volume, etc. Now, clearly such statements, which connect one type of event with another type of event, are not intended to apply to this case only; if they only applied to this one event we should not consider them as explaining it. Nonetheless, it is also clear that these laws are only invoked in this particular case because we wish to explain *it*. Neither the ordinary man nor the scientist would be interested in laws unless they could be used to explain, or to predict, particular cases. With this I am sure that Hempel would not disagree. But we now come to the crucial point, and one on which Hempel's article is singularly ambiguous. Is it the case that in order to explain this particular event, the cracking of this radiator on this particular night, there should be a law concerning the cracking of radiators; or is it sufficient in order to explain this particular event that there should merely be the general laws that connect temperature and freezing, freezing and expansion, and the like? This is a crucial question that demands clarification because in dealing with the question of what constitutes a causal explanation of an event, Hempel makes the following statement:

> The explanation of the occurrence of an event of some specific kind E at a certain place and time consists . . . in indicating the causes or determining factors of E. Now the assertion that a set of events — say, of the kinds C_1, C_2, . . . C_{11} — have caused the event to be explained, amounts to the statement that, according to certain general laws, a set of the events of the kinds mentioned is regularly accompanied by an event of the kind E. (para. 2.1)

This surely sounds as if Hempel holds that in order to explain the cracking of *this* radiator we would have to find some set of events which regularly accompanies the cracking of radiators; but this is precisely the sort of thing which the arguments of Dray and of Donagan have shown that we *cannot* do in history. Nor, I submit, can we do it with respect to the cracking of radiators, the failure of missiles to leave their launching pads, and many other events that no one (I should suppose) would deny to be wholly explicable in terms of physical laws. While we *do* explain these events through the introduction of laws, the laws that we introduce are not laws of cracking radiators or of missile failures: there is, I assume, no one set of conditions which is invariantly linked to a missile failure, nor to a cracking radiator, because (for example) radiators can crack when we pour water into them when they are overheated, no less than when we allow them to stand outdoors on a cold night without antifreeze in them.

In short, what I am contending is that the laws through which we explain a particular event need not be laws that state a uniform sequence concerning complex events of the type that we wish to explain.[7] Rather, they may be laws that state uniform connections between two types of factor which are contained within those complex events we propose to explain. This should be perfectly clear from Hempel's own analysis. What he wishes to explain is "the cracking of an automobile radiator during a cold night," and he holds that that event is explained when "the conclusion that the radiator cracked during the night can be deduced by logical reasoning" from a knowledge of the initial conditions plus "empirical laws such as the following: Below 32 F., under normal atmospheric pressure water freezes. Below 39.2 F., the pressure of a mass of water increases with decreasing temperature, if the volume remains constant or decreases; when the water freezes, the pressure again increases. Finally, this group [of statements] would have to include a quantitative law concerning the change of pressure of water as a function of its temperature and volume" (para. 2.1). In short, there is not a word about radiators in the laws by means of which the cracking of the radiator is to be explained.

Bearing this in mind, we can see that Dray was quite right in objecting to what he significantly called the covering-law model of explanation in history: the law (or laws) by means of which we explain a particular case is not (or surely need not be) a law that "covers" that case in the sense that the case is itself an instance of what has been stated by the law. Rather, the case is explained by the law because those types of factor with which the law is concerned are present in it. If this is true, then it should not be surprising that in history we cannot, for example, find laws that "cover" the case of a particular migration of population in the sense that there is a law of population migration such that this case is an instance of it. Rather, the laws that we could expect to find (if we are to find explanatory laws) would be in one sense more general; in another sense, they would also be more limited than the event that they are to explain. They would be more general, because they would presumably also serve to explain other types of case, and not only population migrations; they would be more restricted because they would not concern all of the aspects of the complex event designated as a population migration, but only some one aspect of it. Thus, for example, we might expect some social psychological law to be useful in explaining a population migration, but such a law, if it were genuinely a law of social psychology, would also be relevant in explaining particular events that are not population migrations. At the same time such a law would be restricted to dealing with some one factor in the population migration, and not with the complex event as a whole. And Hempel, of course, does argue for the importance of precisely such sorts of law in our explanations of historical events.[8] Yet he has opened himself to misinterpretation, if not to error, by insisting that the universal hypotheses by means of which we explain complex events of a given type consist in finding the conditions that always accompany events *of this type*. Thus, in his discussion of population migrations he says:

> Consider, for example, the statement that Dust Bowl farmers migrate to California "because" continual drought and sandstorms render their existence increasingly precarious, and because California seems to them to offer so much better living conditions. *This explanation rests on some such universal hypothesis as that populations will tend to migrate to regions which offer better living conditions.* (para. 5.2; my italics)

Hempel then quickly admits that it would be difficult to state this hypothesis in the form of a general law that is well confirmed by all other cases of migrations. And this illustrates what sort of law he is seeking: he is seeking a covering law that states a regularity of connection between some particular complex type of event and a particular complex set of conditions. However (to revert to my earlier illustration), this is as if in the physical sciences the laws with which we are concerned were laws of radiator crackings or missile failures.

In my opinion, it is not difficult to see how this error—for I believe it to be a fundamental error—cropped up in Hempel's article. As Dray has pointed out, all of the covering-law theorists accept a Humean view of causation.[9] Now, to speak of a Humean view of causation may mean a number of different things, but what I here have in mind is the fact that for Hume, and for those most directly affected by his arguments, the notion of what constitutes the cause of an event is another event that uniformly precedes it in time. To know the cause of an event is, therefore, to know that there is a law that connects this type of event, which we call the effect, with another type of event, which we will call the cause. A causal relation is, then, simply an instance of some empirically established law.

Such a view has certain necessary consequences, two of which we may single out for particular attention. In the first place, if a causal relation is merely an instance of a regularly occurring sequence, a causal attribution does not consist in the analysis of this particular event, but in the formulation of what happens in cases of a particular type, or kind. It is small wonder, then, that those who accept a Humean view of causation should insist, as does Hempel, that causal analysis is really not the explanation of a particular case, but simply of what happens in a kind of case. In the second place, if a causal relation is simply an instance of a regularly recurring sequence, we shall have to distinguish between that particular event that we denominate as "the cause" of a specific event and "the conditions" that merely accompany the occurrence of this event. We must draw such a line of demarcation, if we accept the Humean view, because any particular event will be preceded in time by more than one particular event (or condition), and because, also, more than one event (or condition) will presumably also be spatially contiguous with it. Those aspects of the state of affairs which precede the occurrence of the effect, and which are *not* regularly present whenever an effect of this type occurs, will then be denominated as being merely "conditions" of the effect, but not its cause. What is called "the cause" will be confined to whatever aspect of the total state of affairs obtaining in a particular case is also present in all other cases of the same general type. But this means that the Humean view identifies the cause of an event with what we should consider a *necessary* condition of its occurrence, and does not include as part of its cause the *sufficient*, as well as the necessary, conditions of that effect.

It is small wonder, then, that Dray can charge that Hempel's analysis is really remote from the tasks that most historians have set themselves. In the first place, as Hempel found himself forced to admit, much of the historiography of the past has been concerned with the particular nature of particular events, rather than with describing what a number of events may have in common, and therefore with what constitutes a particular type of event. In the second place, it may be added, the explanations with which historians customarily have been concerned have been explanations that attempt to portray the conditions that were *sufficient* to account for the occurrence of the event; their aim has not been to discover what conditions are *necessary* for the occurrence of events of a given type.[10] In fact, they have not infrequently denied that any statements concerning necessary or invariant conditions would be true. For these two reasons the Humean view of the nature of the causal relation seems singularly inappropriate to deal with what the historian means by "causation", and it seems to me that in point of fact the historian is concerned to explain—in some non-Humean causal sense of the word "explain"—particular events.

However, it would be unfair to Hempel to leave the impression that he could not in any way deal with particular cases on the basis of the covering-law model. What is individual about a particular case is introduced into his account by the fact that the laws that explain events must be applied to the initial and boundary conditions obtaining at a particular time and place. However, what Hempel overlooks is that the establishment of the precise nature of these initial and boundary conditions is a complicated task, *and is itself the task of the historian.*[11] An accurate delineation of these conditions is precisely what I should suppose many historians to mean by "the description of particular events," and Hempel nowhere shows that such an analysis of what actually constituted the initial and boundary conditions under which a given effect occurred can itself be reached by the use of the covering-law model. Later, I shall examine to what extent it is in fact necessary to presuppose a knowledge of certain regularities, or laws, in order to analyze the nature of the relevant initial and boundary conditions. Here it is only necessary to point out that it is misleading to claim that the historian is not interested in describing particular events, if in fact it is necessary for him to do so before he has the data to which he can apply those general laws which purportedly explain the event that he wishes to explain. To say this is merely to say that it is perfectly reasonable to demand of any person who claims to have explained a particular event that he should not only have indicated the *necessary* conditions that presumably always obtain when an event of this type occurs, but that he should also have indicated the *sufficient* conditions for the occurrence of the particular event that he seeks to explain. And in the non-Humean language that I myself used on an earlier occasion, and that Hempel has criticized, this means that the explanation of an event involves a causal analysis of that event, and not merely (or even primarily) the statement of a general law.

By way of drawing together my criticisms of Hempel's position, let me cite the fact that Hempel states that "a set of events can be said to have caused the event to be explained only if general laws can be indicated which connect 'causes' and 'effects'" (para. 3.1.). Now this, I submit, is not what is usually involved when we speak about the cause of a particular event. When I ask what caused a man to fall off a ladder, or what caused a person to commit suicide, I do not expect to be given an answer that states a regular conjunction between any other type of event and the type of event that constitutes falling off a ladder or committing suicide. To be sure, in order to account for the man's fall I must know that usupported bodies do fall. If the man's fall was connected with the fact that he fainted, I must also know that when fainting occurs one's muscles relax, because this will account for the fact that he lost his grip. However, even though Hempel is correct in insisting that my causal explanation presupposes a knowledge of such laws, it is simply not true that there is any law that explains all of the particular cases in which men fall from ladders. Yet Hempel has seemed to insist that a causal explanation would involve the discovery of such a law. Instead, I submit, the causal analysis of any particular case in which a man falls from a ladder involves analyzing that complex event into a component series of subevents, such as the man's fainting, his grip relaxing, his center of gravity shifting, and then his falling to the ground. It is this sort of analysis of a particular complex event into its connected parts which we are called upon to make if we are asked why the man fell when he did and how he did. And to give an answer to this question is (I should suppose) to give a causal explanation of what occurred.

II

It would seem that the preceding argument has brought us around to the position of Professor Dray, in which historical explanation is conceived on the model of what he terms "a continuous series." And this analysis of historical explanation is in many ways similar to what W. H. Walsh has referred to as the historian's task of "colligation."[12]

The paradigmatic case used by Dray is not the case of a radiator cracking, although it too is drawn from automotive mechanics. It is the case of the engine seizure (pp. 66 ff.). Dray wishes to show that causal explanations are not to be given in terms of causal laws, but in terms of tracing a continuous series of subevents that serve to explain what has occurred. His paradigmatic case runs as follows:

> Suppose that the engine of my motor-car seizes up, and, after inspecting it, the garage mechanic says to me: "It's due to a leak in the oil reservoir." Is this an explanation of the seizure? I should like to argue that it depends upon who says it and to whom . . . To me, who am ignorant of what goes on under the bonnet, it is no explanation at all . . . If I am to understand the seizure, I shall need to be told something about the functioning of an auto engine, and the essential role in it of the lubricating system. I shall have to be capable of a certain amount of elementary trouble tracing. I need to be told, for instance, that what makes the engine go is the movement of the piston in the cylinder; that if no oil arrives the piston will not move because the walls are dry; that the oil is normally brought to the cylinder by a certain pipe from the pump, and ultimately from the reservoir; that the leak, being on the underside of the reservoir, allowed the oil to run out, and that no oil therefore reached the cylinder in this case. I now know the explanation of the engine stoppage.

However, it should be obvious that such an explanation presupposes a knowledge of certain uniformities concerning the relations of types of events, that is, it presupposes a knowledge of general laws, and this fact is not pointed out by Professor Dray.[13] For example, the explanation of why the engine stopped presupposes a knowledge of general laws concerning friction and concerning the relation between the absence of lubricants and the presence of friction. It also presupposes a knowledge that liquids flow through openings in the underside of reservoirs, and this too depends upon a knowledge of general laws. In short, Dray's own knowledge of general laws is presupposed in each step of the continuous series explanation, as he has given it. Furthermore, a knowledge of general laws is tacitly involved not only in tracing these connections but in distinguishing between what constitute relevant conditions and what is irrelevant to engine trouble. For example, is the fact that the engine stopped just as another car passed it a circumstance that must be introduced into our account of the cause of the seizure? Our judgment will in this case surely be negative, but that is only because we have learned that, in general, the way most man-made machines function, and in particular the way in which automobiles function, is that they are designed to be independent of what happens in their environments. In short, what alone makes it possible to trace a continuous series between concrete events such as are here in question is a background knowledge of laws describing uniformities among given types of events. Such a knowledge is necessary to tracing such a series in two respects: first, it alone provides the necessary linkage between at least some of the components within the series; second, it is necessary in order that we can rule out features of the environment which are irrelevant to the series.

I am not certain that Dray would deny this, but I think it likely that he would. What he seems to wish to defend is the proposition that a causal analysis of a particular event depends upon what he calls "judgment," and that judgment can function independently of a knowledge of general uniformities or laws. This seems to me to be a mistake. I think that what I have just said about the explanation of the engine seizure shows it to be a mistake.

But why, one might ask, does Professor Dray apparently cast aside all appeal to general laws in historical explanation, if, indeed, that is what he has done? The answer seems to me to lie in the fact that he has inadvertently accepted too much from the Humean position of his opponents, the covering-law theorists. He has assumed with them that in fields other than the sorts of fields with which historians deal, it is appropriate to telescope the notions of cause and law, and he himself does telescope these notions by speaking of "causal laws."[14] But then he finds that he must also speak of "causal explanations" in history, and these explanations he regards as having a logic of their own, distinct from the logic of those explanations that are supposedly given through a use of the causal law model. The distinction one might have expected him to draw between the statement of a *law* concerning a *type* of event and the statement of the cause of a *particular* event is not, to my knowledge, drawn by him. If it were to be drawn, it seems to me unlikely that Dray would have distinguished between the logic of those explanations that scientists give and the logic of the explanations given by historians. Rather, his position, like mine, would then have more nearly approached the position that I take to be essential to Hempel's article: that, in point of fact, at least an implicit appeal to a knowledge of general laws is needed in history.

III

In summary, let me say that the contrast between historians and scientists which we find in the idealists as well as in most of the reactionists is based not only on a misconception concerning the function of general laws in history, but also on a failure to appreciate the role of description in the generalizing sciences. If one asks where, in fact, the generalizations of science must take their rise, it is surely to descriptions of particular complex events and states of affairs that we must ultimately look. And even if we were to regard scientific generalizations as products of the free play of the imagination, which, while they might depend upon some observations, did not demand a painstaking investigation of the particular nature of specific events, still it would remain the case that no confirmation of such a generalization can be given without appealing to specific cases. And these specific cases must be carefully analyzed. In laboratories, where conditions are controlled, the description of the particular event that did occur will not have to introduce as many variables as is the case when the scientist describes what has occurred in a state of nature. Nonetheless, the description of a specific case, even in a laboratory, is not an entirely simple matter. We must describe not merely all of the relevant conditions obtaining at that time and place and all of the equipment used, but we must also state what happened in each successive phase of the experiment. As knowledge of general laws advances, the description of what are the relevant initial conditions, and what are the relevant phases in the experiment, becomes greatly simplified. Yet a concern with what is specific to a particular case, and the contrast between this and what happens in all cases, will presumably always remain to be drawn when we are seeking the confirmation of a general law. And it so happens that in the field of those societal events that historians and social scientists treat, the description of particular events is an extremely difficult task. If I am correct in my argument against Dray, this task can never be fulfilled without utilizing generalizations that state (or attempt to state) what uniformly happens in certain types of cases. However, if I am correct in the point that I have just been making, then the task of the traditional historian will never be rendered obsolete, as Hempel apparently thought and hoped that it would be. For no social scientist will ever be able either to discover or to confirm those generalizations in which he is interested, without making an appeal to the descriptive analyses of historians. Given the impossibility of establishing most of their generalizations under laboratory conditions, social scientists often rely on a comparative method, and this entails that the range of the relevant historical materials will increase, rather than contract, as the range of the generalizations spreads. For this reason what Hempel termed "scientific historical research," a term doubtless disliked as much by the reactionists as by the idealists, will continue to be concerned with the analysis of the concrete nature of particular events, though it will surely continue to utilize, in ever-growing measure, not only the common-sense generalizations of everyday life, but the best available generalizations that social scientists have been able to formulate on the basis of a knowledge of history.

Notes

This paper was delivered at a symposium on historical explanation held at Brandeis University in 1960. The other speakers were W. H. Dray and John Pass-

more. The position that the paper represents has since been more fully developed in my book, The Anatomy of Historical Knowledge *(1977), although in that context it is not specifically tied to a critical consideration of the positions of Hempel and Dray.*

1. Passmore, in his review of Dray's book, seems to identify Dray with the idealist. Cf. *Australian Journal of Politics and History,* 4 (1958):269.

2. The relevant works by Dray, in addition to his book (*Laws and Explanations in History* [Oxford, 1957]) are: "Explanatory Narrative in History," *Philosophical Quarterly,* 4 (1954):15-28; "R. G. Collingwood and the Acquaintance Theory of Knowledge," *Revue Internationale de Philosophie,* 11 (1957):420-32; "Historical Understanding as Rethinking," *University of Toronto Quarterly,* 27 (1957-58):200-215; "'Explaining What' in History," in *Theories of History,* ed. Patrick Gardiner (Glencoe, Ill., 1959), pp. 403-8.

The relevant works by Donagan are "The Verification of Historical Theses," *Philosophical Quarterly,* 6 (1956):193-203; "Social Science and Historical Antinomianism," *Revue Internationale de Philosophie,* 11 (1957):433-49; "Explanation in History," *Mind,* 66 (1957):145-64.

P. H. Nowell-Smith's article, "Are Historical Events Unique?" appeared in *Proceedings of the Aristotelian Society,* 57 (1956):107-60. Concerning the immediately relevant works of Isaiah Berlin, see note 4 below. One further scholar who might be grouped with the reactionists, but who evidently does not share their common origin, is A. C. Danto. Cf. "Mere Chronicle and History Proper," *Journal of Philosophy,* 50 (1953):173-82; "On Historical Questioning," *Journal of Philosophy,* 51 (1954):89-99; "On Explanations in History," *Philosophy of Science,* 23 (1956):15-30. Danto's position apparently grew out of a dissatisfaction with the position of W. H. Walsh; it is also apparently related to the position adopted by Reis and Kristeller in "Some Remarks on the Method of History," *Journal of Philosophy,* 40 (1943);225-45.

3. It is to be noted in this connection that Hempel and Gardiner have severely criticized my views with respect to causation, while Dray seems to have a certain sympathy with them, though he regards them as being inadequate because they do not conform to "the usual sense of the term [cause] in history." Cf. Hempel, "The Function of General Laws in History," *Journal of Philosophy,* 39 (1942):35-48, especially notes 1 and 7; Patrick Gardiner, *The Nature of Historical Explanation* (Oxford, 1952), pp. 83-86; Dray, *Laws and Explanation in History,* p. 110.

4. Isaiah Berlin's "History and Theory: The Concept of Scientific History," *History and Theory,* 1 (1960):1-31 reached me too late to receive the attention it would otherwise deserve. Fortunately, I was already familiar with his general views on the subject, both through his *Historical Inevitability* (Oxford, 1954), and through having been privileged to attend a seminar that he gave on the subject at Harvard University in the fall of 1954. It does not seem to me that his article forces a revision of the position that I here wish to defend, although the particular way in which he casts his argument at some crucial points demands careful analysis.

A second article that came to my attention too late to be taken into account in my paper was Ernest Nagel's "Determinism in History," *Philosophy and Phenomenological Research,* 20 (1960):291-317. I derive considerable satisfaction from finding that I am apparently not in disagreement with Nagel's analysis of the current situation with respect to the theory of historical explanation. In section 3 of his article (pp. 301-4), where he deals with the same problem with which I am here concerned, he, too, points out that it is doubtful whether even in the natural sciences the pattern of deductive explanation is followed in explaining "concrete individual occurrences." However, in his discussion of Maitland's explanation of a concrete historical occurrence (p. 303), he does use the sort of generalization which I shall be criticizing Hempel for employing as a basis for historical explanation; I am therefore unsure as to whether he would accept the argument that I am propounding in this paper.

5. This sentence reads: "The following considerations are an attempt to substantiate this point by showing in some detail that general laws have quite analogous functions in history and in the natural sciences, that they form an indispensable instrument of historical research, and that they even constitute the common basis of various procedures which are often considered as characteristic of the social in contradistinction to the natural sciences."

6. Cf. para. 2.2 of Hempel's article. However, it does not follow that *explanation* is always of a type of event only, and not of a particular event. As I have suggested, I do not think that Hempel wishes to confine explanation to types of event, although his emphasis at this point does not make his intentions clear. However, Hayek adopts this view of explanation, and even of prediction. In an article entitled "Degrees of Explanation," Hayek says: "'Explanation' and 'prediction' of course never refer to an individual event but always to phenomena of a certain kind or class; they will state only some and never all the properties of any particular phenomenon to which they refer" (*British Journal for Philosophy of Science*, 6 [1955-56]:215). One would think that the prediction of a specific solar eclipse, or the explanation of that eclipse, would count as referring to a particular event even if it does not refer to all aspects of the event, such as the temperature of the sun, or the effect of the eclipse on the temperature of the earth, and the like.

7. I use the expression "need not be," rather than "is not," for I wish to leave it an open question as to whether there are any cases in which the laws that explain a particular type of complex event are merely laws in which such an event is related to another type of complex event, or whether *in all cases* the explanation of a particular type of complex event does not demand a resolution into laws of particular component factors within it.

8. For example, in his use in para. 5.2 of the quotation from Donald W. McConnell's *Economic Behavior.*

9. *Laws and Explanation in History*, pp. 3, 60 et passim. A similar point is made by Nowell-Smith.

10. W. B. Gallie in "Explanations in History and the Genetic Sciences," (*Mind*, 64 [1955]:160-80) would seem to hold the exact opposite of this position, viz. that the historian is only interested in the necessary conditions, while natural scientists are interested in the sufficient conditions. The difference, however, is, in part, a difference in the ways in which we are using the terms *necessary* and *sufficient.* In the terminology I am here using a *necessary condition* is one that is invariantly associated with the type of event to be explained.

11. This is why, in the review of Dray already cited, Passmore points out that much of the time the historian's task is really not one of explaining at all, but is merely one of describing, i.e., of "telling how," not "explaining why."

12. W. H. Walsh, *Introduction to the Philosophy of History* (London, 1951), pp. 23-24 and 59-64. For Walsh's views on historical explanation, cf. also pp. 16f., 22-24, 29-47, 64-71.

13. This point is also clearly brought out by J. Pitt, "Generalizations in Historical Explanation," *Journal of Philosophy*, 61 (1959):582f.

14. It is noteworthy in this connection that when Hempel shifts from a Humean type of explanation to an explanation in terms of laws characterizing relations among subevents, Dray simply calls this a more complicated version of the covering-law model (cf. pp. 52-54). However, in my opinion, the shift from what he calls a "holistic" to a "piecemeal" approach represents the adoption of a totally different model of explanation, and not merely a shift in the scale of the events dealt with.

8

The Presuppositions of
Hayden White's *Metahistory*

In the introductory chapter of his *Metahistory*, Hayden White explicitly sets forth the main presuppositions underlying that work. If one were to examine these presuppositions in the light of his other writings, one might uncover his reasons for accepting them. Such, however, is not my aim. I shall confine my discussion to certain of the views he explicitly embraces, selecting those that are basic to the aspects of *Metahistory* I especially wish to challenge.

As a point of entry into the closely articulated system of *Metahistory*, let me first mention the eight persons whom White has chosen as representing the various modes of historical consciousness with which he deals. Four of these he considers to have been the dominant historians of the classic period of nineteenth-century historiography; four he regards as the most important philosophers of history of that century. Michelet, Ranke, Tocqueville, and Burckhardt are the historians chosen; Hegel, Marx, Nietzsche, and Croce are the philosophers of history. To some extent, one may quarrel with these choices; this is a question to which I shall briefly return. What is initially noteworthy is not *whom* he has chosen, but the fact that historians and philosophers of history are treated together, a mode of treatment in direct opposition to the widespread assumption (held throughout the nineteenth century and subsequently) that their aims and methods are not only fundamentally distinct, but are often opposed. His rejection of that view, and his account of what they have in common, is the first of his theses that I shall challenge. What lies behind that thesis is a particular view of what is most fundamental in the writing of history, and it is that view I shall take as his first and perhaps most fundamental presupposition.

It is White's claim that "history proper" and "philosophies of history" grow out of a common root, differing only in emphasis, not in content: philosophers of history simply bring to the surface and systematically defend views that remain implicit in the works of historians (pp. xi, 428). Unfortunately, White fails to specify with any degree of exactitude what he regards as the essential features in a philosophy of history.[1] If (for the time being) we construe philosophies of history as being, essentially, nothing more than reflection on a significant portion of man's past in order to determine what

Reprinted by permission from *History and Theory*, Beiheft 19 (1980):39-54.

"meaning," if any, is to be discerned in it, then one might well say of Michelet, Ranke, Tocqueville, and Burckhardt that each did have a philosophy of history. On the other hand, were one to choose any single work of theirs (with the possible exception of Burckhardt's posthumous *Weltgeschichtliche Betrachtungen*), and were one to consider its aim and its content, one would surely not regard it as similar in these respects to the works usually taken to be representative philosophies of history.

In order to understand what may have led White to overlook or to disregard this obvious point and therefore to hold that there is no deep difference between historians and philosophers of history, one must consider what he took to be the determining factors in all forms of historical inquiry.[2] He held that with the exception of those who are only concerned to write "monographs and archival reports" (p. ix), every historian creates a narrative verbal structure through selecting and arranging the primitive data contained in "the unprocessed historical records"; the elements in such a verbal structure are then arranged in a way that purports to represent and explain past processes; and, according to White, the manner in which these processes are represented reflects the historian's antecedent acceptance of one of four types of "metahistorical" paradigms. White's characterization of the nature of the four types of paradigm will concern us later. What is important to note here is that in labeling them "metahistorical," White is emphasizing the fact that they are not derived from the data with which the historian works; rather, they are "interpretative strategies" that determine to which data he will attend, and in what ways he will envision the relations among them (pp. 428, 430). In short, the narrative structure that a historian creates will have been "*pre*figured" by the particular paradigm in terms of which he sees the historical world (pp. 30-31). Because it is White's contention that exactly the same basic paradigms are to be found in the works of historians and philosophers of history, he rejects the widely held view that the dissimilarities between the two genres are more fundamental than are their similarities.

Before examining what led White to stress what he took to be the similarity between historians and philosophers of history, let us consider some of the respects in which they do in fact differ. In the first place, White fails to note that with the possible exception of some attempts to write universal histories, every historical inquiry is limited in scope, dealing with what is recognized to be only one segment or one aspect of human history. Most philosophers of history, on the other hand, have traditionally embarked on sweeping surveys of what they have regarded as the whole of the significant past, in an effort to establish some one basic principle of explanation which would render intelligible the course it had followed.[3] Their purpose in doing so may be said to be an attempt to justify some particular evaluative attitudes toward various segments or elements in that history. One does not find even the most "philosophical" of historians committing himself to such a project. To be sure, as I have pointed out, one may say of various historians that "they have a philosophy of history," in the sense that they more or less consistently evince certain underlying evaluative attitudes toward the materials with which they deal. To that extent, White is correct in what he claims concerning Michelet, Ranke, Tocqueville, and Burckhardt. Nevertheless, it is implausible to hold that their works, taken either individually or as a whole, were written primarily for the sake of establishing the truth of a particular interpretation of the historical process; yet this is clearly what constitutes the aim of any philosophy of history. The immediate concern of historians may better be characterized in terms of attempts to understand and depict what happened at particular times and in particular places. Therefore, even though their works often reflect a definite and distinctive view of overall characteristics to be found in the historical process, these works are *histories*, not philosophies of history.

A second and related difference between historians and philosophers of history lies in the fact that every philosopher of history seeks to find a principle of explanation, or of interpretation, which illuminates every significant aspect of the historical process. No such belief has been characteristic of historians, at least not since the mid-eighteenth century. Instead, historians have generally come to regard it as essential to preserve flexibility when dealing with different times and different peoples, rather than to expect that there is some particular principle of explanation which is equally applicable to all. Furthermore, most historians are inclined to employ different modes of explanation to deal with different dimensions of social life, rather than using a single set of categories when explaining the nature and changes in, say, the economic, the political, and the intellectual aspects of a society's life. Any insistence on either or both of these forms of pluralism completely undermines the legitimacy of the kind of claim that every philosopher of history must make—namely, that there is some one principle that, when adequately grasped, serves to reveal the meaning of all essential aspects of human history. For this reason, if for no other, the presuppositions of historians and of philosophers of history are strikingly opposed.

A third point at which there are fundamental differences between the aims of a historian and of a philosopher of history lies in the latter's absolute commitment to the view that there is some discernible lesson, or "meaning," in human history. Such a meaning is viewed as providing a way to assess the significance of various past events, to determine the attitude that should be adopted with respect to conflicts within the present, and to help envision what the future will ultimately bring. While philosophers of history have occasionally acknowledged that the meaning they attribute to history was derived from other sources, most have claimed that it arose directly out of an intensive study of the historical past. They have apparently also believed that the same meaning would be acknowledged by all who studied the past in equal depth and with equal intensity.

This claim has often been challenged by historians. They have argued that philosophers of history do not derive meaning *from* history, but attribute meaning *to* history as a way of justifying their own antecedent evaluative beliefs. Not only can historians cite instances in which this appears to have been true, but they can quite convincingly argue that the events of human history, taken as a whole, are far too complex and ambiguous to support the claim that there is any single meaning to be directly derived from them. A philosopher of history might possibly reply that there is no great difference in principle between this and what is involved in such interpretations of history as are to be found in Michelet, Ranke, Tocqueville, and Burckhardt, each of whom had singled out certain forces or tendencies that they regarded as dominant factors in the historical field. However, any supposed parallel between these two endeavors does not hold. Historians such as Michelet, Ranke, Tocqueville, and Burckhardt did not claim to have arrived at their understanding of these forces through a comprehensive survey of the whole past; instead, they had simply dipped successively into the historical stream at various points and were generalizing concerning significant resemblances which they found at these points.[4] Thus, instead of claiming that there is some dominant pattern running through the process as a whole, determining how each of its elements will develop, they were singling out what they took to be the important common elements in various historical situations; it was with respect to their attitudes toward these elements that they may be said to have had "a philosophy of history." This, however, only justifies characterizing them in a very loose sense as "philosophers of history." Their situation exactly parallels that in which, after examining a practicing scientist's works, one might say that he *has* "a philosophy of science," without thereby either asserting or implying that he *is* "a philosopher of science."

As we have noted, what led White to blur the distinction between the works of historians and those of philosophers of history was his view that both reflect an acceptance of one or another metahistorical paradigm that serves to organize the primary data with which they are concerned. Having noted some points at which histories and philosophies of history are obviously different, I shall now consider this presupposition, which led to White's attempt to bring them exceptionally close together.

In offering his account of what he termed "the levels of conceptualization" in a historical work, White took as his starting point the data contained in "the unprocessed historical record" (p. 5). He identified these data as the primitive elements in the historical field. The historian, he held, must first arrange such data in temporal order, thus producing "a chronicle"; he must then connect them in a way that transforms this chronicle into "a story"; this is the beginning of the odyssey that leads to the production of a historical work. This, however, is surely not the way in which any present-day historian would actually work; nor would even the earliest of historians have done so. No historian is confronted at the outset of his inquiries with an *unprocessed* historical record, with a bank of data devoid of all order, to which he must impart whatever order it is to possess. Rather, every historian will, from the outset, be confronted not by raw data but by earlier accounts of the past; embedded within those accounts will be almost all the data with which he is to work. Data not included within one account, but included within another, will lead him to alter one or the other; he must in any case fit these accounts together to obtain a larger, more consistent, and presumably more accurate "story" than any which his predecessors had produced. Nor will all of the accounts of his predecessors appear to be connected: when they deal with different times and places, large gaps may appear between them. In order to fill such gaps, the historian must seek other accounts that will provide data that serve to connect what was previously unconnected; or he must, on his own initiative, seek out such data for himself. In either case, his awareness of the existence of gaps within what White termed "the historical record" conclusively shows that this record does not consist of unorganized raw data—data which are simply "there," and which have no inherent connections with one another until the historian has impressed an order upon them.

It may perhaps be objected that this criticism of White is unfair: that his analysis of the levels of conceptualization which are present in a historical work was intended to be taken as a purely analytic account, and not as an attempt to trace a series of successive steps by means of which any historical work has ever actually been created. Such may indeed have been White's intention, but it would in no way alter the point of the foregoing criticism. Analytically considered, what White designates as "the primitive elements," with which historians work and which serve as their data, are documents, legends, records, and the remains of earlier human activities, or else they are prior accounts concerning the events under investigation. If a historian is to make use of such materials for historical purposes, he cannot regard them as if they were nothing but parchment, slabs of stone, or sheaves of paper; he must view them as relating to various kinds of human activities with which he is familiar through his own direct experience, supplemented by knowledge derived from what has been said by others. Thus, the most basic level on which historical data can be interpreted will be as meaningful elements embedded in an intelligible context. Therefore, from an analytic no less than from a genetic point of view, even the simplest data with which an historian works are not unconnected atomic elements which lack all intrinsic order. What to the historian are "data"—that is, what constitutes "the given" for him—possess connections among themselves which exist prior to, and independently of, the ways in which he subsequently comes to order them. It is for this reason that I reject the first of White's presuppositions.

Turning to a second basic presupposition in *Metahistory,* we find White assuming, without examining alternatives, that the order bestowed by the historian on his materials represents a *poetic* act (for example, pp. x, 4, and 30). It appears as if he took this for granted simply because when one looks at a historical work as "what it most manifestly is," one finds it to be "a verbal structure in the form of a narrative prose discourse" (p. 2). In regarding a historical work in this light and not considering what else it may also be, it is natural that White should turn to the theory of literature in order to identify the various metahistorical paradigms that, as he believes, control the work of historians. He finds such paradigms in four fundamental linguistic tropes. I shall not be concerned with the details of his use of these tropes, but I shall argue that White's approach leaves out of account what has generally—and, I think, rightly—been regarded as the basic intent of historical works: to discover, depict, and explain what has occurred in the past.

I wish first to take note of the fact that simply because every historical work is a verbal structure, and can be considered as such, it by no means follows that this provides the most basic level at which all of its structural aspects are to be understood. An eyewitness may, for example, give a narrative account of the sequence of events that led to an accident, a chemist may describe a series of experiments whereby he succeeded in disproving a previously held theory, a physician may trace the course of a patient's illness from its onset to his death, a traveler may tell us what befell him on his journeys before reaching his destination, and each of these would be a narrative, and would have the general structure that White (following Gallie and Danto) attributes to narratives.

To refuse to regard narratives of this sort as anything more than particular verbal structures would be capricious: as interpreted by a listener, the basic structure of each will be determined by the relationships among the events narrated, not by the manner of their narration. These relationships among the events may have been brought out clearly, or they may have been obscured in the telling, but they will have existed prior to the narration and will be independent of it. So, too, with historical works that, to some extent, these simple narrations resemble. Furthermore, White himself should not attempt to deny that the relationships depicted in a historical narrative exist prior to the act of narration, because that assumption was implicit in his characterization of a historical work. While every such work is, as he tells us, "a verbal structure in the form of narrative prose," it is more than this, for it "purports to be a model, or icon, of past structures and processes in the interest of explaining what they were by representing them" (p. 2). Therefore, unless there is absolutely no basis for the claim that historical narratives *do* represent past structures and processes, and serve as icons which represent relationships that actually obtained, much of their structure—like the structures of the simple narratives I have cited—is not attributable to the narrator but is already present within the elements with which he has chosen to deal.

There doubtless were many reasons why White failed to raise this possibility in his discussion, but he does not suggest what they were, and I shall not speculate concerning them. Instead, it may be more fruitful to inquire what there is in the nature of a historical work itself—totally apart from any of the traditional arguments in favor of historical relativism[5] — that might make it plausible for anyone to regard the narrator as entirely responsible for the structure of his narrative. One such feature seems to me to be the historian's freedom to define the subject matter of his inquiry in almost any way that he chooses.

Every historical work represents a particular choice of subject matter, and in choosing his subject matter a historian is carving out a particular segment of the past from the stream of the historical process; the definition of what constitutes that particular segment — why it does not include either more or less than it does — can be viewed as a creative act on the part of the historian. To be sure, in some cases no genuinely creative act may be involved. For example, a run-of-the-mill historian who decides to write the history of a particular period may simply accept some conventional compartmentalization of the historical process, and work within that framework. In other cases, historians may be puzzled by problems that their predecessors failed to investigate, and their subject matter will be defined by the particular residual problem that they have set out to solve. White would probably be inclined to place works such as these within the same general class to which "monographs and archival reports" belong; it was not with such examples that he was concerned. If, instead, one thinks of the great historians whose works he analyzed, one can see that it is entirely reasonable to regard their ways of envisioning their subject matter as involving original, creative, expressive acts.

On White's analysis of these "precognitive," "precritical" poetic acts the whole argument of his *Metahistory* turns. He distinguishes three "narrative tactics" that all historians employ: an initial "emplotment," an implied form of explanatory argument, and an evaluative, ideological component (p. 7). All of these, White claims, are packed into the historian's original creative act. It is therefore that act that not only "*pre*figures" the general shape of a historical work but determines what kinds of relationships the historian will take into account in analyzing the events with which he deals (cf. p. 430). As White says of such acts, they are "constitutive of the structure that will subsequently be imaged in the verbal model offered by the historian as representation and explanation of 'what *really* happened'" (p. 31).

The various explanatory strategies that the historian can adopt are not, however, unlimited. White holds that each of the three aspects of an adopted strategy — the emplotment, explanatory argument, and ideological component — will assume one of four forms, and he relates these forms to the four fundamental linguistic tropes. He holds that the historian's use of one or another of these tropes represents the deepest level of the historical consciousness, and this is the level at which he seeks to analyze historical works (pp. 30-31). In doing so, he wishes to proceed in a purely "formalist" manner; as he says with respect to his method, "I will not try to decide whether a given historian's work is a better, or more correct, account of a specific set of events or segments of the historical process than some other historian's account of them; rather, I will seek to identify the structural components of these accounts" (pp. 3-4).

So long as he is dealing only with that particular structural component that he identifies as "emplotment," his formalism raises no special difficulties. In fact, it is his analysis of this element which gives point and substance to his claim that in the historian's original way of envisioning his subject there is already prefigured the overall form that his account will ultimately take. With respect to emplotment, White follows Northrop Frye and distinguishes four forms: romance, comedy, tragedy, and satire. These terms are not used in order to characterize distinct literary styles, nor to identify the particular types of subject matter which are present in the works thus emplotted; rather, each refers to a basic attitude on the part of the historian toward the subject matter with which he is to deal. In comedy, for example, what is prefigured is the reconciliation of antagonistic forces; in satire, the attitude is one of irony. Such attitudes are inextricably involved in how the historian envisions his subject: how the beginning of the narrative is related to its end, and which details and what changes in fortune he will emphasize.

Whether White's assimilation of these four forms of emplotment to the four fundamental tropes of poetic discourse can withstand scrutiny is not a matter with which I am concerned: the four forms of emplotment, as White has characterized them, can be accepted independently of any relations they may bear to his theory of tropes. They constitute highly relevant aspects of a historian's work, and White has made an important and suggestive contribution to the theory of historiography in having called attention to them. This cannot, however, be said of his claim that the same linguistic tropes provide the best way to understand the forms of explanatory arguments historians employ, nor the role that ideological factors play in their works. As I shall now suggest, in these cases White's formalist "tropological" account breaks down.

First consider his attempt to reduce the various types of explanatory argument to a linguistic form. Borrowing from Stephen Pepper's *World Hypotheses*, White distinguishes four types of explanatory argument: formist, mechanistic, organicist, contextualist. Let us grant that this may be an adequate typology of four characteristically different modes of explanation; let us also grant the somewhat more dubious contention that different thinkers, regardless of the subject matter with which they deal, tend to accept one of these four types, rejecting each of the others. It would still be necessary for White to show that such a bias is not derived from some specifically *theoretical* considerations, but actually depends upon the way in which *linguistic* forms give structure to the thought of various thinkers. I suggest that when this thesis is considered in relation to the history of ideas, it will be recognized as implausible. If, for example, one examines the thought of a mechanist of the seventeenth century, or of an organicist in the later eighteenth or the nineteenth century, one discovers reasons of a specifically historical and philosophical sort why—once having chosen the subject matter with which he was to deal—such a thinker would view his field in terms of mechanistic or organicist models. For example, in order to account for the dominance of the mechanical explanatory model in the seventeenth century, one has to look to the development of the mechanical sciences in that period; to explain organicist models in late eighteenth- and nineteenth-century thought, one must look to the anti-Newtonian views that developed out of various physical, biological, and specifically historical concerns with which the Newtonian model was unable to cope. To attribute such change to whatever linguistic modes may perhaps have been dominant in the period would almost surely be an example of the hysteron-protoron fallacy, a putting of the cart before the horse: insofar as one trope rather than another was in fact dominant within the period, it was more likely to have been a reflection of the thought of the period than an independent determinant in giving structure to that thought.

Consider also the ideological and ethical stance involved in the work of any historian. White uses the concept of "ideology" in a somewhat broader than usual sense, including beliefs concerning the nature and aims of a study of society, attitudes toward historical change, and beliefs as to when and where a social ideal has been, or might be, realized (p. 24).[6] Even when the concept is used in this extended sense, it is difficult to see how a historian's acceptance of one or another ideological stance can be clarified by relating it to one of the four linguistic tropes with which White's tropological approach is concerned. If one seeks to penetrate to what lies below the surface of the attitudes of the anarchist, the radical, the conservative, or the liberal (the four basic forms of ideology which White takes over from Mannheim), it would seem more fruitful to use other means than those provided by a linguistic analysis. In the first place, it is doubtful whether one can find any common properties determined in terms of linguistic models that would unite all who closely resemble one another in their ideologies. In the second place, it would seem imperative in any given case to try to understand the political and social situation to which the historian was exposed and to consider his ideological stance not only with reference to it, but also in relation to those factors in his personal life which may have led him to view that situation as he did. It is surely far-fetched to interpret his view of the conflicts inherent in his own time, or his stance toward past and future, or his position regarding the possibility of creating a science of society, as if each of these were to follow from some linguistic predisposition on his part. White offers no arguments to dispel this disquietude: from the outset he has simply assumed that the structure of a historical work is to be treated as a literary structure, and that the four fundamental linguistic tropes provide the basic categories to be used in interpreting all linguistic structures.

The inflexibility of White's approach is nowhere more evident than in the manner in which he treats the history of nineteenth-century historiography. His tropological approach is fundamentally ahistorical: the possibility of organizing an historical account in terms of one of these tropes instead of another is not restricted to any one time or place, but is ever-present. Nevertheless, White attempts to trace a development in the dominant modes of historical thinking in the nineteenth century, moving from an ironic realism in the Enlightenment through the postures of romance, tragedy, and comedy, to emerge once again, at the end of the century, in a new mood of irony which he identified with "the crisis of historicism." He failed to establish this developmental schema through any broad-ranging examination of the various lines of development to be found in the historiography of the period. He paid no attention to the impact of nationalism on historiography, to the importance of *Kulturgeschichte,* to how, if at all, evolutionary theory in biology influenced historiography, to the rise of social evolutionism among legal historians and social anthropologists, or to the ways in which a sociological interest in "the masses" affected the consciousness of historians. Nor does one find any extended treatment of many of the foremost historians of the period, of Niebuhr or of Maitland, for example. In fact, one cannot escape the impression that the historians and philosophers of history White chose to discuss were selected primarily in terms of their diversity and because of the contrasts between them. Then, having reduced the number of classic nineteenth-century historians to four, and the number of philosophers of history in the same period to four, it was not a task of great difficulty to establish a relatively clear line of development within the period. What is not evident is that the same line of development would have been discernible had White included many more historians, or had he included Comte, John Stuart Mill, and Spencer along with Hegel and Marx among his philosophers of history, or Dilthey, Rickert, Troeltsch, and Spengler along with Nietzsche and Croce.

I come now to the third and last of the presuppositions I wish to discuss: White's acceptance of relativism. In a sense, this should not be identified as one of his presuppositions, because it is a necessary consequence of his formalistic, tropological approach. Yet, had he not initially been willing to accept relativism, independently of any argumentation for it, he would have been forced to raise the question of whether a historical work can be adequately interpreted solely as a linguistic structure. Consequently, one may regard White's relativism as a basic presupposition, and one that is no less fundamental than his reasons for treating historians and philosophers of history together, or his view that what gives a historical work its structure is not the result of a careful reconstruction of the past but a creative poetic act. Actually, these presuppositions are interlocking, and I find no others that are equally fundamental in his work.

In considering White's relativism, I shall once again refuse to speculate as to how it was that he may have come to accept it; instead, I shall ask to what extent his account of the historian's work legitimates it. The first point to note is that the four historians with whom White chose to deal were engaged in very different enterprises. There was relatively little overlap in the subject matters with which they were concerned; where such overlap existed, the scale of their inquiries differed, and the particular facets of the events with which they were concerned also differed.[7] Therefore, the question whether one of these accounts was "truer" or "more correct" than another would not naturally arise, and White was able to remain wholly within the confines of his formalistic approach. This permitted him to avoid any direct examination of the fundamental issue involved in debates concerning historical relativism: whether it is possible, even in principle, to say of one account that it is truer, or more nearly correct, or more adequate, than another. What took the place of any such direct examination was White's assumption that the structure of every historical account is dependent upon the form that the historian impresses upon his subject matter. Because White found that different historians had distinctively different "styles," and were therefore predisposed to use different ways of giving structure to that with which they dealt, he concluded that the only grounds on which one type of account could be given preference over another would be aesthetic or moral, rather than epistemological (p. xii).[8]

An entirely different situation would have arisen had he compared works concerned with the same subject matter, which worked on the same scale, and with reference to the same aspects of that subject matter. He would then have had to consider whether, in spite of differences in style, accounts that purported to represent the same events were congruent or incongruent, whether one or another had failed to consider certain types of data, and whether the inclusion of those data would have altered the representation of what had occurred.

To this, White might perhaps have answered that there was no need for him to enter into such discussions, because the original way in which a historian envisions any segment of the historical process will always be different from the way in which another historian does. That response, however, would be faulty in two respects. In the first place, even though White sometimes stressed the uniqueness of the structural elements in different historical works (for example, pp. 5 and 29), the basis of his analysis lay in an acceptance of Vico's four linguistic tropes. He took these tropes to be recurrent and typical ways of organizing materials, not idiosyncratic characteristics of specific individuals. He identified the "style" of an historian with the particular combination of modes of emplotment, explanatory argument, and ideological stance that characterized that historian's work. Because, however, each of these modes derived from one or another of the four tropes, and because White acknowledged that not all of the numerically possible combinations were mutually compatible (p. 29), the fundamental variations among historians in basic styles were limited. This is a fact that White explicitly recognized (p. 31). Consequently, it should be both possible and meaningful for anyone examining the works of different historians to compare these works, so long as they resembled one another in their modes of emplotment, explanatory argument, and ideological implication. Because each such mode, according to White, serves to *explain* that which the historian is representing (pp. 2 and 7), one would think it possible to ask with respect to these works whether one or them is in some respects superior to another as a "model" or "icon" of the process represented. White makes no such comparisons, and obviously believed it illegitimate to try to make them (for example, pp. xii, 3, 26-27, 432). The apparent justification for this completely relativistic commitment lay in his decision to treat a historical work solely as a linguistic structure, and so long as that point of view is strictly maintained, there is, of course, nothing against which to compare the two linguistic "models" to determine which is the more adequate representation. It was, then, his linguistic approach, and not ultimately a question of the uniqueness of each historical work, that served as justification for White's relativism.

His rejection of the possibility of comparing different historical accounts is also faulty in a second respect. It is simply not the case that the way in which one historian envisions any segment of the historical process will always be different from another historian's way. Many historians self-consciously set out to show that some account given by a predecessor is mistaken, and they attempt to produce data or arguments to establish their case. It is not that they are looking at the same segment of the past in a different way: they are contending that their predecessor misrepresented the process with which he claimed to be dealing. White failed to discuss inquiries of this sort because they were not typical of the aims and methods of the four historians whose works he had chosen as paradigms. It is even possible that he might be inclined to dismiss these and other problem-oriented types of inquiries as belonging to the class of "monographs and archival reports" (p. ix) or to "the kinds of disputes which arise on the reviewers' pages of professional journals" (p. 13). This, however, would be illegitimate, because among such inquiries there are many full-scale treatments of processes that had a long and complex history, such as those that have been concerned to establish the relations between the slavery question and the American Civil War. Taking into account the fact that historians frequently engage in controversies of this sort and finding that in some cases a consensus develops out of such controversies, White's ready acceptance of relativism is surely inadequate as a characterization of the ways in which practicing historians often view the work in which they are engaged.

On the other hand, if one turns from historical inquiries to consider the works of philosophers of history, one finds that they are almost never in agreement, either with respect to their detailed interpretations or on matters of principle. Nothing on their part in any way corresponds to the responsibility historians accept to document any challenged statement; to their commitment not to exclude from consideration any evidence that may be relevant to the material at hand; and to their recognition of an obligation to consider the criticism of those who do not share their presuppositions, so long as these criticisms directly relate to the accounts they have given of what in fact occurred in the past. We do not find the same scruples in such philosophers of history as Hegel and Marx, who sought to establish a meaning in history through a survey of the past. Instead, they selected only certain aspects of the life of society as a basis for interpreting what was truly significant in that life. They also neglected large segments of the historical past as not belonging within the province of meaningful history. Finally, each tended to take his own interpretative presuppositions as absolute and did not show either a willingness or an ability to find means of reconciling alternative points of view. Nor would the situation be radically altered were we to turn from those who attempt to sum up the total past in order to establish history's meaning and consider only those who, like Croce and Nietzsche, considered themselves primarily as philosophic interpreters and critics of Western man's historical consciousness. Once again the scope of such inquiries tended to be severely limited, and the tenor of the arguments was so dogmatic that only those antecedently committed to similar philosophic presuppositions were likely to find themselves in agreement. Thus, in contrast to historical inquiries, different philosophies of history do not represent potentially compatible interpretations, nor complementary points of view. In fact, had there been as many philosophers of history as there have been historians, we would now find ourselves absolutely confounded by their babel of tongues. Because White—flying in the face of tradition —took philosophers of history to be at least as important as historians for any understanding of the historical consciousness, the wild disparities among their works tended to substantiate the relativism he was already inclined to accept.

As I have indicated, one of the basic reasons why White was so ready to accept relativism lay in the fact that he viewed every historical work as a linguistic entity whose structure wholly depended on the original poetic act that prefigured it. This, however, involved treating the statements that historians make as if they had no referents outside of their own work—as if some theory of the syntactics of poetry could supplant all questions concerning the semantics of everyday speech.[9] I find it one of the oddities of *Metahistory* that in spite of its "lingustic" approach, it failed to include as part of its implicit theory of language any account of how languages function with respect to their referential uses. So long as this is left out of account, one wonders how the individual statements of any historian are to be understood. Some among them refer to past occurrences whose existence is only known through inferences drawn from surviving documents; but it is not to these documents themselves, but to what they indicate concerning the past, that the historian's statements actually refer. Others among their statements depend upon what had been written in earlier accounts, but here again the object of the historian's reference is not these accounts themselves, but is to the very same entities (or to similar entities) as those to which the earlier accounts had themselves referred. Only a person treating a historical account solely as a literary document would not immediately raise the issue of reference, and with it the question of historical truth. So long as that question is not raised, I am forced to wonder in what sense White can properly characterize a historical work as a model or icon purporting to represent past structures and processes and, in doing so, as being able to explain them.

I have confined myself to some of the issues involved in White's "metahistorical" thesis; I have wholly neglected questions raised by the subtitle of his book, "The Historical Imagination in Nineteenth-Century Europe." Such questions might be of two sorts. One would involve an assessment of what occupies by far the largest portion of the book, White's interpretations of the thought of the individual historians and philosophers of history with whom he deals. The other would be a consideration of whether the book as a whole is adequate as "a history of historical consciousness in nineteenth-century Europe" (p. 1). In spite of a high regard for several of White's interpretations of the individuals on whom he focused attention, I find (as I have suggested in passing) that his portrayal of the scope of historical thought in the nineteenth century was far too limited; I also find unconvincing his suggestions as to the general course of development that it followed. These, however, are specifically historical issues, and it would take another and quite different paper to discuss them.

Notes

This paper was one of six critiques of White's Metahistory presented at a symposium held at Wesleyan University in 1979. My aim was to criticize White with respect to some views that he shares with many recent theoretically inclined humanist critics. These views center on treating all written works as texts, to be explicated simply as texts. White was thereby led to obliterate any clear distinction between the works of historians and attempts to construct philosophies of history. This also led him to treat historical works as literary products to be interpreted, rather than as inquiries to be evaluated with respect to the truth or falsity of that which they purport to depict or explain.

1. His closest approach to doing so, when speaking in his own voice, appears in his concluding chapter, where he identifies a philosophy of history as "a second order of consciousness in which [the philosopher of history] carries out his efforts to make sense of the historical process. [He] seeks not only to understand what happened in history but also to specify the criteria by which he can know when he has successfully grasped its meaning or significance" (p. 428).

The foregoing characterization covers both "critical" and "speculative" philosophies of history, as one would expect from White's linkage of Nietzsche and Croce with Hegel and Marx. Nevertheless, in most passages he explicitly refers to "speculative" philosophies of history, and he only rarely cites works that are characteristic of the extensive literature dealing with the problems of a "critical" philosophy of history.

For my own view as to what constitutes a philosophy of history, which I presuppose in much that follows, see "Some Neglected Philosophic Problems Regarding History," reprinted above (ch. 6).

2. For documentation of the following brief summary, cf. especially pp. ix-xii, 2, 4-5, and 30-31.

3. In this respect, so-called universal histories often resemble philosophies of history. Nevertheless, as one can see in both Ranke and Burckhardt, historians attempt to separate themselves from philosophers of history, holding that their primary concern is with the particular and concrete, and not with events merely insofar as they are viewed as exemplifying some particular principle of explanation. On this point, cf. Ranke, *Ueber der neueren Geschichte*, ed., with a preface, by Alfred Dove (Leipzig, 1888), pp. vii-xi and 6-7; Burckhardt, *Force and Freedom: Reflections on History* [translation of *Weltgeschichtliche Betrachtungen*, ed. James Hastings Nichols] (New York, 1943), pp. 80-82.

4. A few philosophers of history, such as Reinhold Niebuhr, attempt to establish their positions in essentially the same way. On the difference between Niebuhr's approach and the dominant tradition among philosophers of history, cf. my article, "Some Neglected Philosophic Problems Regarding History," cited above.

5. As we shall see, White explicitly accepts relativism, but he does not arrive at it, nor defend it, on the basis of any of the traditional arguments for it. Instead, he derives support for it from his view that when different historians give structure to the historical field, they are viewing it in terms of different tropes.

6. He tends to leave out of consideration the specific sense in which Marx and most subsequent analysts have usually used the concept of ideology.

7. For a discussion of how the concepts of *scale* and *perspectives* relate to the issue of relativism, cf. my *Anatomy of Historical Knowledge* (Baltimore, 1977), especially pp. 151-55.

8. Here White's position differs markedly from that of Stephen Pepper, from whose doctrine of "root metaphors" he borrowed. Pepper held that the issues were fundamentally epistemological; he also believed that it is both possible and reasonable to make use of more than one of the four basic systems in our explanations. In this connection he said, "In practice, therefore, we shall want to be not rational but reasonable, and to seek, on the matter in question, the judgment supplied from each of these relatively adequate world theories. If there is some difference of judgment, we shall wish to make our decision with all these modes of evidence in mind, just as we should make any other decision where the evidence is conflicting" (*World Hypotheses* [Berkeley, 1942], pp. 330-31).

9. This is a point also made by Michael Ermarth in his generally favorable review of *Metahistory* (*American Historical Review*, 80 [1975]:961-63.

9

A Note on Thomas S. Kuhn's
Structure of Scientific Revolutions

One of the primary sources of recent forms of what is sometimes referred to as "historicism," and sometimes as "relativism," is Thomas S. Kuhn's *The Structure of Scientific Revolutions*.[1] Although Professor Kuhn has frequently insisted that most such interpretations of his views have distorted his meaning, it is not entirely clear that he has successfully answered those of his critics who have thus interpreted his work, nor that he has so clarified his position that the matter is no longer open to debate. Exegesis is not, however, the point with which this paper is concerned.

Rather, I wish to raise certain historiographical issues that (so far as I know) have not been discussed in a similar form by other critics of Professor Kuhn's position. In the first instance, I shall treat these issues with respect to the historiography of the sciences—a field in which, admittedly, Professor Kuhn has more expertise than have I. I shall then extend my criticism to include those who assume that Professor Kuhn's views regarding the structure of the scientific revolutions with which he concerns himself will apply not only to the sciences generally, but also to all forms of intellectual and cultural history, and, indeed, within historiography generally. The impact of Professor Kuhn's book has been so great that this sort of extension seems seldom to have been challenged. Although Professor Kuhn has urged some degree of caution with respect to such extensions, he has done little to dissuade his admirers from making use of his views in this way (pp. 208-10).[2]

I

I begin with my doubts concerning Professor Kuhn's account of scientific revolutions. Let me say that I shall not in this connection be challenging what might be called the *anatomy* of the revolutions he has traced, but only his account of their *etiology*. This, unfortunately, is not a distinction that Professor Kuhn drew.

As is well known, Kuhn distinguishes scientific revolutions from "normal science." Normal science is a matter of "puzzle-solving" (pp. 35-36), and it is "firmly based upon one or more past scientific achievements, achievements that some particular scientific community acknowledges for a time as supply-

Reprinted by permission from the *Monist*, 60 (1977):445-52.

ing the foundation for its further practice" (p. 10). The basis for normal science consists in the acceptance by a scientific community of particular "paradigms," that is, examples or models of explanation which, "like an accepted decision in the common law," serve as "an object for further articulation and specification under new or more stringent conditions" (p. 23). Scientific revolutions arise when sufficient anomalies develop within normal science to lead to the substitution of new and incompatible paradigms for the old paradigms that underlay the normal science of the preceding period (p. 92).

As Professor Kuhn recognized in his 1969 Postscript, and in his essay in the Suppe volume, there was an unfortunate circularity in his original way of handling the relationships between a particular scientific community and the acceptance of a particular paradigm by that community: the paradigm was characterized in terms of its acceptance by a community, and the community was characterized in terms of its accepting that paradigm (pp. 176-81). Therefore, in his 1969 Postscript, Professor Kuhn attempted to define a scientific community in quasi-sociological terms, which would be neutral insofar as the acceptance of any particular paradigm was concerned. While it is often both useful and important to study disciplines in sociological terms, in some contexts it can be misleading to do so. This I think is generally true if one is attempting to understand what has brought about specific changes as they have occurred in intellectual history, and this was the type of problem with which Kuhn was ostensibly concerned. The difficulty in Kuhn's approach may be illustrated in the following ways.

A scientific community, as characterized by Kuhn, consists of the practitioners of a scientific specialty, although he admits that scientists sometimes belong to more than one such community, either simultaneously or successively (p. 178). Among the marks of those who are practitioners of a scientific specialty are facts of the following sort: they have had similar educations and professional backgrounds, they are acquainted with the same technical literature, and there is a flow of communication within the group. As Kuhn points out, there is an increasing interest among sociologists and historians of science in defining and investigating scientific communities as thus conceived.[3] What must not be overlooked, however, is that every scientist belonging within a scientific community is also a member of other communities, and through them he will have come under other influences. One might suppose that these influences will not be likely to alter a scientist's basic orientation within a period of normal science unless scientific anomalies have arisen, but even this may not always be true. For example, one can reasonably argue that it was not primarily because of anomalies within the accepted systems of classification of plants and animals that Lamarck was led to formulate a sharp and explicit contrast between his evolutionary theory and the doctrine of special creationism. Rather, it has been held that this contrast was closely connected with his general scientific, philosophical, and religious views.[4]

Even were one to argue that such more general concerns can only exert a major influence when anomalies are present within the normal puzzle-solving of a particular scientific discipline, it is frequently the case that a particular science may be profoundly influenced by specific ideas whose origins lie in other disciplines. For example, if one considers how Malthus's views on population influenced the theory of natural selection as it was put forward by both Darwin and Wallace, one will not be likely to underestimate the force of ideas coming from outside a particular scientific community, as Kuhn has defined such a community.[5] The possible impact of outside influences—both specific and general—is also clear in cases cited by Kuhn himself. Not only does he mention the influence of earlier theories on the formulation of later theories, as when he cites the effect of "the impetus theory, a late mediaeval paradigm" on Galileo's analysis of motion (p. 119), but he mentions "the role of sun worship in Kepler's thought" (p. 153 n.). With respect to Galileo's analysis of pendular motion, he also holds that it was Neoplatonism that "directed Galileo's attention to the motion's circularity" (p. 123 f.).[6]

In acknowledging such influences, it is not necessary to reject Professor Kuhn's anatomy of the *structure* of scientific revolutions, but such an acknowledgment entails that one must substantially alter what Professor Kuhn has suggested concerning the dynamics of scientific change (p. 52-53). Even though he admits that other influences must be taken into account in any full analysis of scientific revolutions, it is his contention that "technical breakdown will still remain the core of the crisis" (p. 69). As he then adds, referring to other influences, "issues of that sort are out of bounds for this essay" (p. 69).[7] This suggests that Professor Kuhn's treatise is more limited in scope than it has usually been taken to be, because an analysis of what has occurred when a revolution has taken place is not equivalent to understanding the conditions that brought it about.

This brings me to my second line of criticism, which is directed against the extension of Kuhn's thesis beyond its original limits—an extension for which it would seem that Professor Kuhn himself must share some responsibility.

II

I shall here consider two examples of facile analogies that are briefly suggested by Kuhn and may seem tempting, but that I find unsatisfactory. They consist in taking his view of scientific change and applying it to revolutions in artistic style and to political revolutions.[8]

With respect to changes of style in painting, Professor Kuhn rightly points out that they do not occur in conformity with "some abstracted canons of style," but in accordance with the adoption of new exemplars upon which they are to some degree modelled (p. 208-9). One such change that he mentions (but that he appears to date far too early) is the renunciation of representation as the goal of art (p. 161). He does not concretely suggest what exemplars actually brought about such a change, and it seems doubtful whether he could do so. On the contrary, it would seem that he would probably have to appeal not to scientific exemplars, but to more far-reaching changes within a broader cultural tradition. In fact, he seems to do so, because in discussing the point he alludes to a split that occurred between science and art. Nevertheless, as Kuhn points out (p. 208), there are in fact tradition-bound periods in literature, music, and the other arts, followed by revolutionary breaks in style, and cultural historians are concerned with such changes. It is, however, one thing to indicate the presence of such changes within any field, or among any set of fields, and quite another to trace the influences that brought them about. In the sciences, Professor Kuhn appealed to increasing anomalies that led to sudden revolutionary change, but to what should one compare such anomalies in the arts? It would seem that interests develop out of new experiences, or that artists and writers find new models in traditions other than their own, but such changes usually occur because a given tradition has worn thin, and satiation has set in, or because the tradition seems irrelevant to the interests and needs of the time.[9] If such changes had taken place because difficulties had developed *within* the tradition itself, as the analogy with Professor Kuhn's conception of scientific revolutions would suggest, he has not indicated the nature and the sources of such difficulties. Nor has this been done by others who have attempted to use Professor Kuhn's views regarding scientific change: they have tended to seize on the notion of "paradigms," and on the incommensurability of different paradigms, rather than being concerned with any actual processes of cultural or intellectual change.

I also consider the analogy that Kuhn draws between scientific revolutions and political revolutions (p. 92-94) to be quite misleading. To be sure, one can find at least a rough analogy between scientific anomalies and failures within traditional organizations to solve political problems; one can also find analogies between the oppositions which exist in both fields with respect to the acceptance of change. Furthermore, what occurs when a revolution has succeeded may be similar in both fields. These seem to be some of the reasons why Professor Kuhn was tempted to draw a parallel between the two fields. Nevertheless, there is at least one fundamental difference between those changes that are designated as "revolutions" in these spheres. As Professor Kuhn insists, the scientific community is to a large extent a separate community within the society as a whole (p. 164): it is "a well-defined community of the scientist's professional compeers" (p. 168), and a revolution within a particular science will, in this view, therefore be relatively insulated in its origins and in its effects from any other occurences, and will unfold according to an immanent dialectic of its own. On the other hand, a political revolution, if it is not simply the replacement of one junta by another, represents a genuine upheaval within a society and can affect almost any facet of life in that society. Consequently, the historian dealing with political and social revolutions must trace a complex set of sometimes antagonistic and sometimes interlocking relationships, and this has no parallel in scientific revolutions, if Professor Kuhn's account of such revolutions is assumed to be correct.

The basic difficulty in his account, which seems to me to have been responsible for the ease with which Professor Kuhn and others have extended his view to other fields, is that in *The Structure of Scientific Revolutions*, unlike his study *The Copernican Revolution*, Professor Kuhn was not actually functioning as a historian. Instead, he was defending a particular set of theses against alternative views that had been formulated by historians of science, and perhaps more particularly by philosophers of science. To say that he was not functioning "as a historian" is simply to point out that in treating scientific revolutions his primary focus of interest was on a contrast between "before" and "after," not upon any detailed consideration of the actual processes of change.

One can note this in the frequency with which he speaks of scientific revolutions as involving an element of *conversion* in a point of view (e.g., pp. 150, 152, 198, 202 f., 204). *Conversion*—as the term is actually used in such contexts, and as Professor Kuhn uses it—is typically an "all at once" occurrence, a sudden and total shift in (for example) a moral or religious point of view. Professor Kuhn makes the most of this notion by comparing it with sudden shifts in perceptual organization, in what he terms "a change in visual gestalt" (p. 85; cf. pp. 111 and p. 126 f.) This is not the place to criticize in any detail the use to which Professor Kuhn puts his accounts of a series of psychological studies. Although he holds that such studies are only suggestive and cannot be regarded as conclusive with respect to what occurs in science (p. 113), his theory does in fact lean heavily on them.[10] In this connection it is necessary to point out that even though his theory frequently appeals in a loose way to the concept of a "Gestalt," Professor Kuhn fails to refer to the work of any Gestalt psychologist or to any psychologist whose theoretical position even remotely resembles the point of view made familiar by Wertheimer, Koffka, or Köhler. Had he done so, he could not have assumed that "without what his previous visual-conceptual experience has taught him to see," the world would appear to a person as being—in William James's phrase—'a bloomin', buzzin' confusion'" (p. 113). More importantly, Professor Kuhn's unfamiliarity with Gestalt psychology led him to overlook the stress that school always placed on the fact that perception involves the grasp of "segregated wholes," and that a change in perceptual configurations does *not* carry with it the implication that the whole perceptual world—the world as we experience and describe it—thereby undergoes transformation. Yet it is precisely this assumption that accounts for the fact that Professor Kuhn's critics have held his position leads inevitably to historicism and that he is committed to the acceptance of a form of relativism far more radical than that which he believes he is obliged to accept.

It has not been my aim to argue whether or not Professor Kuhn's views are correct concerning the degree of incommensurability that exists between any two scientific theories or between any cultures. The aim of this note has been restricted to showing that in spite of his deep knowledge of the history of several sciences, Professor Kuhn's argument in *The Structure of Scientific Revolutions* is basically misleading when taken as an analysis of what brings about a revolutionary change either in science or other fields. What it offers instead is an account of the particular respects in which a science changes when a scientific revolution has taken place. It is important to appreciate such changes, but to show what has occurred is not in this case the same as accounting for its occurrence.

Notes

This paper, which antedates my criticism of Kuhn's conceptual relativism, was written for an issue of The Monist *which had as its subject "Historicism and Epistemology." Its aim was more limited, being solely concerned with criticizing Kuhn's analysis of the concept of a scientific revolution and its extension to other fields.*

I believe it only proper to state that Professor Kuhn found my criticism unacceptable, yet I remain unconvinced that this article has done his views an injustice.

1. *International Encyclopedia of Unified Science*, vol. 2, no. 2 (Chicago: University of Chicago Press, 1962); second enlarged edition, with Postscript, 1969.

2. All references, except as otherwise noted, will be to *The Structure of Scientific Revolutions* (Chicago: University of Chicago Press, 1970); second enlarged edition (page numbers in parentheses). Other papers by Professor Kuhn which bear directly on the same topics, but which do not alter the views put forward in the second edition of his book, are "Second Thoughts on Paradigms" (presented in 1969), in Frederick Suppe, *The Structure of Scientific Theories* (Urbana: University of Illinois Press, 1974) and his contributions to *Criticism and the Growth of Knowledge*, ed. by Lakatos and Musgrave (Cambridge: Cambridge University Press, 1970), pp. 1-23 and 231-78.

3. The fact that in the past scientists more frequently belonged to several scientific communities (as Kuhn has defined such communities) than is at present the case suggests that his definition has been mainly influenced by recent science, although his examples of major scientific revolutions are chiefly drawn from earlier periods.

4. One interpretation that stresses the importance of these factors in Lamarck's biology is to be found in C. C. Gillispie, "The Formation of Lamarck's Evolutionary Theory," *Archives internationale d'histoire des sciences*, 9 (1956):323-38. A different interpretation, but one that reaches the general conclusion that "Lamarck's '*biologie*' was a natural philosophy project thoroughly characteristic of the late Enlightenment" (p. 324), is to be found in M.J.S. Hodge, "Lamarck's Science of Living Bodies," *British Journal of the History of Science*, 5 (1971):323-52. A proper interpretation of the roles played by Lamarck's various scientific theories and by his philosophic convictions in the formulation of his views regarding "evolution," does not permit of any simple solution, but nothing that can be established in this connection fits Kuhn's conception of scientific change. For a careful survey of the complex of factors entering into Lamarck's thought, cf. L. J. Burlingame's article, "Lamarck," in the *Dictionary of Scientific Biography*, ed. Charles Gillispie (New York: Charles Scribner and Sons, 1973).

A wider-ranging treatment of the difficulty of applying Kuhn's thesis to the pre-Darwinian period is to be found in John C. Greene, "The Kuhnian Paradigm and the Darwinian Revolution in Natural History," in *Perspectives in the History of Science and Technology,* ed. Duane H. O. Roller (Norman: University of Oklahoma Press, 1971), pp. 3-25. Greene holds that in addition to a paradigm underlying Linnaeus's dominant system of classification there were three pre-Darwinian "counter-paradigms," which he identified with Buffon, with Lamarck, and with the exponents of *Naturphilosophie.* As the discussants of Greene's paper pointed out (pp. 26-37), there are questions as to how one is to conceive of "a paradigm" and of "counter-paradigms" in these cases, and these questions may materially affect the force of Greene's criticism of Kuhn. Nevertheless, in the course of his argument Greene introduced statements that are not likely to be seriously disputed and that are relevant to the point I here wish to make. The following are three such statements. 1. "The Buffonian paradigm was *not* a response to anomalies and contradictions within the Linnean paradigm. Instead, it was a conscious attempt to introduce into natural history concepts derived from natural philosophy, from the seventeenth-century revolution in physics and cosmology" (p. 8). 2. "It appears then that Lamarck's counter-paradigm sprang more from a predisposition toward a uniformitarian view of nature's operations than from a sense of the difficulties to be resolved in the structure of systematic natural history" (p. 14). 3. In speaking of *Naturphilosophie* "as an outgrowth of German idealistic philosophy" (p. 15), Greene says, "But here again, as in the case of the very different views of nature and natural science promulgated by Buffon and Lamarck, paradigm construction did not wait on the emergence of anomalies and crises in systematic natural history. On the contrary, it ran ahead of known facts, postulating a wider unity in nature than could be demonstrated, and delving into the study of embryological development in search of confirmatory data" (p. 16).

5. I have attempted to trace some of these sources as they affected the acceptance of evolutionary theory in "The Scientific Background of Evolutionary Theory in Biology," reprinted below (ch. 24).

6. Also, cf. his discussion of the contributions of Renaissance humanism and of Neoplatonism to the Copernican Revolution, in *The Copernican Revolution: Planetary Astronomy in the Development of Western Thought* (Cambridge: Harvard University Press, 1957) pp. 125-32. There, in speaking of humanism, he says: "Developments like those discussed above can help us understand why the Copernican Revolution occurred when it did. They are essential parts of the climate for astronomical upheaval" (p. 126).

7. Also, cf. page x of his original (1962) preface, where he says that while a consideration of such influences "would surely add an analytic dimension of first-rate importance for the understanding of scientific advance," he does not believe—though he does not show why—that they would "modify the main theses developed in this essay."

8. The extent to which Kuhn's views have spread to other fields is suggestively documented by David A. Hollinger in "T. S. Kuhn's Theory of Science and Its Implications for History," *American Historical Review,* 78 (1973):370-93.

9. The same point is made by James Ackerman in "The Demise of the Avant Garde," *Comparative Studies in Society and History,* 11 (1969):373, where he discusses Kuhn's analogy between scientific revolutions and changes in style. Kuhn, in his comments on this and other papers in that symposium (pp. 403-12), stresses both the parallels and the divergences between the arts and the sciences (e.g., p. 405). Nevertheless, he does not really grapple with the problem of what specific similarities (if any) and what specific differences (if any) there are between revolutionary changes that occur in the two fields. Yet that, presumably, was the focus of his interest when, in *The Structure of Scientific Revolutions* (p. 208), he compared periodizations in the sciences and the arts.

10. With respect to Professor Kuhn's use of the psychological materials he cites, I find his allusions (for they are not discussions) most unsatisfactory. For example, he takes the demonstrations of various perceptual phenomena, as devised by Adelbert Ames at the Hanover Eye Institute, to be experiments and as providing supporting evidence for his own theory of the role of experience in perception (p. 112). He seems to be unaware of the fact that Ames had to assign

to experience a role similar to that which one finds in Herbert Spencer's psychology, according to which the effects of an individual's cumulative experience are genetically inherited.

Professor Kuhn's use of data concerning reversible figures is unusually skimpy, considering the wealth of literature on this subject, for he is content to cite relatively trite examples, such as the Wittgenstein-Hanson duck-rabbit illustration, rather than that of other reversible figures in which his thesis concerning the role of instructions and of experience is open to serious challenge. Similarly, the difficult perceptual problems that are involved when one analyzes what happens when there is inversion of the retinal image due to the introduction of special lenses are left unnoticed in Professor Kuhn's treatment of the original Stratton experiments, which were repeated in the Ames demonstrations.

10

The History of Philosophy:
Some Methodological Issues

One is now so accustomed to consulting histories of philosophy that it is easy to suppose that such works have always been available, but that has not been the case. Aristotle, of course, left an account of his predecessors, and the doxographical tradition as represented, for example, by Theophrastus and by Diogenes Laërtius's *Lives* can also be cited as attempting to recover and portray philosophy's past. Yet one need merely consult Jacob Brucker's five-volume *Critical History of Philosophy* (1742-67), the standard eighteenth-century guide to the history of philosophy, to see that genuinely *historical* treatments of philosophical thought have been in existence for less than two hundred years. Even Brucker organized his work unhistorically, in terms of schools, treating Plato in Book 3, but not discussing Pythagoras until Book 8, and only in Book 9 do Parmenides and Heracleitus appear. Serious concern with the *history* of philosophy did not in fact arise until the end of the eighteenth century and the beginning of the nineteenth; if I am not mistaken, this interest was connected with the historical perspective from which Kant had envisioned his own critical system, and with the reception accorded that system.[1] Subsequently, through the influence of Hegel's historical orientation and through the impact of his *Lectures on the History of Philosophy,* the field was firmly established and occupied an important position in nineteenth-century thought.

It is not, however, my aim to discuss the history of histories of philosophy, analyzing the changing methods that have been followed and the changing uses to which such inquiries have been put. Instead, I wish to raise certain general methodological questions that arise in connection with the historiography of philosophy and that have parallels, I believe, in methodological problems in other fields, such as the history of science, of literature, and of the arts, to name only three. The first of these problems — and a particularly thorny one — is how the historian of philosophy is to delimit the field of his study: that is, how he is to pick out those who are to count as philosophers and, thus, those with whose thought he is to deal.

Were it the case that the term *philosophy* referred to some strictly delimited set of problems, so that any vagueness of reference arose only at or near the boundaries of the field, the problem of definition would not pose a serious methodological issue. That, however, is not the case. Unlike the situation

Reprinted by permission from *Journal of Philosophy,* 74 (1977):561-72.

obtaining with respect to biology or geology, or even astronomy, etymology fails to provide an adequate clue as to what philosophy is, or aims to be. To be sure, there are established traditions that serve to identify some persons as central figures in the history of philosophy, so that no one could, for example, write a history of modern European philosophy without taking into account Descartes, Leibniz, Locke, and Kant. It might then be supposed that by using these and other major figures as touchstones, one could separate philosophers from nonphilosophers by noting a community of interests among these major figures, and proceed by tracing resemblances between them and others who have discussed or challenged their views. This, it would seem, could provide a method of delimiting the field: philosophy would be characterized through ostensive definition, and would consist of that set of problems with which philosophers deal. This form of definition would be comparable to what Jacob Viner is reputed to have claimed with respect to economics: "Economics is what economists do."

I hope it is evident that such an attempt is bound to fail. Viner's proposal will obviously fail unless one is not only able to identify economists but can also say which among the many activities of these persons are to be included in what they, *as economists,* do. Similarly, there must be shared interests among the philosophic figures chosen to serve as touchstones, or they will not be of use in determining whether others are or are not to be regarded as philosophers. This, as we shall see, poses difficulties. Furthermore, it must be noted that although most of the writings of Descartes, Locke, Leibniz, and Kant are surely to be classified as belonging among their philosophical works, not everything that each wrote—not even everything of an intellectual character—would generally be regarded as philosophical. Thus, one must seek some touchstones of philosophy other than that it is something written by one who is generally taken to be a philosopher.

This suggests that one might best proceed by identifying some set of problems that are specifically philosophical in character, with one or more of which anyone who is to count as a philosopher must deal. There are indeed a number of such problems that are readily identifiable; yet, no matter how carefully they are defined, one finds that they are not problems that are discussed only by philosophers. Consider, for example, the issues philosophers raise in their discussions of the theory of knowledge. Many of these are also discussed by natural scientists and by psychologists; they also make their appearance in belletristic essays, or crop up in novels and in conversations in everyday life. A similar situation obtains with respect to questions arising in ethical theory, and, in fact, in almost every other branch of philosophic discourse. Thus, even though some problems can aptly be characterized as "philosophic problems," one cannot assume that everyone who discusses them is a person with whom historians of philosophy need be concerned.

Given this fact, one might be inclined to shift attention to questions concerning method, attempting to distinguish between philosophic and non-philosophic works in terms of some special method that is uniquely philosophical. Yet, were one to attempt to discover any particular form of exposition or argumentation that philosophers use, or any procedures used by most or all philosophers which are not also used in other fields, one would, I think, be bound to fail. One cannot, for example, find any special method that can be claimed to be characteristic of Plato's dialogues, Spinoza's *Ethics*, Kant's *Critique of Pure Reason*, and Hegel's *Phenomenology of Mind*.

In this situation one might be inclined to dismiss the problem of definition and employ some form of a doctrine of "family resemblances" to clarify what philosophy is. I would find that approach more nearly acceptable in this case than in some others, because there are traditions and influences that bind the works of various philosophers together so that the relations among them are not merely relations of resemblance. The existence of these traditions and interlocking influences provides a parallel to the factor of common descent that justifies one in speaking of the resemblances within a family as being not merely a case of resemblances but a case of *family* resemblances.[2] Nevertheless, it is doubtful whether a network of relationships depending upon how the works of philosophers have influenced each other provides an adequate way of distinguishing between those with whom historians of philosophy must be concerned and other persons for whom no place need be found in their works. The difficulty becomes evident as soon as one considers the role played by philosophic doctrines in the history of ideas. Many who are not philosophers are thoroughly enmeshed in doctrines originating in philosophy, and, if the domain of philosophy depended upon a network of influences, it would be far more extensive and far more heterogeneous than any historian of philosophy would acknowledge it to be. Thus, this attempt to avoid characterizing philosophy in a positive way will, I think, also fail.

Although we have seen that it is probably not possible to characterize philosophy in terms of either a particular subject matter or a particular method, at least one other possibility remains: that one can characterize it in terms of some underlying intention or aim common to all philosophers, regardless of the problems with which they deal and of the precise methods they actually employ. Here, I believe, one can hope to meet with greater success.

To be sure, if one thinks of C. D. Broad's distinction between critical and speculative philosophy, it seems unlikely that all philosophers can be said to be motivated by any common aim. Following Broad, one would say that critical philosophers stress the clarification of concepts, the analysis of methods, and the need to untangle intellectual muddles, whereas speculative philosophers tend to build systems that serve to integrate and interpret facts about nature and human experience in some comprehensive manner. Nevertheless, those who follow either of these methods have at least one important characteristic in common: they attempt to overcome contradictions and incoherencies in widely accepted opinions, and they do so through analysis and argumentation. Once again, this may seem to be characteristic of other intellectual endeavors as well. One difference, however, is that it is in the nature of philosophy that its conclusions are not directly derived from particular observations and cannot be refuted by appeal to any restricted body of facts. Unlike other contexts in which men seek to resolve conflicts in belief and intellectual puzzlements, philosophic argumentation sets no limits on the data that are relevant to a resolution of the problems it raises. In philosophy, no assumptions are regarded as immune to challenge, and no barriers can be raised against following wherever an argument may lead in the search for some consistent way of interpreting the world and the nature of human experience. This is why William James could characterize philosophy as an unusually stubborn effort to think things through.

To be sure, there have been many attempts in Anglo-American philosophy during the past decades to draw a sharp line between those issues which are empirical and those which are specifically philosophical; thus, it has often been claimed that there *are* limits beyond which philosophical argumentation should not extend. If, however, one looks back upon such major figures as Descartes, Locke, Leibniz, or even Hume and Kant, one finds that the originality of their contributions was directly related to the ways in which they sought to come to terms with the sciences, religion, and moral convictions of their own times. Although they were also concerned with difficulties and ambiguities in the views of their various philosophic predecessors, their own positive views did not depend primarily upon their critical responses to the views of others, but upon independent convictions of their own. Such basic convictions I shall refer to as a philosopher's *primary beliefs,* distinguishing them from his critical interest in the philosophic positions and arguments of his predecessors. This distinction will, for the time being, lead us beyond the question of who is to count as a philosopher to another methodological issue: the problem of how historians of philosophy are to conceive of the relations between innovation and the ongoing traditions that exist in philosophic thought.

Throughout the history of philosophy one finds that philosophers have been conscious of the views of some of their predecessors, have been stimulated by them, have attempted to emend or refute them, or have developed them in new ways. Thus, in the history of philosophy one finds definite strands of influence, but these strands do not form a single unbroken, continuous tradition; there are shifts of interest which may be more or less sudden, with new continuities developing while others lose their former dominance; these new modes of thought are then supplanted in their turn. Sometimes, what underlies the continuity of a given tradition is a set of shared presuppositions, with each successive philosopher in that tradition criticizing his predecessors without challenging their presuppositions. This, for example, might be said to be the role played by "the way of ideas" that served to connect the thought of Locke, Berkeley, and Hume. At other times a tradition may be built upon a sequence of repeated attempts to correct and expand some particular doctrine of a predecessor, as may be said of the way in which problems in the Kantian philosophy led to the development of German idealism in the first half of the nineteenth century.

Such traditions do not survive indefinitely; it is through the impact of divergent primary beliefs that they come to an end. This is a point to which I shall return. First, however, it is necessary to combat what I am inclined. to call the conventional view of philosophic traditions, a view that dominates many textbook discussions. That view regards each successive figure in a particular philosophic succession as being primarily concerned with emending the system of his predecessor. It is, for example, sometimes supposed that one can best understand the development of British epistemology from Locke to Hume in terms of Berkeley's rejection of Locke's distinction between primary and secondary qualities and his criticism of Locke's supposedly inconsistent acceptance of the existence of material substance. Then Hume, in turn, is viewed as accepting Berkeley's position with respect to the distinction between primary and secondary qualities, and also his criticism of Locke's doctrine of abstract general ideas, but differing from Berkeley in rejecting a belief in spiritual substances on grounds similar to those by means of which Berkeley had criticized Locke. On this view, Hume ends in skepticism, to which, from the outset, "the way of ideas" had been destined to lead.

This is a very neat picture, but it fails to take into account fundamental differences in philosophic motivation and therefore leads to a neglect of the themes that in fact dominated the thought of Locke, Berkeley, and Hume. That this is so evident in the contrasts that exist between the tone of Locke's "Epistle to the Reader" introducing his *Essay,* the subtitle of Berkeley's *Principles,* and that of Hume's *Treatise.* For Locke, the scientific achievements of his contemporaries set the stage for his theory of knowledge, whereas Berkeley's intent was to show "the chief causes of error and difficulty in the sciences," which lead to "skepticism, atheism, and irreligion." Hume, unlike Locke, was primarily concerned not with questions relating to "the origin, certainty, and extent of human knowledge," but with analyzing the principles of human nature, introducing "the experimental method of reasoning into moral subjects." These differences reflect differences in what I wish to call "primary beliefs."

It is the existence of these primary beliefs and of their formative power in the thought of the major philosophers that is usually overlooked in the conventional view of philosophic traditions. This is not to deny that every philosopher engages in a dialogue—whether overt or hidden—with some of his predecessors, and often—though not always—with his immediate predecessors. Nevertheless, the sources of a major philosopher's primary beliefs—whether he be Locke, Berkeley, or Hume, or whether he be Descartes, Spinoza, or Leibniz—are not to be found in his dissatisfaction with the ways in which his predecessors have developed their own views, but derive from religious, moral, or political problems, or from conflicts between contemporary science and antecedent world views, or arise out of an attempt to come to terms with aspects of his experience which led to intellectual or emotional or moral conflicts within his own life.

Thus, I am inclined to contend that major innovations in philosophy do not usually have their roots in a philosopher's criticism of any predecessor, but in those primary beliefs which often lie behind that criticism and serve to channel thought in a new direction. This is not, however, to suggest that philosophers are not cognizant of how other philosophers have dealt with the same or comparable issues. In fact, many of these issues will be of interest to any philosopher just because he is a philosopher and is puzzled or enticed by them. Thus, one can understand the continuity present in philosophic thought through tracing the reactions of successive philosophers to some of their forebears, and one can at the same time understand radical innovations in terms of the way in which a philosopher's primary beliefs have led to a modification, or even to a disruption of that continuity. The situation, I suggest, is comparable to what one finds in the history of litera-ture or of the fine arts: styles develop, and writers and artists work within these styles, modifying or elaborating them, until a new style is set by the intrusion of powerful new influences as expressed in the work of one or more major creative figures who themselves tend to establish a new tradition that others then follow. To be sure, some artists and philosophers—and they have probably always been in the majority—tend to work wholly within an ongoing tradition, and in the case of a philosopher one may not be entirely sure that his work reflects any primary beliefs whatsoverer; he may perhaps be wholly absorbed by the task of criticism, as G. E. Moore claims to have been. This, however, is not to hold that such work lacks importance: the value of the purely critical work that philosophers do, even when it cannot be claimed to be basically innovative, springs from the fact that philosophic method demands argument and dialogue. The debates engendered with respect to the exact meaning and implications of alternative positions may seem to nonphilosophers to be sterile, to be nothing more than technical exercises, but without them and without the self-criticism they foster, philosophy would be nothing but a series of personal pronounce-ments or a set of disconnected systems, rather than a discipline that has a lineage that historians can in fact trace. While it is an important function of historians of philosophy to trace this lineage, it is equally important that they pay ample attention to whatever is distinctive and original in any of the philosophers with whom they deal. In the absence of an insistence on differences, and on elements of discontinuity, it will seem as if each phi-losopher had merely modified what had been transmitted to him, and the significance of radical differences between philosophers will disappear.

In insisting that the historian should not lose sight of the differences between the primary beliefs of different philosophers, I have in effect raised still another methodological issue. To what extent, one must ask, should a historian attempt to explain differences between the primary beliefs of different philosophers, and in what terms can he do so? If primary beliefs were written on the surface of a philosopher's work—if his motivation and his presuppositions were immediately clear—one could simply identify these beliefs and show in what ways they had affected the way in which he had developed his thought. However, even when a philosopher does explicitly state what he is attempting to do, this does not usually indicate why he is attempting to do it: his basic motivation, as well as those presuppositions he takes for granted, but does not discuss, must be uncovered, and an attempt must be made to authenticate the correctness of such attributions.

At first glance this would seem to plunge the historian of philosophy into the depths of psychobiography, but that is not the case. Although the personality of a philosopher and many of his life experiences may be more or less directly reflected in his work, that work would not be intelligible were one to focus attention solely on *him*. The particular problems a philosopher discusses, and how he discusses them, are never wholly independent of the background of his times. It is only when one is able to view a philosopher's work against whatever aspects of this background most directly influenced him that one can adequately understand what he did, and what it was that he did not attempt to do.

As historians of science recognize, one can distinguish two aspects of the background against which one must view a given work in order to come to terms with it. On the one hand, the historian may look at the *internal* history of a discipline, that is, how a given work relates to previous work within that discipline, and thus to a tradition in which it stands or against which it rebels; on the other hand, one may look at it in terms of whatever *external* factors need to be taken into account in attempting to understand it. These external factors may, of course, be of very diverse kinds. In the case of philosophy, for example, one may find that a series of developments within the sciences challenge previously accepted presuppositions as well as previously unquestioned beliefs, and lead to a genuine revolution in philosophic thought such as that which took place in the seventeenth century through the impact of the newer physics and astronomy. Similarly, social change may have a direct effect on the internal history of a discipline, not merely in those cases in which, for example, it leads moral or political philosophers to think in new ways or about new problems, but also when basic institutional shifts occur and those who practice a particular discipline no longer occupy the same place in society, or perform the same functions as they formerly did. Just as the shift from artisan to artist profoundly affected the history of the visual arts, so philosophy has undergone important changes when, for example, it was cultivated no longer in the schools of Athens, in Rome, and in Alexandria, but within the framework of the medieval ecclesiastical system. It obviously changed again when that was no longer the case. More recently, it has again been differently channeled by virtue of the fact that those who engage in systematic discussion of philo-

sophic problems are now—unlike many of their nineteenth-century predecessors—primarily professors of philosophy.

Not all external influences are, of course, quite so general and so pervasive
in their impact as those to which I have just called attention. New scientific
theories, or specific religious controversies, or new social problems can
impinge on some one area of philosophy without necessarily affecting most
others. As the wider-ranging changes in the sciences or in society may bring
about a major redirection of philosophic thought, so many of these more
specific changes are responsible for the particular innovations within a
philosophic tradition. Sometimes these innovations are solely due to the
fact that beliefs formerly accepted come to be discredited in other fields and
as a consequence are widely abandoned within philosophy itself. In many
other cases, however, these specific external influences will impinge so
deeply on the thought of a single philosopher that it becomes a key to his
system of primary beliefs, and through his subsequent influence may alter
what immediately follows within the philosophical tradition in which he
stands.

A historian of philosophy must therefore fulfill a dual role: he must bring
to light whatever external influences affected the course of a particular
philosophic tradition, and he must also be able to trace that tradition,
noting how the work of a given philosopher stands in relation to it. When
historians neglect external influences, not only will it become impossible to
see in what relation the philosophic enterprise stands to other aspects of the
life of the times, but the diversity of views among different philosophers
who nonetheless belong within the same tradition will be left largely unexplained. On the other hand, insofar as historians fail to emphasize the traditions to which particular philosophers belong, and within which they
work, that which is characteristically philosophical in their works will have
been overlooked; to that extent these works will be treated as if they were
nothing more than expressions of the personal characteristics of the philosopher himself, or of forces dominant at the time.

The foregoing remarks entail a consequence for our conception of the
history of philosophy which should not be overlooked; it concerns the
relation that the study of past philosophers bears to the philosophic problems
of one's own time. In many recent studies of major philosophers of the past,
attention has been focused on the particular aspects of their works which
happen to be of most interest to contemporary philosophers. As a consequence, these major figures are viewed in terms of the light they presumably
shed on current philosophic problems. This has, of course, always been one
of the ways in which philosophers have made use of their past. But what
must be said of this practice is that, whatever justification for it there may
be, it should not be considered a substitute for historical study, and those
who engage in it should not be regarded as if they actually were historians
of philosophy. This follows from the fact that, if one discusses a past phi-

losopher in terms of present-day problems, one will not clearly see what made his problems important to him at the time; one will be considering him in terms of *our* problems, not in terms of his relation to the particular philosophic tradition in which he then stood and the influences that, at the time, caused him to formulate his thought as he did.

To be sure, if there were a set of sempiternal philosophic problems impervious to all outside influences, never changing their fundamental forms in spite of the ways in which they had been discussed by succeeding generations of philosophers, one would have a right to treat past philosophers as if they were one's contemporaries. This is not, however, the case. When older problems are seen in a contemporary light they reflect what has transpired in the intervening years, and the original meaning that they had is translated into modern terms. The result may perhaps be compared with what results when a painter chooses to use the work of an earlier painter as providing the theme for a new and original painting: the resulting painting may be better or worse than that on which it was based, and a comparison between the two may be interesting, but the two works will never be confused with each other. Similarly, a later philosopher discussing what is ostensibly the same problem that an earlier philosopher had discussed will be discussing what, in its new context, is no longer the very same problem, and he will be discussing it in a new way. The task of a historian of philosophy is not, however, one of resolving philosophic problems, but of attempting to understand and delineate, as faithfully as he can, all that went into the original work with which has set out to deal, rendering it as intelligible as possible both in its individual parts and as a whole. Because the possibility of approximating to this goal is sometimes challenged, even when its desirability is not, this provides still another methodological issue connected with the history of philosophy.

Finally, and very briefly, I wish to return to the first issue that I raised: Who are to count as philosophers, with whom historians of philosophy are to be engaged? I should suppose that everyone would immediately agree that every person whom I have thus far mentioned is a person with whom every historian of philosophy would have to be directly concerned if his historical account attempts to deal with the periods and countries in which they lived. And to these names many others would have to be added; but what should one say concerning Montaigne and Newton, and what should one say concerning Rousseau or Herder? Each of these names is likely to appear in at least some histories of modern philosophy; furthermore, their views may be discussed in considerable detail. I do not believe, however, that either Montaigne or Newton should be designated as a philosopher. Montaigne presented his views as an essayist does: not in the form of an argument, seriously considering and rejecting alternative views and thus building up and defending his own. Instead, he is a portraitist of aspects of the human condition; he accepts rather than attempting to resolve whatever sources of puzzlement he finds in experience, or in other men's views. As for

Newton, even in his most philosophically pertinent passages, such as his "Rules of Reasoning in Philosophy," the General Scholium to the *Principia,* or the Queries in the *Optics* (to name merely a few), he promulgates philosophical opinions without examining or defending them, or showing how they relate to the assumptions and beliefs of others. Nevertheless, the influence of Montaigne on the history of modern philosophy was appreciable, and the influence of Newton was certainly profound. Thus, many whom it would not be appropriate to regard as philosophers may be expected to be discussed in histories of philosophy because of the influence they had on the development of philosophic thought.

With respect to Rousseau and to Herder there is another, different lesson to be learned: namely, that the history of philosophy does not consist in a single, unbroken, and homogeneous tradition. Historians of philosophy who focus attention on metaphysical and epistemological issues are not likely to feel called upon to consider the views of either Rousseau or Herder. On the other hand, insofar as they may be concerned with the history of political philosophy or with tracing the development of the philosophy of history, they can leave neither Rousseau nor Herder out of account. Similarly, whereas some major figures in the history of ethical theory, such as Hobbes, or Hume, or Kant, will have to be discussed in any history of modern philosophy, others—such as Butler, Hutcheson, Bentham, or Sidgwick—may appear only if the historian concerns himself with the history of modern ethical theory. What is true with respect to these fields is no less true in other fields such as aesthetics, logic, the philosophy of religion, or the like. Thus, there is not, and cannot be, any adequate, single, comprehensive history of philosophy fashioned as Hegel envisioned it: as a single developing whole, in which each stage is expressive of the nature of its age and each contributes to the internal dialectic of that whole. Historians of philosophy will always be forced to choose some aspects of the past with which to be primarily concerned, and one has a right to ask of any historian of philosophy that he be methodologically sophisticated to the extent that he recognizes what it is that he is doing and what he is not doing. If the present paper has served to call attention to some of these methodological issues it will have served its purpose.

Notes

This paper was presented in a symposium on "Philosophy and Historiography" at a meeting of the Eastern Division of the American Philosophical Association in 1977. Willis Doney was the commentator.

An earlier and more extended presentation of the same point of view is to be found in two lectures that I gave in 1974 at an Institute for the History of Early Modern Philosophy, sponsored by the Council for Philosophical Studies and directed by Margaret Wilson. In the first of those lectures I discussed the history of the historiography of philosophy at greater length; the second contained fairly frequent references to recent works dealing with major philosophers of the past. These lectures, entitled "On the Historiography of Philosophy," are available through Philosophy Research Archives, *under the date of July 19, 1976.*

Some problems concerning the relation of the history of philosophy to general intellectual history and to the history of ideas are also discussed in an article of mine that appeared in Beiheft 5 (1965) of History and Theory.

1. I have adduced evidence in support of this conjecture in a paper entitled "On the Historiography of Philosophy," published in *Philosophy Research Archives* (1976).

2. As I argued in "Family Resemblances and Generalization in the Arts," *American Philosophical Quarterly,* vol. 2, no. 1 (1965):1-10, the use to which the doctrine of family resemblances has generally been put in aesthetics is open to challenge precisely because it has been based solely on overt resemblances; the need to connect works of art with one another, apart from these resemblances, has been overlooked.

11

Some Forms and Uses
of Comparative History

If the term *comparative history* is to have significance, not all historical studies should be so designated.[1] Nevertheless, it would be a mistake to assume that the methods and aims for comparative historians are necessarily different from those of other historians. I do not believe that they are. In almost all cases the same methods either are used or could be used by comparativists and noncomparativists alike; in most cases their fundamental aims are also similar. To be sure, certain difficulties may arise in a more aggravated form for comparativists than for noncomparativists. For example, the range of thorough and reliable knowledge which a comparativist needs will not be restricted to the characteristics of a single society, but must embrace the relevant aspects of two or more societies; in many cases he will, therefore, be forced to rely on the work of others who have specialized in these fields. However, the importance of this difference should not be exaggerated: all historical studies demand the use of a greater range of knowledge than any single inquirer will have established for himself. Of course, a comparativist may find it difficult to put the knowledge gained by others to his own use, because their initial purposes and the focus of their interests probably will have been different from his. Other historians, however, face the same difficulty. For example, those who are not expert in economic history, or in legal history, or in intellectual history, must often rely very heavily on highly specialized investigations in these fields if they are to account for the processes with which they are primarily concerned; these specialized histories, too, will have been written with different ends in view and in most cases will have focused on issues with which the nonspecialist is not himself concerned. Nor should it be assumed that the amount of information which a comparative inquiry presupposes is always greater than that which noncomparative studies demand: any historical study that covers an appreciable time span in the life of a single society may presuppose as great a background of detailed and heterogeneous information as is demanded by the study of changes occurring in, say, a single institution in two or more societies over a more limited time. Thus, the background and the tools needed by either a comparativist or a noncomparativist would seem to vary from case to case: no claim that there is a basic difference in this respect between the two types of inquiry seems warranted.

Reprinted by permission from *American Studies International*, 18 (1980):19-34.

In what follows, I shall be primarily concerned to suggest a typology of the forms that comparative histories have usually assumed.[2] Before I do so, however, there is a further preliminary point to be noted. This is the fact that even when a historian is not explicitly drawing comparisons, he must rely on knowledge drawn from similar situations found at other times and places. If he did not, he would not in any case be able to account for what occurred in the case at hand. This is generally recognized with respect to the historian's need to understand "human nature": without a general understanding of how people can be expected to think, to feel, and to act in various sorts of situations, a historian would be at a loss to interpret much that has occurred in the past. Furthermore, unless he also has background knowledge as to how particular institutions functioned or failed to function at various times, he would have no way of interpreting many of the materials on which his own account must be based. While such comparisons may be loose, and while a historian may not be aware of having relied on them, they nonetheless lie at the foundation of his work. The comparativist, too, must initially rely on such loose and merely implicit comparisons as providing a background for his studies, but he then goes on to make some of these comparisons explicit in an effort to show in what ways and to what extent two different sets of occurrences resemble one another and what may be significant with respect to their differences. In addition, some comparativists attempt to put their comparative studies to further use, as leading to a generalized understanding of processes presumably at work in many or in all societies. Such, however, is not always the aim of comparative studies: their concern is often simply focused on comparisons limited to two or a few societies, seeking to gain a better understanding of *them*. Whether there are insuperable obstacles to establishing these wider generalizations that some comparativists have sought is an important theoretical issue but not one with which I can here deal. But because not all comparative historical studies have this as their ultimate goal, my failure to discuss the issue need not adversely affect the typology I propose.

In offering the following typology, I do not claim that the forms I distinguish are in all cases incompatible: many specific studies include the use of more than one of the approaches with which I shall be concerned. What I shall offer as examples are, however, some relatively pure instances of each type.

The Evolutionary Approach

Of the major types of comparative method that I distinguish, the first is that which is best characterized as the *evolutionary approach*. Clear examples of it are to be found in the sociological theories of Auguste Comte and of Herbert Spencer; it also played a major role in determining the way in which Karl Marx envisioned the main outlines of historical change. One finds that the works of anthropologists such as Lewis H. Morgan and

E. B. Tylor were also dominated by the assumption that each society, and also the various forms that its main institutions assumed, could be viewed as representing steps in a single evolutionary history of mankind. It must not be assumed that this widespread conception of social evolution represented a carry-over from evolutionary theory in biology, for it had independent origins; nevertheless, the role that the comparative method played in theories of social evolution exactly paralleled the role played in biology by the comparative data derived from paleontology, anatomy, and embryology. On the basis of such data, gathered from the present and from the past, the social evolutionist was presumably in a position to trace the development of specific institutions from their early and primitive beginnings to their most recent, most advanced forms, thereby presumably arriving at a comprehensive view of the social evolution of the human race as a whole.

So far as comparative history is concerned, the basic assumption of the social evolutionists was that each society, and each of the basic institutions in any society, goes through a set of similar stages, developing from simpler to more complex forms. Therefore, when comparing any two societies, or in comparing the basic institutions in any societies, one should not do so directly, but in terms of the particular stage that each had attained along the path of the developmental pattern assumed to be common to all. For example, in dealing with religion, or in dealing with forms of marriage, one would not compare the practices of contemporary "savages" (as they were then called) with contemporary Western ways; rather, the contemporary savage was to be taken as representing an earlier stage in our own social ancestry, and his practices were regarded as similar, in essential ways, to those practices out of which our own forms of religion or marriage had ultimately come. This was in most cases purely conjectural history. Unlike evolutionary theory in biology, which was based on the transmission of genetically inherited traits from one generation to the next, and which has the fossil record as a means of connecting successive transformations in many biological forms, there was no way of establishing that the different institutions characteristic of different contemporary savage societies represented a series of stages along a single developmental path. Except in the case of material culture traits, where archeological evidence was obtainable, the various serial orders that were proposed by social evolutionists were, to a large extent, artifacts of whatever prior theories they held as to what were the most advanced and civilized forms that these types of institutions could attain. There is a further difficulty in the view that each and every society must pass through the same set of institutional stages, lest its development is prematurely arrested; such a view necessarily neglects the role played by environmental conditions and historical influences on the changes that occur in different societies. Finally, we may note that the evolutionary approach to comparative studies, as exemplified to some extent by Tylor, and to a greater degree by James George Frazer and by Westermarck, led its proponents to consider fragments of a culture apart from their context; as a consequence, the relations between the various aspects of a culture tended to be neglected.[3]

In each of these ways, then, a hypothesis concerning the serial order in which cultural changes always took place tended to dominate the interpolation of the various aspects of a culture and led to a neglect of any detailed treatment of the changes out of which they arose and to which they in turn gave rise. This is most evident in Comte and in Spencer, both of whom held that the historian's concern for detail was inimical to establishing those grand patterns of change which they took to be basic in history.

It is small wonder, then, that the comparative form of historical study, as then understood, was looked on askance by most practicing historians. One landmark document that signalized a change was Marc Bloch's article, "Toward a Comparative History of European Societies," which was published in 1928, one year before he and Febvre founded the *Annales*.[4] Bloch recognized two types of comparative history, the first of which closely resembles that which I have characterized as the evolutionary approach; the second, which he proposed to follow, I shall characterize as a genetic rather than as an evolutionary approach.

The Genetic Approach

The *genetic approach* to comparative history involves an attempt to increase one's understanding of a particular society through investigating what it has in common with—and wherein it differs from—other societies with which it is directly affiliated through lines of descent.[5] Institutional and cultural similarities often rest on the fact that one society descended from the other or that both had a common ancestor from which each had acquired some of its traits. When this is the case, the genetic approach to comparative history may be compared to the comparative method in linguistics.[6] This constitutes one of the two basic forms of the genetic method. Tracing these lineal connections is not always an easy and straightforward task. In some cases similarities that appear to have been due to a common inheritance may be nothing more than accidental resemblances; in other cases they may be due to the diffusion of a particular culture trait through late contacts between two otherwise unrelated societies.[7] Yet, there can be no doubt that a great percentage of the characteristics of any society are due to direct cultural inheritance from its immediate ancestors, and it is with these characteristics that what I have thus far referred to as the genetic approach to comparative history is concerned.[8] To be sure, once having established connections between these similarities, a comparative historian who follows this approach must also take note of concrete differences in the forms and functions of the similarities that are present, accounting for these differences in terms of whatever factors affected the societies differently in the past. Through such interlocking investigations of similarities and differences, a comparative approach adds to the knowledge already gained through the noncomparative investigations that any comparison must always presuppose.

This form of the genetic approach to comparative studies emphasizes the lineal connections between elements present in two or more societies. As one can note in the case of Emile Durkheim, whose influence on the comparative approach was very great, that method seemed able to preserve what was valuable in an evolutionary approach without falling into the trap of having to invent a merely conjectural history of social development.[9] Bloch, who was influenced by Durkheim, tended to emphasize this form of genetic approach in most of his investigations. There is, however, a second and distinct way of accounting for similarities between two or more societies when they are roughly contemporaneous. It does not assume that their resemblances involve a shared lineage; rather, the similarities between them are explained by the fact that each was forced to cope with similar conditions in a common environment, that each made similar responses to those conditions, and, as a result, they converged toward a similar form.[10] As familiar examples that can help to indicate the difference between these two forms of a genetic approach, I might, on the one hand, cite Bloch's *French Rural History* (*Les caractères originaux de l'histoire rurale française* was its more revealing original title), and on the other, Robert R. Palmer's *Age of the Democratic Revolution.* In Bloch's study one finds comparisons of the differences and similarities in the modes of agriculture and the forms of life in different regions, set against the background of change that was traced from the most remote past through the mediaeval period, continuing well into recent times.[11] Thus, his study was primarily longitudinal. Palmer's study, on the other hand, took a number of nations that shared a somewhat similar heritage, and that, having to cope at roughly the same time with the same forces of change, responded in roughly parallel ways. Thus, the parallels he sought were not explained in terms of a transference of traits through social inheritance, but arose through common response to factors contemporaneously operating.[12] It is to be noted, however, that both of these forms of comparative study are concerned with societies closely related, geographically and temporally, and that each proceeded through tracing the actual antecedents of the particular similarities they sought to explain.[13] Because of this they can be classed together as representing subtypes of what may properly be called a genetic approach.

The Analogical Approach

This, however, is not the only form that comparative studies may take. Just as biologists distinguish between analogous and homologous organs, so one may distinguish between genetic approaches and what I shall term the *analogical approach* to comparative studies. This parallel with biology is more or less exact, because the homologous organs found in different species not only resemble one another but are linked through descent; on the other hand, what are termed analogous organs are similar in their functions, and sometimes also in their appearance, but are not directly related from a genetic point of view. Within analogical forms of comparative historical studies, I shall again distinguish two subtypes: a phenomenological approach on the one hand, and an analytical approach on the other. I shall first consider the phenomenological form.

The Phenomenological Form

Phenomenological comparisons—that is, comparisons based on direct descriptions of two or more instances—are exceedingly common in all forms of historical writing; however, it is only when the exploitation of such comparisons becomes one of the essential aims of a historian that we can properly speak of a comparative history. The most familiar examples of this approach are not to be found among historians but among sociologists or philosophers of history. One thinks immediately of Comte, or of Oswald Spengler, and perhaps also of Arnold Toynbee. However, there also have been historians who make no pretense of presenting a general sociology or philosophy of history, yet who have embarked on studies using this approach. Perhaps the example most familiar to contemporary historians would be Crane Brinton's *Anatomy of Revolution*. Unlike authors of genetically oriented comparative studies, Brinton chose to deal with four revolutions that he did not view as springing from a common source. In treating these revolutions—the English Revolution of the 1640s, and the American, French, and Russian Revolutions—he found common structural properties, thus drawing analogies between them. These analogies comprised a particular sequence of stages through which each of the revolutions had presumably passed. His account of these stages is phenomenological—that is, it was descriptive of what he took to be their essential natures; he did not offer detailed causal analyses as to how each stage had developed out of what had come before, nor how it resulted in that to which it gave rise. It was not Brinton's claim that this sequence of stages is to be found in every revolution; he was only concerned with comparisons among these four. Nor did he claim that the sequence had been unavoidable in any one of these cases. Nevertheless, the general tenor of his comparative study leaves no doubt that he regarded this sequence of stages, or "patterns of uniformities" as he called them, as more than accidental. In the analogy he drew between the course of a revolution and the course of a virulent but nonfatal disease one can see that he regarded this sequential structure as the *natural* course that such events tend to follow. Like other appeals to what has been regarded as *natural,* from Aristotle's time to the present day, Brinton's use of this notion concealed the need for offering causal analyses of the specific factors responsible for the changes he observed.[14]

Practicing historians have not in general been inclined to hold that there is some particular sequence of stages through which various types of social phenomena regularly pass: that approach is more frequently found among sociologists, political theorists, and philosophers of history. On the other hand, it is extremely common to find historians drawing parallels between two or more complex social phenomena that are remote in space and time, but resemble one another closely enough to be designated by a common name. For example, feudalism in Japan has often been compared with feudalism in mediaeval Europe on the basis of the constellation of institutional arrangements to be found in each. This sort of phenomenological comparison does not necessarily assume that feudalism passed through comparable stages of development in the two societies. What is presupposed is, simply, the historian's ability to abstract an essential set of factors among those present in a given historical context, to understand their relations to one another, and then, stripping away what are taken to be merely accidental features not generally applicable, to form a conception of the sort that Max Weber referred to as an *ideal-type*. An example of this sort is to be found in the penultimate chapter of Marc Bloch's *Feudal Society*, where (independently of his more usual genetic approach) he briefly discussed feudalism in Japan and in the West. Recently, John Whitney Hall drew the same comparison and in doing so indicated the main features of this form of comparative method, saying, "The utility of the ideal type model is that it permits comparisons to be made without committing the historian to the acceptance of a specific and inevitable sequence of events. What the model does is to identify the variables the historian chooses to recognize as being essential if comparison is to be considered valid."[15]

While this form of the analogical approach to comparative history is an important descriptive tool in both institutional and cultural history (for example, in art-historical studies of style), it fails in two respects: taken by itself, it does not succeed in accounting for the diversity of what occurs in individual cases, nor does it explain change. In fact, as Weber pointed out, there is a tension between the aims of historians and the uses to which the concept of an ideal type can be put. The historian, he said, "aims to provide a causal analysis and an assessment of *individually* culturally significant actions, social systems, and persons"; on the other hand, the formation of the concept of an ideal type has a different function—it aims to characterize essential features that are common to a number of differing individual cases. Consequently, as Weber went on to say, these concepts are "relatively lacking in content as compared with the concrete realities of history."[16] Yet, as Weber's own practice reveals, not only did he consider ideal-type concepts legitimate, but he found them extemely useful in analyzing major forms of religious, political, and economic life. What can be achieved by using such concepts is to focus attention on general structural properties that are evidenced in a variety of similar instances; where it fails, as I have said, is in its inability to account either for individual differences or for overall change.

To be sure, other studies can be used to supplement phenomenological analyses in order to account for what occurred in the various instances subsumed under a particular type. The method best suited to doing this is *not* one in which a historian seeks to treat each of several instances individually, case by case: as Weber saw, this procedure would tend to fragment the ideal type until its generic character would disappear. Instead, there is another form of the analogical method which can supplement the phenomenological approach, helping to account for whatever constellation of factors is common to the various instances of some ideal type. I shall term it the analytical form of the analogical method.

The Analytical Form

Like a phenomenological approach, the analytical form of comparative studies rests on the use of analogies, not on genetic explanations.[17] These two forms of analogical comparison differ, however, in that the phenomenological approach always rests on directly observable resemblances. As the earlier histories of biology and of physics suggest, it is on the basis of overt qualitative resemblances that we ordinarily classify various types of things and assume them to be intrinsically related. However, in both biology and physics there developed an increasing recognition that qualitative resemblances do not always provide a valid basis for scientific classifications: two living forms may be closely related even though there are relatively few directly observable resemblances between them, and in physics the same laws often serve to explain phenomena that, on the surface, seem not to belong together. Now, what I have characterized as the phenomenological form of comparative studies rests on analogies drawn between instances that resemble one another with respect to certain overall characteristics of structure, such as the sequence of stages in revolutions, or some interrelated set of attributes that, taken together, are seen as constituting a specific ideal type. In contrast to this, the analytical form of comparative study aims to establish that there are underlying relationships that may exist even when the overt resemblances between two cases are minimal. However, these two forms of analogical approach are not necessarily incompatible: biologically related forms often *do* resemble one another in their overt characteristics, and what appear to be similar physical phenomena are often explained in similar terms. So, too, as we shall now see, the factors underlying phenomenological analogies may be precisely the factors that an analytical approach reveals.

As a first example of an analytical approach to comparative studies I might mention *The Modernization of Japan and Russia* by Cyril E. Black and his collaborators. Their comparison rests on an analysis of developments in the two countries, developments not to be accounted for by similarities in background or by influences flowing from one to the other.[18] Consequently, their study is not an example of the first form of genetic approach. Nor does it belong squarely within the second form, of which I took Palmer's *Age of the Democratic Revolution* as an example. Black and his colleagues were not attempting to establish that modernization was a single movement that found successive expressions in one nation after another, nor were they attempting to establish its origins and follow its subsequent course. Rather, they posed for themselves one specific analytical question: Why, in the case of two nations that were latecomers in the history of modernization, did the process proceed as rapidly as it did? To answer this question, they sought to establish that there were "areas of commonality" which were present in the early stages of modernization in both of these very diverse societies, and that it was because of these common factors that modernization in these nations took place as it did.[19]

A second example of an analytical approach to comparative studies is to be found in *The Rebellious Century* by Charles, Louise, and Richard Tilly. Using France, Italy, and Germany as examples, they attempted to establish a functional relationship between industrialization and urbanization on the one hand, and collective violence on the other.[20] In doing so, they examined alternative hypotheses as to why such a functional relationship obtained and in each case discarded the theory that increasing violence is associated with disorganization and hardship; instead, they found it to be a by-product of solidarity, clearly articulated interests, and collective action, all of which accompanied industrialization and urbanization.[21] What the example of the Tilly book illustrates is that the analytical approach can sometimes lead— and in some cases will be designed to lead—to generalizations that are possibly applicable in a wide variety of cases.[22] In other comparative studies, such as *The Modernization of Japan and Russia*, the explanatory factors arrived at were recognized to be restricted in their generality: it was not necessary to assume that even though they did render intelligible what had occurred in Japan and Russia, there would be other instances to which they would also apply.[23] However, the generalization proposed by the Tillys on the basis of their studies of three nations was formulated in such abstract terms that if it were to fail to apply in other instances, that fact would suggest that it stood in need of reformulation even with respect to those cases on which it had been based. Thus, there sometimes are fundamental differences between different examples of an analytical approach. What is important, however, is that each of the two examples of the analytical approach which I have given is compatible with the sort of description which the phenomenological approach was designed to supply. Where an analytical approach differs from the phenomenological is that it puts forward hypotheses concerning factors responsible for the essential similarities between those cases which phenomenological comparisons merely describe.[24]

This completes what I wish to say with respect to the typology I have proposed. I need merely reiterate my warning that many comparative studies cross the dividing lines I have drawn, and often do so effectively.[25] Nevertheless, these distinctions seem to me to be helpful, for the uses to which different forms of comparative history may be put often are very different. It is to a very brief consideration of some of these uses that I now turn.

Uses of Comparison

The traditional evolutionary approach has in general been abandoned, and its abandonment does not, in my opinion, involve any loss. Its function was largely one of locating various social and cultural phenomena on what was taken to be a unilinear line of human development. It was not at the time recognized that the very existence of any such single line of development was suspect, that it actually was an artifact of the ways in which sociologists and anthropologists had arranged their materials to conform with the views of progress they antecedently held. The genuine contribution made by the traditional evolutionary form of the comparative method consisted in the impetus given to anthropological interests and to the analysis of basic characteristics common to different forms of social organization.[26]

On the other hand, both the genetic and analogical forms of comparative history have as their primary function the light they are able to cast on the characteristics of specific societies. This may appear paradoxical, because this is also the role attributable to other historical inquiries that do not proceed by way of self-conscious comparative investigations. Yet, it is a point important to stress. Were it to be overlooked, comparative and noncomparative forms of historical inquiry would have little in common even though comparativists must at every point lean on what noncomparative inquiries establish. Without inquiries as to the nature of each of the societies to be compared, there would actually be nothing to compare. Furthermore, as Bloch and almost every other exponent of a comparative method emphasizes, the comparativist is bound to be as much interested in the differences as in the similarities between the societies he compares.[27] Such differences, however, can only be understood in terms of analyses that focus attention not on comparable elements, but on that which led each of the societies to have just those differentiating characteristics that it had. Thus, it is clear that comparative studies of the similarities and differences between two or more societies cannot replace other historical inquiries that are also concerned with the nature of individual societies and the changes that take place in them.[28]

What, then, does the comparativist offer which the noncomparativist does not in equal measure provide? In the first place, if he follows either form of the genetic approach in his inquiries he may be able (as Bloch points out) to show that what might otherwise be thought to be a merely local and even accidental phenomenon is explicable in terms of an otherwise hidden lineage, or is representative of a wider movement going on elsewhere in roughly the same form and at roughly the same time. In the second place, if his comparisons rest on the analogical approach he may be in a position to suggest that some of the relationships that different historians have seen as existing in the particular materials with which they have habitually dealt also exist in other societies. Such suggestions, deriving from comparative studies, are apt to lead still other historians to consider the possibility that the same or similar relationships exist in the materials with which they may subsequently deal; thus, as Bloch saw, these suggestions provide hypotheses that merit testing, and in some cases they may reveal relationships that would otherwise have been overlooked. Extending this possibility still further, such hypotheses may in some cases be sufficiently abstract—and at the same time sufficiently precise to be put to the test—so that they provide insight into relationships that obtain in a very large number of different societies. Were this to turn out to be the case, these empirically grounded generalizations derived from comparative historical inquiries might be of a sort that political scientists, political economists, and sociologists could use. While this has sometimes been envisioned as the only proper goal for historians to pursue, it is a goal to which they as historians—and even as comparative historians—cannot bind themselves. The way to reach such a goal (if there be such a way) is through historical inquiry, starting with inquiries into particular strands of history, and only later explicitly extending their scope to include the comparative studies with which I have been here concerned.

This paper has been entirely taken up with a consideration of comparative historical studies as forms of intellectual inquiry, but I cannot leave the subject without also alluding to an existential purpose that they undoubtedly serve. Through comparative studies, which deal with various types of societies more or less remote from our own, we may come to recognize aspects of our social inheritance and institutional life which we might otherwise overlook. This may help protect us against false analogies that lead us either to overestimate or to underestimate some of our accomplishments.[29] In any case, a concern with comparative history may to some extent free us from an excessive concern with purely national histories and also from that ethnocentrism which, unfortunately, no one of us can ever wholly escape.

Notes

This paper was presented in 1978 to a meeting of the American Historical Association in a symposium, "Can 'Comparative History' Be Defined?" The other symposiasts were Cyril Black and Peter Gay.

1. In what follows, I shall be using the term *comparative history* in a less extended sense than that in which it has sometimes been used. For example, I would reject Fernand Braudel's usage when he says, "Comparative history is the bringing together of history and contiguous disciplines, the exchanging of services between them, and their convergence in selected topics" (in "Marc Bloch," *International Encyclopedia of the Social Sciences*, 2 [New York: Macmillan Co. and Free Press, 1968], p. 94). That definition is both overextended and too closely tied to the program of the *Annales* school. It singles out a characteristic to be found in many comparative studies, but not in all; furthermore, it fails to refer to that aspect of such studies by virtue of which they are designated as "comparative."

2. For another typology, constructed on different principles, cf. Louis Gottschalk, "Categories of Historiographical Generalization," in Louis Gottschalk, ed., *Generalization in the Writing of History* (Chicago: University of Chicago Press, 1963), pp. 113-29.

3. There are, of course, instances in which these general objections do not apply to the ways in which particular anthropologists or sociologists have used the comparative method in their evolutionary theories. For example, the third objection does not apply to Comte or Spencer, or to Marx, because each was concerned with the interrelations among institutions within the culture as a whole.

Similarly, some recent *neo-evolutionists*, such as Sahlins and Service, explicitly insist that environmental factors play an important role in the adaptive processes through which social evolution proceeds. (For a statement of their general evolutionary position, as well as for a discussion of the need to take environmental factors into account, see the Introduction and Chapter 1 of *Evolution and Culture*, by Thomas G. Harding, David Kaplan, Marshall D. Sahlins, and Elman R. Service [Ann Arbor: University of Michigan Press, 1960].)

One final word must be said in order to avoid confusion concerning Julian H. Steward's theory of "multilinear social evolution," which is often linked with neoevolutionist views such as those held by Sahlins and Service. Steward seems to me to avoid each of the criticisms I have directed against social evolutionary theory, but this seems to me to be a consequence of the fact that his views do not actually represent social evolutionism, as I am using that term. Rather, his fundamental aim was "to develop a methodology for determining regularities of form, function, and process which occur cross-culturally among societies found in different cultural areas" (*Theory of Cultural Change* [Urbana: University of Illinois Press, 1955], p. 3. Also, see pp. 18-19, and his essays, *Evolution and Ecology* [Urbana: University of Illinois press, 1977], pp. 43-57.) In short, he appears to me to exemplify a comparative approach to social theory which seeks general laws of coexistence and change, but without assuming that these laws represent any single line of evolutionary development. (For his criticism of "unilinear evolution," in both nineteenth- and twentieth-century thought, see *Theory of Cultural Change*, pp. 19-22. For a summary statement of his position, see Robert F. Murphy's introduction to *Evolution and Ecology*, especially pp. 26-31.)

4. The article appeared in *Revue de synthèse historique*, 46 (1928):15-50. It is now to be found in Bloch, *Mélanges historiques* (Paris: S. E. V. E. N., 1963), 1, 16-40, and in translation in Bloch, *Land and Work in Mediaeval Europe* (Berkeley: University of California Press, 1967), pp. 44-81. It is to that translation that I shall refer.

5. Comparative histories are also concerned with comparisons between societies that are not directly related. I shall discuss such studies as representing an *analogical*, rather than a *genetic*, approach.

6. Bloch explicitly drew this comparison (*Land and Work*, pp. 47f. and 67f.). The comparison is apt, the sole significant difference between the two methods being the direction in which inquiry proceeds. In linguistics, what was originally termed "the comparative method" had as its aim the attempt, through examining a group of related languages, to arrive at the form of the earlier language from which they derived; in the genetic approach to comparative history, however, the earlier stages in a process of change need not be less surely known than what followed upon them. Bloch recognized this difference, noting that comparative history is probably not in a position to discover "detached fragments, broken off long ago from the original mother-society whose existence was previously unsuspected" (p. 68).

7. Bloch quoted Renan as having said, "Historical similarities do not always imply influences," adding that "many similarities cannot be reduced to imitations" (p. 54). These more basic similarities, he held, reveal the "real causes" that account for social phenomena. Thus, it is clear that the genetic method, as Bloch understood it, did not consist in tracing cross-influences between otherwise unrelated societies, but involved explanations of phenomena in terms of continuities and changes within particular social lineages.

8. With respect to the pervasiveness of cultural tradition, it is relevant to note the George P. Murdock roughly estimated that "any two distantly related European cultures will share about six out of ten classificatory elements, whereas only about one in four will be similar when any European culture is compared with any non-European culture" ("Anthropology as a Comparative Science," *Behavioral Science*, 2 [1957]:251.

9. That Durkheim regarded this form of the genetic approach as fundamental for comparative anthropology is evident in his *Rules of Sociological Method* (Glencoe, Ill.: Free Press, 1938), pp. 137-39; for his criticism of the conjectural nature of the evolutionary approach, see pp. 76-78.

10. This use of the concept of *convergence* is analogous to the way in which it is used in evolutionary biology and in social anthropology.

For an example of convergence, taken in this sense, see Barrington Moore's discussion of the difference between the prerevolutionary condition in England and in France, yet the similarity in outcome of the two movements (*Social Origins of Dictatorship and Democracy* [Boston: Beacon Press, 1966], pp. 40-41).

11. *French Rural History* (Berkeley and Los Angeles: University of California Press, 1966), pp. xxiv-xxv and 247-48.

12. Palmer states his objective in the following way: "To deal with Western Civilization as a whole, at a critical moment in its history. . . . It is argued that this whole civilization was swept in the last four decades of the eighteenth century by a revolutionary movement, which manifested itself in different ways and with varying success in different countries, yet in all of them showed similar objectives and principles" (*The Age of the Democratic Revolution* [Princeton: Princeton University Press, 1959], p. 4). Then, after mentioning the American and French Revolutions, he cited numerous lesser revolutionary incidents and said, "All of these agitations, upheavals, intrigues, and conspiracies were part of one great movement" (p. 7). His purpose became that of attempting to set up a "framework, or conceptual structure, in which phenomena that are admittedly different, and even different in significant ways, may yet be seen as related products of a common impulse, or different ways of achieving, under different circumstances and against different degrees of opposition, certain recognizably common goals" (p. 9).

For a discussion by Palmer of his own presuppositions, see "Generalizations about Revolution: A Case Study," in Louis Gottschalk, ed., *Generalization in the Writing of History,* pp. 66-76.

13. As a second contrasting pair of examples, I might on the one hand cite Eugene D. Genovese's comparative account of the history of Afro-American slavery, which interprets it in relation to a single wider process, "the history of the formation of a world market and an integrated international capitalist society" ("The American Slave System in World Perspective," in Genovese, *The World the Slaveholders Made* [New York: Pantheon, 1969], p. 14). Examples of the second form of the genetic approach would be those dealing with topics such as the withdrawals from Africa on the part of various European colonial powers after World War 2. One such study is that of Tony Smith, "A Comparative Study of French and British Decolonization," *Comparative Studies in Society and History,* 20 (1978):70-102.

14. As I have elsewhere tried to show, all attempts to establish a sequential pattern of change without reference to the specific factors that operate from moment to moment to bring about change are, in principle, misguided (*History, Man, and Reason* [Baltimore: Johns Hopkins Press, 1971], pp. 114-24). That argument is not, however, applicable to the nonsequential form of phenomenological approach with which I shall next deal.

15. "Japanese History," in Charles F. Delzell, ed., *The Future of History* (Nashville: Vanderbilt University Press, 1977), p. 183.

16. W. G. Runciman, ed., *Max Weber, Selections in Translation* (Cambridge: Cambridge University Press, 1978), p. 23. For what is perhaps the classic statement of Weber's doctrine of ideal-types, see "Die 'Objektivität' sozialwissenschaftlicher und sozialpolitischer Erkenntnis," in *Gesammelte Aufsätze zur Wissenschaftslehre* (Tübingen: J.C.B. Mohr, 1922) especially pp. 190-212. For a discussion of Weber's use of ideal types, see R. Stephen Warner, "The Role of Religious Ideas and the Use of Models in Max Weber's Studies of Non-Capitalist Societies," *Journal of Economic History,* 30 (1970):74-99, of which pp. 88-97 are the most relevant.

17. In connection with the analytical form of this approach, it is especially important to note that I use the term *analogy* in the broad sense in which all sciences depend on analogical reasoning, not in the corrupt popular sense in which an argument can be dismissed by saying "that is merely an analogy."

18. As they point out, a comparison of Japan and Russia is "a comparison of societies undergoing change from a base of widely different heritages of premodern cultures" (*The Modernization of Japan and Russia. A Comparative Study* [New York: Free Press, 1975], p. xii). Furthermore, as they also point out, the diversity of the two cultures in most other respects is so striking that their parallel modernization, independently of one another, seems almost to be an historical anomaly (pp. 2-3).

19. *Modernization of Japan and Russia*, p. 2. Though obviously not rejecting the idea that there was such a general movement, they provide merely a brief sketch of what they take to have been its major phases (pp. 6-7). On the other hand, Black's *Dynamics of Modernization: A Study in Comparative History* (New York: Harper and Row, 1966) is in essence a discussion of modernization as a general, world-wide movement based on science and technology, but it is not (I should say) strictly speaking an historical account.

20. *The Rebellious Century, 1830-1930* (Cambridge: Harvard University Press, 1975), p. 13.

21. For summary statements of their original analytic problem, and of their conclusions, see pp. 3-9 and 242-45, respectively.

22. Charles Tilly's interest in such generalizations is also apparent in his introductory essay in Charles Tilly, ed., *The Formation of National States in Europe* (Princeton: Princeton University Press, 1975), p. 13 et passim.

23. In fact, because the authors restricted their attention to one particular period in the history of the modernization movement, it is not altogether likely that when other cases arise a similar situation will obtain: actually, it is part of their thesis that modernization in Japan and Russia proceeded differently than had been the case in other nations because of the time at which it took place. (For their discussion of the modernization movement as it might affect other latecomers, see pp. 348-53.)

At this point, it is perhaps apposite to mention another study that compares modernization in two countries, Robert E. Ward and Dankwart A. Rustow, eds., *Political Modernization in Japan and Turkey* (Princeton: Princeton University Press, 1964). That series of comparative essays is primarily concerned with political change in relation to other institutional factors, but like *The Modernization of Japan and Russia* its primary purpose is that of rendering intelligible the similarities and differences in the processes that occurred in two specific countries over a particular period of time, rather than seeking to establish abstract generalizations which would have wide-ranging applicability.

24. If one does not confine one's use of the term *phenomenology* to what was characteristic of the Husserlian school (and I do not), a similar relation between phenomenological description and analytical forms of explanation holds in other fields as well.

25. For example, Barrington Moore's *Social Origins of Dictatorship and Democracy* exemplifies the same type of genetic approach as does Palmer's *Age of the Democratic Revolution* because it, too, claims that the revolutions with which it was concerned represent a single movement (pp. xii, 112, and 414). However, instead of attributing this movement to a particular, transient set of conditions occurring within a limited span of time, Moore approached his problem through an analysis which sought to uncover the political consequences of certain class-relationships, using them as a means of accounting for the changes he traced (p. xvii).

26. Marc Bloch's early article, to which I have repeatedly referred, has some suggestive discussion of them.

27. For example, Black, *The Modernization of Japan and Russia*, pp. 13-14 and 18-21; Bloch, "Toward a Comparative History of European Societies," pp. 45 and 58; Tilly, *The Rebellious Century*, p. 14; also, Charles S. Maier, *Recasting Bourgeois Europe* (Princeton: Princeton University Press, 1975), p. ix.

28. Consequently, the attempts of Comte and of Spencer to substitute a comparative historical sociology for traditional historical inquiries were, from the outset, misguided.

29. On a failure to choose what may have been proper comparisons with respect to the history of the South, leading to a false evaluation of its nature, see C. Vann Woodward, "The Future of Southern History," in Charles F. Delzell, ed., *The Future of History*, p. 142.

III

Methodology in Psychology
and the Social Sciences

12

A Note on "Anthropomorphism"
in Psychology

In what follows I should like to call attention to a paradox that is present in much of our contemporary psychological theory. The paradox is readily discernible and presents no particularly interesting problem to the historian of ideas. However, a recognition of its existence does have significance both for those who are interested in the methodology of psychology and for those who realize that a sound empirical psychology is an essential tool for philosophy.

The paradox may be stated as follows: *those contemporary psychologists who most strongly insist that there is an absolute continuity between animal and human behavior are also the psychologists who most frequently inveigh against "anthropomorphic" interpretations of animal behavior.* This, I submit, is a paradox, even if it is not a contradiction. It is paradoxical because it holds that we can understand human behavior in terms of animal behavior and yet that we can not understand animal behavior in terms that are familiar to us through our observation of human beings. As we shall later see, a tacit assumption accounts for the fact that this paradox is rarely challenged; as we shall also see, this assumption rests on a confusion.

In order to illustrate this paradox let us choose an example that will at the same time serve to reveal one of its implications. Let us assume that a philosopher—or any other "plain man"—were to say in speaking of a dog, "its shame was comical." Most psychologists would immediately charge us with "anthropomorphism." Yet these same psychologists would object most violently if we were to set up the thesis that some of the basic factors in human behavior would forever remain secrets to those who study only animal behavior.

This paradox might, of course, be said to be apparent and not real, because the term *basic factors in human behavior* is vague. Our psychologist might, for example, argue that "shame" is "socially conditioned" in man, and cannot therefore characterize a dog's behavior: the dog behaves much as we do when we experience shame, and we are "anthropomorphic" enough in our language and thought to attribute "shame" to it. Yet this answer does not escape the paradox. For what is generally called "social conditioning" does not actually account for human shame. A man evidences shame only

Reprinted by permission from *Journal of Philosophy*, 40 (1943):246-48.

under certain circumstances, e.g., when he feels that he has acted wrongly or stupidly. "Social conditioning" can (at best) account only for the fact that the individual has been "conditioned" to believe that certain acts are wrong or stupid; it can not account for the shame he feels when he realizes that the act is of this nature. Thus, the doctrine of "social conditioning" might account for *when* an individual feels shame; it would not account for the fact *that* he feels shame.[1] This being the case, anyone who insists on the continuity between animal and human behavior should be willing to speak of "shame" in a dog, rather than dismissing such examples as being instances of "anthropomorphism." Thus, the paradox remains.

Of course, no one would argue that all of the characteristics of human "shame" are necessarily also present in cases of "shame" among animals. In this as in other respects there are doubtless significant differences between the experiences of human beings and of other animals. To attribute to all animals exactly the same perceptual discriminations, motivation, or learning that we find among men would be unwarranted anthropomorphism. But where we find behavioral evidence that animals do discriminate, act, and learn in much the same fashion as do men, we have every right to try to understand their behavior by means of an analysis that starts from human experience. As long as we believe that there is a significant continuity between animal and human behavior, we have as much right to approach animal behavior through what we can discover about human behavior as to proceed in the opposite direction.[2] This is not anthropomorphism.

The customary rejoinder to this contention is that science must always proceed from that which is simpler to that which is more complex. This, however, is a radically mistaken view of the ideal of simplicity in empirical science. This ideal demands: first, that an adequate theory should be simple, i.e., not encumbered with subsidiary, underived hypotheses; and, second, that verification should proceed through the use of relatively simple materials in order to guard against the introduction of extraneous, complicating factors in our experiments. The ideal of simplicity in empirical science is, thus, an ideal of simplicity in theory and of simplicity in experiment. It is not a necessary part of this ideal that we should examine complex phenomena only in the light of those apparently simple cases in which these phenomena are exemplified in *rudimentary* form.

Furthermore, I should like to suggest that there are certain practical dangers inherent in the attempt to proceed from the more "simple" to the more complex. In the first place, by confining our attention to the "simpler instances" we may be excluding from our data those cases in which the basic principles are most manifest; it is by no means sure that "simple" cases are those in which it is simple to see the full nature of the process with which we are concerned. In fact, hypotheses are sometimes more likely to be suggested by the observation of instances that are not themselves simple, for in them the variety of factors which is present suggests alternative hypotheses that can be narrowed down by a comparison of instances and by experiment. Simple data, by virtue of their simplicity, often fail to provide us with a sufficiently large number of clues. In the second place, there is a danger that in first considering simple cases we shall have to heap hypothesis upon hypothesis in order to account for the more complex instances that are related to them. Finally, in the attempt to confine his attention to animal behavior the psychologist is arbitrarily cutting himself off from access to important materials, because we are presumably in a better position to understand our own behavior than we are to understand the behavior of other animals, e.g., the behavior of a rat in a maze.[3]

When we take into account these practical considerations of method, and when we realize that the ideal of simplicity in science does not demand that our investigations start from apparently "simple" materials, there is, I submit, no methodological reason for psychology to frame its concepts solely in terms of animal behavior. I am well aware of the difficulties that are sometimes involved in starting our investigations from experimentation with human subjects. But this is a different matter. What I am concerned to point out is the fact that concepts whose meaning is clear in the field of human experience may often be legitimately used in understanding animal behavior. This is *not* anthropomorphism, and it ill befits any one who wishes to insist on the essential continuity between animal and human behavior to charge that it is.

Notes

This brief note originated as a by-product of my attempt, at that time, to arrive at a position that would provide an adequate psychological basis for some form of ethical naturalism. Eventually, the position formulated in The Phenomenology of Moral Experience *(1955) emerged. The implications of this note, however, are not confined to those which it may have for ethical theory.*

1. In order to account for the latter fact, the doctrine of "social conditioning" would have to establish a view roughly similar to the following: children are punished for performing certain acts; they not only become "conditioned" against these acts, they also become "conditioned" to expect punishment for performing them; when, for any reason, they later perform an act that they have been (in some way) "conditioned" to shun, they expect punishment and shrink from it, attempting to escape; when escape is impossible they feel an emotion; this emotion, aroused by a "conditioned" fear of punishment, is shame.

In addition to the vagueness of the concept of "conditioning," this type of account would be suspect for two reasons: (1) phenomenologically, many (and perhaps all) cases of shame seem to have a direct connection with one's ego, not with a fear of punishment; (2) many forms of effective "conditioning" (even early in a child's life) are themselves based on the phenomenon of shame.

2. I see no reason to suppose that the theory of biological evolution demands a "one-way" interpretation. In would appear to be as plausible to hold that rudimentary characteristics may themselves undergo modification and development as to hold that evolution has proceeded by a mere compounding of elementary, unchanging characteristics.

3. I assume (I hope not without warrant) that when a psychologist deals with a rat in a maze, he is interested in understanding why the rat behaves as it does and is not merely concerned with the score it makes.

13

Professor Ryle and Psychology

In the last chapter of *The Concept of Mind*[1] Professor Ryle states his view of the province of psychology. He warns us not to equate "the official programmes of psychology with the researches that psychologists actually carry on" (p. 319). I shall attempt to avoid this error. One should, however, also avoid the error of basing one's view of the nature and scope of these researches upon a philosophic program of one's own. As we shall see, on one interpretation of what he has written, this is an error of which Professor Ryle himself may be guilty.

In what follows I shall primarily be concerned with the last chapter of *The Concept of Mind,* though reference will also be made to the first chapter of that work and to chapter 7 of *Dilemmas.*[2] For the purposes of this paper I am willing to grant that all of the specific analyses that Ryle gives in *The Concept of Mind* (as distinct from the general discussions of its first and last chapters) are important contributions to the particular problems to which he addresses himself. What I aim to show is that even when the importance of these analyses is granted, there remains at least one wider problem that has been associated with the traditional mind-body problem. This is the problem of how we are to interpret the relation between our ordinary common sense explanations of human behavior and the explanations of human behavior which are frequently given by psychologists.

I

Ryle notes that if we define the province of psychology through examining what psychologists actually do, we shall find that the term *psychology* does not refer to "a unitary inquiry or tree of inquiries," but to "a partly fortuitous federation of inquiries and techniques" (p. 323). With this, I should suppose, all would agree. It seems fair, however, to say that Ryle himself would acknowledge that there is at least a tenuous bond that connects the components of this federation, and in most cases in which he discusses his own view of the province of psychology we find that psychologists deal with "behavior." When, in these passages, Ryle gives us examples of the kinds of behavior with which psychologists deal, it becomes obvious that this behavior

Reprinted by permission from the *Philosophical Review*, 67 (1958):522-30.

is human behavior. Those persons who are concerned with animal psychology or with comparative psychology seem not to be included in his delimitation of the province of psychology. This is not surprising because Ryle apparently dates the beginning of psychology from the time at which the word *psychology* was coined. If we look at this dating, psychology is roughly two hundred years old (cf. p. 319), and if we then consult the *NED* we find that Ryle is quite correct in saying that the program of psychology as a separate study seemed *at that time* to involve the assumption of "the ghost in the machine." If, however, we follow the method of defining psychology in terms of what psychologists do, it is not implausible to argue that in many respects psychology may have changed in both its assumptions and its methods in the course of two hundred years. It then seems not unreasonable to take into account animal psychology, rather than to confine the field of psychology to human actions and reactions.

Closely connected with this point, but more important for what follows, is the fact that those more recent psychologists who have studied the mechanisms of the sense organs, or of the nervous system, are not in general counted as psychologists by Ryle. Though he does at one point (p. 321) mention such inquiries, his characterization of the field of psychology does not usually take their studies into account. To be sure, most persons would probably acknowledge that it made little difference whether investigators who engaged in the study of the sense organs and of the nervous system were to be denominated as *psychologists* or as *physiologists,* or by any other name. Granted that *psychology* is not the name of a unitary inquiry but refers to a federation of inquiries, I too would admit that what we call these persons makes no difference, *unless* their exclusion from psychology represents a particular program for what psychology ought to be. This proviso is crucial, for we shall shortly see that Ryle is in fact giving a prescriptive definition of the province of psychology, and his definition (which excludes both animal psychology and general physiological psychology) is one that is not unconnected with his view that all talk of mind-body problems rests on a category mistake.

For the moment, however, let us grant that the province of psychology is to be confined to human behavior, and let us so interpret what we mean by "human behavior" that it includes only such actions and reactions as we directly observe in ourselves and in others. This is in fact Ryle's prescriptive delimitation of the data of psychology (p. 320). Granted such a definition, Ryle notes that we shall have difficulty in delimiting the field of psychology from a host of other approaches to the same materials. As he points out, historians, philologists, dramatists and novelists, economists, strategists, teachers, detectives, and chess-players all concern themselves with these same materials (p. 320). In fact, of course, we all do so at almost all times in our waking hours. The usual moves to protect psychology as a separate study of these materials are, as Ryle points out, to hold (1) that it differs from these other approaches in being "a science" and thus deals in generalizations (p. 322 f.), and (2) that it differs from them in its attempt to give causal explanations of this behavior (p. 324 f.). Ryle counters these two moves with the following objections: (1) Other sciences, such as economics, sociology, anthropology, criminology, and philology also explain human behavior in terms of generalizations (p. 323). (2) He claims that the "very solemn expressions" "cause" and "causal explanation" should not mislead us: the economist, the novelist (and his reader), and even the schoolboy doing his arithmetic know full well the causes of human behavior (p. 324 f.).

It is here that we at last come to the correct *differentia* of psychology which Ryle has been seeking (cf. p. 322). There are some "actions, fidgets and utterances, the author of which cannot say what made him produce them" (p. 325); these it is the task of the psychologist to explain. Ryle holds, however, that those "actions and reactions which their authors can explain are not in need of an ulterior and disparate kind of explanation" (p. 325). As he says in summary:

> There are plenty of kinds of behaviour of which we can give no such explanations [i.e. explanations in terms of "ordinary causes"]. I do not know why I was tongue-tied in the presence of a certain acquaintance; why I dreamed a certain dream last night; why I suddenly saw in my mind's eye an uninteresting street corner of a town that I hardly know; why I chatter more rapidly after the air-raid siren is heard; or how I come to address a friend by the wrong Christian name. We recognize that questions of these kinds are genuine psychological questions. . . . Even in the field of sense perception and memory the same thing seems to hold. We cannot, from our own knowledge, tell why a straight line cutting through certain cross-hatchings looks bent, or why conversations in foreign languages seem to be spoken much more rapidly than conversations in our own, and we recognize these for psychological questions. Yet we feel that the wrong sort of promise is being made when we are offered corresponding psychological explanations of our correct estimations of shape, size, illumination and speed. Let the psychologist tell us why we are deceived; but we can tell ourselves and him why we are not deceived. (p. 326)

I have quoted this passage at length for fear that my readers may have forgotten, and might therefore not believe, that Ryle holds that psychology deals only with "our mental incompetences," but not with our "mental competences" (p. 326).

The first thing to be said concerning this thesis is that it is factually untrue if we define the province of psychology in terms of what psychologists do. To take Ryle's own examples from the field of sense perception, it may be pointed out that when we perceive what is generally taken to be the true shape of a penny (that is, as circular, not elliptical), or when we perceive what are taken to be the true relations between the size of a man seen at a distance of ten feet and the same man seen at a distance of five feet, we are involved in explanations of constancies of shape and size. Psychologists have devoted a great deal of attention and ingenious experiment to the effort of explaining these constancy phenomena. And the same may be said of color constancy, of brightness constancy, of the apprehension of motion, and the like. Similarly, in experiments on memory, psychologists have studied the conditions under which correct recall takes place, and may perhaps even be said only to have studied errors in recall in order to throw light on the conditions that facilitate correct recall. Further, in the study of associations it is to be noted that while many inquiries have been interested in establishing the existence of certain distorting motivational influences on recall (and Ryle seems to be particularly impressed by these), many other inquiries have attempted to study the facilitating influence of other motivational factors. And precisely the same sort of considerations apply (though even more obviously) to those fields of learning theory which are not confined to the problem of memory. In short, it is simply untrue that the attention of psychologists is confined to those problems to which Ryle apparently believed it *should be* confined. His characterization of the *differentia* of psychology is therefore clearly tendentious.

There is a second and even more important reason for rejecting Ryle's view. Within the field of psychology itself it is clearly impossible to draw a line between the explanations that are to be given of those cases in which we are deceived and of those cases in which we are not. In explaining optical illusions, for example, psychologists talk of the characteristics of the stimulus, of the relation between the stimulus and other parts of the visual field, of the nature of the intervening medium, of what happens on the retina, in the optic nerve, in the visual area of the cortex, and perhaps of other factors (for example, past experience or its traces). To refuse to talk about these factors would be to limit one's self to *listing* hitherto discovered optical illusions. (It is doubtful whether they could even be meaningfully classified without using several of these criteria.) And Ryle himself does not suggest that those cases in which we are deceived should merely be listed: he wants them "explained." However, when we turn from optical illusions to what Ryle would doubtless grant were cases of veridical perception (that is, those acts of seeing which permit the postman to find his way, the farmer to take his pigs to market, the heroine to gather up her letters and take them upstairs), we find that we can analyze these cases in exactly the same terms as we can the cases of optical illusions. Whatever leads us to relate an optical illusion to the characteristics of the stimulus and to the nature of other parts of the visual field, whatever leads us to relate it to the nature of the intervening medium and to processes that go on within the perceiving organism, and whatever relation we attempt to establish between an illusion and past experience will also lead us to relate an act of veridical perception to precisely the same factors. To be sure, we may not be interested in doing so. Perhaps it might be argued that were it not for the epistemologically puzzling cases of illusions men would not have investigated sense-perception at all.[3] However, once this epistemologically generated interest led some people ("psychologists") to investigate those causes of our mental incompetences which are not known by "ordinary good sense" (p. 326), these same people have in fact used precisely the same concepts and methods to explain what happens in other cases of perception. If their explanations are accepted in the one set of cases, and if exactly the same types of factors are also to be found in the other set of cases, some reason must be adduced to show that it is illegitimate—and not merely uninteresting—to apply them there. That it is uninteresting, or perhaps distasteful, to Ryle to apply them in cases of veridical perception does not prove that they cannot be so applied. And Ryle has given no reasons to show that they cannot be.

II

It may be charged that the preceding criticism is based on a misunderstanding of Ryle's views. A defense of what he has meant to say, whether he has said it or not, might take the following form.

(1) Ryle is willing to grant autonomy to all empirical investigations. Empirical research in psychology may deal either with animals or humans; it may also be couched either in physiological terms or in terms of those observable features of behavior with which we are familiar in daily life. Further, Ryle would be willing to grant the right of the empirical investigator to establish correlations between physiological events and instances of everyday behavior.

(2) All that Ryle objects to is a confusion in "logical geography"; confusion that leads us to explain observable human behavior in terms of inappropriate categories. The chief confusion of this kind is the attempt to explain ordinary human behavior in terms of acts of the mind, where the term *mind* is interpreted as referring to a special sort of substance. A second confusion of this kind (to which Ryle devotes more careful attention in chapter 7 of *Dilemmas*) is the mistake of attempting to interpret our ordinary commonsense notion of, say, seeing or hearing in terms of the categories and types of explanation which are appropriate in optics and acoustics.

Such an explication of what Ryle means to say concerning psychology has some plausibility, because in *Dilemmas* (p. 110) he lumps psychology with optics, acoustics, and physiology, and because in one passage in *The Concept of Mind* (p. 321) he does recognize that psychologists have studied animals in mazes, have studied sense-perception as ophthalmologists study sense-perception, and have studied the effects of alcohol and brain injuries on human behavior. It would then follow that what Ryle really means to say when he says that psychology deals only with our mental incompetences is that the problem of explaining perception (or the like) in physiological terms only arises when we make an error. In other words, according to this interpretation, the startling passage that I have quoted and criticized merely affirms that *in daily life* we do not in fact ask why we see two lines as parallel if they are parallel; we only ask such a question when we already know that they are not. The passage, then, would say nothing about what sorts of questions arise *within* the science of psychology; it would only be referring to what sorts of questions generate an interest in pursuing psychological investigations.

It seems to me that it would be hard to substantiate from what he has said concerning the science of psychology that this is all that Ryle wishes to affirm. In both the first and the last chapters of *The Concept of Mind* he is betrayed into a far more extreme position because of a peculiar *non sequitur* in his argument.

Ryle argues that the data which psychologists set out to investigate are data that are accessible to us in ordinary experience. As he correctly insists, if Descartes had not already been able to "distinguish good from bad arithmetic, politic from impolitic conduct, and fertile from infertile imaginations," he would not have "speculated how the applicability of these criteria were compatible with the principle of mechanical causation" (p. 21). And he is quite right in saying that "a researcher's day cannot be satisfactorily occupied in observing nonentities and describing the mythical" (p. 321); we must start from experience, and if our concern is with human behavior then we must start from observing human behavior. From this it does not follow, however, that the concepts that are utilized in explaining these original data are also themselves given in ordinary experience, in the sense in which Ryle uses the term "ordinary experience." Yet he repeatedly speaks as if the one position entailed the other. For example, he criticizes a program for psychology which would "find and examine data inaccessible to teachers, detectives, biographers or friends; data, too, which could not be represented on the stage or in the pages of novels" (p. 320). In opposition to such a program he holds that "those human actions and reactions, those spoken and unspoken utterances, those tones of voice, facial expressions and gestures, which have always been the data of all the other students of men, have, after all, been the right and the only manifestations to study" (p. 320). And he then employs this statement in order to draw the conclusion that psychologists cannot investigate "happenings different in kind from, and lying 'behind,' those bits of human conduct which alone were accessible to the other studies of man" (p. 321). This is his *non sequitur.*

Though psychologists do not in fact possess privileged access to esoteric data but start where we all start in our daily observation of human action, they do explain these actions through recourse to physical and physiological findings that are not capable of being represented on the stage, and that are not usually to be found in the pages of novels. These findings do not constitute their original starting point, their "data," but are materials through which they seek to explain these data. The question then arises whether the explanations which they offer do in fact yield a knowledge of the necessary and sufficient conditions for the data that they seek to explain. Descartes and other adherents of the belief in mental substance would hold that they do not. It is their contention that we must also postulate a mind and its acts if we wish to give an adequate explanation of human behavior. This belief, whether correct or not, has, I submit, been one of the sources of the traditional mind-body problem. It is only because he is not concerned with problems of explanation, outside of those explanations that we give in everyday experience, that Ryle has overlooked or minimized this fact.[4]

III

But let us suppose, with Ryle, that when the snarls of language have been untangled, we shall see that in order to explain behavior we do not have to postulate a mind substance nor any purely mental acts. Does any specifically philosophic problem still remain?

In *Dilemmas,* where he deals most concretely with issues in "logical geography," Ryle shows us differences between our uses of technical, scientific concepts and those concepts which are nontechnical, or less technical; that is, concepts that are used to describe ordinary experience. It is without question important to note these differences. To fail to observe them would be as inappropriate as it would be to muddle our geological maps with arbitrary introductions of state and county boundaries, or our political maps with scattered references to rainfall.

It is also important, however, to show how objects or events which are referred to by our technical concepts are related to the objects or events referred to by our nontechnical concepts. Put in terms of geography—and not merely "logical geography"—it is important to know whether two maps are of the same territory or are of different territories, and this question arises whether the maps are both political maps, or both geological maps, or whether they are of different categories.

Now one of the tasks of philosophers has always been to relate various maps to one another. Even in the case of Descartes we may say that one of his basic purposes was to find some way of relating the mechanical theory of the world, which had implications for the interpretation of the nature of the human body, to the ordinary acts of seeing, choosing, feeling, and reasoning which he as a human person performed.[5] Whatever mistakes were involved in his inference to mental substance as a means of reconciling the two maps, Descartes at least attempted to relate what he found on one to what he found on the other. In order to show that even after he has dissolved the errors that he has found in Descartes the problem remains a problem for Ryle, I shall briefly discuss the two kinds of "explanations" which he permits us to make when we seek to explain human behavior.

Ryle holds that we can and do explain most human actions in a commonsense way and in terms familiar through common, nontechnical usage. He admits that in some cases (errors) we cannot explain them in the familiar way; it is here that we must call on the psychologist. He does not apparently note, however, that in order to explain these cases the psychologist must often resort to concepts which are not familiar through common, nontechnical usage. For example, at many points in psychological explanations we find that physiological terms are employed; similarly, Freudian psychology uses theoretical terms of its own. Now these technical concepts are part of a theoretical structure: they are introduced in order to explain the puzzling behavior, not merely to name it. And if we examine the theoretical generalizations that are contained in the use of this technical language and that are to serve as explanations of the puzzling behavior, we shall find that they are often quite different from the ordinary generalizations by means of which, on the commonsense level, we are apt to explain human behavior. For example, our ordinary explanations of behavior frequently make use of purposive language which is missing in physiological explanations of the same behavior. And if Ryle is not offering a restrictive delimitation of the province of psychology but is willing to allow physiological explanations of behavior even when the latter is "competent," then the same act can, in many cases, be explained in two different ways.[6] It would still be important to insist, as Ryle insists, that we should not confuse these two different explanations. But it would also be important, as I have insisted, for someone to state what are the relations between the territory mapped by one set of explanations and the territory mapped by the other. If all philosophic problems are linguistic problems, then this is not a philosophic problem. It is, however, a problem with which philosophers have often sought to deal.

Notes

Perhaps no recent philosopher was more adamant in attempting to draw a distinction between issues of conceptual analysis and those which involve empirical inquiry than was Gilbert Ryle. As I suggested in the Preface, I regard such an attempt as misguided and unfortunate. While confining its attention to questions concerning the province of psychology, the present article attacks Ryle at this point. For a further attack, on a broader front, the reader could consult the concluding chapter of my book, Philosophy, Science, and Sense-Perception *(1964).*

1. Gilbert Ryle, *The Concept of Mind* (London: Hutchinson's University Library, 1949). All page references in the text refer to this book.

2. Gilbert Ryle, *Dilemmas* (Cambridge: Cambridge University Press, 1954).

3. I do not in fact believe that such is the case, but I should be willing to grant it for the sake of the argument.

4. Cf. Albert Hofstadter, "Professor Ryle's Category Mistake," *Journal of Philosophy*, 48 (1951): 261-64.

5. Cf. the earlier quotation from Ryle (p. 21) concerning Descartes' initial ability to distinguish good from bad arithmetic.

6. If psychological explanations were relevant only to the explanation of behavior that we cannot understand in ordinary terms, and if competent behavior were not subject to psychological investigation, this problem would not arise. But in that case my strictures against Ryle's view of psychology would hold without the modification introduced by the interpretation offered in section II of this paper.

14

To What Does the Term
Psychology Refer?

The problem with which I shall here deal has not to my knowledge been dealt with at length elsewhere, yet it constitutes a type of problem which should be of interest to historians and philosophers of science. Briefly put, the issue I wish to raise is whether it is merely a matter of happenstance that the discipline to which we refer as *psychology* includes the specialties and subspecialties that it does include, or whether, on the contrary, these have arisen because psychologists have at various times been forced to create these specialties in order to solve other problems with which they have attempted to deal. The same type of question can of course be asked with respect to other sciences, such as physics, biology, sociology, or economics, but it should not be assumed that the answers will in all cases be the same. In what follows I shall be confining my attention to psychology, and even with respect to it my argument will be limited in scope. I shall merely attempt to illustrate through one set of examples, chosen from twentieth-century behaviorism, that it is by no means fanciful to claim that the various specialties within psychology form an interlocking system of inquiries, rather than constituting an arbitrary composite that first arose through historical accidents, subsequently becoming institutionalized as *psychology*.[1]

I should also say that the point of view that I am adopting and that I here wish to defend involves a rejection of the familiar Wittgensteinean assumption that it is possible to characterize a type of activity, or a discipline, in terms of 'family resemblances' only. As will later become clear, such an approach has little plausibility when applied to a discipline such as psychology. Instead, what can be taken as linking the various specialties and subspecialties that constitute the discipline of psychology is the fact that there is a network of causal relationships connecting the processes with which these various specialized branches of psychology deal. This is the basic thesis that I wish to defend.

I

As is well known, earlier characterizations of psychology had designated it as either the science of *mind* or *consciousness*; more recently it has come to

Reprinted by permission from *Studies in History and Philosophy of Science*, 2 (1972):347-61.

be characterized as the science of *behavior*. It is to be noted that a willingness to characterize psychology in terms of behavior is not confined to those who accept some form of behaviorism as a methodological or philosophical doctrine. As early as 1905 McDougall broke with the "mentalistic" tradition, defining the province of psychology in terms of "conduct";[2] and in 1912 he contributed a volume to the Home University Library series entitled *Psychology, The Study of Behaviour*. Furthermore, in Koffka's systematic treatment of Gestalt psychology, in 1935, behavior was accepted as the basic psychological category.[3] Thus, to define psychology in terms of the concept of behavior is not to subscribe to behaviorism in psychological theory.

The fact that there is now rather widespread agreement that psychology can best be characterized as a science of behavior should not, of course, be regarded as signifying that psychologists also agree on what constitutes its nature and scope. Unfortunately, that issue has usually been entangled with questions concerning the particular methods and programs of different investigators and different schools, rather than being posed in terms of what relationships may exist among the various tasks that psychologists have actually set themselves. Naturally, no extensive survey of these relationships can be carried out in a single article; instead, I shall attack the problem obliquely, by showing how in one case—that represented by some well-known exponents of behaviorism—it is not possible to limit the sphere of psychology as the programs of these behaviorists have attempted to do. This will serve to indicate a few of the interconnections that exist among various branches of psychology, helping to make plausible the conclusion that it is my aim to propose: that all of the various branches of psychological investigation involve a network of causal connections among the processes with which they are concerned. Therefore, however diverse these investigations may appear to be, psychology as a discipline is not to be viewed as an arbitrary combination of independent investigations.

Let me begin by acknowledging that there seems to be little connection between many of the investigations that were of importance to nineteenth-century psychologists and the investigations of animal and human behavior which have dominated the work of twentieth-century behaviorists. For example, the dimensions of sensation, or the principles of free association and recall, are problems that may seem too "mentalistic" to be relevant to the issues that concern contemporary behaviorists. Yet, it is my contention that even inquiries of this sort could have important bearing upon scientific investigations concerning the behavior of organisms. To illustrate this contention I shall first briefly consider an early and extreme form of behaviorism, that of J. B. Watson.

Watson held that the starting point for any scientific psychology was "the observable fact that organisms, man and animal alike, do adjust themselves to their environment by means of hereditary and habit equipments," and he held that these adjustments depended upon the organism's responses to stimuli; in his view, it was the task of psychology to investigate these stimulus-response connections so that given either stimulus or response one could say what the other would be or had been.[4] As this characterization of a program for psychology suggests, Watson assumed from the very outset that the behavior of any individual is to be analyzed into a series of simple components, and he conceived of these components as simple reflexes.[5] Thus, in terminology made familiar by E. C. Tolman (whose views we shall later consider), Watson's approach was *molecular*, not *molar*, and in this, according to Tolman, he erred.[6]

The distinction between molecular and molar approaches became so familiar and influential through Tolman's critique of Watson, and through his own work, that it is useful to consider it here. Briefly put, the distinction concerns the difference between studying animal or human behavior at the level of goal-directed performances (such as running a maze or operating a steam shovel), which Tolman referred to as "behavior-acts," and, on the other hand, studying the inherited or acquired connections between specific stimuli and particular muscular and glandular responses, which Tolman identified with Watson's physiologically oriented behaviorism.[7] To be sure, Tolman admitted that on occasion Watson had spoken as if he too were interested in molar behavior, seeking to offer a scientific account of human beings engaging in their everyday activities; however, Tolman was correct in his insistence that the underlying principles of Watson's method committed him to the assumption that all behavior could ultimately be analyzed in terms of simple reflexes.

One obvious difficulty that this assumption involved, insofar as molar behavior was concerned, was that animals in their natural environments, and human beings engaging in their everyday activities, are constantly confronted by a host of different stimuli. In fact, as Watson admitted, even under experimental conditions, organisms are rarely confronted by single stimuli, and the organism's adjustment to its environment is rarely confined to a single response. Rather, as Watson pointed out, what an organism confronts is *a situation*, which he defined as "the total mass of stimulating factors," and it is such a mass of stimuli "which lead men to react as a whole."[8] It is precisely at this point that one can recognize the difficulties inherent in Watson's methods and in his attempt to restrict psychology to those domains in which such methods can be applied. If it is the case that even under experimental conditions a number of different stimuli are present in a total situation, it becomes important to ask how, if at all, each of these stimuli may have been affected by the fact that they were simultaneously presented. If there were interaction among them, it would be misguided to investigate single stimulus-response connections, one by one.[9] Consider, for example, the situation with respect to how visual stimuli may affect animal or human behavior. The stimuli making up a visual field are obviously never presented merely one by one. It is therefore important to determine how the copresence of a variety of stimuli may affect the response. To raise this question is, however, to raise a type of question with which experimental theories of visual perception have long been concerned. Although formulated in quite different terms, it is the sort of question which involves experiments concerned with color contrast, others concerned with brightness-constancy, investigations of the factors determining visually apprehended speed of movement, experiments on figure-ground relationships, on camouflage, and a host of other problems which not only have been of importance in the history of psychology but at least some of which are of indisputable importance in understanding the discriminatory responses that organisms make when adjusting to their environments. Without such investigations it would in fact be impossible to bridge the gap between the so-called molecular level of simple stimulus-response experiments and the molar behavior of organisms acting under nonexperimental conditions in their natural environments, which it was Watson's ultimate objective to explain.

What has here been said with reference to only a few isolated areas of the investigation of visual phenomena is no less true with respect to other areas of psychology. For example, within Watson's own field of special interest, the theory of learning, similar questions arise. One need only think, for example, of problems involving proactive and retroactive inhibition, or questions concerning the relation between ease of learning and the conditions under which learning takes place, in order to see that it may not in all cases be advantageous to examine stimulus-response relationships one by one. Thus, Watson's assumption that one need not consider the interaction of stimuli in the determination of the final response was only an assumption and should not be viewed as an established conclusion that is applicable in all cases. To what extent that assumption is correct or incorrect in specific types of cases is a question that many branches of psychology have attempted to solve. Although behaviorists may object to most of the ways in which questions of this sort have sometimes been formulated, most if not all of them can readily be reformulated in terms to which no objection would be raised. Thus, what is here in question is not the issue of behaviorism as such, but the attempts of behaviorists to separate, and indeed isolate, some of the problems of overt behavior from all of the other problems with which psychologists have been concerned in the past.[10]

This shift from what was formerly thought to be included within the province of psychology to an almost exclusive interest in the characteristics of overt behavior is evident in a variety of works within the behaviorist movement. For example, both B. F. Skinner and Clark Hull avoided mention of "psychology," speaking only of a science of behavior. It is probably fair to say that each regarded a science of behavior as identical with psychology, but with a psychology stripped of those pseudo-problems that earlier systems had inherited from the mentalistic assumptions of the past. What I have attempted to suggest, using Watson as an example, is that a great many more—if not in fact all—of the traditional problems of psychology remain of importance within a behavioristic psychology, even though they are unfortunately often left undiscussed. To be sure, no systematic theory in psychology is under obligation to discuss all problems. However, it is my contention that there are some points at which traditional problems may be not only implicitly present and ready to arise, but directly relevant to explaining precisely those features of behavior which behavioristic psychologies seek to explain. The fact that, say, theories of perception or of learning have usually been phrased without reference to questions concerning overt behavior does not, I wish to claim, make them irrelevant to the explanation of that behavior.

II

I now turn to consider the quite different form of behaviorism represented by the system of E. C. Tolman. While Tolman would probably not have questioned the conclusion that I have thus far reached, his own attempt to formulate a consistent theory of the molar behavior of organisms tended to conceal that fact. To be sure, one cannot study his *Purposive Behavior in Animals and Men* without recognizing that Tolman was fully aware of all of the traditional problems of psychologists, and that he was sympathetic to them. Yet it was no part of his purpose to discuss the relations between particular solutions of these problems and his own use of the variables that were to be taken into account in explaining behavior. As a consequence, his system appears to be relatively self-contained, providing an explanation of the behavior of the organism which does not rely upon evidence other than that directly drawn from experiments concerning goal-directed, molar behavior.[11] It will be my aim to show, very briefly, that this appearance is misleading, and that Tolman's system does not in fact provide a complete and self-contained analysis of the factors necessary to explain the forms of behavior with which he was actually concerned.

Consider, for example, Tolman's discussion of how his concepts of demand and of means-end-readinesses are necessary to account for the responsiveness of animals and men to stimuli.[12] In that discussion he was at pains to rebut a simplistic "stimulus-response" psychology. As he pointed out:

> It is the fact that rats and men have hundreds, not to say thousands, of stimuli impinging upon them every instant of their waking lives; and yet to by far the majority of those stimuli they do not, at the given moment, respond. But in order now, in our system, to explain this choosiness as to stimuli, we have merely to refer to these facts of superordinate and subordinate demands and means-end-readinesses. . . .
>
> Consider the case of food-stimuli. It is the hungry rat only who is responsive to food-stimuli. The satiated rat pays no attention to food.[13]

This difference in the behavior of rats when hungry and when satiated does show that if anyone were to assume a simple and unvarying stimulus-response connection to explain behavior he would be mistaken and that either Tolman's explanatory categories or their equivalents in other systems have to be invoked. However, in at least some cases, Tolman's view that "we have merely to refer to these facts of . . . demands and means-end-readinesses" would also appear to be too simplistic: in some cases one must do more than refer to the antecedent state of the animal to explain its responsiveness to the stimuli presented. For example, characteristics of the stimuli, such as their physical intensities, or contrast effects among them, may also have to be considered when explaining the variations in the responses that occur. In other words, it would seem plausible to hold that, in some cases at least, behavior is affected by factors other than a previously existing state of the organism.[14] Whenever this is the case, even a behaviorist would be led to consider and investigate perceptual factors that affect attention and could not confine himself to those experimental investigations which deal with what Tolman designated as complete behavior-acts. Thus, an initial interest in molar behavior may force a psychologist (or his colleagues) to detour in an unanticipated direction; investigations of molar behavior may, temporarily, have to be held in abeyance, while some of the traditional problems of perception are considered. This suggests a more general point: that if one is to explain total behavior-acts, one cannot in all cases consider them as single, unitary events, but must often separately investigate some of their specific segments. In other words, a molar approach to behavior may not always be self-sufficient, but may demand a molecular approach as well.[15]

There are many other instances in which it is clearly necessary to pursue "molecular" investigations, including specifically physiological investigations, if one is to test or round out Tolman's system. For example, Tolman recognized what he designated as differences among "the capacities" of individual organisms and of different species of organism.[16] While one might wish to claim that the only way in which such capacities can be identified is by means of molar behavior, it is surely the case that physiological inquiries often explain their presence or their absence, both with respect to different individuals and to different species. Often, such inquiries also explain the conditions under which particular capacities change. In fact, once one has accepted behaviorism, there is no *a priori* reason to claim—and Tolman has given no arguments to show—that physiological inquiries might not, in the future, be relevant to any, or all, of the other variables that Tolman introduced in order to explain molar behavior.

The preceding discussion of Watson and of Tolman seems to me to make the following position plausible. Even if one holds that the subject matter with which psychology deals is human and animal behavior, none of the major traditional areas of psychological investigation is thereby excluded. To be sure, if one adopts the standpoint of behaviorism many problems that had originally been defined in other terms will have to be reformulated; it may also be that there are a few traditional problems which cannot be reformulated in behavioristic terms. In that case, either some enclaves within traditional areas of investigation would have to be abandoned or (as now seems to be occurring) some of the postulates of behaviorism must be relinquished. However, the crucial issue at this point does not concern behaviorism, for as we have noted not all who define psychology as a science of behavior are behaviorists; rather, the issue is one of the systematic unity and comprehensiveness of psychology as a discipline. I have confined my attention to behaviorists only because their austere doctrines provide a challenge to the position that I wish to defend. That position, as should now be clear, is that the traditional areas of psychology form an interlocking set of investigations, and that even though certain of the areas are not directly concerned with the adjustments of organisms to their environments, nor with any goal-oriented forms of overt behavior, they may nonetheless be directly relevant to analyses of the patterns of response which animals and men exhibit in their natural environments. It is for this reason, I claim, that specific investigations of, say, perceptual illusion or the dimensions of sensation, as well as whole areas such as physiological psychology or developmental psychology, cannot be extruded from the body of psychology, even when psychology is defined as a study of molar behavior.[17]

It may be of interest to note how different this position is from that which would be held were one to claim that what characterizes psychology as a discipline is the fact that the areas and problems of concern to those designated as psychologists are connected only because they manifest what Wittgenstein designated as "family resemblances." In psychology such resemblances would presumably involve a network of overlapping characteristics with respect to similarities in methods, subjects of inquiry, references to the investigations of others, etc. In fact, of course, we do find such networks of relationship in the investigations of those designated as belonging to the "family" of psychologists. However, more than this is needed to establish the relevant relationships of psychologists to one another. As I have elsewhere pointed out,[18] what Wittgenstein failed to make clear is that our ordinary notion of family resemblance, when we use it with respect to the physiognomic characteristics of the members of a family, presupposes not only that these individuals exhibit certain resemblances, but that they are biologically related, sharing a common line of descent. Similarly, that a person is properly regarded as a psychologist is not only dependent upon the fact that his experimental methods, the topics he discusses, and his bibliographic references have some degree of similarity to those of others who have been regarded as psychologists; the investigations of psychologists are connected not only by these external marks, but by the fact that they are directed toward establishing what factors explain the ways in which humans or animals behave under various sets of circumstances. These various factors, as I have suggested in my discussions of Watson and Tolman, are causally interrelated, so that the analysis of one or another aspect of a behavior-act presupposes that other aspects of it are to be investigated as well. This, I suggest, is what psychologists have done, and what provides systematic connection among such fields as perception, learning and memory, physiological psychology, developmental psychology, the investigation of personality differences, etc.

Sometimes, of course, the investigations of others who are not psychologists may make contributions that are important to psychology. For example, physicists and physiologists have contributed to the knowledge of vision and of audition, and neurosurgeons and biophysicists have contributed to knowledge of the neurological processes involved in all aspects of behavior. The existence of these contributions need not lead us to designate those who made them *as* psychologists, if in fact their concern was not with analyzing the factors determining molar behavior. It is surely not unusual for one discipline to borrow knowledge from another in order to solve its own problems, but this does not mean that the problems that each sets itself are the same. In short, the scope of psychology need not be taken as including all of the work of, say, neurophysiologists or biochemists, but can be characterized as being concerned with problems of molar behavior, and these problems—in my opinion—should be taken as including all aspects of the ways in which external and internal changes produce changes in human or animal responses to the environment.[19]

It is at this point that one can recognize that B. F. Skinner's program for a science of behavior sets up more limited objectives, excluding much that a more historically oriented characterization of psychology, such as mine, would certainly include. What I now wish to show, as I attempted to show in the case of Watson and of Tolman, is that a narrower program than that here outlined is almost surely bound to fail.

III

I have already remarked that one difficulty in most characterizations of the scope and aim of psychology is that these characterizations often reflect specific programs of research rather than the investigations that have in fact characterized the work of psychologists in the past and in the present. This is especially true in the case of Skinner's science of behavior which, one may assume, *is* psychology from his point of view. He defines his method as positivistic, which he takes to mean that "it confines itself to description rather than explanation." Its concepts are defined in terms of immediate observations.[20] The immediate observations that came into question were concerned with the responses of organisms to particular stimuli that *elicited* behavior, or responses to stimuli that reinforced the original *emitted* behavior of the organism. These were the analytical units of the system, and Skinner took them to be the ultimate facts of behavior which not only could be observed under controlled conditions, independently of any physiological conjectures, but whose relationships could be determined prior to the examination of more complex behavior.[21] What Skinner assumed with respect to complex behavior was that it depended upon the interaction of these simple units. Of this interaction between units, each of which he regarded as a separate functional part, he said, "Interaction may be studied in a practical way by deliberately combining previously isolated units and observing their effects upon one another."[22] In this respect, his program was distinctly Watsonian.

However, as Skinner admitted in *The Behavior of Organisms* (p. 46), he was not yet in a position to carry out this task except to the extent to which he had, in a limited way, reported on experiments in induction and in the chaining of reflexes. It is only in his later, more popular exposition of his program, *Science and Human Behavior,* that one finds him addressing himself to cases in which, under natural conditions, units may be said to combine to form a complex pattern of behavior. With respect to this gap between his experimental work and the claims he makes in his less technical expositions concerning how his results apply to behavior in the natural environment, Skinner is again reminiscent of Watson.

A difference between any experimental situation and the natural environment is, of course, the fact that in an experiment an attempt is made to reduce the number of relevant variables and to control each of them. Skinner's controls were extremely rigorous; they were designed to reduce the number of stimuli to which his animals were subjected to an absolute minimum.[23] This, of course, is unobjectionable in itself. However, it is important to note that on the basis of his assumption that every behavior act, no matter how complex, consists of a series of specific reflexes, Skinner's analysis of behavior-acts becomes, so to speak, one-dimensional. What is investigated are only those variables which determine the connective relations between stimulus and response. Whatever variables determine the original effectiveness of the stimulus in elicited behavior, or control the effectiveness of the materials that reinforce behavior, or determine under what conditions "induction" takes place (so that one stimulus serves as a substitute for another), are variables which are not investigated in Skinner's system. This is a function of the fact that working originally with only one species of organism, and in all cases reducing the available stimuli as drastically as possible, and by restricting the possible responses equally stringently, all that was left to investigate were the connective relations, under variant conditions, of a single type of stimulus and response. It is this which accounts for what I have termed the one-dimensionality of Skinner's analysis, in which questions regarding the effectiveness and substitutability of various stimuli, and the types of reinforcers which are most effective under different conditions (and a host of other similar questions) are left unexplored. Yet it is with such questions that psychologists interested in perception and in motivation have been concerned. The fact that these psychologists have often formulated their inquiries in mentalistic rather than behavioristic terms is not a reason to look upon their results with suspicion: relevant experiments have often enough been carried out on animals to demonstrate that such investigations need not involve so-called introspective methods.

We may also note that one important aspect of Skinner's methodology was his determination to avoid physiological explanations of behavior, and once again it may be said that the fact that he could avoid such problems was a function of the limits within which he confined his experimental program. For example, it was no part of his task to characterize the kinds of original emitted behavior upon which operant conditioning was based. Nor was it necessary to do so, because the conditions of his experiments were such as to allow for only a very narrow range of activity prior to the onset of conditioning. However, those interested in the comparative study of animal behavior under natural conditions cannot assume that emitted behavior is so narrowly restricted: for example, the whole question of what is native and what acquired in the patterning of the behavior of different species is simply excluded from consideration when one's only controlled observations are carried out within the rigid confines set by Skinner's assumptions and by his limited (albeit extraordinarily ingenious) repertoire of experimental techniques.

Thus I conclude that even though Skinner's system may at first seem to provide an escape from my view that psychology as a science embraces a variety of interlocking fields of inquiry—for example those which have in the past been identified with areas of study such as perception, motivation, or learning, or with physiological, comparative, and developmental psychology—there is every reason to doubt that his system can ultimately bypass the problems which have arisen in these areas. The principles of that system have only been shown to be applicable to certain segments of behavior; his assumption that the behavior of the organism in its commerce with its environment (to use his phrase[24]) can be explained as the sum of such segments remains merely an assumption until it is applied to other aspects of behavior-acts than those which his experimental techniques were designed to explore. In speaking of areas of investigation such as perception, motivation, or learning, I do not wish to be understood as assuming that these are, self-enclosed, or that their boundaries have always been the same; nor would I assume that their present relations might not radically change. In fact, the opposite point of view is precisely that which I wish to maintain: the discipline of psychology includes all fields of inquiry which are involved when one sets out to understand the molar behaviour of organisms, i.e., their behavior-acts. This, I submit, is what characterizes psychology as a discipline, however widely the specific interests of its practitioners may diverge. And what I have here said using three behaviorist systems as examples can equally well be applied to those whose interests or programs have led them to concentrate their attention on other, quite different, fields.

Notes

In the three articles that follow this paper (but that were written earlier) I argue against explaining the societal dimension of human experience in terms of psychological principles or laws. In those articles, my attention was focused on the societal, to the neglect of what can be said concerning the nature of psychology itself. The present paper was an attempt to deal with that problem. To this extent it involves a retraction of a concession granted to Ryle in the preceding paper: I no longer concur with his view that the term psychology *does not refer to "a unitary inquiry or tree of inquiries." By arguing that there are essential connections among the many sorts of investigations which psychologists carry on, I am suggesting an alternative to the Wittgensteinean notion that nothing more than a "family resemblance" is involved in our use of terms such as* psychology. *In this respect the present article resembles the approach I adopted in "Family Resemblances and Generalization in the Arts," published in the* American Philosophical Quarterly *in 1965.*

1. In an interesting article, "Ethnocentrism of Disciplines and the Fish-Scale Model of Omniscience," in *Interdisciplinary Relationships in the Social Sciences,* ed. M. and C. W. Sherif (Chicago, 1969), Donald T. Campbell has argued that the various social sciences *are* "arbitrary composites." He holds that psychology is "a hodge-podge of sensitive subjective biography, of brain operations, of school achievement testing, of factor analysis, of Markov process mathematics, of schizophrenic families, of laboratory experiments on group structure in which persons are anonymous, etc." (pp. 331-32).

While attempting to show that this is a mistaken view of psychology as a discipline, I readily grant that many of Campbell's points regarding the sociology and politics of academic departments are shrewd and well-founded. However, one should not assume that what is true of the structure and growth of particular academic departments provides an adequate basis for generalizing concerning the growth of a discipline as a whole.

2. In *Physiological Psychology* (London, 1905), McDougall said, "Psychology may be best and most comprehensively defined as the positive science of the conduct of living creatures. . . . In adopting this definition we must understand the word conduct in the widest possible sense as denoting the sum of activities by which any creature maintains its relations with other creatures and with the world of physical things" (p. 1).

3. In *Principles of Gestalt Psychology* (New York, 1935), Koffka said: "Although psychology was reared as the science of consciousness or mind, we shall choose behavior as our keystone. That does not mean that I regard the old definitions as completely wrong—it would be strange indeed if a science had developed on entirely wrong assumptions—but it means that if we start with behavior it is easier to find a place for consciousness and mind than it is to find a place for behavior if we start with mind or consciousness" (p. 25). Even earlier in *The Growth of the Mind* (New York, 1925), the following definition of psychology was given: "the scientific study of living creatures in their contact with the outer world" (p. 4).

4. Watson's earliest definitions of psychology are to be found in *Behavior: An Introduction to Comparative Psychology* (New York, 1914), p. 10, and in "Psychology as the Behaviorist Views It," *Psychological Review,* 20 (1913):167.

A few years later, in *Psychology from the Standpoint of a Behaviorist* (Philadelphia, 1919; second edition, 1924), Watson offered a somewhat different definition, but his treatment of the role of stimulus and response in accounting for behavior remained unchanged. (The new definition is to be found in p. 8 of the first edition, and on p. 9 of the second.)

5. Cf. J. B. Watson, *Behavior,* pp. 53-54 and, especially, Watson, *Psychology,* pp. 9-14. (The latter reference applies to either edition of the book.)

6. E. C. Tolman, *Purposive Behavior in Animals and Men* (New York, 1932), pp. 4-12 and 438f.

Tolman acknowledged borrowing the molecular-molar distinction from C. D. Broad, but he apparently did not recognize that in borrowing it he had also altered it. For Broad, "molecular behaviour" referred to "hypothetical molecular movements in the brain and nervous system, and not to muscular and glandular response to stimuli" (cf. *Mind and its Place in Nature* [New York, 1929], p. 616.) On the other hand, it was primarily with reference to the latter that Tolman characterized the molecular level of behavior. This difference is evident in the fact that Broad classified blood pressure, and the convergence and accommodation of the eyes, etc., as examples of molar behavior.

7. The distinction between a molar approach, which concerns itself with behavior-acts, and a molecular approach, such as that adopted by Watson, has sometimes been used as a means of differentiating the provinces of psychology and physiology. It was, for example, so used by Tolman himself in "Physiology, Psychology, and Sociology," *Psychological Review*, 45 (1938):228. An analogous use is to be found in Koffka, *Principles of Gestalt Psychology*, note 3, p. 27.

To be sure, one can raise various objections to the distinction between molar and molecular approaches, and there also are objections that can be raised to defining psychology in terms of molar behavior. However, these are not questions that are crucial to the main issue with which this paper is concerned. Therefore, for my present purposes I shall assume that all such objections can, in principle, be answered.

8. Watson, *Psychology*, p. 11.

9. That this is often a mistake has been recognized by another, later, behaviorist, Clark L. Hull. Cf. his *Principles of Behavior* (New York, 1943), pp. 349f. and 376.

10. As we shall note, this stricture does not apply with equal force to Tolman's system, although even in his case it is not wholly inapplicable.

11. Tolman rejected the view that explanations of behavior had to be formulated in terms of neurological or physiological concepts (cf. Tolman, *Purposive Behavior*, notes 6, 8, pp. 416-17f.). Instead, he regarded it as essential that psychology build its own concepts through analyzing its own subject matter, the molar behavior of animals and men. The types of concepts which Tolman used for this purpose did not refer to specific *segments* of behavior which were separately observable under experimental conditions and which, when aggregated, could account for the behavior as a whole. Rather, they referred to a number of different *variables* that, when taken together in a particular situation, accounted for the behavior observed. Such variables are not directly observable in a behavior-act, for they are not *parts* of it: rather, they are the factors that the psychologist introduces into his analysis in order to account for empirically verified regularities in molar behavior. It is they that have come to be designated as "intervening variables" — a phrase not to be found in *Purposive Behavior*, but introduced by Tolman in his presidential address to the American Psychological Association (*Psychological Review*, 45 [1938]:1-41).

12. For Tolman's definition of *demands* and of *means-end-readiness* as technical terms, cf. Tolman, *Purposive Behavior*, note 6, pp. 441 and 450f.

13. Tolman, *Purposive Behavior*, pp. 35-36.

14. David Katz's experiments on hens, with respect to the role of the situation in eliciting eating responses, are relevant in this connection. (Cf. *Animals and Men: Studies in Comparative Psychology* [London, 1937], pp. 159-65). So, too, are some of the experimental variations reported by B. P. Wiesner and N. B. Sheard in *Maternal Behaviour of the Rat (Biological Monographs and Manuals*, 11 [Edinburgh, 1933]).

We may also note that Tolman himself cites the fact that in certain cases what he terms *discriminanda* may affect maze-running behavior in rats (Tolman, *Purposive Behavior*, note 6, pp. 78f. and 85-88). While he explained these effects in terms of "expectations" (i.e., behavior-supports), he recognized that even this explanation leads into further problems concerning sensory discriminations, and thus into at least some of the problems involved in the theory of perception. This opening wedge might have caused an even more extensive revision of his emphasis on "expectations" had he not been considering the behavior of animals under controlled laboratory conditions; in an uncontrolled environment the stimuli are far more varied and the demands may be less powerful, therefore the influence of the characteristics of the stimuli may be stronger.

15. It may be worth noting that Clark Hull also held that Tolman had drawn too sharp a distinction between molar and molecular approaches, maintaining that this distinction was relative and not absolute. What Hull wished to argue — in contradistinction to Tolman's "emergentist" position — was that, in the end, behavior would have to be explained in molecular, i.e., physiological, terms. (On these points, cf. Hull, *Principles of Behavior*, notes 9, 17, 19-21, and 26.)

Not wishing to discuss this issue, I confine my present point to insisting that to understand complete behavior-acts one must often analyze and take into account their individual segments.

16. Tolman, *Purposive Behavior*, note 6, p. 20.

17. In this connection I should like to cite K. F. Muenzinger's *Psychology; The Science of Behavior* (Denver, 1940). He characterized the subject matter of psychology in terms of what Tolman referred to as "behaviour-acts," but he designated them as movements from starting-phase to end-phase of behavior. He then characterized the problem for psychology in the following manner: "to discover and describe the factors that bring about and determine the psychological movement from start to end-phase" (p. 12). These factors, as the systematic organization of the book makes clear, include the whole range of traditional psychological problems.

For another type of analysis of behavior, which is also compatible with what I say here, I might cite the system of Egon Brunswik, as reported in Postman and Tolman's analysis, "Brunswik's Probabilistic Functionalism" in S. Koch, *Psychology: A Study of a Science* (New York, 1959), vol. 1, esp. pp. 508-11.

18. "Family Resemblances and Generalization concerning the Arts," *American Philosophical Quarterly*, 2 (1965):219-28.

19. I should like to point out that in this respect my position is compatible with the approach of those cognitive psychologists who explicitly reject behaviorism. As one can see in Ulric Neisser's *Cognitive Psychology* (New York, 1967), to choose merely one example, the introduction of the term *consciousness* alongside the term *behavior* does not alter the fact that for the cognitive psychologist the subject matter of human psychology is, basically, what human beings do, how they behave. (Cf. *Cognitive Psychology*, pp. 4-5 and 304-5.)

20. *Behavior of Organisms* (New York, 1938), p. 44.

21. Ibid., pp. 28-29.

22. Ibid., p. 29. In this connection, two related passages may also be cited: "The preceding system is based upon the assumption that both behavior and environment may be broken into parts which retain their identity throughout an experiment and undergo orderly changes" (p. 33); and, "The connections between parts are purely mechanical and may be broken at will. Any section of a chain may be elicited with the same properties which characterize it as part of the total chain" (p. 55).

23. A discussion of his control of extraneous factors is given in *Behavior of Organisms*, pp. 55-57.

24. Ibid., p. 6.

15

Societal Facts

If one adopts Broad's distinction between critical and speculative philosophy, the following paper may be regarded as an attempt to deal
with one of the major problems of a critical philosophy of the social sciences.
Like all such attempts, this paper faces some difficulties that are not encountered in equally acute form by those who deal with the concepts and
methods of the natural sciences. In the first place, the concepts and methods
utilized in the natural sciences have been more sharply defined than have
been those which social scientists employ. In the second place, there is less
disagreement among natural scientists than among social scientists as to the
purposes that actually do underlie, or that should underlie, their studies. In
the third place, the relations among the various branches of natural science
seem to be more easily definable and less subject to dispute than is the case
among the social sciences. It is with one aspect of the relations among the
various social sciences that this paper will be concerned.

There can scarcely be any doubt that there is at present a considerable
measure of disagreement among social scientists concerning the relations
that obtain among their various disciplines. For example, there is little
agreement as to how the province of "social psychology" is related to general
psychology on the one hand or to sociology on the other. There is perhaps
even less agreement as to how sociology and history are related, or whether,
in fact, history is itself a social science. Even the province of cultural anthropology which, in its earlier stages, seemed to be capable of clear definition, is now in a position in which its relations to the other fields of social
science have become extremely fluid. This type of fluidity in the boundaries
of the various social sciences, and the ease with which concepts employed in
one discipline spread to other disciplines, has been quite generally regarded
as a promising augury for the future of the social sciences. One notes the
frequency with which "integration" is held up as an important programmatic
goal for social scientists. But such pleas for integration are ambiguous. On
the one hand, they may merely signify a recognition of the fact that attempts
to understand some concrete problems call for cooperation between persons
trained to use the concepts and methods of different social sciences, or that
workers in one discipline should be aware of the methods and results of

Reprinted by permission from *British Journal of Sociology*, 6 (1955):305-17.

those who work in other fields. On the other hand, what some who plead for "integration" in social science seem to demand is that the various disciplines should merge into one larger whole. In such a view the goal of integration would be the achievement of a state in which all persons who work in the field of social science would operate with the same set of concepts and would utilize the same methods of inquiry. If I am not mistaken, it is sometimes assumed that the social sciences will have made their greatest advance when the individual social sciences that now exist will have lost their separate identities. Insofar as this paper has a practical purpose, its purpose is to indicate that "integration," taken in this sense, is a mistaken goal for sociologists and psychologists to pursue.[1]

In stating that I wish to argue against what some social scientists believe to be the most promising path that their sciences can follow, it is clear that this paper has what might be termed an injunctive character. I am attempting to rule in advance that certain modes of procedure should or should not be adopted by practicing social scientists. To those trained in the critical philosophy of the natural sciences, such a procedure will doubtless seem both foolhardy and perverse. Yet, it is unavoidable. So long as there are fundamental differences among social scientists with respect to the types of concepts and types of method which they actually use, and so long as the criteria by means of which they measure the adequacy of these concepts and methods differ, every attempt to do more than compile a *corpus* of materials for comparison, will involve that the analyst of the social sciences should take his own stand with respect to the matters under debate. Where one can show reasons for the position adopted, the injunctive element in one's analyses cannot be claimed to be wholly arbitrary. It is in proportion to the strength of these reasons that any particular injunctive proposal is to be judged.

However, any proposal as to the relations that ought to obtain between two or more social sciences will presuppose a belief as to what the goal of the social sciences may be. Concerning this topic there is also a considerable amount of debate. However, I believe it possible to formulate a general statement that might be acceptable to all, leaving unprejudiced those specific issues which have divided social scientists into opposed camps. I submit that the following statement would be quite generally acceptable: it is the task of the social sciences to attain a body of knowledge on the basis of which the actions of human beings as members of a society can be understood. This definition of the aim of the social sciences does not rule out the possibility that an understanding of the actions of human beings as members of a society may be instrumental to some further aim, such as that of attaining the means of controlling human behavior or of promoting human welfare. (Nor, of course, does it affirm that this is the case.) Furthermore, it is to be noted that in this statement of the aims of the social sciences I have avoided prejudging this issue as to whether the body of knowledge which is sought can be formulated as a system of laws and whether an understanding of human actions is equivalent to explaining these actions in the sense in which the term "explanation" is used in the natural sciences. Throughout this paper I wish to avoid raising these questions, and insofar as possible I shall confine my discussion to a neutral terminology that does not prejudge any of these issues. Wherever my language seems to suggest that I am using the model of explanation used in the natural sciences, my point could equally well be phrased in terms which are compatible with the view that the methods and concepts of the social sciences are utterly different from those employed in the natural sciences. And, conversely, where I use the language of "understanding," my discussion can equally well be rephrased in terms of the language of scientific "explanation."

Having now defined what I take to be the task of the social sciences, I can state the aim of this paper. My aim is to show that one cannot understand the actions of human beings as members of a society unless one assumes that there is a group of facts which I shall term *societal facts*, which are as ultimate as are those facts which are *psychological* in character. In speaking of *societal facts* I refer to any facts concerning the forms of organization present in a society. In speaking of *psychological facts* I refer to any facts concerning the thoughts and the actions of specific human beings.

An Example of the Irreducibility of Societal Concepts

If it be the case, as I wish to claim, that societal facts are as ultimate as are psychological facts, then those concepts which are used to refer to the forms of organization of a society cannot be reduced without remainder to concepts that only refer to the thoughts and actions of specific individuals.[2] There are many reasons why the type of claim that I am putting forward has been doubted, and we shall note some of these reasons as we proceed. First, however, it will be well to lend some plausibility to the view by means of an example.

Suppose that I enter a bank, I then take a withdrawal slip and fill it out, I walk to a teller's window, I hand in my slip, he gives me money, I leave the bank and go on my way. Now suppose that you have been observing my actions and that you are accompanied by, let us say, a Trobriand Islander. If you wished to explain my behavior, how would you proceed? You could explain the filling out of the withdrawal slip as a means that will lead to the teller's behavior towards me, that is, as a means to his handing me some notes and coins; and you could explain the whole sequence of my action as directed towards this particular end. You could then explain the significance that I attached to the possession of these notes and coins by following me and noting how the possession of them led other persons, such as assistants in shops, to give me goods because I gave them the notes and coins that the bank teller had handed to me. Such would be an explanation of my observed behavior in terms of the behavior of other specific individuals toward me.

And it might at first glance appear as if an explanation couched in terms of these interpersonal forms of behavior would be adequate to cover all of the aspects of the case.

However, it would also be necessary for you to inform the stranger who accompanies you that it does not suffice for a person to fill out such a slip and hand it to just anyone he may happen to meet. It would also be only fair to inform him that before one can expect a bank teller to hand one money in exchange for a slip, one must have "deposited" money. In short, one must explain at least the rudiments of a banking system to him. In doing so one is, of course, using concepts that refer to one aspect of the institutional organization of our society, and this is precisely the point I wish to make. (And the same point can be made with reference to how Malinowski has explained to *us* the Trobriand Islanders' system of ceremonial exchanges of gifts.) In all cases of this sort, the actual behavior of specific individuals toward one another is unintelligible unless one views their behavior in terms of their status and roles, and the concepts of status and role are devoid of meaning unless one interprets them in terms of the organization of the society to which the individuals belong.

To this it may be objected that any statement concerning the status of an individual is itself analyzable in terms of how specific individuals behave towards other individuals and how these individuals in turn behave towards them. Thus it might be claimed that while the explanation of an individual's behavior often demands the introduction of concepts referring to "societal status," such concepts are themselves reducible to further statements concerning actual or probable forms of behaviour. Thus, societal concepts might be held to be heuristic devices, summarizing repeated patterns of behavior, but they would be nothing more: their real meaning would lie in a conjunction of statements concerning the behavior of a number of individuals.

However, this view is open to serious objection. We have seen in the foregoing illustration that my own behavior towards the bank teller is determined by his status. If the attempt is now made to interpret his status in terms of the recurrent patterns of behavior which others exemplify in dealing with him, then *their* behavior is left unexplained: each of them—no less than I—will only behave in this way because each recognizes the teller of a bank to have a particular status. Similarly, it is impossible to resolve the bank teller's role into statements concerning his behavior towards other individuals. If one wished to equate his societal role with his reactions towards those who behave in a particular way towards him, it would be unintelligible that he should hand us money when we present him with a withdrawal slip when he stands in his teller's cage, and yet that he would certainly refuse to do so if we were to present him with such a slip when we met him at a party. Bank tellers as well as depositors behave as they do because they assume certain societally defined roles under specific sets of circumstances. This being the case, it is impossible to escape the use of societal concepts in attempting to understand some aspects of individual behavior: concepts involving the notions of status and role cannot themselves be reduced to a conjunction of statements in which these or other societal concepts do not appear.

[Precisely the same point may be made with respect to attempts to translate societal concepts into terms of the thoughts of individuals rather than into terms of their overt behavior. If one should wish to say that I acted as I did toward the teller because I foresaw that through my actions he would be led to give me money, one would still have to admit that my anticipation of his response was based upon my recognition of the fact that he was a bank teller, and that the role of a bank teller demands that he should act as the bank's agent, and the function of a bank (so far as each depositor is concerned) is that of being a custodian of legal tender, etc., etc. Thus, in attempting to analyze societal facts by means of appealing to the thoughts that guide an individual's conduct, some of the thoughts will themselves have societal referents, and societal concepts will therefore not have been expunged from our analysis.]

Now I do not wish to claim that an individual's thoughts or his overt actions are wholly explicable in terms of status and roles. Not only does it seem to be the case that some actions may be explained without introducing these concepts, but it is also the case that two individuals, say two bank tellers, may behave differently toward me in spite of the identity in their roles. Thus, one may be friendly and the other hostile or aloof, and the nature of my own behavior toward them will then differ. Thus it should be apparent that I am not seeking to explain all facets of individual behavior by means of statements that only refer to societal facts. What I wish to contend is (a) that in understanding or explaining an individual's actions we must often refer to facts concerning the organization of the society in which he lives, and (b) that our statements concerning these societal facts are not reducible to a conjunction of statements concerning the actions of individuals. I take it that almost all social scientists and philosophers would grant the first of these contentions, but that many social scientists and most philosophers would reject the second, insisting that societal facts are reducible to a set of facts concerning individual behavior.

The Criterion of "Irreducibility"

It is now necessary to state the criterion of irreducibility which the foregoing illustration has presupposed.

Let us assume that there is a language, S, in which sociological concepts such as "institutions," "mores," "ideologies," "status," "class," etc., appear. These concepts all refer to aspects of what we term "a society." That there is a language of this type is clear from the works of sociologists, anthropologists, and historians. It is also clear from the fact that we use such terms as *The President of the United States,* or *the unmarried children of X.* In order to define the meaning of the latter terms we must make reference to the Constitution of the United States or to the laws that govern our marriage and kinship systems, and in these references we are employing societal concepts.

There is, of course, also another language, P, in which we refer to the thoughts and actions and capabilities of individual human beings. In making statements in this language (which, for want of a better name, I have called our *psychological language*)[3] we are not using societal concepts. The differences between these two languages may be illustrated by the fact that the connotation of the term *The present President of the United States* carries implications that do not follow from the personal name *Dwight D. Eisenhower,* and statements concerning the personality of Dwight D. Eisenhower carry no implications for our understanding of his societal role. This remains true even though we admit that in this case, as in most others, the status of an individual is often causally connected with the nature of his personality, and even though we also admit that an individual's personality is often connected with the fact that he occupies a particular status, or that he functions within this status as he does.

Put in these terms, my thesis that societal facts are irreducible to psychological facts may be reformulated as holding that sociological concepts cannot be translated into psychological concepts *without remainder.* What is signified by the stipulation "without remainder" must now be made clear.

It would seem to be the case that all statements in the sociological language, S, are translatable into statements concerning the behavior of specific individuals and thus would be translatable into the language P. For example, a statement such as "The institution of monogamous marriage supplanted the polygynous marriage system of the Mormons" could presumably be translated into statements concerning the actions of certain aggregates of individuals. However, it is by no means certain that such translations could be effected without using other concepts that appear in the sociological language. These concepts too might have their translations into P, but the translation of the concepts of S into P would not be complete if such translations still had to employ other concepts that appear in S. It is with respect to incomplete translations of this type that I speak of translations that cannot be effected "without remainder."

An analogue of this situation was pointed out by Chisholm in his criticism of C. I. Lewis's theory of knowledge.[4] According to Chisholm, thing-statements cannot be completely reduced to statements concerning sense-data because one must specify the conditions of the appearance of these sense-data, and in doing so one must again use thing-statements. And this is precisely the situation that we found to obtain in our illustration of the behavior of a person withdrawing money from a bank.

Now, it might be argued (as it has sometimes been argued with respect to Chisholm's contention) that our inability to carry out such translations, without remainder, represents a practical and not a theoretical inability. According to those who take this view, the practical difficulty that is present arises from the indefinitely long conjunction of statements which we should have to make in carrying out our analyses, and from the fact that some of these statements would involve a foreknowledge of future events. But it is claimed that no theoretically important consequences follow from our inability to complete a detailed analysis of a particular statement: such partial analyses as we can actually make may not have omitted any theoretically significant aspects of the statements that we wish to analyze. Such a rejoinder would be open to two objections, so far as our present discussion is concerned.

First, we are here concerned with the problem of the relations between two empirical disciplines. Therefore, if it be admitted that it is impossible in practice to reduce statements that contain societal terms to a conjunction of statements that only include terms referring to the thoughts and actions of specific individuals, the rejoinder in question might conceivably be significant from the point of view of a general ontology, but it would not affect my argument regarding the autonomy of the societal sciences.

Second, it is to be noted that whatever may be the case regarding Chisholm's argument concerning the relation of sense-data statements to thing-statements, the problem of reducing statements that include societal terms to statements that only concern specific individuals is a question not merely of how we may *analyze* action statements, but of how we may *explain* certain facts. It has been my contention that if we are to explain an individual's behavior when, say, he enters a bank, we must have recourse to societal concepts and cannot merely employ terms that refer to the fact that this individual makes marks on paper, approaches a specific point, hands the marked paper to another individual, etc., etc. He who knew all of this, and who also knew all of the other actions performed by the members of a society, would possess a series of protocol statements, or biographical "logs." Even though this set of logs included reference to all of the actions performed by all of the members of the society, no societal concepts would appear in it. However, this information would not make it possible for our omniscient collector of data to explain why the depositor fills out a slip in order to withdraw money, or why the teller will exchange notes and coins for such a slip. Such a transaction only becomes explicable when we employ the concept of *a bank,* and what it means to speak of *a bank* will involve the use of concepts such as *legal tender,* and *contract.* Further, what it means to speak of a *contract* will involve reference to our legal system, and the legal system itself cannot be defined in terms of individual behavior—even the legal realist must distinguish between the behavior of judges and policemen and the behavior of "just anyone." Thus, if we are to explain certain forms of individual behavior we must use societal concepts, and these concepts are not (I have argued) translatable without remainder into terms that only refer to the behavior of individuals.

Yet it is important to insist that even though societal concepts cannot be translated into psychological concepts without leaving this societal remainder, it is not only possible but indeed necessary to make the *partial* translation. It is always necessary for us to translate terms such as *ideologies* or *banks* or *a monogamous marriage system* into the language of individual thought and action, for unless we do so we have no means of verifying any statements we may make concerning these societal facts. Ideologies and banks and marriage systems do not exist unless there are aggregates of individuals who think and act in specific ways, and it is only by means of establishing the forms of their thoughts and their actions that we can apprehend the nature of the societal organization in which they live, or that we can corroborate or disallow statements concerning this organization. Yet, the necessity for this translation of specific sociological concepts into terms of individual behavior in order that we may verify and refine our sociological statements does not alter the fact that the possibility of making such a translation always involves the necessity for using other societal concepts to define the conditions under which this behavior takes place. Thus, the translation can never obviate the use of societal concepts and reduce the study of society to a branch of the study of the actions of individuals.

Objections

In the foregoing discussion I have been at pains to state my position in such a way as to avoid the most usual objections to the general type of view I hold. However, it will be useful to comment on three objections that have frequently been raised against the view that societal facts are irreducible to psychological facts.[5]

The first of these objections may be termed the *ontological objection*. It consists in holding that societal facts cannot be said to have any status of their own because no such facts would exist if there were not individuals who thought and acted in specific ways. Now, to hold the view that I hold, one need not deny that the existence of a society presupposes the existence of individuals, and that these individuals must possess certain capacities for thought and for action if what we term a society is to exist. Yet, this admission does not entail the conclusion that is thought to follow from it: one need not hold that a society is an entity independent of all human beings in order to hold that societal facts are not reducible to the facts of individual behavior. The warrant for the latter position is merely this: all human beings are born into a society, and much of their thought and their action is influenced by the nature of the societies in which they live; therefore, those facts that concern the nature of their societies must be regarded as being independent of them. To be sure, these facts are not independent of the existence of *other* individuals, and it will be from the forms of behavior of these other individuals that any specific individual will have acquired his own societally oriented patterns of behavior. But these individuals, too, were born into an already functioning societal organization that was independent of them. Thus, their societally oriented behavior was also conditioned by an already existing set of societal facts, etc., etc.

To be sure, those who wish to press the ontological objection may insist that at some remote time in the history of the human race there were individuals who were not born into an already existing society, and that these individuals must have formed a societal organization by virtue of certain patterns of repeated interpersonal actions. Thus, they would seek to insist that all societal facts have their origins in individual behavior, and that it is mistaken to argue, as I have argued, that societal facts are irreducible to the facts of individual behavior. However, this rejoinder is clearly fallacious. Whatever may have been the origin of the first forms of societal organization (a question that no present knowledge puts us in a position to answer), the issue with which we are here concerned is one that involves the nature of societies as they exist at present. To argue that the nature of present societal facts is reducible to the facts of individual behavior because the origins of a particular social system grew up out of certain repeated forms of behavior is a clear example of the genetic fallacy. One might as well argue on the basis of our knowledge of the origins of the Greek drama and of the modern drama that every current Broadway play is really to be understood as a religious festival.

However, the above answer to the ontological type of objection is clearly not sufficient.[6] It is, I hope, adequate to show that one usual form of countering my position is untenable; yet, the essential paradox remains. One can still legitimately ask what sort of ontological status societal facts can conceivably possess if it is affirmed that they depend for their existence on the activities of human beings and yet are claimed not to be identical with these activities. There are, it seems to me, two types of answer which might be given to this question. In the first type of answer one might contend that a whole is not equal to the sum of its parts, and a society is not equal to the sum of those individual activities which go to form it. This familiar holistic answer is not the one that I should be inclined to propose. In the first place, it is by no means certain that the principle of holism (as thus stated) is philosophically defensible. In the second place, such an answer assumes that what may be termed the *parts* of a society are to be taken to be individual human beings, and this is an assumption that I should be unwilling to make. All of the preceding argument entails the proposition that the "parts" of a society are specific societal facts, not individuals. If this were not the case, societal concepts could be translated into terms referring to individual behavior if we had sufficient knowledge of all the interrelations among these individuals. Instead, we have found that an analysis of a statement that concerns a societal fact will involve us in using other societal concepts: for example, that what it means to be a depositor in a bank will involve statements concerning our legal system and our monetary economy. Similarly, what it means to be a college student cannot be defined without recourse to statements concerning our educational system, and such statements cannot be analyzed without utilizing concepts that refer to statutory laws as well as to many other aspects of our societal organization. Thus, from the arguments that have been given, it follows that the "parts" of a society are not individual human beings, but are the specific institutions and other forms of organization which characterize that society. Once this is recognized, it remains an open question as to the extent to which any specific society (or all societies) are to be conceived holistically or pluralistically.

The second method of dealing with the ontological objection is the one that I should myself be inclined to adopt. It consists in holding that one set of facts may depend for its existence upon another set of facts and yet not be identical with the latter. An example of such a relationship would be that which a traditional epiphenomenalist would regard as existing between brain events and the contents of consciousness. Whatever objections one may raise against the epiphenomenalist view of the mind-body relationship, one would scarcely be justified in holding that the position must be false because the content of consciousness could not be different from the nature of brain states and yet be dependent upon the latter. If one has reasons for holding that the content of consciousness *is* different from brain states, and if one also has reason for holding that it *does* depend upon the latter, one's ontology must be accommodated to these facts: the facts cannot be rejected because of a prior ontological commitment. And, without wishing to press my analogy farther than is warranted, I can point out that my statement concerning "the parts" of a society has its analogue in what those who hold to the epiphenomenalist position would say concerning the proper analysis of any statement referring to the content of an individual's field of consciousness. Just as I have claimed that the component parts of a society are the elements of its organization and are not the individuals without whom it would not exist, so the epiphenomenalist would (I assume) say that the parts of the individual's field of consciousness are to be found within the specific data of consciousness and not in the brain events upon which consciousness depends.

These remarks are, I hope, sufficient to dispel the ontological objection to the position that I wish to defend. To be sure, I have not attempted to say what position should be assigned to societal facts when one is constructing a general ontology. To do so, I should have to say much more concerning the nature of societal facts, and I should of course also have to discuss the nature of other types of entity. Here it has only been my concern to suggest that what I have termed the ontological objection to my thesis is by no means as strong as it may at first glance appear to be: the admission that all societal facts depend upon the existence of human beings who possess certain capacities for thought and for action by no means precludes the contention that these facts are irreducible to facts concerning those individuals.

The second of the most usual objections to the thesis that societal facts cannot be reduced to psychological facts is an epistemological objection. This objection may take many forms, depending upon the theory of knowledge which is held by the objector. However, the common core of all such objections is the indubitable fact that societal concepts are not capable of being "pointed to," in the sense in which we can point to material objects or to the qualities or activities of these objects. Whenever we wish to point to any fact concerning societal organization we can only point to a sequence of interpersonal actions. Therefore, any theory of knowledge which demands that all empirically meaningful concepts must ultimately be reducible to data that can be directly inspected will lead to the insistence that all societal concepts are reducible to the patterns of individual behavior.

I shall not, of course, seek to disprove this general theory of knowledge. Yet it is possible to indicate in very brief compass that it is inadequate to deal with societal facts. Because those who would hold this theory of knowledge would presumably wish to show that we can be said to know something of the nature of human societies, and because they would also wish to hold that our means of gaining this knowledge is through the observation of the repeated patterns of activities of individuals, a proof that their theory of knowledge cannot account for our apprehension of the nature of individual action is, in the present context, a sufficient disproof of the epistemological type of objection.

In order to offer such a disproof, let us revert to our illustration of a depositor withdrawing money from a bank. In order to understand his overt actions in entering a bank, filling out a slip, handing it to a teller, receiving notes and coins, and leaving the bank, we must view this sequence of actions as one internally connected series. Yet what connects the elements within the series is the person's intention to withdraw money from his account, and this intention is not itself a directly observable element within the series. Thus, unless it be admitted that we can have knowledge of aspects of human behavior which are not directly presented to the senses, we cannot understand his behavior and therefore cannot understand that which we seek to understand; i.e., those societal facts which supposedly are the summations of instances of behavior of this type. To this, it may of course be objected that we have learned to attribute certain intentions to agents on the basis of our own experienced intentions, and when this introspective experience is combined with our observation of overt behavior we learn to interpret human actions. Yet if this enlargement of our modes of knowing is allowed, there is no reason to stop with the facts of individual behavior as the building blocks of a knowledge of societal facts. Within our own experience we are no less directly aware of our own names, of our belonging to a particular family, of our status as youngsters or elders, etc., than we are of our own intentions. To be sure, our societal status must, originally, have been learned by us in a sense in which our intentions need not presumably have been learned. Yet, once again, we must avoid the genetic fallacy: the origin of our knowledge is not identical with that knowledge itself. Just as the concept of number has a meaning that need not be identical with the experiences through which it was learned, so the concept of a family, or of differentiated status due to age or sex, need not (even for a child) be identical with the experiences through which this concept was first made manifest. And to these remarks it should be added that once we have grasped the idea of status, or of family, or of authority, we can transfer this concept to situations that are initially alien to our own experience (e.g., to new forms of family organization) no less readily than we can apply a knowledge of our own intentions to the understanding of the intentions of those who act in ways that are initially strange to us. The problem of extending our knowledge from our own experience of others is not, I submit, more impossible in principle in the one case than in the other. And if this be so, there is no epistemological reason why we should seek to reduce societal facts to the facts of individual behavior. Only if it were true that individual behavior could itself be understood in terms of the supposedly "hard data" of direct sensory inspection would there be any saving in the reduction of societal facts to facts concerning this behavior. But, as I have indicated, this is not the case.

The third type of objection to the view I have been espousing is the objection that such a view interprets individual men as the pawns of society, devoid of initiative, devoid even of a common and socially unconditioned nature, conceiving of them as mere parts of a self-existing social organism.[7] However, such a view I have in fact already rejected. To hold, as I have held, that societal facts are not reducible without remainder to facts concerning the thoughts and actions of specific individuals, is not to deny that the latter class of facts also exists and that the two classes may interact. Those who have in the past held to the irreducibility of societal facts have, to be sure, often gone to the extreme of denying that there are any facts concerning individual behavior which are independent of societal facts. Such has not been my thesis. And it is perhaps worth suggesting that if we wish to understand many of the dilemmas by which individuals are faced, we can do no better than to hold to the view that there are societal facts that exercise external constraints over individuals no less than there are facts concerning individual volition which often come into conflict with these constraints.

Notes

My concern with the issues addressed in this essay, and in the two essays that follow, arose out of my dissatisfaction when, during the Second World War, I was called upon to teach part of an undergraduate course entitled "Social Philosophy," which approached sociopolitical systems such as Communism, Fascism, and Democracy in normative terms. I then started to teach a series of courses and seminars under the rubric "Concepts of the Social Sciences." My own interest in psychology, and the extent to which, at the time, psychology was taken to be the foundation for all the social sciences, led me to examine the issues that appear in each of this series of three articles, and led also to my concern with functionalism as it was being applied in the social sciences.

1. In this paper I shall not be concerned with the other social sciences.

2. The term *ultimate* may, of course, have other meanings as well. In the present paper, however, I am taking the irreducibility of a set of concepts to be equivalent to the ultimacy of that set of facts to which these concepts refer.

3. It will be noted that what I have termed our psychological language does not include terms such as *neural paths, brain traces,* etc. My argument aims to show that societal facts are not reducible to facts concerning the thoughts and actions of specific individuals; the problem of whether both societal facts and facts concerning an individual's thoughts and actions are explicable in terms of (or, are in some sense "reducible" to) a set of physical or physiological correlates is not my present concern. It will readily be seen that this is not the point at issue. Those who seek to reduce societal facts to facts concerning individual behavior are not attempting to speak in physical and physiological terms.

4. Cf. Chisholm, "The Problem of Empiricism," in *Journal of Philosophy,* vol. 45 (1948):512ff. (I am indebted to Roderick Firth for calling my attention to this analogue.)

5. When we consider the type of "irreducibility" which has here been claimed to characterize societal facts, we must be prepared to allow that it may not be the only type of irreducibility to be found among "existential emergents." (On the meaning of this term, which has been borrowed from Lovejoy, cf. my "Note on Emergence," reprinted above [ch. 5].) I am in fact inclined to believe that there is a stronger form of irreducibility than is here in question. This stronger form may be said to exist between, say, the color "red" and brain events or light frequencies. In such cases it might be true that even a partial translation cannot be effected. All that I have wished to show is that while it is undeniable that we can and do make partial translations of societal concepts by using psychological concepts, these translations cannot be complete: we must always use further societal concepts to specify the conditions under which the observed forms of societally oriented behavior take place.

6. In what follows I shall only be discussing human societies. The differences between "animal societies" and human societies are far more striking than are their similarities.

7. It is to be noted that some societally oriented behavior is only intelligible when interpreted with respect to *both* a societal concept and an individual's intention (e.g., in our case, of a person withdrawing money from a bank). However, other instances of societally oriented behavior (e.g., customary observances of age and sex differences) do not involve a consideration of the agent's intentions.

16

Societal Laws

In an earlier paper I argued that societal facts are not reducible, without remainder, to facts concerning individual behavior.[1] In short, I argued against one of the basic theses of *methodological individualism*. However, the issue of whether there are irreducible societal *facts* is not the main problem with which methodological individualism has been concerned. The main problem has been whether or not there are societal *laws* that are irreducible to laws concerning the behavior of individuals. I would uphold the view that there are, and thus would reject a second thesis of methodological individualism.[2] However, before arguing this point it is necessary to disentangle the problem from some of the misleading issues that have become associated with it. In my opinion, these misleading issues have arisen because it is widely and erroneously assumed that those who reject methodological individualism must accept a position that is termed *methodological holism*. It is the primary purpose of the present paper to show that there are in fact several alternatives to methodological individualism, and that not all of these alternatives entail an acceptance of "holism."[3]

I

Let us briefly review the issue between what has been designated as *methodological individualism* and what has been designated as *methodological holism*.[4]

The term *methodological individualism* seems to have been derived from Schumpeter,[5] and two of its chief exponents are Popper and Hayek. As is well known, the writings in which both of the latter have discussed the methodology of the social sciences have been works that have had a special polemical character: they were not merely discussions of methodology but were attacks on historicism, organicism, and social holism. For this reason, Popper and Hayek have tended to equate a rejection of methodological individualism with the acceptance of methodological holism. This oversimplified classification of alternative theories has now unfortunately become standard.

Reprinted by permission from *British Journal for the Philosophy of Science*, 8 (1957):211-24.

To illustrate the usual view of the dichotomy between methodological individualism and holism I shall quote a passage from J.W.N. Watkins' defense of methodological individualism:

> If social events like inflation, political revolution, "the disappearance of the middle classes", etc., are brought about by people, then they must be explained in terms of people; in terms of the situations people confront and the ambitions, fears and ideas which activate them. In short, large-scale *social* phenomena must be accounted for by the situations, dispositions and beliefs of *individuals.* This I call methodological individualism.
>
> You may complain that this is commonsensical and hardly needed saying. The trouble is that some philosophers of history have made the opposite assumption. . . . In the secularized version of [their] theory it is the social whole which so determines matters for the individual that he cannot avoid (or would be foolish to try to avoid: the determinism may be a little loose) fulfilling his function within the whole system. On this view, the social behavior of individuals should be explained in terms of the positions or functions of these individuals and of the laws which govern the system. These laws must be regarded as *sui generis,* applying to the whole as such and not derivable from individualistic principles. This I call methodological holism.[6]

In this passage it is to be noted that a denial of what is defined as methodological individualism is assumed to imply methodological holism. Further, methodological holism is identified with certain forms of the philosophy of history; it is not treated as a methodological principle that might be used by economists, political scientists, anthropologists, or empirical sociologists. Thus it is perhaps not unfair to say that in this passage there is a tendency to assume that the dichotomy between methodological individualism and methodological holism is equivalent to the dichotomy between an empirical explanation of social phenomena and the sort of philosophic interpretation which is characteristic of material philosophies of history.[7] What is more important, however, is that it is assumed that all so-called methodological holists view a social system as an organic whole, the component parts of which are individual human beings. This is not necessarily the case. Some who reject methodological individualism would regard the component parts of a social system as being the institutions that comprise that system.[8] Therefore, *if* they hold that the whole determines the actions of the parts, they are not necessarily arguing that individual human beings are determined by the society as a whole—though they may of course also claim this. And, finally, this passage clearly involves the assumption that if one regards societal laws as being *sui generis* (i.e., as not being in principle reducible to laws concerning individual behavior) then one must hold that such laws concern the society as a whole. In other words, a rejection of the principle defined as methodological individualism has been assumed to involve an acceptance of the thesis that, whatever societal laws there may be, these laws will concern the functioning of a society treated as an organic whole. It would therefore seem that anyone who wished to reject the *metaphysical* theses of holism in general (e.g., "the whole is greater than the sum of its parts") would be committed to accepting the *methodological* principle that has been defined as "methodological individualism."

The root error in all this is, I believe, the assumption that all who deny methodological individualism are committed to exactly the same positions as were those nineteenth-century philosophers who attacked the individualistic approach of the eighteenth century. More specifically, the tenets used to characterize "methodological holism" are precisely those which were held in common by Comte, Hegel, and Marx. This is perhaps understandable in the light of the polemical purposes that we have noted in Popper and Hayek, but it is important to see that a rejection of methodological individualism does not entail an acceptance of an organismic or historicist view of society. This will become apparent in what follows.

I shall proceed by drawing two sets of distinctions concerning lawlike statements. By combining these two sets of distinctions into a four-celled table it will be seen that those who accept the belief that there are (or may be) irreducible societal laws can be holding quite diverse views regarding these laws. Leaving aside those lawlike statements which seek to reduce societal facts to facts concerning individual behavior, a societal law could belong to any of the four classes that I shall distinguish. (At certain points it will become apparent that even these classes can be further divided into subclasses.) It so happens, however, that the theories most frequently discussed by methodological individualists usually fall into only one of these classes. Thus it will be shown that the dichotomy that is usually drawn between methodological individualism and methodological holism is an oversimplified and misleading classification of types of social theory.

II

The first of the distinctions that I wish to draw is between *a law of functional relation* and *a law of directional change*. (I shall usually refer to these as *functional* and as *directional* laws.) The distinction between these two types of laws, which are sometimes referred to as synchronic and diachronic laws,[9] can perhaps most easily be illustrated through reference to the physical sciences. Boyle's law or Newton's inverse square law would be examples of *functional* laws, while the second law of thermodynamics would be the outstanding example of a *directional* law. In the field of history the distinction would be between what I have elsewhere called "laws *concerning* history" and "laws *of* history."[10] Marx's theory of the relation between the economic organization of a society and other institutions in that society (his doctrine of "the superstructure") would be a functional law, i.e., a law *concerning* history. On the other hand, one may interpret his view of dialectical development as an attempt to formulate a law stating a necessary pattern of directional change in history, i.e., as a law *of* history.[11]

These two types of law are obviously different. While either would make prediction possible if we possessed adequate knowledge of the initial and boundary conditions of the state of affairs to which the law was to be applied, the first type of law (a functional law) would only enable us to predict immediately subsequent events, and each further prediction would have to rest upon knowledge of the initial and boundary conditions obtaining at that time. The second type of law (a directional law) would not demand a knowledge of subsequent initial conditions (though it would assume stability of boundary conditions), for if there were a law of directional change which could be discovered in any segment of history we could extrapolate to the past and to the future without needing to gather knowledge of the initial conditions obtaining at each successive point in the historical process.[12]

We now come to the second distinction that I wish to draw: a distinction between what I shall designate as *abstractive* laws and what I shall designate as *global* laws.

In an abstractive law the attempt is made to state a relation between specific aspects or components that are present in a state of affairs and to state this relation in such a. way that it will be applicable in all cases in which these particular aspects or components are present. In formulating such a law, the specific nature of the state of affairs in which these elements are to be found does not enter into the law itself, but is only considered with respect to the initial and boundary conditions that must be taken into account in applying the law.

On the other hand, it is possible to regard some entities in terms of their global properties, to consider them as unitary systems, or wholes. And it may be possible that when we so regard them we can formulate lawlike statements concerning changes in their global properties or concerning relationships between the nature of the system as a whole and the manner in which its component parts behave. In stating such a law we are considering the system as a system, and a reference to the properties of the system is included in the law that we formulate.

Now, in order to avoid an unnecessary misunderstanding, it must immediately be pointed out that the acceptance of a global law (or of the possibility that there are global laws) does not commit one to the position of "emergence," or to any form of "holism." Such laws might be held to be derivative from laws concerning the component aspects of the system, and thus be reducible to abstractive laws. To be sure, one might not so regard them, and in that case one would in all likelihood be accepting the position usually designated as "holism." Yet even this is not necessary. For example, if one were to hold that there are laws concerning the relations between one component in a certain type of system and the nature of any such system considered as a whole, and if one were also to hold that it is this component that determines the properties of the whole, then one would be formulating a law concerning the global properties of a system, and yet not be a "holist" in the most usual sense of that term: it would be a part that determines the nature of the whole, not the whole that determines the nature of its parts.

This last warning may help to elucidate the distinction that I have sought to draw between abstractive and global laws. The distinction is not one between nonholism and holism, but between laws that are formulated in terms of particular aspects or components that have been abstracted from a concrete state of affairs, and laws that are formulated in terms of the nature of particular types of system. In other words, there is a difference in what the laws are *about.* Abstractive laws are about the relationships between two aspects or components that occur in a variety of different concrete situations; the nature of the situations in which these aspects are embedded constitute the initial and boundary conditions that must be taken into account in applying the law. Global laws, on the other hand, are about the properties of systems, attempting to show how these systems change over time or how the system as a whole is related to its component parts.

III

We have now drawn two distinctions: first, a distinction between laws concerning functional relations and laws concerning directional change; second, a distinction between abstractive laws and global laws. These distinctions engender four possibilities concerning law-like statements, and if we now examine the theories of those who have rejected the principle of methodological individualism we shall find that social theorists have attempted to formulate law-like statements of each of the four types. However, methodological individualism has been almost solely concerned with a criticism of the attempt to find *global laws of directional change.* It has in fact tended to identify the view that there are irreducible societal laws with a belief in laws of this type. If we now briefly examine each of the four types we shall be in a position to see to what extent, if at all, each may properly be regarded as holistic.

1. Let us first examine the view that there are law-like statements that are both functional and global. Such laws would relate the global properties of a social system as a whole to one or more of its component parts, i.e., to its specific institutions or sanctioned usages.

As we have already noted, there are two main ways of proceeding in attempting to establish laws of this general type. On the one hand, we may regard the global properties as determinants of the properties possessed by component parts of the system. This is the case in Ruth Benedict's descriptive analysis of particular patterns of culture; it is also the case in Radcliffe-Brown's form of Functionalism in which the need for self-maintenance in a society considered as a whole determines specific usages, such as the punishment of criminals or funeral ceremonies.[13] Marx, on the other hand, would derive at least certain of the global properties of a social system (e.g., the defining characteristics of "feudalism" or "capitalism") from one specific component within that system, viz. the means of production. Others might seek to find a composition law by means of which, given the properties of two or more component parts of the system, the global properties of the system as a whole could be derived. All of these types of law would be instances of an attempt to state global laws of the functional type, i.e., laws that involve the relation of its components to the concrete nature of a system considered as a whole. I believe that it is obvious that not all of these attempts would be "holistic" in the same sense.

2. It would also be possible to attempt to establish laws of directional change concerning global properties. Such laws would not be seeking to relate the properties of a system as a whole to the nature of one or more of its component parts, but would attempt to formulate a law-like statement concerning the successive states of a system. In other words, a law of this type would be a statement concerning a pattern of directional change in a social system considered as a whole, e.g., that there exists a specific sort of unidirectional development, or a cyclic flow, in the overall aspects of a society. Such a law, of course, would not be intended to be merely a description of what has taken place in one social system during a restricted time interval, but would be held to be applicable at all times and with respect to all societies,[14] or with respect to all segments of one all-embracing historical process, viz. to the history of mankind as a whole.

A theory of history which is based on the belief in a law of this type would regard the overall changes that took place as being "inevitable." Furthermore, such theories usually regard the directional law that they seek to establish as being an ultimate law, i.e., one not deducible from functional laws concerning the components of the systems. Where this is the case, we may legitimately speak of "holism." However, we must note that such a law might not be treated as ultimate. For example, it might not be wholly misleading[15] to rephrase Marx's doctrine concerning historical inevitability to make it appear that the law of directional change in history is a consequence of two other laws: a functional law asserting that the global properties of a social system are determined by the means of production, and a directional law concerning changes in this specific component. Such a position would still maintain the thesis that there is a law descriptive of the direction of social change in all social systems, and it would therefore espouse the doctrine of historical inevitability, but it would not be an example of "holism."

The above suggestion is not intended to be a contribution to the exegesis of Marx, but is included for two other reasons. First, it should serve to suggest that not all doctrines of historical inevitability are "holistic," or (at least) equally "holistic."[16] Second, it serves to introduce the third general type of law with which we are concerned: the attempt to find a directional law that is abstractive in the sense that it is concerned with changes occurring in one component of a social system, and not with the social system considered as a whole.

3. Attempt to formulate laws of directional change concerning specific institutions, regardless of the societies in which they are embedded, have been very prevalent in anthropological and sociological theory. Among the

many examples it is only necessary to call to mind theories of the necessary stages in religious development, or in marriage systems; attempts to formulate a law concerning the tendency of language to change from a more complex to a simpler structure, or of the arts to develop from the abstract-decorative toward the representational pole (or vice versa). There have, of course, also been attempts to trace cyclical changes (and to formulate laws concerning the sequence of such changes) in political forms or in styles of art. Whether these directional laws regarding specific institutions have been unidirectional or cyclic, those who have formulated them have not usually viewed them as derivative from abstractive functional laws.[17] Rather, they have generally (but not always) regarded them as derivative from other laws of directional change. These more basic directional laws have usually been of either two kinds: laws concerning the direction of change in the total social system (i.e., directional laws of the global type) or laws concerning the changes in the nature of the human mind. By holding that there is a necessary direction of change in a society as a whole, and by holding that form of global law which states that the whole is so related to its parts that the parts are determined by the whole, a law of change concerning a specific institution follows. Or by holding that there is a particular pattern of growth in the capacities of the human mind, and by making the assumption that each institution will go through stages that reflect this growth, a law of change in a specific institution could be derived. These two alternative ways of deriving a law of directional change in a specific institution from some more ultimate law of change are not incompatible. They are not incompatible because it is possible to hold (and has often been held, e.g., by Comte and, in a sense, by Hegel) that the law of development which applies to the properties of society considered as one systematic whole is a reflection of the development of the human mind or spirit. This should be recalled by those who tend to regard holist views of the structure of society as being primarily due to the tendency to regard societal facts as different from facts concerning human thought and action.

4. The fourth possible type of societal law which follows from our distinctions would consist in the attempt to state functional laws of the abstractive type. Among the examples of attempts to formulate such laws we may cite the following: statements concerning relationships between modes of production and marriage systems; between size of population and political organization; between forms of economic organization and political organization; or, to cite a classic study of Tylor's[18] (which has been amplified and elaborated by Murdock in his *Social Structure*) between certain specific aspects of marriage systems, e.g., rules of residence and rules of descent.

It is to be noted that laws of this abstractive-functional type are different in aim from the laws of the other three types.[19] In being functional laws, they do not assume that there is any necessary direction of historical change, either within specific institutions or within a society considered as a whole. Furthermore, in being abstractive they seek to explain such changes as do occur in terms of the successive initial and boundary conditions that obtain at specific points in time, and do not assume that these conditions must be identical in all societies. In being abstractive they also remain uncommitted on the question of whether any particular society (or every society) can be regarded as a single organic whole; it becomes the task of empirical investigation to determine to what extent the various aspects of a given state of affairs *are* interrelated. Thus, those who hold that there are (or may be) abstractive-functional societal laws are committed neither to historicism nor to organicism, both of which have usually been held to be consequences of the rejection of methodological individualism.

IV

Without entering into the empirical and methodological issues that are involved, I should like to state that I believe there are important reasons for doubting that we shall find irreducible societal laws of the first three types.[20] Therefore I venture the suggestion that *if* there are empirically derivable laws concerning social phenomena, and if these cannot all be reduced to laws concerning individual behavior, those which cannot be so reduced will be abstractive laws concerning functional relations between specific types of societal facts. Whether such laws have been found, or whether we have reason to believe that they may be found, is not the question I have proposed for this discussion. However, before closing, I should like briefly to indicate the various possible relationships that might obtain between psychological laws concerning the behavior of individuals and laws that attempt to state functional relationships between specific aspects of social structures.

If one assumes that there are (or may be) laws that accurately express the functional relations between two or more specific types of fact in all societies (or in all societies of a specific type), it could be the case that these laws follow deductively from laws of individual behavior when one takes into account the conditions obtaining in the societies in question. This is the view held by methodological individualism that rejects *irreducible* societal laws.

If, however, one believes that there are irreducible societal laws, two positions still remain open to one. One *might* hold that such laws are themselves sufficient (granted the initial boundary conditions) to explain all that occurs in societies. To this position methodological individualists would doubtless be no less opposed than they are to a holistic view, because this view would also render human choice and human action nugatory in the realm of social affairs. On the other hand, one might hold that an adequate explanation of social phenomena would have to use *both* psychological laws and societal laws, and that neither of these types of law is reducible to the other.

There would, I submit, be nothing mysterious in such a claim.[21] When, for example, we wish to explain a concrete phenomenon of social history such as the failure of a particular soil conservation program, we need to employ psychological generalizations concerning human behavior, but we also need to employ generalizations drawn from the physical sciences concerning the effects of the conservation steps that were taken. In such cases of interaction between men and their physical environment no one, I should suppose, would challenge the belief that an adequate explanation of the series of events would demand the use of laws belonging to different sciences, as well as demanding a knowledge of the initial conditions relevant to the application of each set of laws. Further, no one, I should suppose, would argue that one set of these laws must be reducible to the other in order that we should be able to use both in explaining this concrete event. And I see no reason why an analogous situation could not obtain with respect to the explanation of social phenomena, i.e., that in such explanations we may need to employ both psychological and societal laws. A belief of this type would not entail the acceptance of historical inevitability, nor would it entail any form of holism. Finally we may note that such a view would not necessarily entail a rejection of the thesis that psychological laws are *always* relevant to the explanation of social phenomena. It could accept this thesis and yet hold that *in some cases*[22] a knowledge of the initial conditions under which individuals act, and a knowledge of the laws of individual behavior, is not adequate to explain the outcome of their actions: for this one must also employ abstractive-functional generalizations concerning societal facts.

The purpose of this paper has been limited to pointing out that a rejection of methodological individualism is compatible with a number of diverse views concerning the nature of societal laws. Therefore the simple dichotomy of methodological individualism *or* methodological holism stands in need of drastic revision. It seems to me that the classification I have offered may also help to point out frequently unnoticed similarities and diversities among social theorists, thus making an analysis of their theories somewhat more manageable. And if, as I believe, there are good empirical and methodological reasons to doubt the feasibility of establishing either abstractive or global laws of directional change or global laws of a functional sort,[23] then the issue of whether there are irreducible societal laws can be confined to one set of claims: that there are (or are not) some irreducible laws governing the functional relationships of specific aspects or components in societal life. The establishment of such laws would not demand that we accept the thesis of historical inevitability or the political and moral implications of either historicism or organicism. Nor would it commit us to either the metaphysics or the explanatory methods of holism.

Notes

This second in a series of three articles was written to show that some attacks (such as those of Popper and Berlin) on the belief in societal laws were only relevant to one of various forms that such laws may assume.

A later, more extended discussion of the differences between functional and directional laws, and of the abstractive character of functional laws, is to be found in my book, History, Man, and Reason.

1. "Societal Facts," *British Journal of Sociology,* 6 (1955):305-17. (Reprinted above [ch. 15].)

2. It will be noted that my view is therefore more radical than that adopted by May Brodbeck in her attack on methodological individualism ("On the Philosophy of the Social Sciences," *Philosophy of Science,* 21 [1954]:140-56). She rejects the view that there are irreducible societal laws (p. 155).

3. In a further paper I hope to show how societal laws are to be distinguished from psychological laws, and to argue on the basis of that distinction for the irreducibility of societal laws.

4. The most important recent formulations of methodological individualism probably are: the articles of Hayek which have been collected in his book *The Counter-Revolution of Science* (Glencoe, Ill., 1952); K. R. Popper, "The Poverty of Historicism," *Economica,* n.s., 11 (1944):86-103 and 119-37; ibid., 12:69-89 (cf. especially p. 80 and p. 88) and his *Open Society and Its Enemies* (London, 1945), vol. 2, ch. 14; J.W.N. Watkins, "Ideal Types and Historical Explanation," *British Journal for the Philosophy of Science,* 3:22-43, and "Methodological Individualism: A Reply," *Philosophy of Science,* 22:58-62. Also relevant is Isaiah Berlin, *Historical Inevitability* (Oxford, 1954).

Perhaps the most important recent attacks on the principle of methodological individualism are those of Brodbeck ("Philosophy of the Social Sciences," p. 211); M. Ginsberg, "The Individual and Society," in his essays *On the Diversity of Morals* (London, 1957) and "Factors in Social Change," in *Transactions of the Third World Congress of Sociology,* 1:10-19; E. A. Gellner, "Explanations in History," *Aristotelian Society,* suppl. vol. 30 (1956):157-76; L. J. Goldstein, "The Inadequacy of the Principle of Methodological Individualism," *Journal of Philosophy,* 53 (1956):801-13.

5. Cf. note 50 of Machlup, "Schumpeter's Economic Methodology," *Review of Economics and Statistics,* 33 (1951):145-51.

6. "Methodological Individualism," 58 sq.

7. This impression is strengthened by the passage omitted in the second paragraph of the above quotation and by much of the argument used by Hayek. (For a discussion of the nature of material philosophies of history, cf. my article "Some Neglected Philosophic Problems Regarding History," *Journal of Philosophy,* 49 [1952]:317-29. Reprinted above [ch. 6].)

8. This is also the view that I would hold. (Cf. "Societal Facts," 314-15.)

9. Cf. Goldstein's discussion, "Inadequacy of Methodological Individualism," 808 sqq. (It is to be noted that Goldstein does not deny the applicability of methodological individualism in synchronic studies, though I would do so.)

In an earlier article Edgar Zilsel referred to these as "temporal laws" and "simultaneity laws" and attempted to establish that both types are to be found in history (cf. "Physics and the Problem of Historico-sociological Laws," *Philosophy of Science,* 8 (1941):567-79). It would seem that Zilsel's position with respect to methodological individualism is essentially similar to that held by Brodbeck.

In his *Philosophy of Science* (Madison, 1957), G. Bergmann draws a distinction between *process laws* and *laws of development* which, I believe, corresponds in many respects to the distinction I have attempted to draw between functional and directional laws. (He also discriminates between these two types of law and two other types: *cross-sectional laws* and *historical laws.* The first of these is not relevant to our present problem; the second, as Bergmann shows, is in many cases reducible to a process law.)

10. "A Critique of Philosophies of History," *Journal of Philosophy,* 45 (1948):365-78.

11. It appears to me that Marx failed to see the difference between these two types of explanation and that the second type constitutes a survival of Hegelianism in his social theory. To be sure, there are passages in Marx which would make it appear that the pattern of directional change is merely the result of the forces that he attempts to analyze in terms of his economic theory and of his doctrine of "the superstructure." Nevertheless, it does seem equally plausible (at the very least) to maintain that he regarded the pattern that he traced in the history of mankind as having an inherent necessity in it, i.e., that it was "inevitable," and was not merely

the actual outcome of forces operating from moment to moment. (Even on the latter interpretation of Marx, there are two possible alternative interpretations: (1) that the inevitability rests on the necessary pattern of development in the means of production, particularly the technology; (2) that the inevitability of the pattern is an expression of the ultimate dialectical process in all reality.)

A somewhat similar confusion between laws *of* history and laws *concerning* history is present in Toynbee. His concept of *challenge and response* purports to throw light on the forces at work at each stage in the course of a civilization's history, but the pattern of change he traces seems to assume the shape of a quasi-inevitable directional tendency. In other words, the concept of *challenge and response* performs the same sort of function as a law *concerning* history would perform in a scientifically oriented theory, while his construction of the histories of civilization in terms of their stages is an attempt to show that there is an inherent tendency for the course of history to follow a definite pattern of development.

12. Cf. the method of Henry Adams. It is to be noted that in those cases in which a directional law is derived from metaphysical principles (rather than being empirically derived), it is not even thought to be necessary to assume stability in the boundary conditions for a society.

13. Cf. Radcliffe-Brown, "On the Concept of Function in Social Science," *American Anthropologist,* 37 (1935):394-402. (The specific illustration used is to be found on p. 396.) Also, "On Social Structure," *Journal of the Royal Anthropological Institute,* 70 (1940):1-12.

It is to be noted that Radcliffe-Brown's form of functionalism is to be distinguished from that held by Malinowski (after 1926). On this distinction, cf. Radcliffe-Brown, "A Note on Functional Anthropology," *Man,* 46 (1946): sect. 30, and "Functionalism: A Protest," *American Anthropologist,* 51 (1949):320-23. Also, cf. my paper, "Functionalism in Social Anthropology," reprinted below (ch. 18).

14. Of course, this may be limited to societies of a given type, e.g., to "civilizations" but not to "primitive societies."

15. Cf. note 11 above.

16. It should also be noted that not all examples of holism in the philosophy of history accept the thesis of historical inevitability, if by "inevitability" is meant that each stage in the development follows necessarily from the preceding stage. In Herder's philosophy of history, for example, the element of necessity is strongly stressed in each part of the process, but the process as a whole is not viewed as proceeding through an overriding necessity. (For example, cf. *Ideen zur Philosophie der Geschichte der Menschheit,* book 13, ch. 7.)

17. This is to be expected, because the attempt to formulate such a directional law of change with respect to a specific institution involves an isolation of that component from the other societal components that are contemporaneous with it.

18. "On a Method of Investigation the Development of Institutions; Applied to Laws of Marriage and Descent," *Journal of the Royal Anthropological Institute,* 18 (1889):245-69.

19. To be sure, the purpose for which Tylor, as a social evolutionist, used his data concerning functional relations was primarily the reconstruction of the evolution of marriage systems. It is also to be admitted that his explanations of *why* "adhesions" took place were often couched in psychological terms. However, he does not appear to have believed that such psychological explanations were alone sufficient to account for the facts (cf. "Development of Institutions," 248).

20. Some reasons for doubting each of these three types are implicit in my earlier article, "A Critique of Philosophies of History." I shall discuss the issue in detail in a future article.

21. I believe that Gellner is correct in thinking that many methodological individualists *would* think this "mysterious." (Cf. Gellner, "Explanations in History," 167-68.)

22. I should not myself be inclined to accept the more radical form of the doctrine here under consideration, viz. that in *all* cases this is true.

23. I am here only referring to laws of this type which are claimed to be "ultimate," i.e., not reducible to abstractive-functional laws.

17

Psychology and Societal Facts

> We must, therefore, consider social phenomena in themselves as
> distinct from the consciously formed representations of them in the
> mind; we must study them objectively as things, for it is this char-
> acter that they present to us.
>
> — Emile Durkheim
> *The Rules of Sociological Method*

Some years ago, in an article entitled "Societal Facts,"[1] I attempted to show that facts concerning social institutions are not reducible to
facts concerning individual behavior. This amounted to a rejection of what
is often termed *methodological individualism,* a position made familiar through
the writings of Karl Popper, J.W.N. Watkins, F. A. Hayek, Isaiah Berlin,
and others. In a subsequent paper entitled "Societal Laws,"[2] I attempted to
show that my position did not in fact entail those forms of holism and historical determinism which most methodological individualists have been
inclined to suppose it must necessarily entail. At the end of the latter article
I indicated that I would soon supplement my original discussion by attempting to clarify the relations between psychology as a discipline and the
nature and existence of societal facts. It is to this problem that I at long last
return.

It is all the more necessary that I do so because some of my critics have
claimed that I characterized psychology in so narrow a fashion that it
followed merely as a matter of definition that there are irreducible societal
facts.[3] Furthermore, the term *the behavioral sciences* has in the interim become
deeply entrenched; to many social scientists this term has come to suggest
that psychology and the social sciences cannot remain fundamentally distinct, with each having its own types of problems. The term first became
widely known through the establishment of the Center for Advanced Study
in the Behavioral Sciences;[4] and while I, like other former fellows of that
admirable institution, remain deeply grateful to it for aid and support, I
persist in what may be errors, still wishing to draw a distinction between

Reprinted by permission from *Logic, Laws, and Life,* edited by Robert G. Colodny (Pittsburgh,
Penn.: University of Pittsburgh Press, 1977).

the science of psychology and the systematic exploration and explanation of societal facts.

I shall lay the groundwork for this discussion by briefly considering the question of what constitutes the province of psychology. I shall then offer suggestions as to the status of societal facts, indicating the reasons why they are not to be identified with those aspects of individual behavior with which psychologists are concerned. Finally, I shall suggest that, in spite of these differences, an independent science of psychology helps to explain social institutions and some of the changes that they undergo.

I

As is well known, earlier characterizations of psychology had designated it as the science either of *mind* or of *consciousness*, but more recently it has most often been characterized as the science of *behavior*.[5] The widespread influence of the behaviorist movement has undoubtedly done much to promote such a definition, but it should be noted that a willingness to define psychology with reference to the concept of behavior is by no means confined to behaviorists. For example, in spite of their sharp opposition to the behaviorist movement, both William McDougall and Kurt Koffka chose to define psychology in terms of behavior, and McDougall had done so well before behaviorism, as a movement, had even arisen.[6] For my present purposes it will be simplest to accept such a characterization of the general province of psychology, although nothing crucial to my argument hinges on the point. What I wish first to do is inquire into the subject matter of *social* psychology, that is, into that branch, area, or field of the science of behavior which seeks to understand and explain the principles of social behavior. This question is obviously related to the topic of this essay, which is the relation of psychology to societal facts.

Although most of the issues with which social psychologists are concerned have a long history, it is not unusual to take 1908 as the date of the first attempts to transform it into a special area of investigation, for that was the year in which two texts in the field appeared: E. A. Ross's *Social Psychology* and William McDougall's *Introduction to Social Psychology*.[7] These two works adopted quite different views as to the nature of the discipline. At the time, McDougall held that all phases of human social life ultimately rest on the instinctive characteristics of men; his social psychology consisted in showing how these instinctive behavioral capacities were the foundations of the institutions characteristic of organized social life.[8] Thus, although his instinctivist approach to psychology, with its reliance upon evolutionary theory and comparative psychology, was relatively novel, his basic concerns within social psychology were wholly traditional: he wanted to discover what traits of human nature made man a social animal with capacities to create such patterns of organized life as the family, tribal organization, systems of law, religion, and so forth. The province McDougall assigned to social psychology was simply one of tracing out these connections. He assumed that once it had been shown that this was possible, it would be acknowledged that all of the other sciences that dealt with social institutions — among which he listed ethics, economics, political science, philosophy of history, sociology, and cultural anthropology—depend for their proper advancement upon the results of the science of psychology.[9]

In contrast to this approach, Ross held that social psychology had a special subject matter of its own, and that it had to proceed empirically, through directly examining each of the problems that arose within the area of its concern. In defining this area, he excluded the study of the structures of social organization, for that study he reserved for sociology. He also excluded from social psychology the behavior of individuals as individuals. Instead, Ross held that the proper province of social psychology lay in the interactions among men, and more particularly in understanding what he referred to as "the psychic planes and currents that come into existence among men in consequence of their interaction."[10] In speaking of these "planes," Ross had in mind the ways in which social interaction operates in bringing about shared actions, experience, attitudes, and beliefs; in speaking of "currents," he wished to call attention to the possibility of following patterns of change that occur within these relationships. His meaning becomes somewhat clearer when we note the key role played by *suggestibility* in his analyses. Suggestibility involves interpersonal relationships, and on the basis of suggestibility he analyzed such phenomena of interaction as crowd behavior, custom, the various ways in which beliefs and attitudes are transmitted, and so forth. All of these, in his view, were the special materials with which he thought that social psychology, as distinct from other disciplines, should deal. Thus, comparing the approaches of Ross and McDougall, it is obvious that from its very inception there were alternative views regarding the nature of social psychology, and these were connected with alternative views concerning its connection with the social sciences generally.[11]

The question of how social psychology is related to other disciplines, including other aspects of psychology, still remains an issue of major theoretical importance. Indeed, it has become even more difficult to handle because the types of problems which are now generally taken to be problems in social psychology have multiplied and at present cover a much greater range than was formerly the case. This is evident in the number of subspecialties that have developed within the general area designated as "social psychology." Nevertheless, in the period following the textbooks of Ross and McDougall, the definition of the field became fairly well standardized;[12] and in spite of recent changes in interest there has been relatively little disagreement among social psychologists as to what gives unity to their endeavors: a common concern with analyzing *the behavior of individuals in their interpersonal relationships.*[13] In other words, the subject of *social* psychology, like that of all psychology, is taken to be the behavior of individuals, but it is specifically designated as social because it is concerned with the ways in which persons interact, rather than analyzing whatever other responses an individual makes to his environment. While interactions between persons may include some factors, such as imitation, which are not as a rule present in other cases of individual behavior, the social psychologist must also be concerned with aspects of behavior with which other psychologists deal. For example, problems of perception and of the relation of perception to the nature of the stimulus, factors determining motivation, the effects of past experience on behavior, the analysis of emotional response, and so forth are of concern to psychologists generally, whether or not they are dealing with behavior that is responsive to the presence of another person. Therefore, it might seem (and has seemed to some) that social psychology is only a matter of applying the general principles of behavior to a special class of instances.

It is precisely here that important methodological questions concerning the relations between social psychology and other psychological investigations arise. In opposition to those who would hold that social-psychological questions should always be handled in terms of general principles that have been established without reference to the special data of interpersonal relationships, one *might* argue that an adequate general psychology that is applicable to human beings can never afford to neglect the factors present in interpersonal relationships. Therefore, one had better start from social psychology, applying the principles derived from these cases to all cases.[14] In defense of this alternative, it might be argued—as has sometimes been done—that insofar as human subjects are used in experiments, the responses elicited in *any* situation will be affected by socially acquired norms, and thus social-psychological concepts are presumably applicable even in experiments where no interpersonal relationships seem to be involved. Or, in opposition to either of these points of view, one might attempt to argue that the problems of social psychology should not be apprehended "from below," nor should cases in which there are no clear interpersonal relationships present be interpreted "from the top down," as if they inevitably did involve such relationships;[15] instead, it could be argued that social psychology should be regarded as a discipline emergent from general psychology, based on the principles applicable to all psychological processes but also possessing a subject matter of its own, and being capable of discovering laws of its own.[16]

I am here interested only in pointing out these possibilities. For my own present purposes the crucial question is not how social psychology may be related to other psychological investigations, but how it is related to the materials with which other social sciences, such as cultural anthropology, deal. In approaching this question it is necessary to recall that social psychology, like general psychology, is concerned with the explanation of the behavior of individuals; more specifically, it is concerned with whatever factors explain the nature of that behavior in those cases which involve interpersonal relationships. Because our lives are lived in organized societies that function only insofar as individuals act and react with respect to one another, we are constantly involved in interpersonal relationships; consequently, it is easy to suppose that social psychology will in fact constitute the single most basic science of society, as McDougall had held. Yet this is precisely the contention I wish to deny; what I wish to show is that the relations between social psychology and the other social sciences are quite different and somewhat more complicated.

As a first step in this direction I wish to point out that even though it is natural for us to identify the field of social psychology with the behavior of individuals in organized social groups, there are other, more primitive situations in which we can observe, and in which we must seek to explain, the interacting behavior of two or more individuals. For example, there is a social psychology of animal behavior, such as the establishment of territorial boundaries in birds, the pecking order of fowl, the mating behavior of seals, or—most obviously in our own everyday life—the behavior of our domestic pets in their encounters with others of their species and in their relations to us. All of these examples of social behavior among animals take place without reference to the organized routines of societal life.

Furthermore, in the case of humans there also are situations in which the roles and expectations that reflect the structure of a society are not the dominant factors in interpersonal relationships. For example, this is the case during the early stages of socialization in the life of the child, for the ways in which a child responds to the presence of adults (as distinct from the behavior of adults toward the child) *must* depend upon factors that cannot have been acquired initially through society, because socialization itself depends upon them. Among the factors that are important in the processes of socialization, as one can see in such studies as *The Ape and the Child* by W. N. and L. A. Kellogg, there are some that involve what might be called a differential responsiveness to *behavior*; that is, both the ape and the child responded differently to each other, and especially toward their experimenter-parents, than they did with respect to other features in the environment. Thus, forces of a specifically social-psychological nature are operative in early behavior, and it is largely on the basis of them that training proceeds. However, these traits do not simply disappear in adult life: we respond differently according to the ways in which others respond to us, and traits, such as unconscious imitation, which are clearly important in the socialization of the child, are present in adult behavior as well. Therefore, it should not be assumed that, in investigating interpersonal behavior, the social psychologist is necessarily studying relationships for which the institutional structures of a society are responsible; in some cases at least, he is dealing with a different stratum of behavior. This difference can perhaps be expressed by saying that the social psychologist investigates behavior from the point of view of how responsive interaction takes place among *individuals*, rather than investigating the sociological questions of how various *roles* are related in the organized life of a society.

This point can also be made with respect to phenomena such as leadership and group formation. While, under normal circumstances, the ways in which persons interact are circumscribed and channeled by socially ascribed roles and resulting expectations, it is possible under experimental conditions to reduce the effect of these factors to a minimum. This has, for example, been done in psychodynamics experiments such as those conducted at Bethel, Maine, where leadership and group formation were studied in what, from a sociological point of view, must be called "empty environments." Because these environments were sociologically unstructured, it would be a mistake to expect (as sometimes seemed to be expected) that the results of such experiments could be directly transposed into the context of everyday life, because in everyday life socially ascribed roles *do* profoundly influence behavior. However, it would be surprising if the factors influencing leadership and group formation under these special conditions did not have an influence upon the dynamics of groups when sociological factors are also present. In fact, there seems to be sufficient evidence drawn from other studies in group dynamics to say that this natural expectation is often fulfilled. What may seem strange is that I should be using this example and that of the socialization of the child as my first step in attempting to show that social psychology is *not* to be considered as the single most basic science of society, because in both examples I have tried to make clear that social psychology investigates factors in interpersonal behavior which do not themselves derive from facts concerning social organization. That my argument is not odd can quickly be made clear.

In showing that there are factors determining interpersonal behavior which are *not* sociologically generated variables, and that these factors are presumably important in understanding personal interactions wherever they are found, I am indicating that the province of social psychology, as an explanatory discipline, does not cover the whole range of those factors to which one must appeal in attempting to explain why, in organized societies, interpersonal relations take the forms that they do. Social psychology does not cover the whole range of these factors precisely because its principles are relevant to *all* interpersonal relationships, including those in which sociological factors fail to play any role. To explain behavior in which the latter factors *do* play a role demands the introduction of concepts that fall outside the scope of social-psychological analyses. As we shall see, these factors are not themselves instances of interpersonal behavior: they serve to structure such behavior without being identical with it. Showing that it is not arbitrary to suppose that this is the case will constitute the next step in the present argument.

II

It should now be familiar, through the writings of Ludwig Wittgenstein and others, that rules and conventions may serve to control human actions without our identifying these rules with the specific behavioral acts they govern. The knight's move in chess and what makes up a home run in baseball are components of the structure of particular games. While the acts

performed by individual players have reference to the rules that are definitive of these games, the rules cannot be identified with the performances of
those whose behavior they regulate. I shall soon use this as an analogy in
order to help clarify my own position. In the meantime, however, I wish to
take note of the fact that some social theorists have used the notion of rule-
governed behavior not merely as *an analogy* that can be helpful in characterizing the nature of social organization; instead, they have *identified* the
structure of a society with the rule-governed behavior of the individuals
within that society.[17] This is an equation I wish to reject.

It is, of course, easy to see that there are many ways in which the functioning of a society is dependent upon the fact that individuals do behave
according to common rules. Unless they followed rules, and unless much of
their behavior were governed by these rules, no consistent pattern of interaction would come into existence, and there would be no societies. In this
connection we may note that, as others have pointed out, a society is not like
an object such as an automobile, which is made up of parts that exist whether
or not they are functioning. The existence of a society is inseparable from
the ongoing functions that individuals perform.[18] Let us refer to the common
ways of doing things as *practices*, stressing the fact that a practice is simply a
widely shared way in which the individuals of a particular society behave.
Let us also note that the consistency and the stability of many practices
depend upon the fact that these practices are governed by specific rules that
people learn, and that they accept. In such a view, a language can be regarded as a rule-governed practice, as can other socially acquired skills,
such as gardening, basket-weaving, canoe-making, healing, and the like.
Given the prevalence of such rule-governed ways of behaving, it might
seem as if one could describe any society in terms of the particular system of
practices engaged in by those who live in that society. In such a description,
sociologists and anthropologists would be expected to analyze the nature of
a society, and of any changes occurring within it, in terms of the interrelated
rule-guided activities of individuals.[19] However, that is precisely the view I
wish to reject, and I shall now briefly point out certain difficulties in it.

In the first place, and most obviously, there are some factors that are
important in analyzing the structure and functioning of a society which are
not themselves instances of rule-guided behavior. For example, any anthropologist must take into account the size and density of a population and the
resources in land and water available to those inhabiting a particular territory. To be sure, factors of this kind may themselves be affected by rule-
governed practices, as size of population is affected by female infanticide, or
as irrigation alters the availability of arable land. However, regardless of
the ways in which these factors are to be explained, the actual size and
density of a population, and the resources available at any time, are not
themselves *practices*. Nonetheless, they do affect practices—including, perhaps, the fact that a society begins to practice, and continues to practice,
female infanticide, or employs irrigation to develop the land. Therefore, if

one attempted to analyze societies in terms of rule-governed interactions of individuals *only,* what is characteristic in these practices, and the changes which they undergo, would in many cases (and perhaps in most cases) be left unexplained.

This situation obtains not merely with respect to factors such as size of population or available resources, which might in some sense be regarded as nonsocial, "physical" factors; it applies in other instances as well. For example, a tribe may come into contact with a neighboring tribe and may develop magical practices and warlike practices that it takes to be essential to its own defense. In such cases, what is involved is the initiation of a new set of internal practices because of fear of some external factor, and the new practices based on such fears may then affect other practices of the tribe.[20] Thus, just as the soil and the climate or the size and the density of a population affect various features of the life of a society, so too may the presence of neighboring societies. Therefore, in accounting for a particular set of practices and the changes that various practices undergo, one cannot simply describe the ways in which the individuals within a society interact with one another: one source of their practices will be found in beliefs, expectations, hopes, and fears connected with the environment in which they live. The importance of this fact becomes particularly evident when we note that the external environment is not always regarded in a merely naturalistic way; in many cases it is viewed as including all manner of supernatural powers or forces. Thus, if we are to understand the actual practices of a society—that is, the ordered ways in which individuals interact with one another in obtaining their food, constructing their shelters, ensuring their crops, and warding off their enemies—we must take into account what, for want of a better term, I shall call the *representations* they share.[21]

While the shared representations to which I have thus far called attention have been beliefs, expectations, hopes, and fears that were specifically connected with various aspects of the environment, there also are other types of shared representations that help to account for the behavior of the individuals within a society. For example, there is an awareness of the expectations of others and a recognition of the sanctions that may be imposed for certain types of action. Only to the extent that such expectations are mutually recognized and widely shared are they effective in creating stable sets of relations within a society. The forms of behavior to which they give rise are those which, following present usage, I have designated as *practices.* What I find it important to recognize—and what is often not recognized—is that a distinction is to be drawn between the shared representations that govern practices and these practices themselves. As ethnologists have shown over and over again, if we are to understand a set of practices we must understand the beliefs, expectations, and other shared representations these practices involve. That this is true may be suggested by considering the situation in which one finds oneself when watching an unfamiliar game being played. In order to understand the behavior of those who are playing, one must come to understand the rules of that game, because it is with reference to these rules that their behavior is governed. It is at precisely this point that I find it helpful to draw an analogy between the rules of a game and the structural features of a society.

From the point of view of a participant, the rules of a game are not to be identified with his own behavior or with the behavior of those who participate with him in that game: the rules lay down principles to which the behavior of each of the participants is to conform. Thus, a set of rules is not identifiable with a set of behavioral acts, but has a different status. Such rules are what I have called shared representations. It is in terms of them that one participant can claim a foul against another and can argue whether the action of his opponent did or did not conform to mutually accepted rules. This situation parallels what is to be found in the laws of a society, whether these laws are customary or codified. Whatever the school of the legal realists may have contended, laws are not summary descriptions of the behavior patterns of any set of individuals; they are prescriptions as to how individuals—including judges and policemen—are to behave.[22] Even in those areas in which no established laws or rules exist and no well-entrenched customs have developed, the interaction of persons engaged in common pursuits depends upon their mutual expectations: these expectations govern their behavior and are not to be identified with it. Thus, throughout any society, the interactions of persons engaging in common practices depend upon what I have termed shared representations.

The fact that all expectations, beliefs, hopes, fears, and so forth are always the expectations, beliefs, hopes, or fears of *someone* entails the fact that even though these representations are shared, they are shared by individuals. Consequently, it is all too readily assumed that such representations are in some sense "internal" or "mental"; in other words, that they are to be construed merely as facts about those who recognize them. It is therefore commonly assumed that if one characterizes rules, or other shared representations, as "objective," one is treating that which exists only in the minds of individuals as if it existed elsewhere. The *being* of a rule, it might be said, is merely its being recognized as a rule. However, if this is taken as meaning that a rule is a fact about the individuals who recognize that rule, it is a badly mistaken supposition.

Consider, for example, an analogous case in which a person performs some simple arithmetical operation, such as multiplying two three-digit numbers. This is a mental operation involving a set of rules, but the rules are not themselves to be taken as if they were facts concerning the person who performs the multiplication; rather, they are recognized by him as having a status that is independent of him, and it is with reference to these rules that he performs the operations he does perform. To be concerned with facts about the particular person who performs the multiplication would be to ask, for example, whether he performed it rapidly or slowly as compared with other persons; or it would be to ask at what age, and under what conditions, he learned to multiply numbers, or to multiply numbers of this sort. It is also possible to be interested in psychological facts that are more general, such as how we are to account for differences in the abilities of children to multiply numbers, or what principles of learning are applicable to the teaching of multiplication in schools. Also, one may be interested in even more general psychological questions that concern the ability of human beings to deal with abstract concepts, to remember and apply rules, and the like. However, in these cases the rules—and their acceptance—are taken as given: the problem is not one of understanding the rules themselves, but of understanding something about individuals and about their ability to use these rules. Thus, remaining within the context of this example, we may say that psychology, as a science of human behavior, presumably has a great deal to say about such questions as how individuals learn mathematics; however, rules such as those of multiplication cannot in any sense be considered to be psychological principles or laws.

Similarly, it is my contention that psychology, although it deals with the principles or laws of how individuals behave under varying conditions, is not a science that has as its task the description or the analysis of those conditions. They are taken as *given*. Among the important given conditions that must be taken into account by psychology is the fact that human individuals are born into societies, are reared in societies, and that in these societies they are forced to learn the rules that govern interpersonal relations. It is my contention that, on the analogy of the case of mathematics, psychology can explain a great deal about how individuals learn rules, how they react differentially to rules, and the like. What psychology does *not* explain is the existence and the nature of those rules that govern the behavior of socialized individuals.

While it might be acknowledged that this contention is true with respect to other fields of psychology, some might wish to claim that it is not true with respect to social psychology, that the task social psychology sets before itself is that of explaining the rules to be found in social interaction. In order to conclude my argument I must suggest why this is not the case, and why, therefore, my contention also applies to social psychology.

Let me begin by admitting what is altogether obvious, that shared representations, such as rules of behavior prescribed in various types of situation, presuppose interaction among persons: without such interaction, rules would not come into existence, nor would they be learned. Thus, whatever general principles or laws apply with respect to interpersonal behavior will be of possible relevance to an explanation of how (through the interaction of persons) rules come into existence. For example, any general principles that can be formulated concerning relations of dominance and submission might be relevant here. Furthermore, social psychology may well be relevant to various aspects of the processes through which rules are initially learned, or how they are reinforced, or under what conditions their authority over the individual tends to increase or to diminish. However, one must immediately note that any principles that would be effective in answering such questions could not be applicable to one set of rules only, or to one society only, but would have to be of general import, applying under diverse conditions. It is at this point that one can see that social psychology will not provide an explanation of the host of diverse rules that characterize different societies, nor will it explain the subsets of the rules within a society which apply to persons who occupy different stations and who therefore function in different roles.

This limitation of social psychology as an explanation of societal facts may perhaps be made most clear by pointing out that when a psychologist seeks to account for the ways in which individuals behave with respect to one another in a particular society, he must understand the structure and the operative rules of that society and must know how—in societal terms —the individuals in question stand in relation to one another. To be sure, as I have already remarked, in some interpersonal relationships societal roles may not play a determining part, or may play only a minor part. However, for the social psychologist who is dealing with human and not animal subjects, societal facts must always be acknowledged to be among the *possibly relevant* conditions that are to be taken into account. In other words, societal facts may always prove to be among the initial conditions that it is necessary to know if one is to explain the behavior of an individual. As relevant initial conditions, they are descriptive data to which the general principles, or laws, of social psychologists are to be applied. When this is recognized one can see that it is no more the task of empirically minded social psychologists to explain these initial conditions than it is the task of a physicist to explain the existence of a particular set of initial conditions when he applies, say, the laws of mechanics to this set of conditions and deduces what will then follow.[23] The description of what constitutes the relevant initial conditions in cases of interpersonal behavior is not in most instances easy. However, when one recognizes that the situations faced by individuals in most of their relationships with others are partly structured by common expectations and by rules, the task of description is far less hopeless than would be the case if the only determining conditions of individual behavior were facts about the individual himself. Thus, the explanatory task of the social psychologist is simplified because societal facts help structure the individual's world.

If what has been said is true, there is no reason to suppose that social psychology can supplant ethnology and sociology as *the* basic discipline in understanding the behavior of human beings in their interpersonal relationships. However, there is also no reason to suppose that, on the contrary, sociologists or ethnologists can take over the social-psychological task of searching for general laws that adequately explain the behavior of individuals in their interpersonal relations. Nor do I see any reason to believe that a new interdisciplinary behavioral science is called for, in which culture and personality become hyphenated, and social psychology, cultural anthropology, and group-behavior theory become a unified science. In what follows I shall suggest a different way in which a social-psychological approach and a societal approach to human behavior may supplement each other without losing their separate identities.

III

In my article "Societal Laws," to which I have already referred, I argued that the attempt to establish laws concerning social institutions need not involve any objectionable form of holism or of historical determinism. I shall not repeat that argument here. However, it is relevant to suggest—although only briefly—how the existence of shared representations, such as rules, makes it plausible to assume that there are the sorts of societal laws that, in that article, I wished to defend. On the basis of what I shall say in this connection, it will also become clear that I attach more importance to the explanatory power of psychological laws than my emphasis up to this point may have led one to suppose.

In speaking of societal laws I here wish to confine myself to the particular type of law which, in the article cited, I was interested in defending. That type of law would attempt to show that a particular institution is always present with, and varies with, some other institution, or that a similar relationship obtains with respect to two or more aspects of a particular type of institution. Thus, I am *not* here concerned with whether or not there are general patterns or laws in history, but with the sort of law with which, for example, E. B. Tylor was concerned when he attempted to show with respect to kinship and marriage that there was a covariance between rules of residence and rules of descent.[24] I am not, of course, attempting to offer an explanation of the particular covariance that Tylor believed one could establish, nor am I defending the claim that he had established such a covariance. I am only interested in showing that—if what I have said up to this point is true—it is not surprising that there should be connections among specific sets of societal facts and that these connections might be formulable as societal laws.

Let us suppose, as I have argued, that behind any particular practice there do exist shared representations in the form of common beliefs, expectations, and the like. While a variety of different practices might be compatible with the specific nature of these representations, it would surely be true that other practices might not be compatible with them. Such practices would therefore not develop except in communities where other, quite different representations were to be found. On the basis of this assumption, one would be in a position to hold that even when two similar sets of shared representations were dependent upon very different originating circumstances, their consequences would be similar, and generalizations relating particular practices to specific kinds of shared representations might be found. In such cases, the historical question of how these representations might have arisen would be irrelevant to the formulation of a law, just as in the natural sciences it is possible to apply a law describing a functional relationship without first accounting for the set of conditions to which that law applies.[25] This, I believe, lends weight to the functionalist position in anthropology and to functionalist criticisms of a historical approach.[26] Furthermore, the possibility of establishing laws concerning the practices of different societies is not confined to showing that only certain sets of practices are compatible with certain types of shared representations; it is also the case that there may be direct relations of compatibility and incompatibility between various practices themselves. For example, if a specific form of agriculture is practiced in a community, the fact that a set of individuals engage in this practice may make it literally impossible for them to engage in various other activities, thus entrenching a particular division of labor in that society. In many cases such a division of labor will be reciprocal, so that if those who engage in one practice, *a*, cannot engage in some other practice, *b*, and those who engage in *b* may not also be able to engage in *a*. In such cases it would be reasonable to speak of *co-related practices*. In the case of such co-related practices it is obvious that a change in either practice, owing to changes in technology, in the size of population, or in any other factors, would in all likelihood affect the co-related practice. And because any one practice may be co-related to a number of different practices, the repercussions of a change in one may be felt in many aspects of the life of that society.

The type of hypothetical case I have been describing may justifiably be said to be very coarse-grained. Very possibly it would only be approximated in small communities with a relatively simple division of labor. However, the same point concerning the mutual compatibility or incompatibility of specific practices would be found in, say, a sophisticated monetary economy where the supply of money at any one time has repercussions on the practices characteristic of various segments of the population who borrow and lend money for a variety of different purposes. Laws concerning the relations among the variables within an economic system are (I suggest) examples of how co-related practices affect one another when a particular set of initial conditions is given and the relevant boundary conditions are assumed to remain stable. Thus, it need not be supposed that the only type of societal laws one may expect to find are those that concern the ways in which particular types of practices may be related to particular types of shared representations; it is also possible that various practices are co-related in ways that make it feasible to trace functional relationships among *them*. However, it is not my present task to develop this point any further. What I now wish to suggest in concluding this discussion of "psychology and societal facts" is that the existence of such specifically societal laws is not in any way incompatible with the fact that there may *also* be social-psychological laws that are of importance in understanding social organization and in explaining whatever changes a society may undergo.

In this connection it is first important to note that there is nothing surprising in holding that any given set of circumstances may demand that we use multiple sets of laws in attempting to offer an explanation of it. For example, in explaining the action of an internal combustion engine, one must invoke laws concerning the expansion of gases when ignited, the laws of the lever, of the conditions under which friction is reduced, and the like. One need not reduce these various laws to one another, nor to any one set of fundamental and all-encompassing laws; they can, so to speak, be intersecting laws that together explain the events that occur. Thus, it should not be surprising that in offering an account of the nature and the changes in any society one might have to invoke both societal and social-psychological laws. In fact, it would be surprising were this not the case. As we have seen, although it is a mistake to equate the shared representations according to which individuals govern their behavior with that behavior itself, still we are dealing with individuals who are aware of one another and who interact with one another in carrying out the various practices to which these representations give rise. Therefore, whatever general principles of interpersonal behavior social psychologists can establish will be applicable when there is an interaction among persons to carry on the practices characteristic of a particular society or of some differentiated group within that society.

Nor should we suppose that it is only social psychology that is relevant to an understanding of the behavior of individuals within the matrix provided by society. Questions concerning motivation, or learning, or the development of personality, can be expected to be relevant to understanding how a particular form of societal structure will affect the behavior of individuals. Bearing this in mind, it is not enough to insist, as I have been insisting, that even a completed science of psychology would not be sufficient to enable us to understand the structure of societies; it is no less important to insist that if we are to understand how the practices of a society are maintained we must also take general psychological principles into account, not merely seeking to discover co-relations among societal facts. These arguments lead, then, to a single conclusion: To gain any measure of concrete understanding of the nature and the changes occurring in any society, we must apply intersecting sets of laws to existing societal structures, seeking to delimit the psychological possibilities for action under those circumstances and establishing the psychological processes that may be presumed to be operative under such conditions. On the other hand, we must also recognize that psychological factors only operate under specific sets of circumstances, and the shared representations underlying societal life at any one time and place will provide a set of constraining conditions which those who belong to a particular society find themselves forced to take into account. Thus, psychological inquiry and the analysis of connections among societal facts proceed independently, but they must intersect whenever we seek to explain the concrete forces that are present within any society. Were one to seek a more all-embracing set of laws, more general than the formulations to be found in psychology or in the analysis of societal facts, one would be attempting to create that all-embracing social science that includes so much that it fails to allow us to distinguish among the various factors each of which, in its own special way, helps to explain those complex phenomena which the social sciences, taken as a whole, seek to explain.

Notes

This article, though not published until 1977, was presented at the University of Pittsburgh in a 1970 lecture series. It therefore failed to take into account some writings published in the interim.

1. Reprinted above (ch. 15).
2. Reprinted above (ch. 16).
3. See J.W.N. Watkins, "Historical Explanation in the Social Sciences," *British Journal for the Philosophy of Science,* 8 (1957):108n.; and Alan Donagan, "Social Science and Historical Antinomianism," *Revue Internationale de Philosophie,* 11 (1957):444-45.
4. Although there were a few earlier uses of the term *behavioral sciences,* it undoubtedly came into prominence with the founding of the center, which was sponsored by the Ford Foundation. According to Preston Cutler, the former associate director of the center, the term was used with reference to the future work of the center by D. Marquis and J. G. Miller during the planning conferences that led to its establishment. (Concerning immediately prior uses of the term at the University of Chicago, see J. G. Miller in *American Psychologist,* 10 [1955]:513-14. It is also to be noted that in *Principles of Behavior* [New York: Appleton-Century-Crofts, 1943] Clark Hull spoke of "the behavior sciences" and regarded it as possible to construct a systematic theory of behavior which would be foundational for "social" sciences [pp. 17 and 398-401].)

In the present announcements of the center, which suggest to fellowship candidates the areas of advanced study which are appropriate, no definition of "the behavioral sciences" is offered; there is simply a list of a wide variety of disciplines, such as anthropology, education, psychology, economics, philosophy, and so forth. However, in two earlier documents (the *Report of the Behavioral Science Division of the Ford Foundation* of June 1953, and a staff memorandum dated June 5, 1954, written by Ralph W. Tyler, the first director of the center), it is clear that a distinction was intended to be drawn between the behavioral sciences and the social sciences. Neither document attempted to state the distinction in rigorous fashion; each relied upon a few illustrative examples to suggest its nature. The two sets of examples are not incompatible, but they have little in common; consequently, their joint use is not particularly helpful in clarifying the original meaning which was to attach to the term *behavioral sciences.*

The fullest account of the introduction of the term, with an indication of its widespread adoption in recent literature, is to be found in B. Berelson's article "Behavioral Science," in the *International Encyclopedia of the Social Sciences.*

5. For an extended discussion of the province of the science of psychology, see my article "To What Does the Term 'Psychology' Refer?" reprinted above (ch. 14).
6. In 1905, in his *Physiological Psychology* (London: Dent, 1905), McDougall defined psychology as "the positive science of the conduct of living creatures" (p. 1); in 1912, he contributed a volume to the Home University Library series entitled *Psychology: The Study of Behavior* (New York, Holt).

In *The Growth of the Mind* (New York: Harcourt Brace, 1925), Koffka defined psychology as "the scientific study of living creatures in their contact with the outer world" (p. 4); in the *Principles of Gestalt Psychology* (New York: Harcourt Brace, 1935), he said:

Although psychology was reared as the science of consciousness or mind, we shall choose behavior as our keystone. That does not mean that I regard the old definitions as completely wrong—it would be strange if a science had developed on entirely wrong assumptions—but it means that if we start with behavior it is easier to find a place for consciousness and mind than it is to find a place for behavior if we start with mind or consciousness (p. 25).

7. As John Dewey pointed out in "The Need for Social Psychology" (*Psychological Review*, 24 [1917]:266ff.), the year 1890 might also have been chosen, for in that year William James published his *Principles of Psychology*, which called attention to some important social-psychological problems, and Gabriel Tarde published his influential work, *Les Lois de l'imitation.*

8. Later, in *The Group Mind* (1920), McDougall took a quite different approach that was nearer that of Ross. He had planned a further volume, which might have established the connections between the first two, but that volume was never written; as matters stand, his two contributions to the field are not contradictory, but they proceed on the basis of wholly different assumptions. (On this and other problems in the history of social psychology during the nineteenth century and the first two decades of the twentieth, see F. B. Karpf, *American Social Psychology* [New York: McGraw-Hill, 1932].)

9. *Introduction to Social Psychology*, rev. ed. (Boston: Luce, 1926), pp. 1-19.

10. *Social Psychology* (New York: Macmillan, 1908), p. 1.

11. Still another view was, of course, characteristic of Auguste Comte's position. Psychology did not exist as a separate discipline, according to him: individual psychology was a branch of biology, whereas social psychology was included within sociology.

12. For a tabulation of definitions of social psychology drawn from twenty-two textbooks published between 1908 and 1934, see H. Cantril, "The Social Psychology of Everyday Life," *Psychological Bulletin*, 31 (1934):297-330. His extensive use of references provides an interesting bibliography of over three hundred items published within the same period.

13. My remarks are based chiefly, but not exclusively, upon the following: David Krech and Richard Crutchfield, *Theory and Problems of Social Psychology* (New York: McGraw Hill, 1948); S. E. Asch, *Social Psychology* (New York: Prentice-Hall, 1952); Muzafer Sherif and Carolyn W. Sherif, *Social Psychology*, 2d ed. (New York: Harper and Row, 1956); David Krech, Richard Crutchfield, and E. L. Ballachey, *Individual in Society* (New York: McGraw Hill, 1962); E. E. Sampson, *Approaches, Contexts, and Problems in Psychology* (Englewood Cliffs, N.J.: Prentice-Hall, 1964); and E. E. Jones and H. B. Herard, *Foundations of Social Psychology* (New York: Wiley, 1967).

As one among several exceptions to my generalization regarding the definition of social psychology in terms of the behavior of individuals I should especially call attention to Daniel Katz and Robert L. Kahn, who, in the introductory chapter of their *Social Psychology of Organizations* (New York: Wiley, 1966), have explicitly taken note of the methodological issues involved. Their attempt to apply social-psychological concepts to the behavior of organizations, rather than to individuals only, resembles the approach of McDougall in *The Group Mind*; however, unlike McDougall, they avoid any semblance of speaking of organizations as if such organizations possessed mental traits.

As another, and earlier, exception the position of J. F. Brown should be noted. Although he defined the province of social psychology as being the investigation of "the behavior and reactions of the individual with regard to his fellow men, whether as other individuals or as groups" (*Psychology and the Social Order* [New York: McGraw-Hill, 1936], p. 3), and thus seems to be concerned only with factors influencing individual behavior, his actual procedure led him to apply his explanatory concepts, not only to social institutions, but to individuals as well.

14. This was the position apparently advocated by Dewey, in expressing the hope that the development of social psychology would exert influence on general psychology ("The Need for Social Psychology").

The position of George Herbert Mead also deserves mention here. While he admitted the independence of physiological psychology from social psychology, he regarded these two disciplines as parallel inquiries; all nonphysiological inquiries into mind or self he took to be dependent upon the basic principles of social psychology. Among his discussions of this topic, two may be singled out for attention: "Social Psychology as Counterpart to Physiological Psychology," *Psychological Bulletin*, 6 (1909):401-8; and *Mind, Self, and Society* (Chicago: University of Chicago Press, 1934), pp. 222-26.

15. I borrow these phrases from the introductory chapter of Gustav Fechner's *Vorschule der Aesthetik* (Leipzig: Breitkopf and Härtel, 1876).

16. A position of this general stamp would seem to be adopted by S. E. Asch in his *Social Psychology*. Particularly relevant are his first and ninth chapters.

17. The most extreme example of this seems to me to be the position adopted by Peter Winch in *The Idea of a Social Science* (London: Routledge and Kegan Paul, 1958), in which he conceives of all social relations as being expressions of the ideas men hold regarding reality (see, for example, pp. 23-24). His conception of the philosophy of science makes it unnecessary for him to argue for that interpretation through any appeals to matters of empirical fact (see pp. 17-18 and 20); yet it is nonetheless strange that he fails to inquire what can be supposed to shape men's ideas of reality in such a way that, at different times and places, different "forms of life" arise.

18. I borrow this contrast from Daniel Katz and Robert L. Kahn, who phrase it as follows:

Physical or biological systems such as automobiles or organisms have anatomical structures which can be identified even when they are not functioning. In other words, these systems have an anatomy and a physiology. There is no anatomy to a social system in this sense. When a biological organism ceases to function, the physical body is still present and its anatomy can be examined in a post-mortem analysis. When a social system ceases to function, there is no longer an identifiable structure (*Social Psychology of Organizations*, p. 31).

19. If I am not mistaken, this would be an implication of the view held by Alan Ross Anderson and Omar Khayyam Moore in "Toward a Formal Analysis of Cultural Objects," *Synthèse*, 14 (1962):144-70. After surveying alternative definitions of culture, they conclude that cultural objects should be defined as consisting of all, and only, things that are *learnable*. As they point out (pp. 165-66), such a definition focuses attention on such things as "propositions, techniques, values, rules, and the like," rather than on institutional structures, or other *products* that result from the fact that people act in the ways in which they have learned to act.

An analogous position may perhaps be attributed to Melville J. Herskovits on the basis of his discussion of "Culture and Society" in *Man and His Works* (New York: Knopf, 1947), ch. 3. It also seems to be implicit in David Bidney's view that it is only for heuristic purposes that facts of interest to anthropologists and sociologists can be treated apart from the activities of the human organisms on which they depend (*Theoretical Anthropology* [New York: Columbia, 1953], pp. 48-49, 106-07 et passim).

20. Concrete evidence for the internal relatedness of the various practices of a society was one of the major contributions of early functionalist theory in anthropology. On the history of functionalist views, see my "Functionalism in Social Anthropology," reprinted below (ch. 18).

21. It will be recognized that my use of this term has some degree of affinity with Emile Durkheim's concept of *collective representations*, and I gladly acknowledge that affinity. However, as will become clear, the unfortunate assumption of some sort of "collective mind" which has frequently (and with some justice) been attributed to Durkheim's view of *collective representations* has no place in my use of the term.

I also wish to point out that I am using *representations* as a technical term and am not borrowing from the notion of representation as that term has been used in discussions of art or as it has sometimes been used in epistemological theories.

22. The question of what brings about changes in custom or in laws, and in the interpretation and enforcement of laws, is not my present concern. These are the areas in which the views of legal realists may appear most convincing. However, it should be noticed that it is with reference to the behavior of *judges* and of enforcement agencies that they define the law, not with respect to the behavior of other persons in the society. Thus, from the point of view of the members of a

society (including judges and policemen), behavior is expected to conform to the law, and the law is not taken to be identical with the behavior it governs.

23. To be sure, both the physicist and the social psychologist may formulate for themselves the problem of explaining how a particular set of initial conditions came to occur. They may do so in terms of general laws. However, in *that* explanation they must assume another, anterior set of initial conditions which it is not their purpose to explain.

24. Tylor, "On a Method of Investigating the Development of Institutions: Applied to Marriage and Descent," *Journal of the Royal Anthropological Institute*, 18 (1889):245-69.

25. For a discussion of what I regard as functional laws I should like to refer the reader not only to my article, "Societal Facts," which has already been cited, but to my book *History, Man, and Reason* (Baltimore: Johns Hopkins Press, 1971), pp. 114-27.

26. I regret having failed to notice this possibility when I wrote the article "Functionalism in Social Anthropology," which I have already cited. While my present suggestion does not alter the particular criticisms which I leveled against the functionalist school, it would have altered the tone of my conclusions by showing that there are other respects in which the functionalist thesis can be of positive use.

It may also be that the assumptions I am making here concerning the relation between representations and practices, and the relations among practices that I shall immediately discuss, throw some light on the phenomenon of "convergence." For a brief discussion of this concept, see Alfred Kroeber, *Anthropology* (New York: Harcourt Brace, 1948), pp. 539-41.

18

Functionalism in Social Anthropology

Few philosophers of science in our generation have been as scrupulous as Ernest Nagel in taking into account the actual methods and the actual results of the sciences, and probably none has ranged so widely over the whole territory of contemporary scientific thought. These characteristics of his work, as well as its clarity, have given him unique distinction and have placed many scientists and almost all contemporary American philosophers deeply in his debt. To be asked to join in honoring him is itself an honor. Nonetheless, in what follows it will be my aim to suggest that in one case the model that he has given us has been misleading and, unlike his other analyses, has departed too widely from the methods and goals of those whose works it sought to explicate. To use the present occasion to bring forward this suggestion is not, however, perverse: one cannot have had contact with Ernest Nagel, nor with his work, without appreciating the extent to which, under all circumstances, he has sought to clarify issues and to do justice to theories, positions, and problems, following where the facts lead.

What I wish to propose is that the actual historical movement in social anthropology which has been called *functionalism* should be treated independently of questions concerning functional explanations in the biological sciences and independently of issues concerning teleological explanations. This proposal involves a departure from Nagel's position. In "A Formalization of Functionalism," and later in *The Structure of Science,* his analysis of functionalism leaned very heavily upon the analysis he had given of functional explanations in biology; and that analysis he first proposed in an article entitled "Teleological Explanation and Teleological Systems."[1] In this respect Nagel's work has been typical of most of the work done by philosophers who have been concerned with functionalism in the social sciences.[2]

It is of course true that those who sought to establish the functionalist position in social anthropology frequently called attention to parallels with biology, and similar statements are to be found among those who are gen-

Reprinted by permission from *Philosophy, Science, and Method: Essays in Honor of Ernest Nagel,* edited by Sidney Morgenbesser, Patrick Suppes, and Morton White (New York: St. Martin's Press, 1969), pp. 306-31.

erally identified with a functional position in sociology.[3] More specifically, it must be admitted that some of the biological parallels that have been drawn by anthropologists and sociologists do suggest a connection between functionalism in the social sciences and the acceptance of an organismic, or holistic, approach in biology. Nevertheless, not all aspects of functionalism draw on such sources. In the relevant literature many of the statements that suggest parallels between social processes and biological phenomena do so with respect to problems of adaptation and survival; however, a concern with these topics is assuredly not confined to those who adopt a holistic position in biology. Nor should such interests be interpreted as demanding that functional explanations be considered as examples of teleological explanations: it would surely be stretching the concept of teleology in a most unwarranted fashion to consider Darwin's theory of the origin of species as an example of a teleological theory.[4] Under these circumstances, it seems to me worthwhile to go back to two of the primary sources of functionalism, the theories of Malinowski and of Radcliffe-Brown, in order to see whether current discussions of functional explanations really conform to the types of understanding which were originally sought by those who looked upon functionalism as a new and more promising approach in the field of social anthropology.

The Functionalism of Malinowski

In Malinowski's earlier writings one does not find that *functionalism* is used as the name for a specific scientific theory of culture.[5] Yet, as early as *Argonauts of the Western Pacific* (1922), a quite definite theory of culture was clearly implicit in Malinowski's method, and he was aware of this fact. When, in the first chapter of that work, he was describing his own invesigative procedures, he stated it as his view that "an ethnographer who starts out to study only religion, or only technology, or only social organization cuts out an artificial field for inquiry."[6] And in the last chapter of the same work this point of view was made perfectly explicit, and Malinowski contrasted his own views with those of the previously dominant schools of ethnography. He wrote:

> We have seen that this institution [the *Kula*] presents several aspects closely intertwined and influencing one another. To take only two, economic enterprise and magical ritual form one inseparable whole, the forces of the magical belief and the efforts of man moulding and influencing one another. . . .
> It seems to me that a deeper analysis and comparison of the manner in which two aspects of culture *functionally* depend on one another might afford some interesting material for theoretical reflection. Indeed, it seems to me that there is room for a new type of *theory*.[7]

The particular theories with which Malinowski then went on to contrast his own view were the evolutionary studies of anthropologists such as Tylor,

Frazer, and Westermarck; studies of cultural influences by means of contact and diffusion, as represented by Graebner, Schmidt, Rivers, and Elliot Smith, among others; and studies, such as those of Ratzel, concerning the influence of the environment on institutions. It was Malinowski's conviction—and in this he was surely correct—that in the future a much greater role would be played by theoretical studies that, unlike those of his predecessors, took as their field of inquiry "the influence on one another of the various aspects of an institution, the study of the social and psychological mechanism on which the institution is based."[8] It is this view that I shall term the *early* functionalism of Malinowski, a view that defined both a method and a theoretical position.

One can readily see the connection that existed between this theoretical position and Malinowski's very insistent rejection of historical considerations in anthropology. When the interdependence of the various aspects of a culture is stressed, and when it is claimed that any attempt to understand these aspects singly constitutes a misleading form of abstractionism, then the diffusionist method of tracing the migration of specific culture traits must be rejected as inadequate: an understanding of any trait (or any complex of traits) is to be derived from understanding its functioning within its own particular context, rather than from tracing its migrations. Similarly, the attempt to construct an evolutional history of specific institutions would be misleading: it is the nature and functioning of these institutions in their actual contexts, and not their place in a linear temporal series, that is of ethnological significance. Thus one can see that the theory of functional interdependence was in itself sufficient to lead to Malinowski's rejection of a historical approach in his actual field work and in his theoretical orientation.[9]

That a stress on the interdependence of institutions within any given social context was in fact the basic postulate of Malinowski's early functionalism can be documented through the testimony of anthropologists who were, at the time, deeply influenced by him. For example, Raymond Firth's *Primitive Economics of the New Zealand Maori* (1929), which was dedicated to Malinowski and at numerous points gratefully acknowledged his influence, used this functional approach and explicitly rejected a separation of specific economic practices from their environing conditions. The same assumption was stressed—though perhaps less obviously—in H. I. Hogbin's *Law and Order in Polynesia* (1934), which was also closely connected with Malinowski's views, and for which the latter wrote a lengthy preface. For example, in his concluding summary paragraph, Hogbin insisted that there was danger in "isolating single aspects of culture from their context," and he stressed the view that Polynesian societies are to be regarded "as organic structures in which all the parts are interrelated." Furthermore, one finds in Gregory Bateson's *Naven* (1936) the following opening sentence: "If it were possible adequately to present the whole of a culture, stressing every aspect exactly as it is stressed in the culture itself, no single detail would appear bizarre or strange or arbitrary to the reader. . . ." Bateson then ascribes this point of view to "Radcliffe-Brown, Malinowski, and the Functional School": The "Functional School" is then characterized as having set itself the task of describing "in analytic, cognitive terms the whole interlocking—almost living —nexus which is a culture" (p. 1 f.).[10]

Bateson's treatment of functionalist views is enlightening in several respects, marking the confluence of a variety of differing but related functionalist conceptions. In the first place, as has just been noted, he was aware of what I have termed the early functionalism of Malinowski, taking this thesis as the distinguishing mark of all who might be said to comprise the Functional School. (As we shall see, Bateson was correct in regarding this view as also characteristic of Radcliffe-Brown.) In the second place, however, Bateson's own conception of the *ethos* and the *eidos* of a culture marked a step beyond the position adopted by Malinowski, a step that took him toward a view of cultural unity which one might designate as "organismic." With reference to this aspect of his thought, Bateson acknowledged the importance he attached to that specific form of a functionalist position which was adopted by Ruth Benedict.[11] He also apparently recognized that Malinowski's stress on specific institutions was at odds with an organismic interpretation of the unity of culture (cf. p. 27); and in this, as we shall see, he was correct. In the third place, Bateson noted that Malinowski's own thought had begun to shift (and in this context he quoted from the article "Culture" in the *Encylopedia of the Social Sciences*): he pointed out that Malinowski was coming to use the concept of "function" primarily with reference to the functioning of institutions in satisfying specific human needs.[12] In this connection Bateson indicated (quite rightly) that there was a fundamental ambiguity in the way in which the term "function" was being used (cf. pp. 26-27). Finally, we may note that Bateson also recognized that the primary stress of Radcliffe-Brown's functionalism was not merely an emphasis on the interdependence of the elements within a society but upon the contribution that each of these elements makes to the solidarity and integration of the group (cf. p. 29). A view similar to that of Radcliffe-Brown is present in Bateson himself, for he tended to lay stress upon the function performed by the elements in a culture in maintaining states of equilibrium (cf. pp. 108-109).

To pass from the first to the second of the points just singled out for attention in connection with Bateson's modification of Malinowski's own earlier views, we may note that in spite of an emphasis on the interdependence of the elements within a culture, Malinowski never looked upon a culture (or upon a society) as possessing a complete unity. The degree of pluralism inherent in his system is to be seen (at one level) in the emphasis he placed on individuality among the members of any society. In his criticism of the thought of Durkheim, for example, and most clearly in the major thesis of his *Crime and Custom*, Malinowski explicitly rejected the view that the members of a primitive society should be viewed as constituting a single group that was homogeneous in attitudes and in behavior.[13] In this respect he differed profoundly from Ruth Benedict's position, which had noticeably influenced Bateson. And he differed from her also in not looking upon a culture as a single whole. The focus of Malinowski's attention was always upon institutions, or upon what might better be called institutional complexes, in which human beings carried on multiform, interrelated activities. To be sure, these institutional complexes were intimately connected with one another in any culture, but Malinowski never (so far as I am aware) spoke in a way that would lead one to assume that he thought of a culture as being something different from these interrelated parts. And the focus of his attention was always on the parts.[14] Put more generally, the interrelationships of the various aspects of a culture were never of a sort that would (in Malinowski's view) lead one to speak of the culture as a single, supervenient entity different from its various, specific institutional aspects. In contrast, however, one may note that it was precisely such a view, which can appropriately be called an *organismic view,* that Ruth Benedict espoused. One typical theoretical statement from her *Patterns of Culture* runs as follows:

> The whole, as modern science is insisting in many fields, is not merely the sum of all its parts, but the result of a unique arrangement and interrelation of parts that has brought about a new entity. . . . Cultures, likewise, are more than the sum of their traits. We may know all about the distribution of a tribe's form of marriage, ritual dances, and puberty initiations, and yet understand nothing of the culture as a whole which has used these elements to its own purpose.[15]

In contrast to this position we may note that in Malinowski's articles in the *Encyclopaedia Britannica* ("Anthropology" in the thirteenth edition, 1926; "Social Anthropology" in the fourteenth edition, 1929) his application of what he defines as the functional approach proceeds through analyses of the functioning of what I have called institutional complexes, i.e., "Marriage and the Family," "Economic Organization," "The Supernatural," and "Primitive Knowledge" (viz. Language and Mythology). Furthermore, of course, the series of his studies of Trobriand life proceeds along essentially similar lines. However, we need not merely *infer* an opposition between Ruth Benedict's theoretical presuppositions and those of Malinowski concerning what constitutes a proper method for anthropological study.

In the first place, in his article "Culture" in the *Encyclopedia of the Social Sciences* (1931), Malinowski was perfectly explicit as to how a functional analysis of culture should proceed. As the following quotations from that article show, his insistence on the interrelationships of activities within a cultural context (an insistence directed against diffusionists, evolutionists, and those whom he in other places accused of "antiquarian" interests) did not lead him to deny the existence of institutional components, or units, within societies. In his view, functional anthropology is an analytic discipline, which seeks to understand cultures through the ways in which their true components function, and these components are institutional in nature.

This can be illustrated through a series of excerpts from that article, in which Malinowski's reliance on *analysis* and *elements* should be clear:

> Culture is a well-organized unity divided into two fundamental aspects—a body of artifacts and a system of customs—but also obviously into further subdivisions and units. The analysis of culture into its component elements, the relation of these elements to one another and their relation to the needs of the organism, to the environment and to the universally acknowledged human ends which they subserve are important problems of anthropology. (p. 623 b)

> The primary concern of functional anthropology is with the function of institutions, customs, implements and ideas. It holds that the cultural process is subject to laws and that the laws are to be found in the function of the real elements of culture. The atomizing or isolating treatment of culture traits is regarded as sterile, because the significance of culture consists in the relation between its elements, and the existence of accidental or fortuitous culture complexes is not admitted. (p. 625 a)

> The real component units of cultures which have a considerable degree of permanence, universality and independence are the organized systems of human activities called institutions. Every institution centers around a fundamental need, permanently unites a group of people in a cooperative task and has a particular body of doctrine and its technique of craft. (p. 626 a)

In the second place, we may note that in addition to Malinowski's insistence on the existence of genuine *elements* within a culture, the foregoing passages make clear another fundamental difference between his views and those of Ruth Benedict. (This difference brings us to the third point in Bateson's account of the variant meanings of the term *function.*) In these passages Malinowski speaks of "human needs" and of "universally acknowledged human ends." Ruth Benedict explicitly rejected Malinowski's views at precisely this point: she denied the existence of any set of human needs which is the same in all cultures, or—to put the same point in another way —she denied that there are any psychological invariants underlying the forms of organization in different cultures.[16] Malinowski's interest in such invariants presumably antedated the publication of his article on "Culture" in the *Encyclopedia of the Social Sciences.* For example, it was at least implicit in his willingness to generalize concerning primitive man in his 1925 essay "Magic, Science, and Religion," and its was assuredly present in his treatment of instinct in Part IV of *Sex and Repression in Savage Society,* which dates from 1929. However, it was his 1931 article on "Culture" that introduced the question of fundamental human needs as an essential aspect of his position, and it is this emphasis to which we shall refer in speaking of Malinowski's *later* functionalism.[17]

This later functionalist position is best summarized in a 1939 essay entitled "The Functional Theory," posthumously published in *A Scientific Theory of*

Culture, and also in the longer theoretical monograph that gave that volume its name. What characterized Malinowski's later position, as distinguished from his earlier statements of his views, is an insistence on relating institutions, which he always regarded as the genuine elements in a culture, to human needs. Among these needs there were some that Malinowski regarded as *basic,* and he held that most, though not all, of man's basic needs were rooted in biological factors. In addition to these basic needs, Malinowski held that a set of *derived* needs always arises through the operation of cultural factors. The general nature of these derived needs (though not the specific ways in which they are satisfied) is, according to Malinowski, the same in all cultures: as a consequence, one can find common characteristics in all societies. And it was with these common features and their relations to human needs that Malinowski's later functionalism was concerned. The details of his theory need not here occupy us. What is important to understand is that there is no necessary incompatability between Malinowski's later focus of interest and his earlier form of functionalist theory. Thus, it would be mistaken to assume that Malinowski's later functionalism superseded or altered his earlier position. Rather, it operated on a new level of theory, and it can be either accepted or rejected independently of one's acceptance or rejection of Malinowski's original position.

In order to see that there is no inconsistency between Malinowski's earlier and later views, one need merely recognize that he always viewed those institutional complexes which he took to be the genuine elements within culture as being characterizable in terms of reciprocal relationships between individuals. The notion of reciprocity was fundamental in Malinowski's analysis of gifts within the Kula cycle (*Argonauts of the Western Pacific*); furthermore, in his introduction to Hogbin's *Law and Order in Polynesia,* the same notion of obligations and counterobligations was taken to be basic for an analysis of primitive law. In fact, in that preface (p. xxxiii), Malinowski came close to defining the concept of "an institution" in terms of reciprocal relationships of obligation. He said: "From the point of view on which it is necessary to focus our attention at present an institution is nothing but a network, a closely-knit system of rules which define the mutual behaviour of partners in marriage, in parenthood, in kinship, clanship, economic cooperation, and so on."[18] Granted this position, it is easy to see that the institutions that are present in any society will tend to form a coherent and interlocking pattern of relationships, since if this were not in general true the individuals within that society would be caught in a trap of mutually inconsistent reciprocal obligations: they would have obligations they could not fulfill, and one or the other of the mutually incompatible institutions simply could not survive without substantial alterations.[19] Once we recognize that Malinowski regarded institutions in this way, it is apparent that there need be no conflict between the emphases that one finds in his earlier and his later forms of functionalism: the reciprocal relations that *are* institutions could be precisely those forms of relationship which fulfill a particular set of basic human needs. And this was, of course, Malinowski's position.

However, it is also possible that there should be no single set of basic needs that are constant, in the sense of being unaffected by the culture. In that case the reciprocal obligations, or systems of rules, in any one culture might differ substantially from those to be found in any other. In general, this might be said to have been Ruth Benedict's position. To be sure, she would not have denied that whatever set of rules did exist in any society would have to result in at least a minimal satisfaction (for a significant proportion of that population) of such basic needs as those for food, shelter, security, etc.: if a society failed to provide such satisfaction of needs it would, of course, simply cease to exist. And Malinowski sometimes made use of this obvious fact in arguing for his position.[20] However, such an argument is not only too weak to establish the types of cross-cultural invariance which he sought to establish; as we shall later see, it does not serve to define any position that can appropriately be designated as functionalism. What Malinowski actually attempted to establish in his *later* functionalism was much stronger: he held that there are definite types of rules to regulate reciprocal obligations in all cultures and that these types of rules derive from a specific set of basic needs that are common to all men, regardless of variations in their cultural inheritance. It was through the existence of such common basic needs that Malinowski, in his later work especially, sought to account for the types of rules which he held to be present in every society. For example, he sought to explain the negative, proscriptive rules that are directed against infidelity after marriage in terms of a basic need for sexual satisfaction in the marriage relationship; he also sought to explain the reciprocal obligations demanded of kinsmen and clansmen in terms of sentiments, such as those of friendship, which developed in social interaction.[21] As Malinowski made clear in his *Scientific Theory of Culture,* what he took to be the fundamental structure present in any society rested on a basis of common human needs. And it was because of the universality of these needs that he believed it possible to present a general theory of culture, which was applicable to all specific cultures, however variant their superficial qualities might seem to be to those who did not offer functionalist analyses of them.

We come now to the fourth characteristic isolated by Bateson as a variant use to which the concept of functionalism was applicable: the view that in any culture each element must be examined in the light of what it contributes to the solidarity, integration, and survival of the group. At this point the theory of functionalism leaves aside consideration of how various institutions satisfy specific human needs and considers these institutions in terms of the contributions that they make to the stability and survival of the group as a whole.

There is, of course, a possible connection between functionalism as thus understood and what we have termed Malknowski's early functionalism. The former position stressed the interconnections existing among the various institutional elements within a culture, and such a position is wholly compatible with viewing the functions of these institutions as contributory to the persistence of the group as a stable whole.[22] And it was (as we shall see) an emphasis upon this connection between the two theses which was definitive of Radcliffe-Brown's position. Or, put in another way, Bateson was correct in viewing Radcliffe-Brown as sharing Malinowski's view that all aspects of a culture were interconnected, and he was also correct in seeing that it was Radcliffe-Brown, and not Malinowski, who laid primary stress on the notion that a society as a whole was to be understood as tending to maintain itself as a stable, self-equilibriating system. This stress was not compatible with Malinowski's insistence that culture was to be understood primarily as a means of satisfying the biological and psychological needs of individuals, and the crucial difference between the functionalism of Malinowski and that of Radcliffe-Brown lies precisely here. Radcliffe-Brown rejected Malinowski's attempt to connect social institutions with individual needs and stressed instead the notion that a society has needs of its own to which its various institutional elements are to be related and through which they are to be understood. While Malinowski did not so frequently criticize Radcliffe-Brown as the latter criticized him, there is clear evidence that he too recognized where the difference between their two theories really lay. As he said in *A Scientific Theory of Culture*:

> Functionalism would not be so functional after all, unless it could define the concept of function not merely by such glib expressions as "the contribution which a partial activity makes to the total activity of which it is a part," but by a much more definite and concrete reference to what actually occurs and what can be observed. As we shall see, such a definition is provided by showing that human institutions, as well as partial activities within these, are related to primary, that is, biological, or derived, that is, cultural needs. Function means, therefore, always the satisfaction of a need.[23]

One finds only rare occasions on which Malinowski is willing to speak in terms of what might be considered as the needs of a social group as a whole,[24] and in this, as we shall see, he is fundamentally at odds with Radcliffe-Brown.

The Functionalism of Radcliffe-Brown

In 1922, the year in which Malinowski's *Argonauts of the Western Pacific* appeared, Radcliffe-Brown published *The Andaman Islanders*. In that work —which had been written some years earlier—he set forth the main contentions of his functionalist position, and they remained substantially unaltered throughout his career.[25] His basic theory had two main characteristics, in one of which he was wholly in agreement with Malinowski, and in the other not. This may be shown by separating into two parts a single passage in which he stated the conclusions to be drawn from his extended interpretation of ceremonial customs among the Andaman Islanders.

The passage begins as follows:

It is time to bring the argument to a conclusion. It should now, I hope, be evident that the ceremonial customs of the Andaman Islands form a closely connected system, and that we cannot understand their meaning if we only consider each one by itself, but must study the whole system to arrive at an interpretation. This in itself I regard as a most important conclusion, for it justifies the contention that we must substitute for the old method of dealing with the customs of a primitive people—the comparative method by which isolated customs were brought together and conclusions drawn from their similarity—a new method by which all the institutions of one society or social type are studied together so as to exhibit their intimate relations as parts of an organic system.[26]

Here it is obvious that Radcliffe-Brown is in accord with Malinowski: each stressed the interrelationships among the various aspects of a culture, and on this basis each rejected the current comparative methods, whether evolutionary or "antiquarian" (to borrow Malinowski's phrase).

Furthermore, Radcliffe-Brown was no less skeptical than Malinowski concerning the scientific value of attempts to trace the *origins* of elements in a culture: both maintained that the relevant question to be asked concerning any element in a culture was not one concerning its origins, but one directed toward establishing the role that element played in the functioning of the society in which it was found.[27]

However, even though Malinowski and Radcliffe-Brown laid equal stress on the principle of interrelatedness as applied to the elements of a culture, there was an important difference between them with respect to the uses to which they put this principle. In his earlier work, Malinowski regarded the principle as being explanatory in character. It was his view that the concrete nature of each element in a culture was determined by its interrelationships with the other activities carried on by the same individuals in satisfying their wants; therefore, in following out the interconnections among these various activities, one was in fact explaining why the culture had the form that it did. In Radcliffe-Brown's functionalism, however, the principle of interrelatedness was not regarded as having explanatory power. In order to understand the elements in a society it was not sufficient to view them in their relationships to one another: they served as mechanisms whereby the society as a whole maintained itself, and each element was to be understood through examining the way in which it enabled the system of which it was a part to function as a stable and continuing whole. As we shall see, it was precisely this principle of explanation which Radcliffe-Brown identified with the notion of function.[28]

That there was at this point a difference between the theoretical position of Radcliffe-Brown and the early functionalism of Malinowski can be illustrated through the succeeding sentences of the passage that I am citing, for Radcliffe-Brown continues:

> I have tried to show that the ceremonial customs are the means by which the society acts upon its individual members and keeps alive in their minds a certain system of sentiments. Without the ceremonial those sentiments would not exist, and without them the social organization in its actual form could not exist.

It should by now be obvious that in his analyses of a culture Malinowski did not tend to speak in this way. He did not treat a society as a quasi-entity that was to be differentiated from the activities of its members and that was capable of acting upon them through particular ceremonial customs, or the like. Given such passages in the writings of Radcliffe-Brown, it is clear why Malinowski linked the theory of Radcliffe-Brown with that of Durkheim and contrasted it with his own.[29]

Legitimate as such a contrast may be, it would be mistaken to suppose that Radcliffe-Brown rejected an appeal to individual, psychological factors in offering his explanations concerning the nature and functioning of social systems. This mistake has frequently been made because of the ways in which Malinowski and Radcliffe-Brown expressed their opposition to one another's theories and because Malinowski's thought is so often identified with his later psychologically oriented functionalism. Even though it is true that Radcliffe-Brown attempted to draw a sharp line of demarcation between "psychology" and "social science," he at no point accepted the view that one could establish laws of society which were not dependent upon psychological mechanisms for their operation. For example, in the passage just quoted —and indeed throughout *The Andaman Islanders*—the psychological concept of *sentiments* plays a crucial role.[30] This concept, made familiar by McDougall and by Shand, provided the sole link by means of which Radcliffe-Brown connected the existence and nature of ceremonial rites with the needs of society.[31] While most of his later investigations and theoretical discussions do not place an equally heavy emphasis on the specific concept of sentiments, in such studies as "The Mother's Brother in South Africa" (1924) and "On Joking Relationships" (1940), Radcliffe-Brown continued to appeal to psychological mechanisms when analyzing the manner in which particular social arrangements were able to function in preserving a social system. And in his Frazer lecture, "Taboo" (1939), he stated his conviction on this matter quite explicitly. He said: "Clearly it is impossible to discuss the social function of a rite without taking into account its usual or average psychological effect."[32] Furthermore, in an essay written as late as 1945, he again affirmed the view that sentiments are the psychological mechanisms through which ceremonial rites exercise their social function. In that essay, he said:

> Rites can be seen to be the regulated symbolic expression of certain sentiments. Rites can therefore be shown to have a specific social function when, and to the extent that, they have for their effect to regulate, maintain and transmit from

one generation to another sentiments on which the constitution of society depends.[33]

Given, then, the fact that Radcliffe-Brown deliberately used psychological concepts in offering functional explanations of the elements in a society, on what basis could he claim that a sharp line was to be drawn between psychology as a science and what he termed "social science"? The work in which one finds the most explicit treatment of this issue is *A Natural Science of Society,* which constituted a recording of discussions held at the University of Chicago in 1937. In them he presented the view that all theoretic natural sciences deal with *systems,* and that

> the social scientist and the psychologist are not concerned with the same system and its set of relations. The social scientist is concerned with relations he can discover between acts of diverse individuals; the psychologist with relations between acts of behavior of one and the same individual.[34]

According to this view, the raw data for both the psychologist and the social scientist were the same: each started from observations concerning acts of behavior. The distinction between psychological and social-scientific investigations depended not upon any difference in data, but upon the systems to which these data were related.

In speaking of "a system," Radcliffe-Brown referred to a complex organized whole, whose parts were so interrelated that one would alter their natures if one attempted to abstract them from the system of which they were parts. Thus, he frequently used the example of a human organism as a paradigmatic case of what constituted a system; but it was not, of course, with the human organism that he believed either the psychologist or the social scientist should deal. As the above passage suggests, that with which the psychologist deals are acts of behavior (including thoughts, beliefs, feelings, etc.), and these acts form the system that constitutes the mind of a given individual; the social scientist, on the other hand, deals with acts by which persons are related to one another, and Radcliffe-Brown assumes that such acts too form a system.[35]

Unfortunately, in discussing what were the elements or parts of the systems with which social scientists deal, Radcliffe-Brown was less careful and explicit than one should like him to have been. On the one hand he sometimes spoke as if the related elements that comprise a social system were individual persons, but he also spoke as if they were what he generally called "social usages."[36] However, in spite of possible misunderstandings with respect to this issue—which, as we shall see, is an important issue for the problems which concern us—I believe that Radcliffe-Brown did have a consistent position that runs through all of his works and that can be stated in the following way.

The data of the social scientist are drawn from observations of those acts of behavior which relate individuals to one another; therefore, the essential elements of a social system are individuals, and without human individuals no social system would exist.[37] Thus, in one sense, the units of a social system are individuals, and Radcliffe-Brown sometimes explicitly says that they are.[38] However, because it is not the task of the social scientist to relate the acts of any one individual to his other acts, it is not the individual as such who can be regarded as comprising a genuine unit in a social system.[39] Such units must be those acts which relate individuals to one another, and Radcliffe-Brown calls attention to this fact in saying that the units of a social system are "human beings regarded as sets of behavioral events" — namely as the behavioral events through which they are related to one another.[40] And when he is most careful in discussing the units of a social system, Radcliffe-Brown specifies another characteristic that such behavioral events must have: they must be recurrent.[41] Furthermore, we may say that his view demands that these recurrent behavioral events lead to continuity in the relatedness between individuals, because every system (according to Radcliffe-Brown's use of that term) must have structural continuity over a span of time.[42] The acts that fulfill these conditions are referred to by Radcliffe-Brown as "*social usages*," and of them he says:

> A social usage is not merely a common mode of behavior. . . . [It] always involves a rule of behavior: there are proper or appropriate ways of behaving under certain circumstances. . . . A social usage is more than simply something which people do. A, B, and C make bows; D recognizes that that is the way to make a bow. The fact (1) that some or many people observe it, and (2) the fact that a large number of people recognize it as a rule constitutes the reality of a social usage.[43]

It is through such usages that individuals are related to one another in persisting social systems. As Radcliffe-Brown put the matter:

> It is the structural form of the society which the social scientist has to describe. (One might call that form "non-mental" or "super-psychic" if one liked.) It [the structural form] is explicit in the social usages.[44]

For this reason it is proper to consider social usages as the specific units whose interrelationships form a social system.

In this connection there is one final point to be noted, and that is the stress that Radcliffe-Brown placed on the fact that the total set of social usages form a single, coherent system. As we have noted, he shared with Malinowski an acceptance of the principle of interrelatedness: that the various elements of a culture affect one another. When translated into terms of social usages, this principle demanded that the specific, repeated forms of behavior evinced by individuals in their relations to one another form a coherent pattern, and it was to this principle that Radcliffe-Brown referred when he discussed "the functional consistency of social systems."[45] That there is functional consistency within any particular system implies that (in the long run) various social usages cannot be in conflict with one another. However, Radcliffe-Brown pointed out that in addition to this minimal form of consistency, in most societies these usages react upon each other and reinforce one another, thus leading to a marked degree of integration within the social system.[46]

Having defined Radcliffe-Brown's position with respect to the elements that enter into and form the nature of a social system, we are in a better position to understand what he was claiming when he insisted that the elements of such a system were to be understood through understanding their functions in maintaining the coherence and continuity of that system as a whole. When he says, as he did in *The Andaman Islanders,* "Every custom and belief of a primitive society plays some determinate part in the social life of the community, just as every organ of a living body plays some part in the general life of the organism,"[47] this is not to be understood as signifying that there is, so to speak, some selective power in the society as a whole which accepts or rejects specific beliefs and customs, only allowing those to continue which are of benefit to it. Customs and beliefs are social usages, and no such usage can long persist if it stands in conflict with other usages that are present within the system. It is in this sense that the system as a whole may be said to "select" or to "reject" particular forms of behavior. Bearing this interpretation in mind, one need not read Radcliffe-Brown as if he were holding that a social system, considered as a whole, exercises a selective power and control over each of its components, in some way guiding them for its own good.[48]

To be sure, one may wish to criticize Radcliffe-Brown's theory for having failed to indicate that the relationship between *some* elements and the functioning of the system as a whole is a very indirect relationship (as is also the case with respect to some features of organic systems). Were such a criticism justified (as I believe it to be), it would considerably weaken Radcliffe-Brown's contention that the proper way to understand *every* social usage is through relating it to the role which it plays in maintaining the coherence and the continuity of the system as a whole.[49] One might also wish to criticize him (as has often been done, and as I should be inclined to do) for having overstressed the elements of coherence and continuity in social systems, and for having failed to see how various institutions may change radically, and even suddenly, and alter the system in more drastic ways than he was inclined to take into account.[50] Yet, such possible criticisms do not suggest that his view of the relationships among the elements in a social system rested on false analogies to biological systems or on methodologically objectionable forms of teleological explanation.

What has generally been considered methodologically objectionable in classic formulations of teleological explanations is, basically, the fact that they failed to establish any means by which the purposiveness attributed to an organism could be effective in the present and could lead that organism to the future goal that the teleologist claims that it may be said to "seek."

Whatever other faults his views may have, no such charge can justifiably be leveled against the type of functional explanation which Radcliffe-Brown offered in his accounts of anthropological facts.[51] As we have seen, his theory did not deny the existence of psychological determinants in functional explanations, and such explanations (as he employed them) in fact rested upon the existence of these determinants. And we are now in a position to see why this should have been the case. A social system is a set of interrelated social usages; social usages, however, are acts of individuals; they are acts which "while they characterize a certain number of individuals . . . are the product in these individuals of the action upon them of other individuals within a specific social system."[52] This being so, the whole dynamism of any social system will rest upon the interactions of individuals, not upon an unspecified and "occult" relationship whereby the supposed needs of the system as a whole presumably make themselves directly felt in each of its component parts. That Radcliffe-Brown's emphasis on the role of individuals in a society was basic to his functionalism throughout his career can perhaps best be seen through citing a passage from the preface to the revised edition of The Andaman Islanders (1933), in which he attempted to specify the meaning of function:

> The notion of function in ethnology rests on the conception of culture as an adaptive mechanism by which a certain number of human beings are enabled to live a social life as an ordered community in a given environment.[53]

However, if this is taken as his view of the nature of functional explanations, and if he too emphasized psychological determinants in such explanations, what—one may wonder—was the basic difference between his view and the later functionalism of Malinowski?

The difference, I submit, may be stated in terms of the very different roles psychological determinants played in each theory. Both Radcliffe-Brown and Malinowski viewed a social system as constituting a whole, and both conceived of any such system as having a number of institutional components, or elements. Furthermore, each regarded it as necessary to appeal to psychological determinants in analyzing the functioning of social systems. However, according to Malinowski's view (and now I am only discussing his later functionalism), it was not possible to understand the structural elements within a society without viewing them as reflections of a set of basic, universal needs. In Malinowski's system, therefore, the psychological determinants of a society consisted in a set of psychological constants which underlay all of the actions of individual human beings: the comparability of social systems depended for him on the universality and stability of these basic needs.[54] Radcliffe-Brown, on the other hand, denied that any generalizations of the science of psychology could provide such a basis for social anthropology. While he did admit that one could meaningfully speak of a basic human nature, which it was the business of general psychology to study, he did not regard generalizations concerning these universal features of human beings as providing a basis for the analysis of social institutions. It was his contention that, in addition to whatever factors all human beings had in common, there were "special psychologies" for different social groups.[55] In his view, men were malleable, and thus special characteristics were imparted to them by the social usages under which they lived. Therefore, psychological determinants could not be regarded as the *foundations* upon which the nature of social usages rested; they were the mechanisms by means of which these usages tended to agglutinate into a single, coherent, self-maintaining system. As a consequence, Radcliffe-Brown's view differed from Malinowski's in the fact that he rejected the assumption that the comparability of social systems rested upon constancy in the nature of human beings. Instead, he believed that the constants in social anthropology were to be found in the means by which social systems maintained themselves. In his view, it was the task of social science to discover these constants and to state them as laws. In short, according to Radcliffe-Brown, a science of society was independent of a theory of psychological constants: its task was to state the abstract general conditions under which systems of social usages maintained themselves and the conditions under which they underwent change.[56]

Such a definition of the task of the comparative study of societies not only distinguishes the functionalism of Radcliffe-Brown from the later functionalism of Malinowski, it also serves to distinguish it from Malinowski's earlier views. Those views were not put forward as a means of establishing a basis for comparative studies: unlike Radcliffe-Brown, it was only late in his career that Malinowski showed an interest in such studies. In what I have termed his early functionalism, Malinowski regarded the principle of interrelatedness as having a genuinely explanatory function in social anthropology: one could understand the character of one element in a culture through seeing how it was related to all of the other elements in the same culture. Radcliffe-Brown, however, must be interpreted as having rejected the view that a descriptive method of this sort can be regarded as "explanatory"; he insisted most strongly on drawing a sharp distinction between ideographic and nomothetic enquiries, and it was his contention that a *science* of society was exclusively concerned with establishing acceptable general propositions.[57] Malinowski, too, in his later theory, sought to go beyond the principle of interrelatedness and attempted to formulate a substantive theory that could serve to explain the basis of each essential feature of man's social life. Thus, in one respect at least, Malinowski's later thought and the views of Radcliffe-Brown were at one: both conceived of a proper social science as being one that was capable of explaining what all societies had in common. Malinowski sought to relate such features to a universal set of basic needs; Radcliffe-Brown rejected this psychological approach and sought to find the common features in the needs of the society as a self-maintaining system. Each assumed that a generalizing science of social life had to be general in a very special way: before it set out to explain any particular feature of social systems it had to establish the most general features of all such systems and account for them.[58] When this aspect of the thought of Malinowski and of Radcliffe-Brown is stressed, one can see why philosophers have been skeptical as to whether functionalism can provide an adequate theoretical framework for explanations in anthropology and in sociology. It is to a brief elucidation of this point that I shall now turn.

Conclusion: Functionalism and the Nature of Explanation

In the foregoing account we saw that the basic starting point of functionalism for both Malinowski and Radcliffe-Brown was the doctrine that all elements within a social system are mutually related; as Bateson pointed out, it was this thesis that characterized the Functional School. However, as we also saw, Malinowski's later functionalism operated on a quite different theoretical level: its purpose was to account for the universal elements in cultures, rather than being confined to a thesis concerning the relations obtaining among the coexisting elements in any one culture. It should be obvious that even if we assume both aspects of Malinowski's views to have been sound, they were independent of one another; and we may note that, if sound, they would play quite different roles in the economy of our knowledge of societies. Malinowski's early functionalism was a descriptive thesis concerning specific cultures, and his later functionalism was concerned with comparisons of the elements to be found in all cultures. Radcliffe-Brown's theory operated on these same two levels. As we have seen, he shared Malinowski's descriptive thesis concerning the interrelatedness of the elements within any one culture, and he also sought to generalize concerning the features which all societies have in common. In his view, however, these common features were structural principles making for the cohesiveness and continuity of societies rather than being specific, repeated elements tied to individual needs.

Now, it seems to me clear that the first, or descriptive, principle in each of these theories ought not to be treated as if it were intended to provide an empirical law. To view it as a law would be either to render it empirically false or so to modify it that it would become too weakened to possess any explanatory power. This can be suggested in the following way.

If the principle of interrelatedness were to be formulated as a law, it would very probably be stated in something like the following form: in any culture, all elements within the culture are related to all other elements in such a way that none would be as it is if the other elements were different from what they are. However, such a law would imply that any change in any element of any culture would entail that all other elements in that culture would also undergo change. This principle can surely not be thought to be true, and neither Malinowski nor Radcliffe-Brown can easily be interpreted as having believed it to be true.[59] However, if the principle were to be weakened in a manner that would make it empirically plausible, it would probably have to be stated as holding that *many* elements in a culture have *some* effect on one another; that no element can be understood as a unit that stands in isolation from *all* others. This weaker principle was indeed advocated by Malinowski and by Radcliffe-Brown, and their work—as well as the work of their followers—has assuredly established its plausibility; it is a principle that has, in their hands, undermined some of the assumptions shared by most earlier diffusionists, and before them by most who approached social anthropology from an evolutionary or an "antiquarian" point of view. However, when phrased in this weakened form, the principle no longer permits one to deduce specific consequences in specific instances. It could therefore not perform the explanatory function of a law on the classical deductive-nomothetic model. Nor is it likely that it could be successfully rephrased in probabilistic terms and be used in explanatory generalizations of a probabilistic type.

Under these circumstances, one might seek to interpret the descriptive principle of interrelatedness (as this principle was used by Malinowski and by Radcliffe-Brown) as a merely methodological principle of heuristic significance. In such a view, these functionalists would be interpreted as having merely held that one should always look for interrelationships among the elements of a culture, for fear of misunderstanding them or of misdescribing them, because one may have overlooked their relationships to other elements with which they were connected.[60] However, I believe that this strictly heuristic interpretation of the principle of interrelatedness would assuredly be too weak an interpretation to be an accurate reflection of Malinowski's thought, and I believe—though with perhaps less assurance—that it would also be too weak an interpretation to do justice to the views of Radcliffe-Brown and of functionalism in general. What was at stake in functionalism was not merely an important heuristic device but an explanatory principle: the various elements in a culture were held to be what they actually were because of their interconnections with one another. This explanatory principle, it should be noted, was descriptive in character, and was not a lawlike generalization from which further specific consequences were expected to be deduced. Thus, if I am not mistaken, the position of functionalism—so far as the principle of interrelatedness was concerned—presupposed that, in some cases at least, *descriptive analyses constitute explanations* of particular phenomena. A position of this sort—though making use of a different type of descriptive analysis—has become familiar to us through William Dray's discussion of "the continuous series model of explanation."[61] In Malinowski's early functionalism, the characteristics of a particular phenomenon were held to be explained when it was shown why this phenomenon was as it was; and an explanation of its nature was assumed to be attainable through pointing out how it was related to a wide variety of other contemporary phenomena in the same culture.[62] Thus, while functionalist explanations of this type stand opposed to genetic investigations, they attempt to produce synchronic analyses that in other respects resemble the diachronic approach of traditional historical investigations. This being the case, it is obvious that insofar as one takes it to be true that all "explanation" must conform to the classical deductive-nomothetic model, or else to probabilistic models, descriptive analyses of the foregoing type will not be taken to be explanatory. As a consequence, neither the functionalism of Malinowski nor that of Radcliffe-Brown will appear to be adequate to many philosophers of science.

Turning now to the second level of theory which is to be found in both Malinowski and Radcliffe-Brown, we can see why their cross-cultural generalizations have also failed to satisfy philosophers of science. And here, I may say, my sympathies lie wholly with their critics. It will be recalled that Malinowski sought to establish a general scientific theory of culture by relating a set of universal cultural elements to a set of universal human needs. However, as numerous critics have pointed out, he never succeeded in showing in concrete instances that the specific forms that those elements assumed were *necessary* to the satisfaction of these needs; nor did he ever attempt to show that the existence of these needs (assuming them to be universal) provided *sufficient* conditions for the existence of the particular elements whose universality he claimed to have established. Thus, there was a looseness of connection between the purportedly universal and constant factors in human nature and human culture and the specific elements that Malinowski and other descriptive anthropologists found to be present in different cultures. Nor was Radcliffe-Brown's theory of the necessity of certain practices for the survival of a society any less vulnerable to criticism from the same point of view.[63] Thus, the attempt to establish laws of social organization on the assumptions of either Malinowski or Radcliffe-Brown ended in failure: their generalizations permitted no deductive consequences with respect to the specific nature of the practices of the peoples that they, and other descriptive anthropologists, investigated.

Given the inadequacies of this second level of theory in functionalism, and given the present reluctance of many philosophers of science to accept descriptive analyses as offering explanations, it is small wonder that the movement known as functionalism in social anthropology should have fallen into serious disrepute among philosophers of science. The blame, however, can scarcely be attributable to narrowness or rigidity on the part of the philosophic crticis of functionalism. If, instead of seeking highly general principles that would delineate what all cultures, as wholes, have in common, Malinowski and Radcliffe-Brown had moved more continuously from the first level of their theories—their insistence on the principle of interrelatedness—to a comparative study of the ways in which the various elements of culture are related to one another, more accurate and more testable generalizations might have resulted. This, however, would have involved abandoning the attempt to find what I have elsewhere termed *global laws* in favor of seeking *abstractive laws* concerning the specific relations of elements within societies.[64] Such abstractive laws would attempt to correlate the specific nature and changes of specific elements of social structure with one another and would thus be *functional* in one of the classic senses of that term: two properties, events, or other characteristics may be said to be *functionally* related if there exists a nonaccidental covariance between them.[65] If I am not mistaken, it was—at least in part—this conception of *function* which had been suggested by the original descriptive analyses of Malinowski and of Radcliffe-Brown, but which had unfortunately been minimized by them in their emphasis upon a general theory of societies. And it is this original and important aspect of their theories which is, in my opinion, apt to be neglected when functionalism in social anthropology is assumed to be modeled on organismic biology and when it is interpreted as an example of teleological explanation—whether the teleology in question be that connected with traditional vitalism, or whether it be the quasi-teleology imputed to self-regulating mechanisms that operate through negative feedback.

Notes

In 1952, at the Eastern Division of the American Philosophical Association, Ernest Nagel and C. G. Hempel participated in a major symposium on functionalism in the social sciences. It seemed to me that in their discussions, and in much that was being written by sociologists and by political scientists, not enough attention was paid to distinguishing the various ways in which anthropologists used the concept of functionalism. Nor did I find this adequately rectified in a 1959 article by Hempel (now most readily available in his Aspects of Scientific Explanation*) or in Nagel's discussion in his* Structure of Science *(1961). In 1969 I took the opportunity of examining this question when asked to contribute to the* Festschrift *for Nagel.*

Unfortunately, I had overlooked Raymond Firth's article "Function," contained in the Yearbook of Anthropology *— 1955, edited by William L. Thomas, Jr. When I sent Professor Firth a copy of my article, he wrote a most generous reply, and also called his own article to my attention. It gives me satisfaction to be able, at last, to add this important reference to the other works I have cited.*

1. "Teleological Explanation and Teleological Systems" was published in 1953 in *Vision and Action*, edited by Sidney Ratner. "A Formalization of Functionalism" dates from the same year but was first published in 1956 in *Logic Without Metaphysics*. Because the latter paper was closely tied to Robert K. Merton's essay on "Manifest and Latent Functions" (cf. note 3 below), many of its aspects are not incorporated in *The Structure of Science*; it should therefore be separately consulted. However, so far as I can see, the position expounded in *The Structure of Science* does not depart from this earlier formulation of Nagel's view. (A much briefer discussion of functionalism is to be found in his contribution to a symposium on "Problems of Concept and Theory Formation in the Social Sciences," *American Philosophical Association, Eastern Division*, 1 [1952].)

2. It has, of course, also been one of the chief sources of much of this work. Among the philosophers of science who have dealt with the problem, I might mention Sidney Morgenbesser's "Role and Status of Anthropological Theories," *Science*, 128 (1958):285-88; Carl G. Hempel's "The Logic of Functional Analysis," originally published in 1959, but reprinted in a revised version in his *Aspects of Scientific Explanation* (1965); Israel Scheffler's

Anatomy of Inquiry (1963), especially secs. 5 and 9 of part 1; and chap. 9 of Robert Brown's *Explanation in Social Science* (1963).

In Dorothy Emmet's *Function, Purpose and Powers* (1958), one finds a very similar linkage of functionalism in social anthropology with questions concerning teleological systems.

3. In the present paper I shall not deal with functionalism in sociology. It is a considerably later movement. Functionalism in social anthropology can be regarded as originating with publications by Malinowski and Radcliffe-Brown in 1922, whereas 1949 is the year in which functionalism became an important issue in general sociology: it was in that year that Talcott Parsons's *Essays in Sociological Theory* appeared and Robert Merton published his classic article, "Manifest and Latent Functions," in *Social Theory and Social Structure*. The connection between functionalism in anthropology and Parsons's views is evident in the latter's essay on "The Theoretical Development of the Sociology of Religion," which is included in the 1949 volume of essays. In the case of Merton's article, the evidence of connection is unambiguous. (For example, cf. *Social Theory and Social Structure*, second edition, pp. 20-37.)

Among the other important discussions of functionalism in sociology, the reader may be referred to Marion J. Levy's *The Structure of Society* (1952), and to the following articles: Harry C. Bredemeier, "The Methodology of Functionalism," *American Sociological Review*, 20 (1955): 173-80; Bernard Barber, "Structural-Functional Analysis: Some Problems and Misunderstandings," *American Sociological Review* 21 (1956):129-35; Kingsley Davis, "The Myth of Functional Analysis," *American Sociological Review*, 24 (1959):752-72; Ronald P. Dore, "Function and Cause," *American Sociological Review*, 26 (1961):843-53.

In addition, George C. Homans has dealt with the meanings of functionalism on frequent occasions; the last of these being his presidential address to the American Sociological Association in which he severely criticized the position. (Cf. "Bringing Men Back In," *American Sociological Review*, 29 [1964]:809-18.) For his earlier analyses, see *The Human Group* (1950), pp. 268-72; his review of Radcliffe-Brown, *Structure and Function*, in *American Anthropologist*, 56 (1954):118-20; and *Sentiments and Actions* (1962), et passim.

4. Recent uses of the term *teleology* have extended its application to a wider variety of phenomena than had previously been regarded as being *teleological*. For example, the term is presently applied to man-made physical systems regulated by negative feedback and to those instances in which human action is motivated by attempts to attain future goals, as well as being applied to biological phenomena as these phenomena are interpreted by vitalists. One can, of course, find connections among these three types of use, as well as connections with other traditional uses (e.g., the theological uses of the term). However, so far as I can see, no one of these three uses has any necessary connection with functionalism as a theory in social anthropology, and it will be my purpose to suggest that Hempel was mistaken when he said: "Historically speaking, functional analysis is a modification of teleological explanation, i.e., of explanation not by reference to causes which 'bring about' the event in question but by reference to ends which determine its course" ("Logic of Functional Analysis," p. 303).

5. A useful bibliography of Malinowski's writings, and of the literature concerning him, is to be found in Raymond Firth (ed.), *Man and Culture, An Evaluation of the Work of Bronislav Malinowski* (1957). Some of the articles cited in that bibliography have more recently been reprinted in a collection entitled *Sex, Culture and Myth* (1962).

6. *Argonauts*, p. 11. Although Malinowski's first book, *The Family Among the Australian Aborigines* (1913), was based upon presuppositions that he soon abandoned, one finds in its concluding chapter expressions of precisely the same point of view as that cited above: the institution of the family, Malinowski argues, cannot be understood in isolation from its social conditions, e.g., from territorial and tribal structure, land ownership and economic practices, and moral, customary, or legal norms (cf. p. 293 and p. 301 of the 1963 edition, edited by J. A. Barnes).

7. *Argonauts*, p. 515 (italics mine). That the interplay of various aspects of a culture was basic in Malinowski's earlier views regarding methodological and theoretical issues also becomes clear in his special preface to the third edition (1932) of *The Sexual Life of Savages* (cf. especially p. xx).

8. *Argonauts*, p. 516.

9. I do not deny that the unsatisfactoriness of many diachronic studies and their highly conjectural nature, as well as a variety of personal factors, played a part in Malinowski's anti-historical bias. I merely wish to point out that if one takes his antiabstractionist thesis as seriously as he himself did, then there are good theoretic reasons for the position that he adopted. This point comes out very clearly in *Sex and Repression in Savage Society* (1927), pp. 181-82.

To be sure, one might accept this early functionalism and yet be interested in tracing some dynamic, directional process in the society as a whole. However, on Malinowski's premises, any such interest could only be satisfied *after* the primary, synchronic studies had been adequately carried out. Thus, he rejected diachronic studies as not germane to his own immediate task. However, as the closing sentences of *Crime and Custom in a Savage Society* (1926) make clear, he did not exclude the possibility of future studies of historical and evolutional factors in society; and this position was one which he repeated at frequent intervals, e.g., in the foreword to the third edition (1932) of *The Sexual Life of Savages*, and in Chapter 3 of his posthumously published *Dynamics of Culture Change* (1945).

10. In his *History of Ethnological Theory* (1937), R. H. Lowie gives an account of Malinowski's thought which may be characterized as vituperative in tone, but which is accurate in content; he, too, finds the emphasis on an interdependence of the aspects of a culture as the characteristic feature of Malinowski's early functionalism.

A similar interpretation of Malinowski's early functionalism is implicit in remarks made by J. A. Barnes in his helpful introduction to the 1963 reprint of Malinowski's *The Family Among the Australian Aborigines* (q.v., p. xix). One may also note that Audrey Richards comments on how mistaken it is to identify Malinowski's functionalism with a theory of human needs and to contrast it in this respect with the functionalism of Radcliffe-Brown (cf. "The Concept of Culture in Malinowski's Work," in Firth, *Man and Culture*, p. 17, n. 2). I shall return to this point in discussing Malinowski's later form of functionalism.

11. Cf. *Naven*, pp. ix, x, 112n., 258, et passim.

12. In retrospectively calling attention to his concern with the concept of basic human needs, Malinowski himself specifically referred to the same article, which had been published in 1931 (cf. his posthumous *Scientific Theory of Culture*, p. 22).

13. This, of course, is a fundamental thesis in *Crime and Custom*, and in this respect Malinowski is frequently critical of the work of Durkheim. A further, and not wholly separable, criticism of Durkheim is that the latter's emphasis on the collective nature of social phenomena led him to neglect (according to Malinowski) the biological basis of cultural facts (cf. his preface to Hogbin, *Law and Order*, p. xxxviii, and Malinowski, *The Dynamics of Cultural Change*, p. 42). In the latter respect, Malinowski linked Radcliffe-Brown with Durkheim, as the first of the latter passages will show.

14. Even in his last work, when—as we shall see—the focus of his interests had somewhat changed, and he had come to emphasize psychological needs as underlying institutions, Malinowski had insisted on viewing these institutions as what he termed "the legitimate isolates of cultural analysis" (*Scientific Theory of Culture*, pp. 160-61; also, p. 54). For him, such isolates were entities to be utilized both in observation and in theoretical discourse (ibid., p. 27). Furthermore, as we shall see, he disagreed profoundly with Benedict's denial of universals in culture, i.e., with her view that specific cultures fail to satisfy the whole range of man's basic needs (ibid., p. 40).

15. Benedict, *Patterns of Culture*, pp. 42-43 of Mentor Books edition. As Boas pointed out in his introduction to this book, Ruth Benedict's interest in the total configuration of a culture "is distinct from the so-called functional approach to social phenomena in so far as it is concerned rather with the discovery of fundamental attitudes than with the functional relations of every cultural item."

16. Ibid., pp. 45-46. For an example of Malinowski's contemptuous rejection of Benedict's views, cf. "Culture As a Determinant of Behavior," in *Factors Determining Human Behavior*, (1937), p. 143.

17. It is now not unusual to find that Malinowski's functionalism is solely identified with his later attempt to relate social institutions to biological and psychological needs. As I have indicated, Audrey Richards comments on this interpretation (cf. her contribution to Firth, *Man and Culture*, p. 17, n. 2). It is implicit in the views of E. R. Leach (cf. his contribution to the same volume and his essay on Malinowski and Frazer in *Encounter*, November 1965), and the same truncated view of Malinowski's theoretical position is present in Leon J. Goldstein "The Logic of Explanation in Malinowskian Anthropology," *Philosophy of Science*, 24 (1957):156-66. In his polemics against Malinowski, Radcliffe-Brown in the end is also guilty of this error (cf. "Functionalism: A Protest," *American Anthropologist*, 51 [1949]:320f.). However, to view Malinowski's position in this way is to fail to understand the theoretical views that originally guided his field work, and the nature and extent of his influence on an important generation of anthropologists.

18. One would not, of course, have to conceive of rules in terms of reciprocal obligations, but it is clear that Malinowski did so conceive of them. (For example, cf. p. xxxv of the same preface, as well as Malinowski's own analysis of law in *Crime and Custom*.)

19. To be sure, incompatibilities of obligations may exist in the experience of any one individual and may even be fairly characteristic of certain groups of individuals; however, such incompatibilities cannot (in Malinowski's view of the nature of an institution) be general and continuing.

20. For example, in his preface to Hogbin, *Law and Order*, p. xxxi.

21. Ibid., pp. xxxviif. Malinowski's doctrine of sentiments owed much to the psychology of A. F. Shand, as is clear in the preface to *Sex and Repression in Savage Society*. (Cf. also the remarks on this point in the essays of Firth and of Fortes in *Man and Culture*, edited by Firth).

22. Audrey Richards tends to hold that this emphasis was present in Malinowski's early functionalism (cf. her essay in Firth, *Man and Culture*, p. 17), although she admits that it is difficult to know whether the idea of the unity of a culture preceded the idea of the interconnectedness of its elements, or whether it followed from it (ibid., p. 18). The interpretation I am offering assumes that the latter is Malinowski's most usual view. That there is an ambiguity in this matter can perhaps best be seen by examining the concluding paragraph of Malinowski's *Crime and Custom*, where both points of view are stressed. A combination of both points of view is also present in a brief passage quoted from an early (1912) article of Malinowski's in Radcliffe-Brown, "A Note on Functionalism," *Man*, 47 (1946):30, 38b.

23. *A Scientific Theory of Culture*, p. 159. As we have noted, in his preface to Hogbin's *Law and Order*, Malinowski remarks that the fundamental difference between his views and those of Radcliffe-Brown (as well as the school of Durkheim), lies in the fact that the latter neglect the individual and the biological factor (i.e., the factor of individual needs) in culture (cf. p. xxxviii). The same point is repeated in "The Group and the Individual in Functional Analysis," *American Journal of Sociology*, 44 (1939):939 (Now also available in Malinowski: *Sex, Culture, and Myth*, p. 224n.)

24. An early, isolated passage of this sort is to be found in Malinowski's 1925 essay "Magic, Science, and Religion" (cf. Anchor edition of the volume bearing the same title, pp. 39-40). However, the chief passage of this sort is in pp. 168-70 of *A Scientific Theory of Culture*. However, the latter passage ends with the remark that such a use of the concept of function is to be considered primarily as a heuristic device, and Malinowski immediately returns, in the next pages, to his theory of biological and psychological needs.

25. Of course, Radcliffe-Brown amplified his theoretical position in his later works (cf. *A Scientific Theory of Society*, recorded in 1937, but not published until 1948, and the later contributions included in the posthumous volume, *Method in Social Anthropology*). However, it seems fair to say that the chief *alteration* in his various later formulations of his position was that he came more and more to state his theory as a theory of "the structure of society." This later insistence that social anthropology deals with "society," and not "culture," and his growing emphasis on the term *structure* were in large measure to be understood as reactions against — and, indeed, as protests against — Malinowski's position. (For Radcliffe-Brown's most explicit statement concerning his relationships to Malinowski, cf. "A Note on Functional Anthropology," *Man*, 46 [1946]:30, 38-41.)

26. *The Andaman Islanders,* p. 324. I quote from the 1933 edition, but the body of that text appears to be unchanged. However, the preface was substantially altered, and Appendix B (on the Andaman Languages) was entirely rewritten.

27. Cf. *The Andaman Islanders,* p. 229. For a passage in which Radcliffe-Brown acknowledged the convergence of his view and those of Malinowski and of Margaret Mead with respect to this issue, cf. his address "The Present Position of Anthropological Studies" (1931), reprinted in *Method in Social Anthropology.* (The reference is to be found on page 70 of that volume.)

28. Among the many statements Radcliffe-Brown made concerning the essential nature of functional explanations in social science, perhaps the clearest are to be found in his article "On the Concept of Function in Social Science," *American Anthropologist,* 37 (1935):394-402. However, it may be well to cite additional passages, starting with *The Andaman Islanders,* pp. 229-230, and continuing in chronological order through a statement in *Method in Social Anthropology,* p. 62, to *A Natural Science of Society,* pp. 85 and 154-56, and to the introduction to *Structure and Function in Primitive Society,* p. 12. These are, of course, merely a few of the references that are directly relevant.

29. Cf. above, note 13. The same linkage is to be found in R. H. Lowie's treatment of Radcliffe-Brown in his *History of Ethnological Theory*: he discusses Radcliffe-Brown in connection with "the French School," rather than in connection with Malinowski and functionalism.

Radcliffe-Brown readily acknowledged his debt to Durkheim and to the latter's followers. For example, see the prefaces to *The Andaman Islanders,* and also the important acknowledgment in the footnote on page 325 of that work. Among the many other passages that establish this connection, I shall cite only the following: *Structure and Function in Primitive Society,* pp. 14, 166, 176, and 200. However, I should like also to call attention to the fact that in his article "On the Concept of Function in Social Science," (*American Anthropologist,* 37 [1935]:394) Radcliffe-Brown attributed the basic concept of the function of a social institution to Durkheim.

30. According to Radcliffe-Brown, one of the major factors on which the existence of any society depends is the existence in it of a shared body of moral customs, and these he regarded as dependent upon sentiments (cf. *The Andaman Islanders,* pp. 400ff.). Thus he says: "These sentiments and the representations connected with them, upon the existence of which, as we have seen, the very existence of the society depends, need to be kept alive, to be maintained at a given degree of intensity. Apart from the necessity that exists of keeping them alive in the mind of the individual, there is the necessity of impressing them upon each new individual added to the society, upon each child as he or she develops into an adult" (p. 404).

31. For a concise statement of the empirical assumptions involved in Radcliffe-Brown's position, see the five points that he takes as his working hypothesis: in each of them the concept of a sentiment is central (*The Andaman Islanders,* pp. 231-32).

While Radcliffe-Brown did explain some ceremonials, such as the rite of weeping (p. 245) and ceremonial dancing (p. 252), in terms that were entirely consistent with this working hypothesis, it may be doubted whether the same can be said with respect to his explanations of bodily ornamentation (cf. pp. 320-23). In the latter explanations he failed to show how sentiments were actually involved. This suggests that he had either failed to state his working hypothesis with sufficient clarity or that he had failed to test it with sufficient rigor.

32. All three essays cited above are reprinted in *Structure and Function in Primitive Society.* The quotation from "Taboo" is to be found on page 144 of that volume.

33. *Structure and Function in Primitive Society,* p. 157. Similarly, he says: "The social function of the rites is obvious: by giving solemn and collective expression to [a particular system of sentiments] the rites reaffirm, renew and strengthen those sentiments on which the social solidarity depends" (ibid., p. 164).

34. *A Natural Science of Society,* p. 45. This work was originally published in 1948, but I shall cite the 1957 reprinting of it.

For a discussion of Radcliffe-Brown's use of the concept of systems, their distinction from classes, and their relation to his view of natural laws, cf. especially pp. 19-22 of the same work.

35. Ibid., p. 47. In my opinion it is true that social scientists do deal with what Radcliffe-Brown terms systems of acts through which individuals are related to one another. However, to

define the province of social science (as distinct from psychology) in this way cannot be considered adequate. In the first place, not every set of acts through which persons are related forms what Radcliffe-Brown characterizes as a system. In the second place, it is not likely that we would regard it as within the province of a social scientist, rather than a psychologist, to investigate all cases in which behavior evinces systematic connections between the interrelated acts of individuals. (For example, an extreme case of sibling rivalry in a particular family would not usually be assigned to the field of social science rather than psychology.)

36. In his last, unfinished work—a projected portion of a text on social anthropology—he used the term *institutions* in much the way he had formerly used the concept of *social usages*. This fragment is published as Part 2 of *Method in Social Anthropology*, and his use of the term *institution* is to be found in his discussion of "Social Structure" in that place.

37. I here exclude from consideration the question of whether one can speak of animal societies as being "societies" in the same sense as human societies. In doing so, I am following Radcliffe-Brown, who distinguishes between them on the ground that animal societies are based exclusively (or almost exclusively) on instinct rather than on instinct plus culture (cf. *A Natural Science of Society*, p. 91).

38. For example, in *A Natural Science of Society*, p. 49.

39. Radcliffe-Brown uses the term *unit*, rather than *part*, to refer to the *relata* within a system, as contrasted with the members of a class (cf. *A Natural Science of Society*, p. 22).

40. *A Natural Science of Society*, p. 26. And in a posthumous fragment published in *Method in Social Anthropology*, he suggested that "the matter" of human societies consisted in human beings, whereas their "forms" consisted in the ways in which these individuals were connected by institutional relationships (cf. p. 176).

41. Cf. *A Natural Science of Society*, p. 53.

42. *A Natural Science of Society*, pp. 24-26.

43. *A Natural Science of Society*, p. 56.

44. *A Natural Science of Society*, p. 56.

45. Cf. *A Natural Science of Society*, pp. 124-28; cf. also *Structure and Function in Primitive Society*, p. 43.

While Malinowski would not have denied that an overall functional consistency normally characterizes the culture of any society, in *Crime and Custom in Savage Society*, and elsewhere, he emphasized the existence of deviant behavior among individuals. To what extent Radcliffe-Brown's theory of the mechanisms underlying the formation of social usages permits him to account for deviant behavior is, I believe, an important open question.

46. At this point it may be useful to call attention to the fact that Radcliffe-Brown did not share what may be termed the *organismic* conception of a culture that one finds in Ruth Benedict, among others. Like Malinowski, he saw a social system as composed of elements, and it was the interrelatedness of these elements that gave the system the degree of unity it possessed. In various of Ruth Benedict's utterances, however, she spoke as if she intended to hold that it was the system as a whole which determined the characteristics of the units that comprised it. Though Radcliffe-Brown also used the catch phrase "the whole is greater than the sum of its parts," distinguishing dynamic systems from mere aggregates, he never suggested that the system as a whole was to be regarded as self-determining. In fact, it was the essence of his functionalism that the persistence of the whole was only made possible by the ways in which each element contributed to it. In this respect, then, his position was closer to that of Malinowski than it was to that of Benedict.

47. *The Andaman Islanders*, p. 229.

48. There are, however, passages in *The Andaman Islanders*, and elsewhere, which might be regarded as setting forth such a view. For example, in that work he puts forward the following statement:

> By its action upon the individual the ceremonial develops and maintains in existence in his mind an organized system of dispositions by which the social life, in the particular form it takes in the Andamans, is made possible, using for the purpose of maintaining the social

cohesion all the instinctive tendencies of human nature, modifying and combining them according to its needs (p. 327).

Although one can clearly see in such a passage that Radcliffe-Brown wished to emphasize the needs of a society conceived as a whole, if my interpretation of his thought has been correct, one need not interpret such passages as being meant to convey the view that a society has the power to select which social usages shall and shall not have a place within it. It is the combination and mutual reinforcement of these social usages, through their effects on individual behavior, which support the system as a whole.

49. He does in fact usually state his view in such a way as to imply that *every* element contributes directly to the system as a whole. Cf. the passage cited above from page 229 of *The Andaman Islanders*. In his article "On the Concept of Function in Social Science," he is, however, somewhat more cautious: he only takes this to be a "working hypothesis" (cf. *American Anthropologist*, 37 [1935]:399).

50. To be sure, Radcliffe-Brown did recognize the pervasiveness of social change and did regard it as an important problem for the social anthropologist (cf. *A Natural Science of Society*, pp. 86-89). However, his emphasis was upon synchronic analyses, and he regarded it as legitimate to treat these independently of questions regarding processes of change.

51. Radcliffe-Brown did not discuss biological explanation in sufficient detail to make certain that the charge *might not* apply to him in that sphere—though from the general tenor of his discussions of scientific explanation in *A Natural Science of Society*, I should be surprised if such a charge were justified with respect to his biological views. However, I am here solely concerned with the charge as it is presumed to apply to his social anthropology.

52. *A Natural Science of Society*, p. 106.

53. P. ix. It is of interest to note that in *The Andaman Islanders*, and in his other earlier works, Radcliffe-Brown used *culture* and *society* as roughly equivalent terms. It was only later that he held it a mistake to view social anthropology as dealing with *culture*. In his essay "On Social Structure" (1940) he attempted to argue that a society is "observable" in some sense in which *culture* is not (cf. *Structure and Function in Primitive Society*, p. 189f.). It is difficult to see how this thesis can be supported.

As I have suggested above (cf. note 25), this change in terminology, and Radcliffe-Brown's emphasis on it, may have been due, in part at least, to his desire to distinguish his doctrine from that of Malinowski. Whether the terminological issue was of importance for anthropology, or whether it had a merely personal basis, seems to me an open question.

54. Cf. "Culture as a Determinant of Behavior," in *Factors Determining Human Behavior*, Harvard Tercentenary Publications (1937), pp. 137-39 and p. 146.

55. Cf. "Meaning and Scope of Social Anthropology" (1944), in *Method in Social Anthropology*, pp. 103-4; also, *A Natural Science of Society*, p. 49.

56. In his later works, Radcliffe-Brown evinced an increasing interest in problems of social change, although it cannot be said that he ever completely overcame his antihistorical bias. For his later concern with problems of change, cf. *A Natural Science of Society*, pp. 86-89, and *Method in Social Anthropology*, pp. 178-89. To some extent, although to a lesser degree, the same may be said of Malinowski. However, Malinowski's concern with the problem of change seems to have been motivated less by theoretical considerations than by the pressing practical concerns connected with problems of cultural contact (cf. the posthumous work, *The Dynamics of Culture Change*, edited by Phyllis M. Kaberry).

57. The importance that Radcliffe-Brown attached to the distinction between ideographic and nomothetic enquiries can be seen in the opening pages of the introduction he wrote for the papers collected in *Structure and Function in Primitive Society* (1952). The same sharp distinction was present in his frequent attempts to differentiate between *ethnology* and *social anthropology*. (The latter term he equated with *comparative sociology*, and in effect with *social science*.) For an early example of this distinction, cf. "The Methods of Ethnology and Social Anthropology" (1923), reprinted in *Method in Social Anthropology* (cf. especially p. 7). As that essay makes clear,

one important reason for his having drawn this distinction was his desire to free contemporary anthropology from its earlier concern with questions about the historical origins of specific elements in a culture.

Radcliffe-Brown's actual use of the contrast between *ideographic* and *nomothetic* seems to me fundamentally mistaken. The fact that one can distinguish between ideographic and nomothetic *statements* does not justify the assumption that these terms refer to two distinct and independent types of *inquiry*. Of course, confusion with respect to this point has not been confined to the methodological views of Radcliffe-Brown.

58. I should not expect this statement to be challenged by those who know Malinowski's *Scientific Theory of Culture*. On the other hand, it may be thought to constitute something of a caricature of the position of Radcliffe-Brown. I do not believe that this is actually the case. Consider, for example, the following passage from "Patrilineal and Matrilineal Succession": "Any social system, to survive, must conform to certain conditions. If we can define adequately one of these universal conditions, i.e., one to which all human societies must conform, we have a sociological law. Thereupon if it can be shown that a particular institution in a particular society is the means by which that society conforms to the law, i.e., to the necessary condition, we may speak of this as the 'sociological origin' of the institution" (*Structure and Function in Primitive Society*, p. 43). Such a sociological origin, rather than any historical origin, is what he views it as the aim of the comparative method to establish. A similar passage — though perhaps less unambiguous — is to be found in *Method in Social Anthropology*, pp. 40-41. Cf. also *Structure and Function in Primitive Society*, p. 86f.

59. It might also be objected that the foregoing principle cannot be taken to be a law at all, because from it one could not deduce the specific nature or the degrees of the changes that would be entailed. However, even though this is the case, I am not certain that these limitations should lead one to say that a general principle of this form would not, if true, be an empirical law.

60. In his first analysis of functionalism, Nagel suggested that this might be the only empirically warranted interpretation of the functionalist thesis. (Cf. pp. 47-48 of his "Problems of Concept and Theory Formation," as cited in note 1, above.) This is also the position adopted by Dorothy Emmet (cf. *Function, Purpose and Powers*, pp. 81-82).

61. Cf. *Laws and Explanation in History* (London, 1957): pp. 66ff.

62. In reviews of two of Malinowski's posthumously published works, Max Gluckman has bitterly attacked Malinowski's functionalism as remaining on a primarily descriptive level. (Cf. "An Analysis of the Sociological Theories of Bronislaw Malinowski," *The Rhodes-Livingstone Papers, Number Sixteen*; reprinted from *African Studies* [1947] and from *Africa* [1947].

"Viewed sympathetically, Malinowski's position regarding the explanatory function of descriptive analyses seems to be unobjectionable. Viewed critically, however, it appears to be circular, for if one element, *a*, is to be explained in terms of other elements *b* and *c*, how is one then to explain the latter? According to Malinowski's early functionalism, are not the natures of *b* and *c* as much dependent upon *a*, as its nature is dependent upon them?"

An answer to such a charge of circularity lies in the fact that in advancing any explanation one must take *some* facts as given: the field worker finds that *b* and *c* are the case, but is puzzled by *a*. Thus *a* is explained through noting how it fits with *b* and with *c*; or, if *a* were taken as given, *b* and *c* might be explained through their relations to it. In this connection, it is especially to be noted that Malinowski's early functionalism was not in any way concerned with questions relating to the origins of specific cultural characteristics, but only with questions concerning influences upon their present natures. Viewed in this light, I do not find it misleading to regard descriptive analyses of the type he offered as explanatory.

However, in holding this view, I do not wish to suggest that such analyses can proceed without at least covertly using generalizations concerning psychological and institutional factors. (Cf. my criticism of Dray in "Historical Explanation: The Problem of 'Covering Laws'," reprinted above [ch. 7].) However, there is no reason to suppose that Malinowski would have objected to this contention.

63. For a lucid and more careful exposition of these matters, cf. Carl G. Hempel, "The Logic of Functional Analysis," reprinted in revised form in *Aspects of Scientific Explanation*, especially pp. 308-19.

64. Cf. "Societal Laws," reprinted above (ch. 16).

It may with some justice be argued that many of the analyses of Radcliffe-Brown did in fact establish generalizations concerning the specific relations that various elements in societies bear to one another. I am inclined to share this view. However, the deducibility of such relationships from his general theory of the needs of society for cohesiveness and continuity might still be challenged.

65. Cf. the first sense of the term *function* as discussed by Nagel in *The Structure of Science*, pp. 522-23. As Nagel rightly says: "The word [*function*] is widely used to signify relations of dependence or interdependence between two or more variable factors. . . . Such "functional" relations of dependence or interdependence are often established by functionalists in their analyses of social processes. However, if functional analysis means no more than this, it does not differ in aim or logical character from analyses undertaken in any other domain with the objective of discovering uniformities in some subject matter." If I have not been mistaken in my interpretations of their thought, both Malinowski and Radcliffe-Brown would be wholly in accord with this conclusion.

19

A Note on Homans's Functionalism

In this essay I seek to point out certain difficulties in the argument put forward by Homans and Schneider in *Marriage, Authority, and Final Causes*.[1] It is not my aim to defend the particular theories that these authors attack or to challenge the correlations they have pointed out; in both respects I find myself entirely willing to accept their views. I wish only to suggest that their own view regarding the efficient, operative causes in social organization remains wholly unproven so far as this particular book is concerned.

On pages 28-29 the authors first delimit their task; they then state their general theory and formulate the specific hypothesis that they are to test. I shall number these propositions to facilitate reference to them.

Their task is defined as follows:

> Prop. 1: "*Given* unilateral cross-cousin marriage . . . What will determine the adoption of one form of unilateral cross-cousin marriage rather than the other?"

Their general theory holds:

> Prop. 2: "The form of unilateral cross-cousin marriage will be determined by the system of interpersonal relations precipitated by a social structure, especially by the locus of jural authority over ego."

Their special hypothesis, which is deduced from this theory and which they are to test, is:

> Prop. 3: "One kind of unilateral cross-cousin marriage will be associated with patrilineal society, the other kind with matrilineal."

Or, more fully stated (cf. p. 28):

> Prop. 3a: "Societies in which marriage is allowed or preferred with mother's brother's daughter but forbidden or disapproved with father's sister's daughter will be societies possessing patrilineal kin-groups, and societies in which marriage is allowed or preferred with father's sister's daughter but forbidden

Reprinted by permission from *British Journal of Sociology*, 14 (1963):113-17.

or disapproved with mother's brother's daughter will be societies possessing
matrilineal kin-groups."

Now what I wish to point out is that if we take Proposition 2, the general
theory stated by the authors, and delete twelve words from it, their special
hypothesis (Props. 3 and 3a) will still follow from the theory as revised.
However, in that case, the social psychological underpinnings of their general hypothesis will have disappeared. The twelve words in question are
those which are not italicized, but are placed within brackets in the following
repetition of Proposition 2:

> *Our general theory holds that the form of unilateral cross-cousin marriage will be de-*
> *termined by* [the system of interpersonal relations precipitated by a social struc-
> ture, especially by] *the locus of jural authority over ego.*

That my contention is true can be seen when, on page 51, the authors say:

> To sum up our findings . . . : among those societies on our list for which we
> have some information on interpersonal relations and the locus of jural author-
> ity, there is only *one* that stands as a true exception to our general theory — the
> Yir-Yoront. . . . Specifically, the following is a highly significant proposition:
> *Societies in which marriage is allowed or preferred with mother's brother's daughter but*
> *forbidden or disapproved with father's sister's daughter will be societies in which jural*
> *authority over ego male, before marriage, is vested in his father or father's lineage, and*
> *societies in which marriage is allowed or preferred with father's sister's daughter but for-*
> *bidden or disapproved with mother's brother's daughter will be societies in which jural*
> *authority over ego male, before marriage, is vested in mother's brother or mother's*
> *brother's lineage.*

It is to be noted that in this summary of findings the causal efficacy of the
"interpersonal relations precipitated by a social structure" are not mentioned. Nonetheless, the authors obviously place special emphasis on these
interpersonal relationships as efficient causes in the social process, for in
their general conclusion (pp. 57-58) they write:

> Our general theory did more than predict a relation between the locus of
> jural authority over ego and the form of unilateral cross-cousin marriage: it also
> explained why this relation should exist. It argued that the locus of jural au-
> thority in father or mother's brother would be an important determinant of
> ego's sentimental ties with kinfolk.

However, if one looks through this book for evidence that has been carefully
marhsalled in favor of *this* proposition — in contradistinction to the carefully
formulated findings regarding the specific hypothesis (Props. 3 and 3a) — one
finds little such evidence, and the discussion of it (cf. pp. 36-39) might be
characterized as being almost impressionistic. To be sure, some references

to supporting materials are given; however, when these references are actually traced, one finds, startlingly enough, that such evidence as is used by Homans and Schneider does not, of itself, help establish their form of functionalism. I shall attempt to show this very briefly in the following two ways.

First, it is to be noted that the authors cite chapter 10 of *The Human Group*, in which Homans analysed Raymond Firth's account of the Tikopia, paying special attention to the interpersonal relationships to be found in the Tikopia kinship system. However, in making use of Homans's earlier analysis (p. 23), the authors fail to make explicit the fact that the Tikopia do not represent an example of cross-cousin marriage: among them, such marriages are in fact forbidden. Therefore, whatever may be the value of the general theorems concerning interpersonal relationships which Homans derives from his consideration of Firth's materials, the inferential connection between data concerning the Tikopia and the Homans-Schneider theory of cross-cousin marriage should be scrutinized with care: the relevance of the one to the other cannot be taken for granted.

Second, on page 3 Homans and Schneider cite Radcliffe-Brown's classic paper "The Mother's Brother in South Africa"[2] as the source of their own efficient-cause theory (cf. also p. 21). However, in that paper there are two main points at issue, and neither involves their own theory of the origins of a specific type of family organization. The first of Radcliffe-Brown's two points consists in his criticism of an historical conjecture made by Junod: that certain customs involving the relationships between a male and his mother's brother were vestiges of a previous matrilineal phase in that society. The second point is the development of Radcliffe-Brown's own view of how "a strongly marked tendency to merge the individual in the group to which he or she belongs" leads to "a tendency to extend to all the members of a group a certain type of behaviour which has its origin in a relationship to one particular member of the group" (op. cit., p. 25). Now, the first of these points concerns the question of whether a particular, present form of family organization did in fact originate from a different form. This obviously is a question concerning the origin of an institution, but it is not with it that Homans and Schneider are concerned. Rather, their theory is ostensibly derived from Radcliffe-Brown's second point. This second point, however, is *not* concerned with the question of the origin of a particular form of family organization; instead, it discusses patterns of behavior *within* a given form of family organization. That this is the case can perhaps be most quickly demonstrated by quoting from Radcliffe-Brown's own summary of his view:

4. In patrilineal societies of a certain type, the special pattern of behaviour between a sister's son and the mother's brother is derived from the pattern of behavior between the child and the mother, which is itself the product of the social life within the family in the narrow sense. (p. 29)

In this there is no attempt to explain the origin of the type of family which is present; rather, what is at issue is the extension of patterns of behavior from the mother to the mother's brother (etc.) within a particular type of family system. Thus, Homans and Schneider are putting forward a far different thesis from that which is either explicitly formulated or logically entailed by Radcliffe-Brown's paper.

Taking into account these criticisms of the way in which Homans and Schneider use materials drawn from Firth and from Radcliffe-Brown, one can only wonder how two such careful analysts could have strayed so far from what is actually entailed by the evidence they cite. The answer, I believe, lies in the following statement (p. 39):

> Prop. 4: "We believe present association betrays ultimate origin; the history of some institutions is repeated every generation; to some unknown degree the energies that maintain a system are the ones that created it."

That this *may* be the case cannot be denied. However, before assuming that it *must* be the case one would do well to ponder Durkheim's equally forceful maxim:

"When, then, the explanation of a social phenomenon is undertaken, we must seek separately the efficient cause which produces it and the function it fulfils."[3]

And if the question at issue is in part an issue between efficient causes and final causes, as Homans and Schneider imply that it is, then one might do well also to ponder the matter in terms of evolutionary explanations in biology. Were one a Darwinian and not a Lamarckian, it is clear that ultimate origin is independent of function. To be sure, that a variation continues to survive bespeaks the fact that its functions are not so maladaptive as to lead to extinction, but from this fact one cannot infer (as Darwin himself later came to see)[4] that every variation is of *positive* use. And, surely, in the case of those psychological forces with which Homans and Schneider deal, comparative anthropology would not suggest that the elimination or frustration of the sentiments in question would be sufficiently maladaptive to lead to the extinction of any social group in which these sentiments could not thrive. Thus, even the continuing existence of the societies with which Homans and Schneider were concerned fails to afford evidence that their functionalism is true.

In short, it has been my claim that Homans and Schneider did not provide evidence for the social-psychological form of functionalism which they adopted. Instead, they simply took it for granted that "present association betrays ultimate origin" (Prop. 4). That this assumption is not proved, but is merely assumed, can be seen if we now return to their original definition of their task (Prop. 1). There they took unilateral cross-cousin marriage of two different types as *given*, and they asked what had determined the adoption of one of these types rather than another. To ask such a question, namely what will determine the "adoption" of any social institution, is presumably to ask a question concerning origins. However, the specific hypothesis that they proposed as an answer to this genetic question was a hypothesis concerning the presently existing relations of this form of marriage to other co-existing social institutions (Props. 3 and 3a). Thus, the very definition of their task only makes sense if, as they say, "present association betrays ultimate origin" (Prop. 4). Furthermore, strictly taken, even the acceptance of this proposition would not entail an acceptance of their social-psychological form of functionalism, because Proposition 4 does not tell us which of the two associated elements embodies those energies which both create and conserve the social system: on the basis of this proposition one could hold the very sort of functionalism which Homans and Schneider attack.

It is not my aim to disprove the functionalism which Homans accepts, nor do I here wish either to defend or attack any alternative version of the functionalist theory. I only wish to deny that *Marriage, Authority, and Final Causes* is a monograph that gives us good grounds for believing that Homans's functionalism is a theory capable of explaining the origins of particular forms of social organization.

Notes

When attending a seminar of mine, several graduate students in Social Relations at the Johns Hopkins University objected to my views regarding the autonomy of societal facts, claiming that my paper was undermined by the monograph of Homans and Schneider to which reference is here made. This led to my writing the present article.

1. George C. Homans and David M. Schneider, *Marriage, Authority, and Final Causes: A Study of Unilateral Cross-Cousin Marriage* (The Free Press, 1955).

This monograph has been republished in George C. Homans: *Sentiments and Activities* (Routledge & Kegan Paul, 1962), and to it Professor Homans has added an appendix: "Postscript: Five Years Later" (pp. 250-56). That postscript calls for no changes in the following argument.

Mention may also be made of a monograph that came to my attention after the present paper was written; it is Rodney Needham, *Structure and Sentiment, A Test Case in Social Anthropology* (University of Chicago Press, 1962). Needham's criticism proceeds on a quite different basis, but there are some parallels between what he says in his concluding section of chapter 2 (pp. 50-52) and what is here said.

2. Reprinted in Radcliffe-Brown, *Structure and Function in Primitive Societies,* pp. 15-31.

3. *The Rules of Sociological Method,* p. 95. (In the original, *Les Règles de la méthode sociologique,* p. 112.)

4. In *The Descent of Man* he wrote: "I did not formerly consider sufficiently the existence of structures, which, as far as we can at present judge, are neither beneficial nor injurious; and this I believe to be one of the greatest oversights as yet detected in my work. I may be permitted to say, as some excuse, that I had two distinct objects in view; firstly, to shew that species had not been separately created, and secondly, that natural selection had been the chief agent of change,

though largely aided by the inherited effects of habit, and slightly by the direct action of the surrounding conditions. I was not, however, able to annul the influence of my former belief, then almost universal, that each species had been purposely created; and this led to my tacit assumption that every detail of structure, excepting rudiments, was of some special, though unrecognized service." (Quoted from page 442 of The Modern Library edition [Random House, n.d.], which includes both *The Origin of Species* and *The Descent of Man.* The same passage, with minute stylistic changes, is to be found in the first edition of *The Descent of Man* [1871], vol. 1, p. 146f.)

20

G. A. Cohen's Defense of
Functional Explanation

In chapters 9 and 10 of *Karl Marx's Theory of History*,[1] G. A. Cohen offers an analysis and defense of functional explanations in general and, more specifically, of the functional explanations to be found in Marx's theory. In my opinion, Cohen's book is outstanding among all recent analyses of Marx's thought, and I find him correct when he contends that Marx relied heavily on functional explanations. Nonetheless, I believe that much of what Marx held regarding the structure of societies and the factors responsible for social change could be retained even though one were to relinquish his reliance on functional explanations; that, however, is another issue, and one with which I shall not here be concerned. The sole purpose of the present paper is to argue that Cohen's defense of functional explanations is seriously flawed because he misinterprets Darwinian theory in using it as a standard example of a functional explanation. The flaw is serious because he relies on our acceptance of Darwinian theory to gain our acceptance of the functional explanations to be found in Marx (cf. pp. 269-71, 285-89, 291).

In his preliminary characterization of what constitutes a functional explanation, Cohen cites a number of statements that purport to explain a phenomenon in functional terms; of them he says, "the intelligibility of these statements creates a *prima facie* case for the existence of a distinctive explanatory procedure, in which *reference to the effects of a phenomenon contributes to explaining it*" (p. 250, emphasis added). He then states the hypothesis that "there is a *special* type of causal explanation advanced in these and like instances, deriving its peculiarity from generalizations of distinctive logical form." In the remainder of Chapter 9 he develops this hypothesis, considering some alternative views regarding functional explanations and carefully constructing his own analysis of their distinctive logical form.

I shall not examine the manner in which Cohen develops his analysis of functional explanations, but shall proceed immediately to his short, nontechnical statement of what is involved in any such explanation. As he says when he shifts his attention from his general discussion of the logic of functional explanations to a consideration of their presence in Marx's theory, "We have said that central Marxian explanations are functional, which means, *very roughly*, that the character of what is explained is determined by

Reprinted by permission from *Philosophy of the Social Sciences*, 12 (1982):285-87.

its effect on what explains it" (p. 278). He then chooses as one example Marx's explanation of the rise of Protestantism in terms of what Protestantism was able to contribute to the growth of capitalism. In this connection he interprets Marx as holding that "Protestantism arose when it did because it was a religion suited to stimulating capitalist enterprise and enforcing labour discipline at a time when the capital/labour relation was preeminently apt to develop new productive potentials of society" (p. 279). Thus, the rise of Protestantism, which is the phenomenon to be explained, is explained in terms of what it contributed to the rise of capitalism. Cohen makes clear that this is what Marx meant, for he adds: "When Marx says that 'Protestantism, by changing almost all tradiitonal holidays into workdays, plays an important role in the genesis of capital' he is not just assigning a certain effect to the new religion, but proposing a (partial) explanation of its rise in terms of that effect" (p. 279).

As Cohen points out (p. 281), there is a standard objection to this view: "that what comes later does not explain what comes earlier." He argues, however, that the functional statements with which he is concerned do not violate this rule. It is here that his argument relies on his interpretation of Darwinian theory (p. 285; cf. p. 269). If a species survives in a particular environment it does so because it has characteristics that are of benefit to it in that environment; lacking these characteristics it would not have survived. This is the case no matter how the species came to have these particular characteristics; in this connection, Cohen admits that the characteristics themselves need not have developed in order to promote the survival of the species (cf. pp. 281-82). What he maintains is that no matter what the origin of these characteristics may have been, this constitutes an example of a functional explanation because the superior adaptation that resulted from the presence of these characteristics serves to explain why the characteristics themselves have survived. It is for this reason that the proffered explanation conforms to his characterization of functional explanations: the effect of a phenomenon contributes to explaining that phenomenon itself.

There is, I submit, a confusion in this interpretation of Darwinian theory. That confusion can best be seen if we begin with Darwin's own basic problem, the origin of species, rather than taking as a point of departure his explanation of specific adaptations. In explaining the origin of species, Darwin's account rested on two independent theses. One concerned the origin of the differences between the traits of one generation of individuals and the traits of their immediate forebears; the other concerned the conditions under which the presence of such traits led to the formation of new species. Each was an indispensable part of his theory. The explanation he gave of the origin of new traits is usually stated in terms of the phrase *chance variations,* though he held that other factors were also at work; in explaining how these traits then contributed to the origin of new species he appealed to the twin concepts of *struggle for survival* and *natural selection.* It should be evident that these two major aspects of his theory were based on different forms of evidence and that they involved different mechanisms, because Darwin was dealing in the one case with the inherited constitution of specific individuals and in the other with ecological questions concerning the relations between these individuals and their environments. In neither case was his explanation one in which a phenomenon was explained in terms of the effect it promoted; thus, neither major aspect of his theory relied on a functional explanation in Cohen's sense of the term.

In order to understand why Darwin's theory might nevertheless be interpreted as exemplifying a functional mode of explanation, we need merely recall that the operation of these two independent principles had as their joint consequence the fact that the types of organisms which did survive were suitably adapted to the environments in which they were found. Now, if we were to interpret Darwin's theory as being primarily intended to offer an explanation of this fact, then that theory could be construed as conforming to Cohen's model of a functional explanation: the presence of these particular traits is explained by what they contribute to the survival of this type of organism in the specific environment in which it is found. Nevertheless, it is a mistake to interpret Darwin's theory in this limited way. The fact that organisms are well suited to their environments was simply a *consequence* of the factors he had invoked when explaining how new species came to be formed. In analyzing that process, which included variability and the struggle for survival as well as selection and which stretched over extremely long periods of time, Darwin was not relying on functional explanations, and Cohen does not attempt to show that he was. On the other hand, Lamarck *did* attempt to explain the origin of new biological forms in a manner exemplifying Cohen's model of a functional explanation. According to him, such forms arose because of the inherent tendency of organisms to expand in ways that would fulfil their needs in the environment in which they found themselves. Thus, in Lamarck, the effect achieved was used to explain the phenomenon to be explained.

Now, Cohen recognized the difference between Darwinian and Lamarckian modes of explanation, but he subsumed both under the head of functional explanations. It was his view that any functional explanation can be further elaborated (p. 271), and he took the theories of Darwin and of Lamarck to be two different ways of elaborating the functional explanation of adaptations that he regarded as being common to both (pp. 287-89 and 291). Yet, if as I have claimed, the adaptation of organisms to their environments is simply a *consequence* of the joint operation of the basic principles involved in Darwinian theory, and if it is the case that these principles, taken individually, do not themselves conform to Cohen's model of a functional explanation, can it be held that Darwin, like Lamarck, explained adaptations in functional terms? What led to Cohen's confusion on this point is, as I have suggested, that he interpreted Darwin as if the latter's primary aim had been to explain adaptations, not to explain the origin of species. He was therefore able to bypass any concrete discussion of Darwin's actual explanatory principles, focusing attention on the adaptations that had resulted from the processes that Darwin had attempted to isolate and trace. In short, Cohen confused a consequence of Darwin's theory with the structure of that theory itself.

Had it not been for this interpretation of Darwinian theory, Cohen would have been hard put to find any parallels between the explanations to be found in the natural sciences today and the functional explanations he finds in Marx's works. In fact, apart from his references to Darwin, Cohen fails to refer to any concrete examples in which contemporary natural scientists actually use functional explanations of phenomena. Of course, this does not prove that Marx was wrong to appeal to functional explanations in the way that Cohen has shown that he did. On the other hand, it might be possible to revise Marx's form of argument in such a way that his functional statements would follow as consequences of his theory, rather than being foundational to that theory itself. Were this possible, I am inclined to think that his theory would prove to be more plausible than it otherwise is.

Note

My interests in functionalism and in interpreting Marx coalesced in the following brief paper. It was written immediately after Cohen's book appeared but was delayed in publication. It is only fair to say that since that time Cohen has somewhat modified his position (cf. Inquiry, 25 [1982]:27-56). Yet, because his book will undoubtedly be more widely known than that article, I feel justified in publishing this paper — at the same time calling attention to his article.

1. Karl Marx's Theory of History: A Defence (Princeton, 1978). All page references in the text refer to this volume.

IV

Historical Interpretations

21

The Distinguishable and the Separable:
A Note on Hume and Causation

In this essay, I shall be concerned with only one part of Hume's doctrine of causation, and my criticism of this feature of his position will leave much of the remainder untouched. This is not to say that my point is unimportant, for I shall challenge Hume's right to claim that there cannot in any case be a direct impression of connection, force, or power. He attempted to establish this claim by argument, and I wish to show that there is a fatal flaw in that argument.

In order that what follows shall not be misunderstood, two points must be noted. First, I would not claim that we have an impression of connection, force, or power in *all* cases in which we hold that events are related as cause and effect. There are many instances in which this is not true, and the number and even the varieties of these cases could be greatly expanded beyond the illustrations that Hume gave in the *Treatise* and the *Enquiry Concerning the Human Understanding.* I shall only argue that he did not offer adequate reasons for holding that there are *no cases* in which we can possibly have such impressions.

Second, it must be noted that Hume very generally linked the notions of *necessity* and *connection,* referring to *necessary* connection, and it was with our belief in the existence of a *necessary* connection between a cause and its effect that his analysis was primarily concerned.[1] One may, however, be willing to grant any or all of his arguments against the possibility of justifying the belief that the relation between two events is, in his sense, a *necessary* relation, yet these arguments might not be regarded as proving that in any particular case it is unjustified to hold that the two events were in fact connected and that the cause brought about, or produced, the effect. The possibility of separating these issues did not clearly emerge in Hume's treatment of the causal relation because he assumed that the terms *efficacy, agency, power, force, energy, necessity, connexion,* and *productive quality"* are "nearly synonymous."[2] However, this assumption is extremely doubtful if "necessity" is used in the sense of "logically necessary," and that is the way in which Hume used it time and again in his argument.[3] For my present purposes, I wish to put aside the question of whether there is any sense in which we can attribute "necessity" to the causal relationship; this is the second point I wished to make clear in order to obviate possible misunderstandings. I shall, then, only be concerned with that portion of Hume's argument which led him to hold that there cannot in any case be a direct impression of connection, efficacy, or power.

This contention was of obvious importance to Hume's formulation of his position, as can be seen from the statement at the outset of his discussion of the causal relation:

> To begin regularly, we must consider the idea of *causation,* and see from what origin it is deriv'd. 'Tis impossible to reason justly, without understanding perfectly the idea concerning which we reason; and 'tis impossible perfectly to understand any idea, without tracing it up to its origin, and examining that primary impression, from which it arises.[4]

Given this principle, it follows that if we do not in any cases have a primary or direct *impression* of force, efficacy, power, or of connection between what we regard as cause and effect, the *idea* of the causal relation must be accounted for in some other way. Hume, of course, offered such an account in his analysis of how the effects of constant conjunction and the operations of the mind lead us to attribute a necessary connection to events that are, in themselves, "entirely loose and separate" (*Enquiry,* p. 74). I shall not here challenge his account of how this idea arises in the absence of a primary impression; I am only interested in the way in which Hume attempted to prove that there is not, and cannot be, such an impression. So far as I have been able to determine, no other commentator has called attention to the particular flaw in Hume's argument with which I am concerned.[5]

In arguing against the possibility of there being any direct impression of force, power, or connection, Hume sometimes claimed to appeal to direct experience, but he repeatedly argued in terms of one basic principle that can in fact be regarded as an axiom in his system. In one of its formulations it reads: "Whatever objects are different are distinguishable, and whatever objects are distinguishable are separable by the thought and the imagination."[6] Hume's misuse of this axiom, to which I wish to call attention, lies in the fact that if it is to serve as a proof that we have no direct or primary impression of power, force, or connection, he would have had to show that it applies to our impressions; in fact, however, when he uses this axiom with reference to the causal relation he applies it not to our impressions, but only to complex *ideas.*

My point can initially be illustrated by appealing to Hume's remarks concerning "distinctions of reason" in his treatment of abstract ideas. The difficulty he attempted to resolve in that particular passage was how, on his principles, he could interpret what were called "distinctions of reason." He put the matter as follows:

> Before I leave this subject I shall employ the same principles to explain that *distiction of reason,* which is so much talk'd of, and is so little understood, in the

schools. Of this kind is the distinction betwixt figure and the body figur'd; motion and the body mov'd. The difficulty of explaining this distinction arises from the principle above explain'd, *that all ideas, which are different, are separable.* For it follows from thence, that if the figure be different from the body, their ideas must be separable as well as distinguishable; if they are not different, their idea can neither be separable nor distinguishable.[7]

Hume did not hold that the ideas are separable in such a case, even though they are different. He then solved this apparent contradiction in the following way, choosing impressions of color and shape as examples:

When a globe of white marble is presented, we receive only the impression of a white colour dispos'd in a certain form, nor are we able to separate and distinguish the colour from the form. But observing afterwards a globe of black marble and a cube of white, and comparing them with our former object, we find two separate resemblances, in what formerly seem'd, and really is, perfectly inseparable.

I need not proceed, for what is evident here is that Hume's axiom, as it is applied to our impressions, does *not* permit us to separate shape and color; we must learn to regard them as distinct through acts of comparison with other sets of impressions, that is, by transforming what were originally complex impressions into ideas. In fact, as this passage continues, Hume even acknowledged that some memory-images (which are, of course, ideas) are like impressions in this respect. All that can be done in such cases, if we are to separate the aspects of objects between which we can draw a distinction, is to focus attention on one of these aspects rather than another through summoning up other complex ideas and noting a respect in which they resemble one another, neglecting those respects in which they differ. In such cases at least, Hume's axiom that what is distinguishable is separable holds only in relation to what results from acts of thought and imagination; it is not properly construed as a description of what is given in experience.

This passage, which supposedly only concerns the way in which we come to form "distinctions of reason," is highly instructive with respect to Hume's doctrine of causation. It shows that there are elements that are in fact inseparable in experience, but that are later distinguished and treated as separable when they have been reproduced in our mind's eye and we have considered them under some of their aspects only, separating and combining them in new ways. This, I submit, is precisely what Hume did in all cases in which he applied his axiom to the relation between cause and effect. Consider, for example, the following passage, in which he is not describing actual impressions, but is considering those ideas which may afterwards be formed on the basis of earlier impressions:

The effect is totally different from the cause, and consequently can never be discovered in it. Motion in the second Billiard-ball is a quite distinct event from motion in the first; nor is there anything in the one to suggest the smallest hint of the other. . . . . When I see, for instance, a Billiard-ball moving in a straight line towards another; even suppose motion in the second ball should by accident be suggested to me, as a result of their contact or impulse; may I not conceive, that a hundred different events might as well follow from that cause? May not both these balls remain at absolute rest? May not the first ball return in a straight line, or leap off from the second in any line or direction? All these suppositions are consistent and conceivable.[8]

Had Hume been considering actual *impressions,* rather than ideas, could he have said that what a person actually observes when one billiard ball strikes another is a case in which "the effect is totally different from the cause"? Can it also be said that an observer clearly distinguishes and can separate the motion of one billiard ball from that of the other at the moment at which he witnesses their impact, or can this only be done in his imagination when he recalls his earlier impressions, transforming them into sets of complex ideas?[9]

Complex ideas are readily handled in the imagination: one can separate them and recombine them in a multitude of ways. Therefore, if we apply Hume's axiom to our complex ideas only, we can show—as Hume sets out to show—that there is no logically necessary connection, or relation of implication, between any type of cause and any specific type of effect. This, however, does not prove that what can be distinguished within our direct or primary impressions is also separable; in fact, as we have seen, this point is conceded by Hume in his discussion of "distinctions of reason." Consequently, we may say that he misused this axiom when he attempted to argue on the basis of it that our impressions never disclose a relation between a cause and its effect.

Those who wish to circumvent this argument and defend Hume's position on this point may be inclined to resort to the same challenge that Hume repeatedly offered his readers: that they should produce for him any example of a case in which we do have a direct impression of a connection between a cause and its effect.[10] It is to be noted, however, that while such a challenge may appear to involve an appeal to everyone's experience, it cannot properly be said to have that character. In support of this fact we may note that Hume not only admitted that in many cases we believe that we see a bond of necessary connection between cause and effect, he attempted to explain just how this pseudo-impression arises. Thus, in order to deny that we have any primary or underived impression of connection, power, or force, Hume had to rely upon argument, and not upon an appeal to experience. That he did rely upon the axiom concerning the distinguishable and the separable and that this axiom failed him has now I hope been shown. Yet one may still wonder why Hume did not notice that it was illegitimate to use this axiom in connection with our *ideas* when that which he wished to establish was a point concerning what could or could not be present in our *impressions.*

A possible answer to this question is, I submit, Hume's acceptance of still another axiom, which he also misused. In Book I, Part I, Section 7 of the *Treatise* we read: "Now since all ideas are deriv'd from impressions, and are nothing but copies and representations of them, whatever is true of the one must be acknowledged concerning the other. Impressions and ideas differ only in their strength and vivacity" (p. 19). Granted this assumption, it would seem that one could argue either from what is true of impressions to what is true of ideas, or from what is true of ideas to what is true of impressions. The latter possibility would seem to make it legitimate to use this axiom as a basis for the view that if our ideas of events are distinguishable and separable, then the impressions from which they were derived must have been so as well. Some tacit use of this axiom may have infected Hume's position. However, an unrestricted application of this axiom would be a misapplication of it. The axiom not only states that "all ideas are derived from impressions," but holds that our ideas "are nothing but copies and representations of them." Hume, however, obviously did not accept this principle with respect to our *complex* ideas: it was a principle he espoused only in connection with the relation between simple impressions and simple ideas.[11] Because those cases in which Hume argued that the cause was distinguishable and separable from the effect were cases in which he was dealing with complex ideas, and because (as we have seen in those cases in which we draw "distinctions of reason") there are cases in which simple impressions are inseparable, this axiom has no appropriate application to the question of whether an impression of power, force, or connection is present in what we directly observe.

While there may be many reasons that would lead one to deny that we do in any sense directly perceive power, force, or connection, I am not here concerned with those questions. Nor have I argued that Hume's analysis of the role of past experience and expectation is wrong in all cases in which we make causal judgments. My aim has been restricted to showing that in one of his frequently recurring arguments concerning the cause and effect relation, Hume misused what amounts to an axiom in his system: the dictum that whatever is different is distinguishable, and whatever is distinguishable is separable. If I have also succeeded in indicating that axioms concerning the elements included in his system play a greater role in Hume's thought than has often been remarked, this essay will have fulfilled a further, although secondary, purpose.

Notes

Hume's epistemology has been of continuing interest to me. This examination of one of his basic axioms is directly relevant to at least two of my other discussions of his views, namely those in Philosophy, Science, and Sense-Perception *(1964) and in* The Anatomy of Historical Knowledge *(1977).*

1. If it be doubted that this was Hume's primary concern, that doubt can be dispelled by noting the manner in which he formulated his problem near the end of section 2 (p. 78) and at the end of section 3 (p. 82) of book 1, part 3 of the *Treatise*. (All citations of the *Treatise* and the *Enquiry* will refer to Selby-Bigge's editions of these works.) Hume's *Abstract* of the *Treatise* is also relevant with respect to this point. (Cf. the Keynes and Sraffa edition, pp. 13-14.)

2. *Treatise*, book 1, part 3, sect. 14 (p. 157). For other points at which there is a similar equation of power, force efficacy, or connection with *necessity*, see pages 90-91 and 161-62 of the *Treatise*, and pages 62 and 73-74 of the *Enquiry*. B. M. Laing makes the same point, saying "He [Hume] identifies the notion of necessity with that of power, or force, or energy" (*David Hume*, p. 121); however, Laing does not criticize Hume for doing so.

3. An extreme statement of the view that Hume's primary concern was with the question of whether the causal relation is a logically necessary relation is to be found in R. E. Hobart, "Hume Without Scepticism," where it is said: "With regard to cause and effect, Hume pried apart certain ideas that were really distinct but had grown together. A proposition may imply another proposition, but a thing cannot imply another thing. That is the whole discovery; there is nothing more" (*Mind*, 39 [1930]:273). The statement is extreme because it suggests that this was not merely the primary but the exclusive concern of Hume's analysis. However, he was also obviously interested in offering a psychological account of the origin of our belief in the necessity that we attribute to the relation of cause and effect.

4. *Treatise*, book 1, part 3, sect. 2 (pp. 74-75). The same general point is made in the *Enquiry*, p. 22.

5. In addition to articles, I have consulted the books and monographs of the following students of Hume: Robert F. Anderson, A. H. Basson, R. W. Church, A. Flew, T. H. Green, C. W. Hendel, T. H. Huxley, B. M. Laing, J. Laird, A.-L. Leroy, D.G.C. MacNabb, C. Maund, A. Meinong, R. Metz, J. Passmore, H. H. Price, Alfred Schaefer, N. K. Smith, G. della Volpe, J. Wilbanks, and F. Zabeeh. I might add that of these works only those of Anderson, Church, and Meinong place what I consider to be adequate emphasis on Hume's use of the axiom to which I shall be calling attention, and Meinong's discussion of it was primarily related to its role in Hume's doctrine of abstract ideas.

The closest modern approximation to some of the points that are to follow is to be found in sect. 62 of Jonathan Bennett's book, *Locke, Berkeley, and Hume: Central Themes*. However, Richard Popkin has called to my attention that a reviewer of the *Treatise*, writing in the *History of the Works of the Learned* in 1739, did find fault with Hume's use of the axiom that whatever is distinguishable is separable, saying "This Axiom is somewhat like a Conjurer's *Hocus-Pocus*: it works Wonders and is at every Turn repeated" (quoted by Laird, *Hume's Philosophy of Human Nature*, p. 9).

6. *Treatise*, book 1, part 1, sect. 7 (p. 18). For some other passages in which this axiom is used in the *Treatise*, see pages 2, 10, 27, 36, 38, 54, 79-80, 87, 221, 223, 233, 259, 632, 634, 636, and 637. A comparable passage is to be found in the *Enquiry*, p. 29.

7. *Treatise*, book 1, part 1, sect. 7 (pp. 24-25). Although Hume attributed this distinction to "the schools," Laird cites Descartes and the *Port Royal Logic* as the targets of the discussion. (Cf. *Hume's Philosophy of Human Nature*, p. 63.)

8. *Enquiry*, pp. 29-30. For another passage that illustrates the same point, cf. the *Treatise*, pp. 86-87.

9. That Hume's position is exceedingly dubious with reference to both of these points can be seen in many of Michotte's experiments on the perception of causality. In them it is readily possible to *imagine* the movement of one of the objects independently of the presence of the other, but what is *seen* is a connection between them. For example, cf. experiment 2 on "entrainment" in A. E. Michotte, *The Perception of Causality*, p. 21.

10. For examples of such passages, cf. the *Treatise*, pp. 76-77, 159, and 162.

11. Laird makes the same point in another connection. Speaking of Hume's doctrine that ideas copy impressions, Laird remarked, "Strictly speaking, he had attempted to prove it with regard to *simple* ideas only" (*Hume's Philosophy of Human Nature*, p. 31). If the point be doubted, the reader need merely consult the *Treatise*, book 1, part 1, sect. 1 (p. 3).

22

On Interpreting Mill's *Utilitarianism*

It is doubtful whether any text in the history of ethical thought is better known to contemporary British and American philosophers than John Stuart Mill's *Utilitarianism.* Nevertheless, those who discuss Mill's views have usually been content to isolate and analyze particular positions, rather than offering an interpretation of the essay as a whole. Among the propositions most often discussed are those connected with Mill's introduction of the notion of higher and lower pleasures and those connected with his proof of the principle of utility. To the various questions associated with these passages, there has recently been added the further issue of whether Mill is to be classified as a "rule utilitarian," or whether he holds the classic position of unrestricted utilitarianism.

I do not believe that, on the whole, this method of fragmentary criticism has been particularly unfair or that it has led to distorted interpretations of Mill's doctrine on those issues with which most critics and commentators have been concerned. However, many passages have been left needlessly obscure, and in fact baffling. Consider, for example, the manner in which Mill uses the term *virtue* and its cognates. In a passage that immediately succeeds his discussion of the proof of the principle of utility, Mill acknowledges the distinction that is made in common language between a desire for happiness and a desire for virtue.[1] Rather surprisingly, he then goes on to say that the utilitarian doctrine "maintains not only that virtue is to be desired, but that it is to be desired disinterestedly, for itself."[2] This thesis, he claims, is in no way incompatible with holding that "actions and dispositions are only virtuous because they promote another end than virtue." The method by means of which Mill can reconcile these two apparently contradictory statements is an important aspect of his ethical theory, but it is not an aspect that can easily be understood without reference to some of his generally neglected ethical writings or without relating it to a number of other views which he held. A similar claim can be made with respect to the issue of whether Mill should or should not be classed as a rule utilitarian, but I shall not deal with that issue in the present paper.[3] In what follows I shall draw on the whole corpus of Mill's writings, rather than attempt to deal with *Utilitarianism* in isolation. By this means, I believe, one can best explicate what is otherwise obscure in that work.[4]

Mill on Bentham

I suppose it will be granted that if we are to understand Mill's ethical theory we must keep in mind its relationship to the thought of Bentham. It will be recalled that in speaking of the time when he first read Bentham, Mill said: "The feeling rushed upon me, that all previous moralists were superseded, and that here indeed was the commencement of a new era of thought."[5] Even when, after his mental crisis, his own views began to diverge from those of Bentham (and of his father), he never abandoned the conviction that, in its most essential aspects, Benthamism was true. In his *Autobiography* he referred to the fact that although he found the fabric of his old opinions giving way in many places, he never allowed it to fall wholly to pieces;[6] and if one examines the series of articles which contain Mill's discussions of Bentham, dating from 1833 through an essay on John Austin published thirty years later, one finds no reason to doubt this self-estimate on his part.[7]

Nonetheless, as every reader of *Utilitarianism* knows, the differences between Mill's position and Bentham's are striking. One may in fact view each of the chapters of that work, except the first, as being, in part, an attempt to correct what Mill took to be either errors or lacunae in the position of Bentham. For example, the emphasis in chapter 2 is placed upon rebutting what Mill took to be the most serious charge against Benthamism: its failure to acknowledge distinctions in value among various types of pleasurable experiences.[8] The relation of chapter 3 of *Utilitarianism* to Bentham's views is equally obvious: it provides a supplement to the Benthamite doctrine of external sanctions by adding the internal sanction of a feeling, the feeling of obligation. In so doing it also remedies what Mill took to be a distorted picture of man which came from Bentham's emphasis on the role of a calculation of consequences in determining human action.[9] Mill's fourth chapter, which is concerned with the question of how the principle of utility is to be proved, remedies what he regarded as a flaw in Bentham's system: the failure of that system to provide any positive argument for utilitarianism, relying instead on a rejection—through what was almost a caricature—of alternative principles.[10] With respect to the fifth chapter, which was originally begun as the draft of an independent essay on justice,[11] the connection between *Utilitarianism* and the need to correct Bentham's system is less immediately obvious, but there are in fact even more points at which it may be seen as offering a corrective. For example, in other writings Mill had criticized Bentham for having failed to distinguish between benevolence and justice—a failure that this chapter can be seen as correcting.[12] In addition, justice provides a case, consistent with utilitarianism, in which one can safely appeal to a secondary principle or rule and need not calculate the consequences of an action in the cumbersome way the Benthamite formula would seem to demand.[13] And, finally, in this chapter Mill is able to explain why the secondary principle of justice could truly appear to men as being "incomparably the most sacred and binding part of all morality,"[14] thus showing, in the particular case most often cited as an objection to the principle of utility,[15] that utilitarianism could acknowledge the strength and the justification of precisely the same moral sentiments as those to which Bentham's opponents appealed.

It is usually assumed that when Mill departs from Bentham's system, enlarging the scope of what is to be regarded as humanly important, he is making concessions to the opponents of the utilitarian school, rather than building a positive moral theory of his own. Typical of this interpretation, and ably expressing it, are remarks made by A. D. Lindsay:

> We find him in all his books enunciating with firmness the Utilitarian principles, then compelled by his fairness and openness of mind to admit exceptions and insert qualifications which the older Utilitarianism, complete but narrow, had never recognized. The resultant picture is much fairer to the facts, but presents much less of a consistent doctrine, and the critical reader is always wondering why, if Mill admits this or that, he persists in maintaining general principles with which the facts admitted are clearly inconsistent.[16]

However, it is also possible to view most (though not all)[17] of the changes that Mill incorporated into utilitarianism as attempts to offer a moral theory more in line with a careful psychological account of human motivation: a theory that was to be based on Hartley and James Mill, not on the crude form of psychological hedonism which Bentham espoused. On the whole, I would stress the second of these alternative interpretations. And if we now consider Mill's early criticisms of Bentham's psychology, one can (I hope) see reason for doing so.

In his "Remarks," Mill summarized Bentham's psychological assumptions in the following propositions:

> . . . that happiness, meaning by that term pleasure and exemption from pain, is the only thing desirable in itself; that all other things are desirable solely as means to that end . . . and moreover, that pleasure and pain are the sole agencies by which the conduct of mankind is in fact governed, whatever circumstances the individual may be placed in, and whether he is aware of it or not.

And continued:

> Mr. Bentham does not appear to have entered very deeply into the metaphysical grounds of these doctrines; he seems to have taken those grounds very much upon the showing of the metaphysicians who preceded him.[18]

Now, it is clear that Mill is here using the term *metaphysical* as equivalent to what we should designate as *psychological*, the noun metaphysics having frequently been used by Adam Smith and Hamilton, and by others, to refer to *pneumatology* as contrasted with *physics*.[19] The general criticism Mill leveled against Bentham's psychology was its attempt to explain human action in terms of the notion of self-interest and its failure to see that motives not originally part of man's endowment could arise through the associative process. In an argument reminiscent of Bishop Butler, Mill pointed out that the view that self-interest dominates men is only plausible because it involves an ambiguity in terms.[20] Furthermore, he rejected Bentham's assumption that men always act for *future* pleasures or the avoidance of *future* pains. According to Mill, this form of hedonism makes it impossible to explain so-called disinterested actions, for example, actions that spring from patriotism, benevolence, or conscience.[21]

The hedonistic theory that, in these passages, Mill himself explicitly accepts (and which he seems never to have abandoned) states that men act in accordance with the pleasantness or unpleasantness of their *present* ideas. To explain how ideas of particular actions take on pleasantness or unpleasantness, Mill invokes associations dependent upon past experience. And by this means he materially enlarges the range of motives which Bentham had attributed to men.[22] As he says in this essay:

> The attempt to enumerate motives, that is, human desires and aversions, seems to me to be in its very conception an error. Motives are innumerable: there is nothing whatever which may not become an object of desire or of dislike by association.[23]

In this connection it is important to note that Mill cites Hartley against Bentham, praising Hartley on the ground that "although he considers the moral sentiments to be wholly the result of association, [he] does not therefore deny them a place in his system, but includes the feelings of 'the moral sense' as one of the six classes into which he divides pleasures and pains."[24] This passage is suggestive of Mill's own positive views, for (as we shall see) he insists on the emergence of an effective moral sense through what we should now term *functional autonomy*.[25] It will be my contention that this departure from Bentham's psychological views constitutes a crucial factor in Mill's ethical theory.

The second point of criticism of Bentham which it is important to note for the sake of interpreting *Utilitarianism* as a positive and consistent formulation of a utilitarian position is Mill's rejection of the view that the rightness or wrongness of an action is to be calculated in terms of its "specific consequences." Mill states his criticism as follows:

> Now, the great fault I have to find with Mr. Bentham as a moral philosopher, and the source of the chief part of the temporary mischief which in that character, along with a vastly greater amount of permanent good, he must be allowed to have produced is this: that he has practically, to a very great extent, confounded the principle of Utility with the principle of specific consequences, and has habitually made up his estimate of the approbation or blame due to a par-

ticular kind of action, from a calculation of the consequences to which that very action, if practiced generally, would itself lead.[26]

Now, what we must note is the additional factor, other than "specific consequences," that Mill holds must be taken into account if the utilitarian doctrine is to be acceptable. This type of factor is *not* the more remote consequences: Bentham, after all, had taken such consequences into account, as is evident in the roles played by purity, fecundity, and extent, in his felicific calculus. Instead, what Mill holds to have been neglected by Bentham is the sort of "consequence" which lies in the effect of an action on the agent's own character. The thesis that such effects are themselves relevant to the moral judgment of actions is an aspect of Mill's moral theory which, as we shall see, is of sufficient importance for quoting at length from the passage in his anonymous essay on Benthem:

He [Bentham] has largely exemplified, and contributed very widely to diffuse, a tone of thinking according to which any kind of action or any habit, which in its own specific consequences cannot be proved to be necessarily or probably productive of unhappiness to the agent himself or to others, is supposed to be fully justified; and any disapprobation or aversion entertained towards the individual by reason of it, is set down from that time forward as prejudice and superstition. It is not considered (at least, not habitually considered), whether the act or habit in question, though not in itself pernicious, may not form part of a *character* essentially pernicious, or at least essentially deficient in some quality eminently conducive to the "greatest happiness." To apply such a standard as this, would indeed often require a much deeper insight into the formation of character, and knowledge of the internal workings of human nature, than Mr. Bentham possessed. But, in a greater or less degree, he, and every one else, judges by this standard.[27]

This appeal to the effects of an action, or type of action, upon the agent's own character (and, presumably, also upon the characters of those who might emulate the agent) is an aspect of Mill's theory which had not—so far as I can recall—been duly noted. That its expression in this anonymous essay was not an isolated instance of an ephemeral view can be seen in its repetition in Mill's attack on Sedgwick, where he says:

In estimating the consequences of actions, in order to obtain a measure of their morality, there are always two sets of considerations involved—the consequences to the outward interests of the parties concerned (including the agent himself); and the consequences to the characters of the same persons, and to their outward interests so far as dependent upon their characters. . . . It often happens that an essential part of the morality or immorality of an action or a rule of action consists in its influence upon the agent's own mind; upon his susceptibilities of pleasure or pain; upon the general direction of this thoughts, feelings, and imagination; or upon some particular association.[28]

As we shall see, if we take this doctrine seriously, accepting the view that we are to count among the consequences of an act the effects of the performance of that act on the agent's own character, we shall be in a better position to interpret some of the more baffling aspects of *Utilitarianism.*[29]

On Virtue and Utility

The preceding discussion places us in a better position to understand why Mill considered it justifiable to claim that even though utility is the standard of morality, the concept of virtue possesses a meaning distinct from that of utility. His use of the psychological principle of functional autonomy enabled him to explain how men come to act for ends other than those included among their original desires. Furthermore, a recognition of the functional autonomy of these new motives is reconciled with psychological hedonism through Mill's insistence that human action is to be explained through the pleasantness-unpleasantness of *present* ideas, not through the calculation of future pleasures and pains. Finally, in including among the consequences of an action the effects of that action on the agent's own character, Mill was able to show that the principle of utility did not regard the morality of an action as solely dependent upon its overt consequences: the motives and the character of an agent were no less to be considered by the utilitarian than by his opponents. Bearing these points in mind, it is clear how Mill could answer the question that we originally raised: whether it is possible to say that virtue "is to be desired disinterestedly, for itself," and yet consistently hold that actions and dispositions "are only virtuous because they promote another end than virtue." That Mill's answer depends upon his adoption of a particular set of psychological assumptions is clear in the following passage:

> Whatever may be the opinion of utilitarian moralists as to the original conditions by which virtue is made virtue, however they may believe (as they do) that actions and dispositions are only virtuous because they promote another end than virtue, yet this being granted, and it having been decided from considerations of this description what *is* virtuous, they not only place virtue at the very head of the things which are good as means to the ultimate end, but they also recognize as a psychological fact the possibility of its being, to an individual, a good in itself, without looking to any end beyond it.[30]

Up to this point, then, the interpretation of Mill's doctrine of virtue poses no obstacles that cannot be overcome by looking to his other works for the relevant psychological assumptions that he accepts. However, neither in *Utilitarianism* nor elsewhere do I find an explicit characterization of the specific nature of that which he calls virtue. In order to determine the substantive content designated by that term, we must examine in context the passages in which he uses it, its cognates, or their antonyms.

Following this method, it would seem that virtue is to be regarded as a dispositional property of persons, and that anything that is to be described as "virtuous" is connected with the existence of this property in human agents. (Thus, for example, I find no occasions on which Mill designates an action as virtuous because its specific consequences are good.) As examples of instances in which he uses the term as I suggest, one may note that he twice speaks of "a person of confirmed virtue,"[31] and he remarks that in conflicts of obligation the conflict can only be partially overcome through "the intellect and virtue of the individual."[32] He also says of the readiness of a person to make an absolute sacrifice of his own happiness for the sake of the happiness of others, that this readiness—which is clearly a dispositional trait—is the highest virtue one can find in man.[33] Furthermore, this remark reveals what Mill actually took to be the substantive character of that dispositional trait he designated as virtue: it was a readiness to act for the greatest good of mankind, in place of acting for one's personal good. That this is an accurate interpretation of Mill's position can perhaps be seen most clearly in a passage from *On Liberty*. In that passage Mill lists those objects which deserve the strongest moral reprobation. These objects include not only acts in which one person injures another, but the dispositions that lead men to perform such acts; these dispositions, Mill says, "are moral vices and constitute a bad and odious moral character."[34] This being so, one may justifiably infer that virtue, or a virtuous character, consists in a readiness to respond to the needs of others, a disposition to act not out of self-interest but for the happiness of others. Obviously, praise of such a disposition is wholly in conformity with an acceptance of the utilitarian principle, because nothing can in the long run better serve to promote the happiness of mankind than fostering that trait of character which involves a readiness to respond sensitively to the needs of others, placing their needs above one's own. And thus Mill was wholly justified in insisting—as we noted in his criticism of Bentham—that it is not only the "specific consequences" of an action, but the effects of that action on the character of the agent himself, that a utilitarian must take into account.

Now, the trait of character which leads an agent to place the good of others ahead of his own pleasure was a trait which Mill held to be both a proper and a possible object for the individual to desire for himself. To be sure, if virtue failed to afford pleasure, we would not seek it; but it *does* afford pleasure—not through the specific consequences which it brings us, but in the idea which we have of *being* virtuous (and by the pain that would be occasioned by the realization that we were not). Thus, through functional autonomy, virtue—which would not be virtue if it did not foster happiness—becomes for an agent a goal sought for itself. If one were to object and say that a man is not truly virtuous, but is self-righteous and a prig, if he seeks virtue because the idea of his virtue is agreeable to him, one would have misunderstood how, according to Mill, the functional autonomy of motives comes about. The only reason that pleasure can be derived from a consciousness that one has acted virtuously is that there was an original bond between pleasure for ourselves and the happiness of others. This bond is dependent upon our original possession of feelings of sympathy, of love, and of all those other-regarding tendencies that Mill refers to as "the social feeling."[35] Thus, unless one were first interested in others, one could not derive pleasure from the thought of acting virtuously. In short, while it is compatible with functional autonomy that the attempt to be virtuous may *eventually* lead some men to become prigs, Mill's analysis makes it clear that the pursuit of virtue originally springs from the existence in us of other-regarding sentiments, and not from a concern with our own self-image. In other words, the pursuit of virtue for its own sake is possible only for those whose social feelings have rendered them sensitive to the needs of others; for them it can be among the strongest of motives; and it can impart an immediate happiness, independent of the future. In this connection Mill says:

> Virtue, according to the utilitarian doctrine, is not naturally and originally part of the end, but it is capable of becoming so; and in those who love it disinterestedly it has become so and is desired and cherished, not as a means to happiness, but as a part of their happiness.[36]

Assuming the accuracy of the foregoing account of Mill's use of the term *virtue*, one can see why—apart from all reasons of composition[37]—his treatment of justice proceeds independently of his remarks concerning virtue. In the first place, Mill apparently recognized that the concept of justice, unlike that of virtue, does not have at its root a reference to the dispositional properties of persons: in its primary meaning, he tells us, it is a characteristic attributable to certain "modes of action" or "arrangements of human affairs."[38] This being so, an analysis of the concept of justice and of its relation to the standard of utility, would not follow a path like that involved in the analysis of virtue. In the second place, we may note that in his account of justice, unlike his account of virtue, Mill distinguishes sharply between what constitutes the *standard* of justice and what constitutes the *origin* of the sentiment that attaches to it.[39] Furthermore, we may note that in his account of the origins of the sentiment attaching to justice Mill does not make use of the principle of functional autonomy, as he did in the case of the origin of our idea of virtue. Instead, he placed reliance upon a recognition of self-interest as bound up with the recognition of rights, as well as upon a basic impulse to retaliate against injuries.

In spite of these differences, however, there is one basic similarity between Mill's account of virtue and his account of justice: he recognizes each as capable of being pursued as an end in itself, even though the moral legitimacy of each depends wholly upon its relation to the principle of utility. That this is the case with respect to virtue, we have already shown; that it is Mill's view with respect to justice is (so far as I know) universally acknowledged. And it is at this point that we can see why it is frequently held that Mill is to be regarded as a rule utilitarian. However, it is not with that complex issue that I am here concerned. My aim in this paper has been to show the very great extent to which a careful interpretation of Mill's

Utilitarianism presupposes that we take seriously those psychological doctrines which most commentators neglect.

Now, it should not be surprising to find that Mill's ultimate conclusions in the theory of morals rest upon psychological principles, and that in establishing these conclusions his associationism played a particularly important part. One thinks immediately of his *System of Logic* and of his *Examination of Sir William Hamilton's Philosophy* as two other instances of a similar sort. And if, in interpreting *Utilitarianism*, we bear in mind Mill's treatment of axioms in the *Logic* and his treatment of our belief in an external world in the *Examination*, we shall derive more assistance than by looking only to those works of political philosophy from which critics generally seek help in their interpretations of his moral theory.[40] Axioms, one will recall, have their sources in the total, cumulative effect of experiences, but it is not necessary for us to refer them back to those sources in order to understand their mathematical or logical import and to use them. Similarly, in our conception of independent, external objects, and in that paradigmatic case to which Mill often refers—our ability to judge distances—we rely in these cases on the effects of a congeries of past sensations, but our practical judgments do not demand that we refer back to these ultimate sources before we actually judge. Such examples suggest that even though the ultimate *source* of our moral notions is in all cases to be found in simple experiences of pleasure and pain, the shapes that morality can assume are highly complex and in many cases appear as wholly independent of that in which they had their origin. Thus, the ideas and feelings connected with morality possess characteristics that one would not expect to find associated with so humble a source.[41] It is, then, not necessarily an inconsistency on the part of Mill to recognize that there are (in some sense) "nobler" or "higher" feelings and states of character than those leading us to view every action in terms of the future effects it will have on our own pleasures and pains.[42] To recognize the emergence of new forms of action is not, however, to deny that pleasure and pain lie at their base. It was for the sake of showing how Mill thought that he could derive the nobler sentiments from their primitive source in experience that we have examined his criticism of Bentham and have analyzed his use of the concept of virtue.

Notes

In my preface to this volume I indicated what led to this and the following article. Originally, they comprised a single article, but being too long for publication in that form I separated them in a way that might make each appear to be more or less independent of the other.

1. *Utilitarianism*, chap. 4, para. 4 (Everyman's edition, p. 33).
[In citing Mill's *Utilitarianism* I shall make use of Mill's paragraphing, so that the reader may readily find the passage regardless of the edition he uses. However, in each case I shall also add the pagination of the Everyman edition.]

2. Chap. 4, para. 5 (p. 33).

3. I discuss it at length in an article entitled "Two Moot Issues in Mill's *Utilitarianism,*" published in *Modern Studies in Philosophy: John Stuart Mill,* ed. Jerome B. Schneewind (New York, 1968). Also reprinted below (ch. 23).

The question of whether Mill is to be regarded as a rule utilitarian was first raised in its present influential form by J. O. Urmson. His essay, "The Interpretation of the Moral Philosophy of J. S. Mill," was originally published in *Philosophical Quarterly* (January, 1953); it too appears in the volume edited by Schneewind.

4. In what follows I shall make every effort to interpret Mill's thought as a carefully expounded and consistent position. While I am prepared to acknowledge that his style does not lend itself to that degree of explicitness and precision which contemporary modes of thought demand, it seems to me a mistake to assume, as has sometimes been assumed (e.g., by Sidgwick in *Methods of Ethics* [7th ed.], p. 93, n. 1; and by Urmson, "Moral Philosophy of J. S. Mill," p. 38), that because *Utilitarianism* was originally published in *Fraser's Magazine* it can be considered as merely a "popular" exposition, in which looseness of phraseology and of presentation are to be expected. Such a suggestion presupposes a dichotomy between popular and technical writing which did not exist for Mill. It also fails to take into account the consistency between *Utilitarianism* and every other exposition of Mill's ethical views, as well as its consistency with the relevant statements in his *Autobiography.*

5. *Autobiography,* chap. 3, para. 3. (Cf. *The Early Draft of John Stuart Mill's "Autobiography,"* ed. Jack Stillinger [Urbana, Ill., 1961], pp. 74f.)

In citing from the *Autobiography* I shall quote from the text as given in the Columbia University Press edition, referring to that text by chapter, and by the paragraphing it follows. However, the *Early Draft,* as edited by Stillinger, is in many respects so valuable that I shall refer to it by page.

6. Cf. *Autobiography,* chap. 5, para. 14 (*Early Draft,* p. 133).

7. The articles in question are: an anonymous essay entitled "Remarks on Bentham's Philosophy," published in 1833 as an appendix to E. L. Bulwer's *England and the English*; his essay "Professor Sedgwick's Discourse on the Status of the University of Cambridge" (1835); his essay "Bentham," *London Review* (1838); his attack on Whewell's moral philosophy (1852); and his essay on Austin, which postdates the publication of *Utilitarianism.* (All but the first of these are to be found in Mill's *Dissertations and Discussions,* hereafter cited as *Dissertations.* In quoting from that collection, I shall use the five-volume New York edition of 1874.)

It is worth remarking that the anonymous essay on Bentham contains Mill's most explicit account of some of the points on which he disagrees with Bentham. It is strange that the essay is not better known, for Mill mentions it in the *Autobiography,* chap. 6, para. 7 (*Early Draft,* p. 157). One can now also find references to it in the *Early Letters of John Stuart Mill* (*Collected Works,* 12 [Toronto, 1963], pp. 152 n. 12 and 236. Fortunately, J. B. Schneewind has included this essay in his recent edition of *Mill's Ethical Writings* (New York, 1965). I shall refer to this essay as "Remarks," to avoid confusion with the more celebrated later essay entitled "Bentham"; page references to it will be those of the fourth edition of Bulwer's *England and the English* (Paris, 1836), followed by reference to the Schneewind anthology.

8. Mill attributed this deficiency in Bentham's system to Bentham's own personal limitations, not to his basic philosophic insights. He rightly saw Bentham as a person who lacked imagination and did not learn from others, and whose own range of experience was exceedingly narrow (cf. *Dissertations,* 1, 378). As a consequence of these personal limitations, the concrete moral standard to be found in Bentham seemed to Mill to "do nothing for the conduct of the individual, beyond prescribing some of the more obvious dictates of worldly prudence, and outward probity and beneficence. There is no need [Mill continues] to expatiate on the deficiency of a system of ethics which does not pretend to aid individuals in the formation of their own character; which recognizes no such wish as that of self-culture" (ibid., p. 388). This complaint is echoed in *Utilitarianism,* chap. 2, para. 4 (p. 7), when Mill says that "utilitarian writers in general have placed the superiority of mental over bodily pleasures chiefly in the greater permanency, safety, uncostliness, etc., of the former—that is, in their circumstantial advantages rather than in

their intrinsic nature." Mill's objection to the portrait of human nature which utilitarians had thus painted was, no doubt, founded on moral conviction—and moral conviction which *may* not have been consonant with any form of utilitarianism. Nonetheless, it should be noted that he was here also rebelling against a psychological theory: as we shall see immediately below, one of his objections to Bentham was that the Benthamite psychology overstressed the intellectual calculation of consequences as a motive for human action, and failed to acknowledge the plurality of human ends.

9. This criticism, implicit in the paragraphs cited in the preceding note from Mill's "Bentham," is even clearer in his anonymous essay, where he says: "The prevailing error of Mr. Bentham's views of human nature appears to me to be this—he supposes mankind to be swayed by only a part of the inducements which really actuate them; but of that part he imagines them to be much cooler and more thoughtful calculators than they really are" ("Remarks," p. 325; in Schneewind, p. 60).

10. Mill expressed this point strongly in "Remarks," pp. 315-16 (Schneewind, pp. 46-47). (Though later, in his unusually bitter and polemical essay on Whewell, he defended Bentham against the same charge: cf. *Dissertations*, 3, 146-55). In "Bentham" he also pointed out the latter's failure to appreciate the positions of those who did not accept the principle of utility (cf. *Dissertations*, 1, 370, 375). What he found to be original in Bentham was a *method* of handling moral questions, not the discovery of any new moral principle (ibid., pp. 370-72). Thus, one may infer that Mill felt that it was left to him to establish the truth of the principle of utility, and it would seem to be a fair reading of the last two paragraphs of the introductory chapter to say that it was primarily for the sake of filling this lacuna that *Utilitarianism* was written.

11. Cf. the remark of Helen Taylor in her preface to *Three Essays on Religion* (London, 1874).

12. For Mill's criticism of Bentham in this respect, cf. "Remarks," p. 322 (Schneewind, p. 56), and *Dissertations*, 1, 384 and note. The relation of these remarks to chapter 5 of *Utilitarianism* is to be seen if the reader will consult Mill's comment in his edition of James Mill's *Analysis of the Phenomena of the Human Mind*, 2, 2nd ed. (London, 1878), p. 324.

13. While Mill strongly criticizes Bentham for overlooking the importance of secondary principles (cf. *Dissertations*, 1, 409-10), his own treatment of such secondary principles (including justice) should not, in my opinion, lead one to interpret him as a rule utilitarian.

14. Chap. 5, para. 32 (p. 55).

15. Cf. chap. 5, para. 1 (p. 38).

16. Preface to Everyman's edition of Mill: *Utilitarianism, On Liberty*, p. viii.

17. I find the chief exception to be his introduction of the notion of higher and lower pleasures; that innovation can, I believe, be regarded as a case in which his own moral and aesthetic judgments forced him to a conclusion inconsistent with his basic theory. I might add, however, that he probably could have argued for at least *some* of those values which he linked with the higher or nobler pleasures on grounds consistent with his other views. That he did not attempt to do so suggests that in this case Lindsay's characterization is correct.

18. "Remarks," p. 315 (Schneewind, p. 46).

19. Cf. *Oxford English Dictionary*, "Metaphysics," entry 1c.

For other instances of Mill's use of *metaphysician* and *metaphysics* in this sense, cf. his characterizations both of his father and of Helvetius as metaphysicians in "Bentham" (*Dissertations*, 1 (New York, 1874-75), pp. 360, 408, respectively); also his remark that the relation between the question of whether moral feelings are simple or complex (and whether, if they are complex, of what simple feelings they are composed) "is a metaphysical question," "Professor Sedgwick's Discourse" (*Dissertations*, 1, 149).

Among the many other references that might be cited are the following: *Utilitarianism*, chap. 4, para. 10 (p. 36); *Dissertations*, 3, 164; and the concluding paragraphs of the introduction to the *System of Logic*.

The importance of noting that *metaphysical* is to be taken as meaning *psychological* can be seen from the fact that as able a critic as Mary Warnock holds that Mill viewed it as *logically* contradictory that we should desire anything but pleasure, and she cites his use of *metaphysical* in support of that contention (cf. Preface to the Meridian edition of Mill's *Utilitarianism*, p. 26).

20. "Remarks," pp. 322-23 (Schneewind, p. 57).

21. Cf. "Remarks," pp. 321, 323 (Schneewind, pp. 55, 58).

22. Unlike many later commentators, Mill notes that Bentham admitted sympathy to be an underived motive in man (cf. "Remarks," p. 322 [Schneewind, p. 56]. Also, *Dissertations*, 1, 383). However, he criticized Bentham for failing to account for benevolence as "a steady principle of action" (cf. "Remarks," p. 323 [Schneewind, p. 58]). Without taking into account the results of the associative process, sympathy (according to Mill) can only explain those cases of benevolent action in which it is actually felt.

In both of his essays on Bentham, Mill stresses the importance—and the inadequacy—of Bentham's "Table of the Springs of Action" (cf. "Remarks," p. 321 [Schneewind, p. 54]. Also, *Dissertations*, 1, 383).

23. "Remarks," p. 321 (Schneewind, p. 55). The clearest expression of Mill's views on this point is to be found much later, in a context in which he is not discussing Bentham. One finds that expression in notes added to his father's *Analysis of the Phenomena of the Human Mind*, 2, 233-34, 307-9.

24. "Remarks," p. 322 (Schneewind, p. 56). Mill's criticism of Bentham's psychology in his later essay, "Bentham," follows the same general lines as those laid down in his anonymous essay, even though the later exposition is less detailed. For example, it contains an equivalent reference to Hartley (*Dissertations*, 2, 387); it also contains a criticism of Bentham's failure to include motives that are not original, but are derived through the effects of association:

> Man is never recognized by him as a being capable of pursuing spiritual perfection as an end; of desiring, for its own sake, the conformity of his own character to his standard of excellence, without hope of good or fear of evil from other sources than his own inward consciousness. Even in the more limited form of conscience, this great fact of human nature escapes him. Nothing is more curious than the absence of recognition in any of his writings of the existence of conscience, as a thing distinct from philanthrophy, from affection for God or man, and from self-interest in this world or in the next. (*Dissertations*, 1, 384)

In interpreting Mill on association it is of course necessary to bear in mind that the principle of association, as he used that term, was not only applicable to memory but was at the same time "the law of imagination, of belief, of reasoning, of the affections, of the will." (From "Blakey's History of Moral Science," *The Monthly Repository*, n. s., 7 [1833]:664. Also, *Dissertations*, 4, 112-13.

25. This term was apparently coined by Gordon W. Allport and first used by him in *Personality: A Psychological Interpretation* (New York, 1937), pp. 191ff.

26. "Remarks," p. 317 (Schneewind, p. 49).

27. "Remarks," pp. 317-18 (Schneewind, pp. 49-50). This passage follows, without interruption, upon the passage which was quoted immediately above.

28. *Dissertations*, 1, 156-57.

29. How important Mill regarded the consequences of an action on the agent's own character can be suggested by the following psychological assertion:

> It may be affirmed with few exceptions, that any act whatever has a tendency to fix and perpetuate the state or character of mind in which it itself has originated. ("Remarks," p. 318 [Schneewind, p. 50])

I find no evidence that Mill ever broke with this assumption.

30. *Utilitarianism*, chap. 4, para. 5 (p. 33).

31. Ibid., para. 11 (pp. 36, 37).

32. *Utilitarianism*, chap. 2, concl. para. (p. 24).

33. Ibid., para. 16 (p. 15).

34. The complete passage, which deals with acts that are injurious to others, reads as follows:

> Encroachments on their rights; infliction on them of any loss or damage not justified by his own rights; falsehood or duplicity in dealing with them; unfair or ungenerous use of ad-

vantages over them; even selfish abstinence from defending them against injury — these are fit objects of moral reprobation, and, in grave cases, of moral retribution, and punishment. And not only these acts, but the dispositions which lead to them, are properly immoral, and fit subjects of disapprobation which may rise to abhorrence. Cruelty of disposition; malice and ill-nature; that most anti-social and odious of all passions, envy; dissimulation and insincerity, irascibility on insufficient cause, and resentment disproportioned to the provocation; the love of domineering over others; the desire to engross more than one's share of advantages . . . the pride which derives gratification from the abasement of others; the egotism which thinks self and its concerns more important than everything else, and decides all doubtful questions in its own favour; — these are moral vices, and constitute a bad and odious moral character. (*On Liberty*, chap. 4, para. 6 [*Utilitarianism*, p. 135])

35. *Utilitarianism*, chap. 3, para. 10 (p. 29).

36. *Utilitarianism*, chap. iv, para. 5 (p. 34).

37. Cf. note 11, above.

38. *Utilitarianism*, chap. 5, para. 4 (p. 40). Also, cf. paras. 2 and 3 (p. 39) for instances in which Mill speaks only of modes of action in connection with justice.

39. For a crucial passage in which the distinction stands out clearly, cf. *Utilitarianism*, chap. 5, paras. 21, 23 (pp. 48, 49).

40. It is worth noting that in his essay "Bain's Psychology," Mill explicitly classes Duty and Virtue with Extension, Solidity, Time and Space, as notions that "are not exact copies of any impressions on our sense." In his contrast between a priori and a posteriori theories of knowledge, he is insisting that in his view (and Bain's) it is necessary to seek to give an account of the origin of such ideas (*Dissertations*, 4, 108).

41. This can be taken as an example of what Mill called "chemical" composition, distinguishing it from "mechanical" composition (*System of Logic*, bk. 3, chap. 6, "The Composition of Causes"). In other words, it would be an example of what we, following G. H. Lewes, call "emergence."

There are two points at which Mill is relatively explicit in using this conception in connection with the results of associations: *Dissertations*, 4, 114-15, and a note he added in his edition of his father's *Analysis of the Phenomena of the Human Mind*, 2, 321.

42. Mill says:

The cultivation of an ideal of nobleness of will and conduct, should be to individual human beings an end, to which the specific pursuit either of their own happiness or of that of others (except so far as included in that idea) should, in any case of conflict, give way. But I hold that the very question, what constitutes this elevation of character, is itself to be decided by a reference to happiness as the standard. (*System of Logic*, bk. 6, chap. 12, sect. 7).

This passage is not present in the first edition; however, it is to be found in the third edition (1851).

23

Two Moot Issues
in Mill's *Utilitarianism*

In the present paper I shall be concerned with two points at which I believe Mill's *Utilitarianism* is frequently misinterpreted. The first, which is a relatively new issue, is whether Mill should be regarded as subscribing to a *rule-utilitarianism*, rather than to that unrestricted form of utilitarianism which is presently termed *act-utilitarianism*.[1] The second is whether Mill's proof of the hedonistic principle does in fact commit the elementary blunder that most critics, following G. E. Moore, have been ready to assume that it does.[2] In discussing each of these points I shall make more extensive use of Mill's other writings than has been usual among commentators. As I have elsewhere sought to establish, it is a mistake to attempt to interpret *Utilitarianism* apart from a consideration of Mill's less well known ethical writings and especially apart from his psychological theory and his explicit rejection of Bentham's psychology.[3]

Mill and Rule-Utilitarianism

Whether or not Mill is to be interpreted as a rule-utilitarian depends in part on how we are to characterise rule-utilitarianism. As we shall finally see, our answers may be different (though only in part) if we characterize that theory as primarily concerned with "a method for determining what acts are right," or if we characterize it as a way of saying how, in a particular case, the use of a moral predicate such as "right" is to be justified.[4] I shall take its primary meaning to be the latter. In so doing I am (I believe) in agreement with the usage of J. O. Urmson, whose views I wish to discuss. This conformity with his usage can be seen in the first of the four propositions that he gives as characterizing rule-utilitarianism:

> A particular action is justified as being right by showing that it is in accord with some moral rule. It is shown to be wrong by showing that it transgresses some moral rule.[5]

Taken alone, this proposition concerning the moral justification of particular actions would of course fail to characterize rule-utilitarianism. To constitute a species of utilitarianism at all, the notion of utility (that is, of the general welfare, or the maximization of good consequences) must be introduced. This Urmson does in the second of his propositions:

> A moral rule is shown to be correct by showing that the recognition of that rule promotes the ultimate end.[6]

The ultimate end is, of course, utility.

That Mill did justify moral *rules* in terms of their utility and that he held that there was no other way in which they could be justified is a point on which there is agreement among all commentators. We may then take it for granted that Mill's thought conforms to Urmson's second proposition. Does it, however, conform to the first? Here the crucial question is whether it was Mill's view that moral predicates such as "right" and "wrong" are to be applied to particular actions *because* these actions were instances of what specific moral rules prescribed or proscribed. Formulating this question by means of a familiar technical term, one may ask whether, according to Mill, rule-conformity is in itself a *right-making characteristic* and rule-infringement a *wrong-making characteristic.* While some ethical writers would surely accept a position of this sort (one thinks immediately of W. G. Sumner), I have found no passage in Mill that can be fairly interpreted as committing him to it.[7]

To be sure, one might use the term *justify* in a weaker sense than the above, when speaking of justifying moral judgments through moral rules. For example, if you ask me why I praise or condemn a particular action, I may, in my answer, tacitly appeal to some particular moral precept or maxim: I may say, "It was an unusually kind thing to have done," or I may say, "It was practically stealing." A response of this sort might be taken as offering a justification of my original judgment; in that case the precept to which appeal was made would have been taken as serving as a justifying ground for my praise or condemnation. However, such a response would only be seen as a justification by those who not only accepted the precept as itself being a justified precept, but regarded it as a precept applicable to this case, and one that was not overridden by any other considerations. In thus limiting the conditions under which the precept or rule serves as a justification of the judgment, one is using "justification" in a much weaker sense than is usual in ethical theory. Used in this way, it does little more than provide a clue as to what particular aspect of the action led me to praise or condemn it.[8] Thus, if it is to count as a justification it does so only because it is linked with other premises relevant to the moral assessment of the act in question. Under these circumstances, the function that a general moral maxim or rule performs is to indicate the locus of one of the main right-making or wrong-making aspects of the action, our expectation being that this will suffice to evoke agreement on the part of those who have asked us, or who might ask us, to justify our judgment. In this weaker sense of *justify,*

Mill does hold that general maxims can be used to help justify a particular moral judgment.[9] However, in his view, one of the tacit premises that is involved in such a justification is the acceptance of the principle of utility: one cannot, in that view, justify a judgment by appealing to a rule unless at the same time one takes that rule to be justified by its utility. To separate the justification of particular moral judgments from the justification of the precepts that they instantiate is not, so far as I can see, a position which Mill ever adopted; though this is what Urmson's argument demands.[10]

Mill's general position (which we shall shortly supplement with further details) can best be made clear through two major passages that Urmson fails to analyze. One is in the opening paragraphs of *Utilitarianism*, in which Mill contrasts the role of the first principles in the sciences and their role in morals; the second is in the concluding chapter of the *Logic*, where Mill addresses himself to the differences between the sciences and the practical arts.

The point of the passage in *Utilitarianism* is clear, in spite of the fact that Mill uses qualifying phrases such as "one might think." After noting the lack of agreement concerning the ultimate principles of morality, he proceeds:

> It is true that similar confusion and uncertainty and, in some cases, similar discordance exist respecting the first principles of all the sciences, not excepting that which is deemed the most certain of them — mathematics, without much impairing, generally indeed without impairing at all, the trustworthiness of the conclusions of those sciences. An apparent anomaly, the explanation of which is that the detailed doctrines of a science are not usually deduced from, nor depend for their evidence upon, what are called its first principles. . . . The truths which are ultimately accepted as the first principles of a science are really the last results of metaphysical analysis practiced on the elementary notions with which the science is conversant; and their relation to the science is not that of foundations to an edifice, but of roots to a tree, which may perform their office equally well though they be never dug down to and exposed to the light. But though in science the particular truths precede the general theory, the contrary might be expected to be the case with a practical art such as morals or legislation. All action is for the sake of some end, and rules of action, it seems natural to suppose, must take their whole character and color from the end to which they are subservient. When we engage in a pursuit, a clear and precise conception of what we are pursuing would seem to be the first thing we need, instead of the last we are to look forward to. A test of right and wrong must be the means, one would think, of ascertaining what is right or wrong, and not a consequence of having already ascertained it.

That the qualifying phrases in this passage are not to be taken as indicating reservations or a disclaimer on Mill's part, can be seen from the next paragraph, which must be read as a continuation of the same argument. Mill there refers to those who appeal to a native faculty of conscience as the arbiter of right and wrong in specific cases, and he argues against them that morals must be a matter not of direct perception, but of reasoning and general rules.[11] However, he remains dissatisfied with the appeal to a series of rules unless they be shown to be exhaustive and unless they be shown to have a fixed order or to derive from one first principle. Thus, he argues for the necessity of one fundamental moral standard as the basis for our concrete judgments of right and wrong.

If it should be doubted that this is the point which he is seeking to make in these paragraphs, one need merely turn to the following paragraph in which Mill raises the question of why, if a single principle must serve as the basis for our judgments of conduct, the absence of any clear recognition of such a standard has not had more deleterious effects than it apparently has. To this he answers: "Whatever steadiness or consistency these moral beliefs have attained has been mainly due to the tacit influence of a standard not recognized."[12] Bearing this statement in mind, the fact that we often find that a particular moral judgment in a concrete case is ostensibly being justified through the appeal to some moral rule, should not preclude us from saying that justification by such a rule only carries conviction where, behind it, there is a tacit appeal to the standard without which the rule itself would lack justification.

The second passage in which there is a general discussion of the same subject is, as I have said, in the concluding chapter of the *System of Logic,* a chapter entitled "Of the Logic of Practice, or Art; Including Morality and Policy." In this place Mill explicitly says:

> In all branches of practical business, there are cases in which individuals are bound to conform their practice to a pre-established rule, while there are others in which it is part of their task to find or construct the rule by which they are to govern their conduct. The first, for example, is the case of a judge, under a definite written code. The judge is not called upon to determine what course would be intrinsically the most advisable in the particular case in hand, but only within what rule of law it falls.[13]

In contrast to the judge, Mill cites the legislator:

> As the judge has laws for his guidance, so the legislator has rules, and maxims of policy; but it would be a manifest error to suppose that the legislator is bound by these maxims in the same manner as the judge is bound by the laws, and that all he has to do is argue down from them to the particular case, as the judge does from the laws. The legislator is bound to take into consideration the reasons or grounds of the maxim.

And it is clear that for Mill the proper function of the legislator can only be fulfilled by reasoning in terms of the ultimate end which legislation is to serve:

To the judge, the rule, once positively ascertained, is final; but the legislator, or other practitioner, who goes by rules rather than by their reasons, like the old-fashioned German tacticians who were vanquished by Napoleon, or the physician who preferred that his patients should die by rule rather than recover contrary to it, is rightly judged to be a mere pedant, and the slave of his formulas.[14]

This contrast between the judge and the legislator should be borne in mind when one reads the contrast which Mill later drew (1863) between Austin and Bentham. In his essay "Austin on Jurisprudence," Mill says:

> Mr. Austin's subject was Jurisprudence, Bentham's was Legislation.
> The purpose of Bentham was to investigate principles from which to decide what laws ought to exist—what legal rights, and legal duties or obligations, are fit to be established among mankind. This was also the ultimate end of Mr. Austin's speculations; but the subject of his special labors was theoretically distinct, though subsidiary, and practically indispensable, to the former. It was what may be called the logic of law, as distinguished from its morality or expediency. (*Dissertations and Discussions,* vol. 4, p. 160)

This surely in part explains why it is so much easier to find clear cases of the "practice" conception of rules in Austin. However, as Rawls points out (pp. 19-21), even Austin is probably not to be characterized as having rejected the "summary" conception.

Originally, in the first edition of the *Logic,* Mill explicitly discussed how the problem of moral decision was to be construed in terms of the contrast between judge and legislator. He said:

> Questions of practical morality are partly similar to those which are to be decided by a judge, and partly to those which have to be solved by a legislator or administrator. In some things our conduct ought to conform itself to a prescribed rule; in others, it is to be guided by the best judgment which can be formed by the merits of the particular case.

He then proceeded to state in what kinds of cases morality consists in the simple observance of a rule:

> The cases in question are those in which, although any rule which can be formed is probably . . . more or less imperfectly adapted to a portion of the cases which it comprises, there is still a necessity that some rule, of a nature simple enough to be easily understood and remembered, should not only be laid down for guidance, but universally observed, in order that the various persons concerned may know what they have to expect: the inconvenience of uncertainty on their part being a greater evil than that which may possibly arise, in a minority of cases, from the imperfect adaptation of the rule to those cases.
> Such, for example, is the rule of veracity; that of not infinging the legal rights of others; and so forth.[15]

And in this connection we may note that in *Utilitarianism* Mill cites breach of friendship and breach of promises (two types of case in which, as he points out, expectations count heavily) as cases in which a species of conduct is generally reprehensible apart from its specific consequences.[16]

Now, it is to be noted that in his discussion Mill explicitly limits to a single type those cases in which rules are to be followed without considering the specific circumstances under which the action is to be done. In this exceptional type of case, rules are made necessary in order that individuals may be clear as to what sort of conduct they may expect of others. Bearing this in mind, it would surely be false to interpret him as holding, *tout court*, that in these cases a judgment of rightness or wrongness was justified *because* the action fell under a rule. To capture his meaning we should surely have to say that abiding by a rule, rather than consulting circumstances, was justified only because the action was one of a special class of actions in which it was *for the general good* that all persons act in accordance with set rules. Thus, as justification of the use of the predicates "right" and "wrong" it is not sufficient, even in these special cases, only to cite the relevance of the rule to the action: the rule must be understood to be a socially necessary rule. And it is to be noted that Mill does not shrink from saying that there are exceptional cases in which even *such* rules may be abrogated.[17]

With respect to all cases in which the foregoing condition does not obtain, Mill is quite explicit in advocating the view that it is the general principle of utility, not the specific rule, which serves as the morally justifying factor with respect to particular actions. He says:

> In cases, however, in which there does not exist a necessity for a common rule, to be acknowledged and relied upon as the basis of social life; where we are at liberty to inquire what is the most moral course under the particular circumstances of the case, without reference to the authorized expectations of other people; there the Method of Ethics cannot differ materially from the method of every other department of practice. Like other arts, it sets out from a general principle, or original major premiss, enunciative of its particular end.[18]

And this end is, for Mill, that which is defined by the principle of utility.

In the light of these passages it is hard to find grounds for saying that there is any type of case in which Mill would hold that rule-conformity is, by itself, a justifying ground of obligation. Why then can one find passages in *Utilitarianism* which seem to provide justification for attempting to ascribe rule-utilitarianism to Mill? The answer to this query is, I believe, to be found in the same chapter of the *Logic* from which our other evidence has been taken. There Mill says that *as a practical matter* in actual deliberations, a particular rule or maxim may sometimes be helpful in the following way:

> [It] may very properly serve as an admonition that a certain mode of action has been found by ourselves and others to be well adapted to the cases of most com-

mon occurrence; so that if it be unsuitable to the case in hand, the reason of its being so will be likely to arise from some unusual circumstances.[19]

However, this admission of the usefulness of rules in practice is in effect a concession on the part of Mill, for it is introduced only after he has said:

> By a wise practitioner . . . rules of conduct will only be considered provisional. Being made for the most numerous cases, or for those of most ordinary occurrence, they point out the manner in which it will be least perilous to act, where time or means do not exist for analysing the actual circumstances of the case, or where we cannot trust our judgment in estimating them. But they do not at all supersede the propriety of going through (when circumstances permit) the scientific process for framing a rule from the data of the particular case before us.

This passage makes it clear that Mill should not be classed as a rule-utilitarian, even if one were to characterize rule-utilitarianism as a theory primarily concerned with a method of saying what acts are right. Nonetheless, the content of these passages serves to suggest why, in the second chapter of *Utilitarianism*, there are a number of places in which Mill emphasizes the usefulness of secondary principles in morality. In that chapter, it will be recalled, he was replying to those who had criticized the principle of utility. Among their criticisms were charges that the utilitarian standard was not (for various reasons) practically applicable. It is in this connection that Mill would obviously feel himself justified in pointing to the practical use that can be made of ordinary moral rules. However, the utility of secondary principles in affording rule-of-thumb guidance does not suggest that the use of such rules is a necessary condition for deciding which acts are morally right acts. Nor did Mill hold that there is any case in which knowing that an act conforms to a specific rule is a sufficient condition for knowing it to be a right act—we must first know that the rule is itself a justified rule, as is true in the case of justice. Thus, even if we were to follow R. B. Brandt in his characterization of rule-utilitarianism as a theory that "consists primarily of the proposal of a method for determining what acts are right,"[20] Mill should not be classified as a rule-utilitarian. And if rule-utilitarianism holds that "a particular action is *justified* as being right by showing that it is in accord with some moral rule," then Mill cannot, on any grounds whatever, be identified with that position.

The Proof of Hedonism

In Mill's critical examination of Bentham's ethical theory, he found it a major weakness that Bentham had failed to offer any positive argument for his utilitarianism, relying instead on a rejection of alternative principles.[21] Furthermore, Mill criticized Bentham for an inability to treat opposed positions with adequate sympathy and understanding.[22] Such a charge cannot with justice be leveled against Mill, who was generally able to appreciate why the theories of his opponents seemed convincing to honest and enlightened men. Nonetheless, he was no more inclined than was Bentham to test a moral theory through its conformity with judgments and practices that were widely accepted: he wished to find a standard, criterion, or test — the terms were equivalent for him[23] — by means of which those judgments and practices which were morally right could be shown to be so and those which were wrong could be legitimately condemned. It was to such a standard that he referred when he used phrases such as "the foundation of morality" or "the fundamental principle of morality and the source of moral obligation."[24] This standard or test was the principle of utility, and it is with Mill's attempt to establish that principle — or, rather, the hedonistic aspect of that principle — that we are now concerned.[25]

Mill had one basic *negative* argument that he frequently used when he was arguing for the principle of utility. It consisted in the charge that those who rejected the principle would be forced to rely upon a theory of knowledge which was erroneous. In most instances, Mill identified this erroneous theory as the a priori view, but it was not only the rationalist appeal to a priori insights which was the object of his attacks. In a passage to which we have already called attention in criticizing Urmson,[26] Mill linked any appeal to a native faculty of conscience (that is, any belief in a moral sense) with the a priorist's claim that certain rules of conduct are self-evidently correct. The connection between these two dissimilar doctrines, and the sense in which they may be said to form a single philosophic school, is that both are "nativistic": both appeal to some sort of native, inborn capacity to distinguish moral truths, whereas utilitarianism holds that moral discriminations are to be accounted for through the effects of experience.[27] One of the discussions in which it is clear that Mill is concerned to attack nativism as such and not merely one or another of its variant forms, is to be found in his article on Sedgwick's *Discourse:*

It is a fact in human nature, that we have moral judgments and moral feelings. . . . Concerning their reality there is no dispute. But there are two theories respecting the origin of these phenomena, which have divided philosophers from the earliest ages of philosophy. One is, that the distinction between right and wrong is an ultimate and inexplicable fact; that we perceive this distinction, as we perceive the distinction of colors, by a peculiar faculty; and that the pleasures and pains, the desires and aversions, consequent upon this perception, are all ultimate facts in our nature, as much so as the pleasures and pains, or desires and aversions, of which sweet or bitter tastes, pleasing or grating sounds are the object. This is called the theory of the moral sense, or of moral instincts, or of eternal and immutable morality, or of intuitive principles of morality, or by many other names; to the differences between which, those who adopt the theory often attach great ..portance, but which, for our present purpose, may all be considered as equivalent.[28]

In discussing what sort of theory stands opposed to these unsatisfactory beliefs, Mill cites only one example: the theory of utility. And time and again he returns to this contrast, in which only utilitarianism is cited as an alternative to the various forms of nativism.[29] Because it was Mill's most basic epistemological conviction that nativism was fundamentally mistaken even in those areas, such as mathematics and logic, in which it appeared to have its greatest strength,[30] the fact that his opponents were committed to that theory provided him with what he took to be a strong negative argument in favor of his own position.

In addition to using this very general argument that ethical theories other than utilitarianism rest on false epistemological assumptions, Mill attacked these theories by claiming that whatever acceptability their principles possessed was dependent upon a tacit and unrecognized use of the utilitarian standard. This form of argument appears in his brief criticism of Kant's first formulation of the categorical imperative;[31] it is also present in his criticism of Whewell.[32] Furthermore, Mill brought forward what was essentially the same argument, but put in a more concrete form, when he suggested that the standards upheld by his opponents provided no guidance where practical questions were in dispute. For example, he held that if one is to adjudicate among the conflicting claims as to what is just with respect to punishment, one cannot try to do so by a direct appeal to one's conscience or to self-evident maxims: one must turn for guidance to the utilitarian standard.[33] Mill also used an analogous argument with respect to questions of moral motivation. Like most of his predecessors (and like his opponents), Mill assumed that moral philosophy must provide an answer to the question of what motives can lead men to act in accord with that which the moral standard demands.[34] What he was able to point out against his opponents was that they—no less than the utilitarians—appealed to pleasure and pain as fundamental motives in so far as the *external* sanctions of morality were concerned:[35] thus, what they were inclined to regard as ignoble motives played precisely the same role in their own systems as was the case in the utilitarian system. (And whatever noble motives were connected with the external sanctions were, he claimed, also the same.) Furthermore, Mill's argument that a person's sense of duty, which is the inner sanction of morality, is itself a *feeling* to the mind, can be interpreted as an attempt to show that his opponents are able to explain the efficacy of this noblest of human motives only by themselves appealing to a hedonistic psychology: to be moved by a feeling of duty is to respond to the immediate pleasure or pain of the ideas to which that feeling attaches.[36] Thus, once again, what his opponents claim turns out to be in accord with the very principles which they criticize utilitarians for upholding.

Mill makes such points only in passing, for he explicitly states that in *Utilitarianism* he is not concerned to discuss other theories, but to "attempt to contribute something toward the understanding and appreciation of the 'utilitarian' or 'happiness' theory, and toward such proof as it is susceptible of."[37] We turn, therefore, from his negative arguments to his attempted positive proof.

Mill's proof of hedonism, which he offers in chapter 4, is often claimed to involve a confusion between normative and non-normative propositions, because he apparently attempts to show that happiness is *desirable* by showing that it is in fact *desired*. Now, regardless of how we are to interpret this famous passage in which Mill draws an analogy between proving that something is desirable and proving that a thing is either visible or audible,[38] it is necessary to note that he is *usually* very insistent on the need to distinguish between normative and factual propositions. For example, time and again one finds him distinguishing between *can* and *should*,[39] between *is* and *ought*,[40] and between the *origin* of something and its *validity* (to which he usually refers as its *binding force*).[41] Furthermore, in the fourth chapter, which is the chapter devoted to the proof of the principle of utility, the very first paragraph contains an explicit acknowledgment that the way in which one can establish a first principle of *conduct* may be different from the way in which one establishes a first principle of *knowledge*. If, then, we are not to do violence to the actual text of *Utilitarianism*, we must admit that Mill was fully aware of the distinction to be drawn between normative and factual questions. It would therefore seem necessary to interpret his proof in such a way that one is not forced to find him guilty of a wholly naïve confusion between that which is actually desired and that which is truly desirable.

It must be admitted that the charge that his proof contains such a confusion is made somewhat more plausible by his use of the analogy between the visible and the audible on the one hand, and the desirable on the other. Although (as we shall see) I do not believe this analogy to be misleading in every respect, there is certainly at least one respect in which the desirable is not to be compared with the visible or the audible. This can be seen in noting that it is *not* a sufficient proof of the desirability of an object to show that the object is sometimes actually desired, although it is regarded as a sufficient proof of the visibility of an object that it is sometimes actually seen. However, I do not believe that the point Mill may be assumed to have been making is really damaged by this flaw in the analogy. To show this, I need merely point out that in speaking of what men desire, Mill is *not* here speaking of particular, specific objects of their desires, but of what they desire as an ultimate end, as the *summum bonum*. Considering the context of the passage, it would not be unnatural for Mill to take it for granted that this would be understood by his readers. Interpreting the offending passage on the basis of this assumption and adding in italics the phrases that would be necessary to make this meaning unambiguous even when the passage is torn out of context, what we should understand Mill to be saying is the following:

> The only proof capable of being given that an object is visible is that people actually see it. The only proof that a sound is audible is that people hear it; and so of the other sources of our experience. In like manner, I apprehend, the sole

evidence it is possible to produce that anything is desirable *as an ultimate end* is tha people do actually desire it *as such an end.*

And this, I submit, is precisely the way in which Mill's much maligned sentence is to be interpreted when one also takes into account the sentence that immediately follows it:

> If the end which the utilitarian doctrine proposes to itself were not, in theory and in practice, acknowledged to be an end, nothing could ever convince any person that it was so.[42]

Now, it is to be borne in mind that Mill specifically says that in this passage he has only proved that happiness is *one* of the ends of conduct. "It has not," Mill says, "by this alone proved itself to be the sole criterion."[43] Therefore, Mill immediately proceeded to ask whether there were any other ends that men desired as ultimate ends; if there were, then his argument would also involve holding these ends to be intrinsically desirable. Now, in making this examination of other possible ultimate ends, Mill apparently thought it sufficient to consider the case of virtue. That he should take virtue to be a possible end in itself, and an end that might be independent of happiness, was not surprising: as he himself pointed out, in common language virtue and the absence of vice are regarded as being quite different ends from pleasure and the absence of pain. It is at this point, therefore, that Mill was led into his discussion of virtue as an end in itself, and until he had completed that discussion he could not be regarded as having established the principle of utility.[44]

With respect to virtue, Mill argued that it—like money, power, or fame—is a specific end that men do seek and that they may be said to seek disinterestedly, for its own sake.[45] However, he also argued that such ends are sought only because there is a direct connection between pursuing them and experiencing pleasure. Thus Mill believed that he had shown it to be a fact of human nature that all human desires are either desires for happiness or are derivative from that desire, being desires for ends that have come to constitute what a person considers to be a part of his happiness. Having proved this, he concludes:

> We have now, then, an answer to the question, of what sort of proof the principle of utility is susceptible. If the opinion which I have now stated is psychologically true—if human nature is so constituted as to desire nothing which is not either a part of happiness or a means to happiness—we can have no other proof, and we require no other, that these are the only things desirable.[46]

If it be doubted that this constitutes a proof of what is desirable, consider the alternative. Let some one say: "This goal, X, is desirable in itself; it is the goal which all human beings *should* desire." Now, suppose that, upon inquiry, it turns out that X is something that, as a matter of psychological fact, no human being is *capable* of desiring. Could it still be held that X is desirable? Is it not a necessary condition—though not a sufficient condition—of the desirability of something that it should be capable of being desired?[47] I know of no one who has sought to uphold the contrary position. And if we are speaking of human goals, it follows that it is a necessary condition of the desirability of such a goal that human beings should be capable of desiring it. However, Mill has argued that, as a matter of fact, there is no goal other than happiness which human beings *are* capable of desiring. Should this psychological point be granted, then I see no escape from his conclusion. Because we cannot desire any end but happiness, no other end is capable of fulfilling what is a necessary condition of desirability. Thus—by default—what is desired turns out in Mill's system to be both a necessary *and* a sufficient condition of desirability.[48]

The foregoing discussion shows that Mill's proof of hedonism is not to be identified with the brief passage in which he draws an analogy between the visible and the desirable. The contention on which his positive proof rests is not merely that men do desire happiness, nor that they do desire it as an end in itself, but that this is in fact the *only* end they do so desire. And Mill's proof of this last point, as should now be abundantly clear, rests on a particular set of psychological principles. If one is to overthrow his proof, I should contend, one cannot merely attack the logical form in which his argument is cast; one must be prepared to show that he is mistaken in adopting the principles by means of which he explains the specific ends that men actually seek.

Perhaps recent trends in ethical theory will have cleared the way for a more sympathetic treatment of Mill with respect to his argument for hedonism, once that argument is understood. It has been my aim in the foregoing discussion to place Mill's proof in the context in which it properly belongs; and I have attempted a similar task with respect to the question of whether Mill is to be interpreted as a rule-utilitarian. If I am not mistaken, his theory—whatever its difficulties—is at once more coherent and less open to reinterpretation or to easy objection than it is now frequently taken to be.

Notes

1. This issue was first raised in its present form by J. O. Urmson in "The Interpretation of the Moral Philosophy of J. S. Mill," *Philosophical Quarterly*, 3 (1953):33-39. Urmson's interpretation was discussed by J. D. Mabbott in "Interpretations of Mill's Utilitarianism," *Philosophical Quarterly*, 6 (1956):115-20. Another article on the same topic, but only incidentally concerned with Mill, was J.J.C. Smart's "Extreme and Restricted Utilitarianism," *Philosophical Quarterly*, 6 (1956): 344-54. In the many subsequent discussions of rule-utilitarianism there has been little attempt to deal with the issue of whether Urmson was in fact correct in attributing to Mill the position that he did.

2. There have been a number of recent reexaminations of this issue; for example, Carl Wellman, "A Reinterpretation of Mill's Proof," *Ethics*, 69 (1959):268-76 and E. W. Hall's article, "The 'Proof' of Utility in Bentham and Mill," *Ethics*, 60 (1949):1-18.

3. Cf. "On Interpreting Mill's *Utilitarianism*," reprinted above (ch. 22).

4. According to R. B. Brandt, the primary purpose of rule-utilitarianism is to offer "a method for determining what acts are right" (*Ethical Theory* [Englewood Cliffs, 1959], p. 253). However, his formal definition of the position (p. 396f.) would be wholly compatible with the second interpretation of what rule-utilitarianism aims to do. A considerable diversity in the definition of rule-utilitarianism has in fact developed, but the consequent differences in usage are not, I believe, directly relevant to my present aim. I wish to establish what Mill's position actually was. How one then labels that position is not of primary interest to me.

5. Urmson, "Moral Philosophy of J. S. Mill," p. 35. To be sure, Urmson also appeals to rule-utilitarianism as a method for determining what acts are right, but this (I take it) follows from the proposition quoted above.

6. Ibid. Mabbott points out in his rejoinder to this article ("Interpretations of Mill's Utilitarianism," p. 115) that two slight emendations must be made in this second proposition if it is to be accurate.

I shall not discuss the last two of Urmson's four propositions because I am here concerned only with Mill's position, and as we shall see that position is not in fact consonant with the first of the four propositions.

7. Urmson challenges those who do not regard Mill as a rule-utilitarian to explain a passage in *Utilitarianism* in which it is held that the differentiating characteristic of moral acts, as distinct from expedient or inexpedient acts not regarded as "moral," is to be found in the notion of punishment. Cf. ch. 5, para. 14 (p. 45); cf. Urmson, "Moral Philosophy of J. S. Mill," pp. 36-37.

In reply, I should like to point out that in this passage Mill never mentions specific moral rules. He says: "we do not call anything wrong unless we mean to imply that a person ought to be punished in some way or other for doing it." He then explicitly recognizes three classes of such punishments: punishment by law, by the opinions of one's fellows, and by one's own conscience. Now, insofar as punishment by law is concerned, it is natural enough to equate the justification of such punishment with the agent's breach of some specific rule. However, I see no reason to interpret Mill as holding that the sanctions of one's conscience *do* operate only when specific rules are broken, nor that they *should* operate only under these conditions. (Nor do I believe that he would hold this position with respect to the opinions of one's fellows.) Thus, this passage, taken by itself, does not (in my opinion) establish the fact that Mill should be regarded as a rule-utilitarian. My doubts on this score seem to me fortified by a letter that Mill had previously written to W. G. Ward (cf. *Letters of John Stuart Mill*, edited by Elliot, vol. 1, pp. 229-31). In that letter he analyzes the meaning of "ought" and refers it to punishment. However, the punishment that he explicitly mentions is that of the "internal and disinterested feeling" of conscience.

Furthermore, exegesis of this passage aside, if one turns to Mill's lengthier discussion of precisely the same problem in his edition of his father's *Analysis of the Phenomena of the Human Mind*, one sees that his account does not in the least conform to rule-utilitarianism. (Cf. the last part of his note to his father's chapter on "The Acts of Our Fellow-Creatures," vol. 2, pp. 324-26.)

8. Cf. my article, "On the Use of Moral Principles," *Journal of Philosophy*, 53 (1956):662-70.

9. Examples of this are frequently suggested in *Utilitarianism*, and two of his general statements on the need for subsidiary principles provide evidence that such was his view. Cf. *Utilitarianism*, ch. 2, the next to the last and the last paragraphs (pp. 22-23 and p. 24). (In citing Mill's *Utilitarianism*, I shall make use of Mill's paragraphing, so that the reader may readily find the passage regardless of what edition he uses. I add the pagination of the Everyman edition.) However, the clearest expression of it comes in his praise of Bentham in the essay devoted to attacking the doctrines of Whewell. Mill says:

Bentham was a moralist of another stamp. With him, the first use to be made of his ultimate principle, was to erect on it, as a foundation, secondary or middle principles, capable of serving as premises for a body of ethical doctrine not derived from existing opinions, but fitted to be their test. . . . He was the first who, keeping clear of the direct and indirect influences of all doctrines inconsistent with it, deduced a set of subordinate generalities from utility alone, and by these tested all particular questions. This great service, previous to which a scientific doctrine of ethics on the foundation of utility was impossible, has been performed by Bentham (though with a view to the exigencies of legislation more than to those of morals) in a manner, as far as it goes, eminently meritorious, and so as to indicate the way to complete the scheme. (*Disserations and Discussions,* vol. 3, p. 143)

10. In "Two Concepts of Rules," *Philosophical Review,* 64 (1955):3-32, John Rawls distinguishes between a "summary" conception of rules, and a "practice" conception. In terms of this distinction, Urmson's interpretation of Mill makes him an upholder of the practice conception, whereas my interpretation (with one qualification, to be explained below) makes him an upholder of the summary conception. Rawls, it may be noted, interprets Mill as an upholder of the summary view (cf. p. 21 of his article).

11. It is at this point in the argument that Mill makes the statements cited by Urmson ("Moral Philosophy of J. S. Mill," p. 35) as the first of his four illustrations of rule-utilitarianism in Mill. However, as the context makes clear (as I am about to suggest), Mill immediately goes on to attack any attempt to rest our moral justification of actions on an uncoordinated set of moral rules.

12. *Utilitarianism,* ch. 1, para. 4 (p. 3). This statement must, I believe, be taken as Mill's explanation of the fact (which was acknowledged by him in the preceding paragraph) that utilitarians and apriorists agree to a significant extent concerning specific moral rules. Thus, Urmson's use of Mill's recognition of this agreement is misleading.

For another passage in which Mill cites this agreement, cf. *Dissertations and Discussions,* vol. 1, pp. 409-10.

13. *System of Logic,* bk. 6, ch. 12, sect. 2. (This passage is to be found in all editions of the *Logic,* and appears as section 2 of the concluding chapter. However, book 6 originally had only eleven chapters, the chapter on the science of history having been added in the fifth edition [1862].)

In the passage quoted above, Mill is saying that the judge must adopt what Rawls referred to as the "practice" conception of rules. However, as Rawls points out, this is not Mill's own view of the place of rules in *moral* justification. (Cf. above, note 10.)

14. *System of Logic,* bk. 6, ch. 12, sect. 2.

15. This quotation, and that immediately preceding it, appear in section 6 of the same chapter. Cf. first edition (London, 1843), vol. 2, pp. 621-22.

There is no reason to suppose that Mill suppressed this passage in later editions of the *Logic* because he disagreed with it. It is wholly consistent with the other passages that I have cited from the same chapter and that Mill allowed to remain in all editions of the *Logic.* And, as I am claiming, it is wholly consistent with *Utilitarianism* as well. Rather, its deletion is correlated with an enlarged discussion of the relations of science and art, which constitute the theme of the chapter as a whole. Furthermore, one may note that, in the first edition, section 5 ended with fulsome praise of Comte, whereas the changed version of section 6 (including a new section 7) is to be read as critical of Comte. It is its theme that *ought* cannot be reduced to *is, should be* to *will be,* and that there is "a Philosophia Prima peculiar to Art, as there is one which belongs to Science." This contention is clearly to be taken as a rectification of Mill's former praise of Comte. However, Mill's discussion of the role of first principles in art, and (more specifically) in morality, in no wise contradicts the views on *this* topic which he had earlier expressed.

16. Cf. *Utilitarianism,* ch. 5, fifth paragraph from the end (p. 56f.).

17. Immediately after the passage last quoted from the *Logic,* Mill admits the possibility that it might be permitted to deviate from the rule in cases "of a very peculiar and extreme nature."

And in *Utilitarianism* he points out that even with respect to cases in which we should normally say that justice was at stake, it is in some cases morally justifiable to abrogate a person's rights (cf. ch. 5, next to last paragraph [p. 59]). Finally, it is to be noted that in a letter in which Mill argues that the obligation of veracity depends upon the social utility of there being such a rule, he nonetheless cites the fact that we must, in particular cases, look to the particular results that are to be achieved. (This letter—which is not entirely clear, because we do not have the objections to which it is an answer—is to be found in Elliot's edition of the *Letters of John Stuart Mill*, vol. 2, p. 73.)

18. This is also from section 6 of the early editions of the last chapter of the *Logic.*

19. From section 3 of the concluding chapter of the *Logic.* (This section is to be found in the same form in all editions.)

20. *Ethical Theory*, p. 253.

21. Cf. "Remarks on Bentham's Philosophy" in J. B. Schneewind (ed.), *Mill's Ethical Writings* (New York, 1965), pp. 46-47.

It is usually overlooked that Mill wrote two essays on Bentham. The first, "Remarks on Bentham's Philosophy," was anonymous (but is mentioned in Mill's *Autobiography*); it was published in 1833 as an appendix to E. L. Bulwer's *England and the English.* Fortunately, it is now readily available in the collection cited above. Mill's second essay, which was simply entitled "Bentham," is the well-known companion piece to his essay on Coleridge; it will be cited as it appears in Mill's *Dissertations and Discussions*, published in five volumes in 1874.

For a discussion of the relation of Mill's thought to Bentham's, see "On Interpreting Mill's *Utilitarianism*," reprinted above (ch. 22).

22. Cf. "Bentham," *Dissertations and Discussions*, vol. 1, pp. 370 and 375.

23. Among the instances in which he uses *standard* in *Utilitarianism*, cf. ch. 2, para. 10 (p. 11) and para. 19 (p. 17); for his use of *criterion*, cf. ch. 1, para. 1 (p. 1) and ch. 4, para. 9 (p. 36); in the latter passage he also uses the term *test*, as he does in ch. 2, para. 19 (p. 17). All three are also used as equivalent terms in his other works.

24. For these phrases, cf. *Utilitarianism*, ch. 1, para. 1 (p. 1) and para. 4 (p. 3), respectively.

25. In the present article I shall not deal with Mill's attempted proof of the *universalistic* aspect of the principle of utility. His attempt in ch. 4, para. 3 (p. 32f.) to establish the desirability of the general happiness seems to me to fail, as he has formulated it. Nor do I believe that his later explication of his argument (*Letters of John Stuart Mill*, ed. by Elliot, vol. 2, p. 116) extricates him from the difficulty.

If the purpose of the present article were to defend Mill's moral theory, I should of course have to deal with this question. However, it does not seem to me to affect the main issues with respect to which Mill has been misinterpreted, and I shall not discuss it here.

26. *Utilitarianism*, ch. 1, para. 3 (p. 2).

27. From the point of view of ethical theory the two schools also form one class, which is to be differentiated from utilitarianism: neither appeals to the *consequences* of actions in determining the rightness or wrongness of those actions.

It is to be noted that Mill not infrequently conflated this specifically ethical characterization of his opponents with his epistemological charges against them. Although the two sets of objections do not actually have any necessary connection with one another (as one can see if one calls to mind various forms of noncognitivism), Mill failed to see that it was possible to abandon nativism and *not* hold that actions are designated as right or wrong on the basis of their consequences. We shall, I think, better understand Mill's failure in this respect if we recall that he assumed (as the opening paragraph of *Utilitarianism* clearly shows) that there *must be* some universally valid standard or test of morality, and that it is the business of ethical thought to determine the nature of that standard.

28. *Dissertations and Discussions*, vol. 1, p. 148.

29. As examples, see "Remarks on Bentham," in Schneewind, p. 47. Also *Dissertations and Discussions*, vol. 3, pp. 137-39, and vol. 4, pp. 106-7; and *Utilitarianism*, ch. 3, para. 7 and para. 8 (p. 28).

30. Cf. *Autobiography*, ch. 7, para. 4; (*Early Draft*, pp. 168-69).

31. *Utilitarianism*, ch. 1, para. 4 (p. 4).

32. *Dissertations and Discussions,* vol. 3, pp. 177-79.

33. *Utilitarianism,* ch. 5, para. 27 and 28 (p. 51f.), and following.

34. Cf. *Utilitarianism,* ch. 3, para. 1 (p. 24).

35. *Utilitarianism,* ch. 3, para. 3 (p. 25f.).

36. It is often overlooked that the theory of motivation which Mill espoused was what is usually termed "a psychological hedonism of the present moment": that it is the pleasantness-unpleasantness of present ideas, and not that of future consequences, which move us to action. (Cf. his "Remarks on Bentham's Philosophy," and my own discussion of his psychology in the article already cited.)

37. *Utilitarianism,* ch. 1, para. 5 (p. 4).

38. Cf. ch. 4, para. 3 (p. 32f.).

39. For example, in *Utilitarianism* he does so explicitly in ch. 2, at the end of paragraph 15 (p. 15), and implicitly in distinguishing between a rule of action and the motive of the action (ch. 2, para. 19 [p. 17]). He again does so implicitly when he separates the existence of habits from questions concerning the moral standard (ch. 4, next to last paragraph [p. 38]).

40. For example, in the later editions of the *Logic,* bk. 6, ch. 12, sect. 6. It should also be noted that such a distinction is at least implicit in any criticism of a social custom, and it comes out very strongly throughout Mill's criticism of Whewell (cf. *Dissertations and Discussions,* vol. 3, p. 154f.).

41. A clear and explicit example is to be found in his treatment of the sentiment attaching to our idea of justice (cf. *Utilitarianism,* ch. 5, para. 2 [p. 38f.], et passim). The same distinction is equally sharply drawn in a letter to Thornton (*Letters of John Stuart Mill,* ed. by Elliot, vol. 1, pp. 291-92), and in his review of Blakey (*Monthly Repository,* 7 [1833]:666). (The latter passage is also to be found in Schneewind, *Mill's Ethical Writings,* p. 70.)

42. It is not essential to my interpretation to do so, but I should like to point out that it is not difficult to see how Mill came to draw the analogy between the visible and the desirable, even though this analogy is bound to be misleading in various respects.

In the first place we may note that if men did not have the capacity to see certain objects, one could scarcely argue them into acknowledging that these objects *are* visible. Similarly, Mill wishes to hold that if men did not have the capacity to find certain ends good in themselves, it would be futile to try to argue them into believing that these ends *really* were so. What Mill is concerned to show (as his own words should serve to make clear) is that there must be some form of experience with which we are directly acquainted which can serve as the source of our notion of what is desirable. This form of experience, Mill holds, is provided by our consciousness of the ends that we seek, and the ends sought by others. As he says in another place, the court of appeal in this matter is "practiced self-consciousness and self-observation, assisted by the observation of others" (*Utilitarianism,* ch. 4, para. 10 [p. 36]).

43. *Utilitarianism,* ch. 4, para. 4 (p. 33), referring back to paragraph 3.

44. How Mill uses the term *virtue,* and what relation it bears to happiness as an end in itself, is the subject of one section of my article, "On Interpreting Mill's *Utilitarianism,*" reprinted above (ch. 22).

45. For other instances in which Mill compares the disinterestedness of virtue and the pursuit of wealth and power, cf. his notes to his father's *Analysis of the Phenomena of the Human Mind,* which he edited, 2nd ed., vol. 2, p. 233f. and p. 307f.

46. *Utilitarianism,* ch. 4, para. 9 (p. 36). Cf. also the paragraph that follows (p. 36).

47. In this context we may quote a statement from R. B. Brandt, made in connection with Mill's proof:

I think we may take it as uncontested that attitudes are at least relevant guides, reliable at some points. Take the case of desires and the desirable. Will anybody in fact deny that a certain kind of thing is desirable, if in fact everybody would desire it in all circumstances? Or will anybody in fact deny that a thing is not desirable, if nobody would desire it under any circumstances whatever? We may doubt whether anybody would in fact deny either of these things. (*Ethical Theory,* p. 262)

I might add that it seems to me that most contemporary philosophers have erred in thinking that the term *desirable* must be taken to mean *worthy of desire,* and that this phrase must, in its turn, mean *ought to be desired.* If one consults dictionaries (including those current in Mill's time), one finds this pair of assumptions to be unfounded. In this connection, we may quote Sidgwick on the meaning of *desirable,* remembering that few philosophers have been more scrupulous in attempting to distinguish *ought* from *is.* In the following passage he explains his use of *desirable*:

> —meaning by 'desirable' not necessarily 'what *ought* to be desired' but what would be desired, with strength proportioned to the degree of desirability, if it were judged attainable by voluntary action, supposing the desirer to possess a perfect forecast, emotional as well as intellectual, of the state of attainment or fruition. (*Methods of Ethics,* p. 111)

48. My interpretation of Mill's proof may be challenged on the ground that in the introductory chapter of *Utilitarianism* Mill himself said that "questions of ultimate ends are not amenable to direct proof" (ch. 1, para. 5; p. 4). However, as that paragraph makes clear, Mill was only speaking of "what is commonly accepted as proof"; he proceeds to say that considerations may be presented capable of determining the intellect either to give or withhold its assent to the doctrine; and this is equivalent to proof." In short, if by "proof" be meant a chain of deductive argument which depended upon some more ultimate premise, then it is obvious that no proof of the ultimate moral principle could be given. However, the argument that the foregoing exposition has attempted to reconstruct is not of that nature: it consists in a set of considerations that are "equivalent to proof."

24

The Scientific Background of
Evolutionary Theory in Biology

The aim of this paper is to show how a variety of scientific problems, and the solutions proposed concerning them, helped pave the way for the formulation and eventual adoption of the biological theory of evolution. No attempt will here be made to trace the influence of certain more pervasive philosophic doctrines on the development of evolutionary modes of thought.[1] Nor shall I attempt to treat any one of the scientific problems here discussed in an exhaustive fashion. In spite of these limits, it is to be hoped that this paper may contribute to the understanding of the history of evolutionary theory by offering a brief conspectus of various scientific issues which were widely discussed, and each of which was relevant to the formulation of evolutionary views in biology.

To understand the significance of most of these problems it is important to remember that they were viewed in the context of their bearings on religious orthodoxy. This close connection between scientific and religious concerns was not the result of any fear of science on the part of the orthodox: on the contrary, science was quite generally viewed as lending support to orthodoxy. This harmony between science and revealed religion was a continuation of the tradition laid down by Boyle and Newton. Even those who attacked *revealed* religion, wishing to equate true religion with natural religion, did not challenge the belief that through scientific inquiry man could discover in nature the handiwork of God the Creator. Thus, for the Deist as well as for the orthodox, the sciences of nature were the allies of religion. It was therefore the case that when the specific problems that absorbed men of science were discussed, these problems were regarded as being of religious import, and were (more often than not) explicitly discussed in these terms.

The close connection between religion and those scientific developments which paved the way for biological evolutionism is most clearly evidenced in geology. The story of this connection, as well as the story of the influence of geology on the development of evolutionary theory in biology, is so well known that I shall treat it only in the most summary fashion.

Reprinted by permission from the *Journal of the History of Ideas,* 18 (1957):342-61. Copyright © 1957 by the Journal of the History of Ideas, Inc.

The History of the Earth

Even before the eighteenth century there was an interest in the relations between newly discovered geologic facts and religion. This was evident in the early speculations concerning the nature and origins of fossils, and clearly evident, as their titles show, in such speculative cosmogonies as Burnet's "Sacred Theory of the Earth, containing an Account of the Original of the Earth, and of all the general Changes which it hath already undergone, or is to undergo, till the Consummation of all Things" (1684) and Whiston's "A New Theory of the Earth, wherein the Creation of the World in six Days, the Universal Deluge, and the General Conflagration, as laid down in the Holy Scriptures, are shewn to be perfectly agreeable to Reason and Philosophy" (1696). However, it is also evident in some of the forerunners of a more empirical geology, such as Hooke, Ray, and Woodward. As Lyell remarked concerning Ray: "We perceive clearly from his writings that the gradual decline of our system, and its future consummation by fire, was held to be as necessary an article of faith by the orthodox, as was the recent origin of our planet. His Discourses, like those of Hooke, are highly interesting, as attesting the familiar association in the minds of philosophers, in the age of Newton, of questions in physics and divinity."[2] And as Lyell was regretfully forced to point out in his discussion of eighteenth-century geology, the controversy between Neptunists and Vulcanists took place within an atmosphere of bitter theological recriminations.[3] Lyell felt that with the end of this dispute, and with the laying of the foundations for a new science of geology by the introduction of more accurate empirical studies of geologic formations, and by the development of the close linkage between paleontology and geology which had been inaugurated by Cuvier, a more fruitful period could begin.[4] However, Cuvier's Catastrophism stood opposed to Lyell's Uniformitarianism, and once again theological issues intruded into geological debates. In *Genesis and Geology*, C. C. Gillispie has traced in detail the later as well as the earlier stages of these controversies, but one point may here be made clear. After Lyell's *Principles of Geology* was published (1830-33) the scope of the problem became enormously widened: geotheological debates no longer centered merely in the history of the surface of the earth, but came to include the nature of living creatures. This widening of the issues under dispute had come about through the fact that paleontology—as both Cuvier and Lyell recognized—was the most important key for unlocking the secrets of the history of the earth.[5] Thus, the problem of the origin of different types of living creatures and their adaptations to their environments, as well as the problem of the extinction of certain species, and the distribution of those still extant, were in the forefront of attention among geologists. All these problems, of course, raised issues concerning special creation versus transformism (as evolution was then called), and these issues were placed in the forefront of attention by such works as Chambers's widely read *Vestiges of the Natural History of Creation*

(1844) and Hugh Miller's *Footprints of the Creator* (1849). It can scarcely be wondered that when Darwin's *Origin of Species* was published in 1859, the theological implications of the work were stressed by all reviewers.

The Problem of Species

A second scientific problem that was instrumental in developing an interest in biological evolutionism and that also bears the marks of the close association between theological and scientific problems in the eighteenth and early nineteenth centuries was the problem of species.

Early Discussions

One major aspect of Aristotle's biology was the problem of classification, and it was in this connection that the concept of *species* arose.[6] However, Aristotle's own employment of this concept as a means of classification was not consistent, and it was not until Linnaeus introduced his system of ordering plants into *class, order, genus, species, varieties* that the term *species* was a useful instrument in classification.[7] The main criterion of species, originally suggested by Aristotle and developed by Ray in 1686, was that of capacity for reproduction: only those varieties which could be crossed belonged to the same species. This criterion was adopted by Linnaeus, but his most famous utterances concerning the concept of species were couched in theological terms: there are as many species as God originally created.[8] The harmony between these two modes of definition is obvious: both rule out the possibility of transformism.

Granting this Linnaean characterization of species, the question arises as to what distinguishes classes, orders, genera, and varieties. Here Linneaus's conviction that the world constituted a perfect *Scala naturae*, with each type of plant filling a necessary niche in an overarching pattern, was an important influence on his classification. In addition to this conviction, however, Linnaeus also sought a *useful* classification of plants, and the arrangement of plants according to their modes of reproduction and the introduction of his system of binary nomenclature provided just such a system. Linnaeus himself did not identify his useful system with the natural system, though he always strove to make the former approximate the latter, and he hoped that the latter would at some future time be achieved. This hope rested on a faith in the strict orderliness of the divinely created world of living things. Since this created world was orderly, a perfect natural system of classification was possible, even though it had not yet been attained.[9]

The distinction between an artificial and a natural order of classification had a profound influence on later discussions of the problem of species. In the first place, it opened the door for criticism of the actual system of classification that Linnaeus had worked out,[10] and this criticism was fortified by the discovery of new specimens, which demanded either an immense expansion of the number of distinct species or the lumping together of very disparate forms. In the second place, it suggested that species were not real. Those who—on general philosophic grounds—were inclined to deny the reality of universals (or who took the more moderate position of denying their importance for the empirical investigation of nature) could readily make the transition from Linnaeus's distinction between a useful and a natural classification to the thesis that all groupings into *orders, classes, species,* and even *varieties* were man-made conventions that did not correspond to real distinctions in nature. In such a view, only the concrete individual plant or animal is real. This was the position taken by Linnaeus's contemporary and critic, the great naturalist Buffon.

Buffon shared with Linnaeus the conception of a system of nature, but for him this system was not a statically ordered array of classes, but a dynamic whole[11] in which individuals vary from each other in sometimes imperceptible degrees: "La marche de la nature se fasse par nuances et par degrés." And to this he added that classification of plants or animals into *families* is our work, which we have performed only for the sake of our purposes, and that if we are unsuccessful in this task it is our fault, and not the fault of nature "qui ne connaît point les prétendues familles et ne contient, en effet, que des individus."[12] Buffon's antagonism to the reality of class concepts was so great that he even denied that our lines of demarcation between plants and animals represented a necessary break in the unity of nature.[13] In his view, Linnaeus' classifications "degraded and disfigured nature, instead of describing it."[14]

As is well known, Buffon himself came to hold the doctrine of transformism, largely through his comparative studies of the fauna and flora of different continents. His contributions to the development of evolutionary theory need not occupy us; what is here important to note is that his attack on the very concept of species was taken up and amplified by three younger biologists whom he had aided and influenced; Lamarck, Lacépède (the man whom he authorized to complete his *Histoire naturelle*),[15] and Geoffroy de Saint-Hilaire.

Lamarck

The evolutionary views of Lamarck were closely connected with his attack on the concept of species, as that concept had been employed by Linnaeus. In the first place we may note that Lyell, who knew Lamarck's work well and introduced a knowledge of it into England, traced the origin of Lamarck's evolutionary theory to his investigations in conchology: in classifying species of fossil shells, he found that the resemblances some of them bore to extant species were so close that the lines drawn among the extant specimens tended to break down. He was thus led to the assumption that there was a common bond of descent between the present types of individuals and formerly extant ones and that a definition of species must include a genealogical factor as well as the factors of resemblances and capacity to reproduce.[16] Now, it is to be noted that the genealogical factor is (ideally) alone sufficient for the demarcation of species because individuals linked by descent resemble one another and because they have obviously had the capacity to produce their descendants. But what is ideally true may not be actualized, and we may expect that from the point of view of learning about which individuals should be classified together we must rely upon the conventional criteria of resemblance and reproductive capacity. Thus, Lamarck is willing to define *species* as "any collection of individuals which were produced by others similar to themselves."[17] Such a definition is compatible either with the older view of the fixity of species or with transformism. It is to be noted, however, that throughout the first five chapters of his *Zoological Philosophy,* which center on the problem of the classification of species, Lamarck is concerned with the distinction between *artificial* and *natural* classifications. Chapter 1 opens as follows:

> Throughout nature, wherever man strives to acquire knowledge he finds himself under the necessity of using special methods; 1st, to bring order among the infinitely numerous and varied object which he has before him; 2nd, to distinguish, without danger of confusion, among this immense multitude of objects, either groups of those in which he is interested, or particular individuals among them; 3rd, to pass on to his fellows all that he has learnt, seen and thought on the subject. Now the methods which he uses for this purpose are what I call the *artificial* devices in natural science — devices which we must beware of confusing with the laws and acts of nature herself.
>
> It is not merely necessary to distinguish in natural science what belongs to artifice and what to nature. We have to distinguish as well two very different interests which incite us to the acquisition of knowledge.
>
> The first is an interest which I call *economic* . . . . From this point of view he is only interested in what he thinks may be useful to him. The other, very different from the first, is that *philosophic* interest through which we desire to know nature for her own sake, in order to grasp her procedure, her laws and operations, and to gain an idea of what she actually brings into existence. This, in short, is the kind of knowledge which constitutes the true naturalist."

The conclusion he reached was to draw a distinction between "classifications" and "arrangement," the first being *artificial* and the second *natural.* The first "furnishes points of rest for our imagination, by means of lines of demarcation drawn at intervals in the general series"; the second "represents as nearly as possible the actual order followed by nature in the production of animals."[18] And he further points out that as knowledge advances, and more varieties are discovered, our knowledge of the natural arrangement will increase, and at the same time the utility of our artificial classifications will diminish because the intervals upon which it depends will be filled in.[19]

The motivation of this attack on the traditional view of species did not stem solely from Lamarck's own observations and from the growing difficulties in classification which he noted. Lamarck shared his age's Newtonian distrust of "systems and hypotheses," contrasting them with the results of observation.[20] His theory of knowledge is explicitly stated when he says: "Toute connaissance qui n'est pas le produit réel de l'observation ou des conséquences tirées de l'observation est tout à fait sans fondement et véritablement illusiore."[21] Furthermore, he shared his age's Lockean denial of innate ideas[22] and its distrust of explanations that presumed that our abstract ideas mirrored reality: as he said in discussing the concept of fixed species, "In reality only individuals exist in nature."[23] These lines of linkage between Lamarck and his predecessors are often overlooked because we today tend to think of him as a "vitalist." In fact, however, Buckle was at least equally near the truth when he classified Lamarck as a materialist, because Lamarck held that the "habits of man are entirely a result of his physical organization."[24] In the light of this discrepancy between our present interpretations of Lamarck and the interpretations of those who stood closer to him in time, it may be useful to summarize his general philosophic position.[25]

As we have noted, Lamarck's theory of knowledge would seem to commit him to a rigorous "positivism." However, like many men of his age, he saw no conflict between holding that all knowledge that was not based on observation was illusory and holding that he could know something concerning the ultimate nature of the material world, and could also know that God exists as creator of the universe. When we survey the whole of created nature we find that all entities are physical, that they change state and position according to laws, and that motion accounts for these changes.[26] However, we also find that there is a sharp distinction between the inorganic and the organic with respect to the principle of their motions: the former is characterized by passivity because its motion depends upon *transmission*, while the latter is characterized by activity because its motion depends upon *stimulus*. Thus, it would appear that Lamarck should be regarded as a vitalist, because he draws this absolute distinction between the living and the non-living.[27] However, it is to be noted that organic activity (the reaction to stimuli) depends upon "the vital fluids" and these are themselves physical: they are the caloric and electric fluids.[28] Furthermore, these physical fluids act according to their physical natures, and the vitalistic view of a purposiveness immanent in all living things is explicitly rejected by Lamarck:[29] "La vie [est] une véritable puissance qui donne lieu à des phénomènes nombreux. Cette puissance cependant n'a ni but, ni intention, ne peut faire que ce qu'elle fait, et n'est elle-même qu'un ensemble de causes agissantes, et non un être particulier." Teleology is therefore banned from the realm of science: even though as philosophers we may know that God created the universe, our scientific explanations must be in terms of what came to be known in the controversies that followed as "secondary causes."[30] In the words of Buffon, Lamarck's teacher, it is the object of natural philosophy (i.e., science) to know "the *how* of things," not to search to divine "the *why* of facts."[31] And

Lamarck insists, as did his evolutionary successors, that there is no reason to deny that God could have created an order of nature which gave rise to organic beings *successively* rather than having created them simultaneously with the creation of the earth.[32] Thus, basing his theory on the difficulties that he encountered in his observations of what were supposedly distinct species, and motivated by some of the major philosophic concerns of his age, Lamarck boldly contrasted his hypothesis of evolutionary development and its causes with the Mosaic account.[33]

Later Developments

While Lamarck's hypothesis was rejected by his evolutionary successors,[34] his analysis of the problem of species must be acknowledged to have had an influence even on the opponents of the doctrine of transmutation. This is to be seen in Cuvier's views on the problem of species. In the first place we may note that Cuvier's own definition of the concept of *species* introduces the genealogical element as the only rule that is not "merely hypothetical, and destitute of proof."[35] In the second place (and more importantly), Lamarck's hypothesis of the transmutation of species laid stress on the relations between species and their environments, and this adaptation of animals to their environments became the leading principle of Cuvier's fundamental principle of "the Conditions of Existence": "As nothing can exist if it does not combine all the conditions which render its existence possible, the different parts of each being must be coordinated in such a manner as to render the total being possible, not only in itself, but in its relations to those which surround it."[36] This view, taken merely as a biological principle, is not only connected with Lamarck's insistence on viewing animals in their relations to their environments, but it echoes Lamarck's view that a true arrangement of species (as distinct from an abstract classification) depended on the affinities of the organs of individuals.[37] However, Cuvier was willing to equate his principle of "the Conditions of Existence" with the principle of "Final Causes"[38] and held fast to the view that God had created the species with relation to their environments. To be sure, Cuvier and his followers were forced to admit that, as Whewell put it, there is "a capacity in all species to accommodate themselves, to a certain extent, to a change in external circumstances. . . . There may thus arise changes of appearance and structure . . . but the mutations thus superinduced are . . . confined within certain limits. Indefinite divergence from the original type is not possible. . . . In short, *species have a real existence in nature*."[39] Thus the view was held that secondary causes accounted for the differences among the *varieties* of a species, but not for the differences between species.[40] But when the advance of observations and collections of specimens proceeded far enough—especially when comparative studies were made in new areas of the world —the early quandary of Lamarck reasserted itself, as Lamarck had prophesied it would: the lines to be drawn between species (as distinct from mere varieties) became more and more difficult to draw.

One can see this quandary at work in Hooker, whose difficulties with the question of species in his *Florae Novae-Zelandiae* prepared him to adopt Darwin's theory of transmutation, to the confirmation of which he made such great contributions.[41] Darwin's theory furnished Hooker, and all others who accepted it, a way out of the difficulty of distinguishing *species* from *varieties,* and Darwin himself (with some justice) believed that this would be of considerable help in systematic biology, i.e., it would help those who were interested in classifying biological phenomena.[42] Through Darwin's genealogical approach, that which Linnaeus and all of his successors had sought—a natural, and not an artificial, classification—seemed to have been assured. As Lyell said: "Mr. Darwin labors to show, and with no small success, that all true classification in zoology and botany is, in fact, genealogical, and that community of descent is the hidden bond which naturalists have been unconsciously seeking, while they often imagined that they were looking for some unknown plan of creation."[43] In these words, as well as in our survey of Linnaeus, Lamarck, and Cuvier, it is apparent how closely linked were the problem of species and questions of religion. There is one further scientific problem of the age which also focused interest on evolutionary theory and which also came to be discussed against the background of religious thought. This problem was that of the relation between the human species and the rest of the animal kingdom.

Problems of Man's Place in Nature

The question of the relation of man to the rest of the animal kingdom had three facets. The first concerned the problem of classification: how should the human species, regarded as a part of the *Scala naturae,* be defined? The second concerned the antiquity of the human species. The third, which was related to both of the others, was the problem of the races of men: did they constitute distinct species or were they merely varieties of the same species, and what was the origin of their distinctness from one another? All three of these facets of the question of man's relation to other animals were widely discussed, and all three had obvious connections with questions of religious orthodoxy. In the pre-Darwinian period, however, no general consensus of opinion developed: it was not until Darwin's general theory of biological evolution by natural selection was put forward, and its applicability to man was seen, that these problems came into the forefront of attention. I shall therefore not go into detail on the history of ideas concerning these topics, but merely indicate that they were of concern to many persons in the first half of the century. This is of importance because it throws light on two facts: (1) that even while he was developing his theory of evolution by natural selection Darwin himself frequently considered the problem of the relation of his theory to the nature and history of man; and (2) that the reception accorded *The Origin of Species* by those who condemned it was in large measure dominated by the views it entailed regarding man, rather than the views it set forth regarding the origins of plant and animal species.

1. With respect to the task of classifying man in the *Scala naturae,* two major possibilities were open: one could classify him as a part of the hierarchy of animal species, or one could view him as constituting a new order, distinct from the animals no less than these are distinct from plants. If the second alternative were adopted, it would be because of man's mental endowments, not because of his physical structure: as a physical structure he could be compared with other animals, and his specific differences from other species could presumably be found. Therefore, from the point of view of systematic biology it was necessary to adopt the former alternative, and this Linnaeus did. He classified man as one genus (or family)[44] among the primates. Blumenbach, however, attempted to set man apart from the apes by holding that he constituted a different order, i.e., that of *Bimana,* or two-handed animals, distinguishing them from the order of *Quadrumana* to which the apes belonged. This classificatory schema was adopted by Cuvier, but was gradually abandoned; nonetheless, as late as 1861 Huxley still felt obliged to attack it in his lecture *On the Motor Organs of Man compared with those of Other Animals.* And other attempts were made—notably by Richard Owen—to separate man from the apes in terms of physiological structures; in fact, it was in terms of his theory of the differences between the human brain and the ape's brain that Owen opened his famous attack on the Darwinian theory at the 1860 meeting of the British Association.[45]

However, these debates need not occupy us.[46] Two examples should be sufficient to illustrate the point that the question of man's relation to the animal kingdom was a problem recognized to be intimately connected with the question of whether or not the transmutation theory was true. The first of these examples is from the thought of Lyell. As Lyell later wrote to Darwin, he had long believed "that the case of Man and his Races and of other animals, and that of plants, is one and the same,"[47] and he later wrote that what originally had kept him from adopting Lamarck's transmutation theory was that he was put off by Lamarck's view of the continuity between man and the animals—he did not want to "go the whole orang."[48] The second example is to be found in Hugh Miller's *Footprints of the Creator,* a book written as a reply to Chambers' *Vestiges of Creation.* In opening his discussion of "the development hypothesis,"[49] Miller acknowledged that an evolutionary view of species does not necessarily lead to atheism. However, he held that if this view is extended to include man, so that man is believed to be continuous with the animals, having evolved from them by small changes, then either one must ascribe immortal souls to monads and mites, fishes and reptiles, birds and beasts, or one must deny that humans have such souls. Herein lies the real danger of the development hypothesis, according to Miller, and it is for this reason that he sought to combat it by means of an examination of fossil evidences.

In brief, then, the examples of Lyell and of Miller show that the question of the truth of the theory of transmutation among plants and animals was viewed in the light of what implications it would have for the nature of man: was his nature continuous with that of the rest of the animal kingdom, or was it not? And, as Geoffroy de St. Hilaire pointed out,[50] even those who debated this point with reference to man's bodily structure were really motivated by a desire to distinguish man as a moral being from all the rest of nature. And, if further evidence be needed, the strength of this conviction in the disparity and lack of continuity between man and other animals can be seen in others as well as in Lyell and in Miller. For example, in his very popular *Twelve Lectures on the Connexion between Science and Revealed Religion,* Nicholas Wiseman says in connection with Lamarck's doctrine "it is revolting to think that our noble nature should be nothing more than the perfecting of the ape's maliciousness";[51] and Sedgwick in his long review of *The Vestiges of Creation* criticizes Chambers as having "annulled all distinction between physical and moral."[52] And in 1845 Humboldt, the great naturalist, expressed his belief in the radical discontinuity between man and nature, saying: "A physical delineation of nature terminates at the point where the sphere of intellect begins and a new world of mind is opened to our view."[53] It is therefore of small wonder that Darwin's theory of evolution, recognized as being in the "developmental" tradition of Lamarck and of Chambers, should have had its critics focus attention on its implications for a theory of man even though Darwin had hoped to avoid arousing prejudice against his theory by not discussing the question.[54]

2. In addition to the foregoing debates concerning whether it was possible to view man as having arisen in the course of evolution out of remote anthropoid forebears was the question of *when* man had his origins. Here the question had to be decided in terms of the discovery of human remains or human artifacts in the sequence of geological strata. And throughout the first decades of the century, no traces of human life were found to be anything but "recent"; on this the Catastrophist Cuvier and the Uniformitarian Lyell were agreed.[55] Therefore, insofar as one was to be guided by the available empirical evidence, man was of recent origin and no links were to be found which connected the present state of man with earlier manlike creatures. Speculations, such as those of Lamarck, on how man *might have* arisen from the anthropoid apes, were mere speculations. So, too, were the suggestions of Chambers, and others, that the course of human embryonic development recapitulated an evolutionary development.[56] The evidence drawn from the investigation of geological strata seemed conclusive: man had come onto the scene in relatively recent times (long after the extinction of the last prehistoric species) and had shown no development in his characteristics from the earliest times to the present. Thus, it was natural that man should have been viewed as a special creation.

As Lyell later noted,[57] the more one was impressed by the adequacy of the geologic record, the more it was necessary to assume the truth of the doctrine of the special creation of man. And the extent to which this record was trusted in so far as the history of man was concerned can be seen in Darwin. As we know, Darwin already held his theory of evolution before 1848 when he read Boucher de Perthes' *Antiquités celtiques*, which proved that man coexisted with extinct mammoths; yet Darwin dismissed it as "rubbish."[58] It was not until Darwin's friends Falconer and Lubbock visited the Abbeville excavations,[59] and Darwin, having completed *The Origin of Species*, turned his attention to the problems of *The Descent of Man*, that he came to appreciate the value of these discoveries. Thus it would seem fair to say that the question of the history of man went through two stages with relation to the development of evolutionary theory. In the first stage those who were most painstaking concerning the evidence of geologic investigations emphasized the recency of man and the need for special creation. In this state, the debate over transmutation of species was intimately connected with the question of man's origin, and the evidence seemed to indicate that with respect to this question transmutation was a less plausible view than special creation. However, at precisely the period when Darwin published *The Origin of Species*, new discoveries were being made which upset the conclusions formerly reached, and Lyell's *Antiquity of Man* (1863), which summarized the new evidence, made it clear—though not so clear as Darwin and his friends would have liked[60]—that even with respect to man the doctrine of transmutation was in accord with the evidence.

3. We turn now to the relation between the question of transmutation and the question of how one is to account for the differences among the races of man. The latter question was originally connected with debates concerning the classification of species and with debates concerning the antiquity of man; however, the discussion of those problems later came to have an important relation to discussions of how *varieties* could assume the form of widely diffused and apparently fixed *species*.

Two opposed theories concerning the races of mankind were possible: (1) that all races were descended from a single original stock, or (2) that different races were ultimately different in their ancestry. Either of these theories could be held by those who believed that man was directly created by God, and either could also be held by those who believed that man had an evolutionary origin. For example, Linnaeus held that all of mankind descended from a single divinely created pair of humans, whereas Cuvier, who was also a creationist, held that each of the different races was separately created.[61] On the other hand, those who rejected a separate creation for man, believing him to have evolved from other animal forms, could either hold to the unity of the human race, as did Lamarck, or they could hold to separate origins, as did Virey.[62]

However, the struggle over the unity of the human race was of short duration. Investigations in physical anthropology, inaugurated in a systematic way by Blumenbach, and carried forward by Prichard and Sir William Lawrence, had shown that the similarities between individuals of different races were far more striking than their differences. But this posed a significant problem: if all human beings had a common origin how could one account for the wide variations that we find among the different races? Prichard posed this problem for himself when he listed the facts that seemed to predispose others to believe in plural origins.[63] These facts were: (1) the differences in "figure and complexion which are observed in different nations"; (2) the existence, throughout all known history, of distinct languages; (3) "moral and intellectual diversities . . . thought to characterize particular races"; (4) the existence in all newly explored territories of uncivilized tribes "destitute of those common arts and resources which it seems difficult to suppose that men could ever have forgotten or have lost when once acquired." To undercut these objections Prichard took a decisive step: he attempted to show that in both the plant and the animal kingdoms great variation in type accompanied dispersion in space without necessitating the assumption of independent origin. After this argument he turned to a consideration of the comparative anatomy, comparative physiology, and comparative psychology of the different races of men and reached a similar conclusion.[64] These investigations, as well as those of Lawrence, had an influence on the development of evolutionary theory,[65] for the question that they attempted to answer was how distinct varieties could be accounted for in terms of the diffusion of distinctive peculiarities ("chance variations") that cropped up in some individuals. Still, so far as man was concerned, their views suffered under one major handicap: the assumed time span since the origin of man was too short to make it plausible that the races of man had originated in this way. It was only when Lyell and others had pushed back the history of man that the doctrine of a single origin lying behind all of the present races became plausible. And once this had become plausible, it was possible to argue on the basis of evidence—and not mere speculation—whether man's origin was or was not traceable to nonhuman forebears.[66]

Epigenesis vs. Preformation

There were two other scientific problems that, like the problems we have already discussed, paved the way for the acceptance of evolutionary theory. Their relations to this problem were, however, less intimate than were the struggles over the definition of species or the attempts to place man with respect to the animal kingdom. The first of these problems lay within the field of the theory of reproduction, and its solution cleared away one obstacle to the acceptance of transmutation. I refer to the overthrow of the preformationist hypothesis and the establishment of the doctrine of epigenesis.

The doctrine of epigenesis, i.e., that organisms developed by the successive differentiation of the fertilized ovum, was the dominant and orthodox theory of generation from the time of Aristotle. However, with the discovery of the microscope, Leeuwenhoek and Swammerdam put forward the pre-formationist theory, i.e., that the complete and perfect organism was already preformed in the sperm, and merely grew in size. In the late seventeenth and early eighteenth centuries this controversy was also connected with the controversy between ovists and animalculists (spermists), as to the relative importance of the egg and the sperm in the generative process. In general, the preformationists (some of whom were ovists, and some spermists) domi-nated the field in the eighteenth century. The problem of accounting for the differentiation of parts in embryonic development seemed an insuper-able obstacle to accepting the epigenetic view. It was not until the researches of C. F. Wolff were published (1759) that the doctrine of epigenesis was shown to be necessitated by the observable facts of embryonic developments; but Wolff's work was not widely known until 1812, when it was translated from the Latin by Meckel, another epigenesist. From that point on, the preformationist doctrine was abandoned.[67]

Now it is easy to see what bearing this controversy had upon the incipient controversies over the transmutation of species. So long as one held the pre-formationist doctrine, it was impossible to give up the doctrine of the fixity of species: every individual organism was simply an expanded version of that which was contained in either the egg or the sperm from which it developed, and the characteristics of this egg or sperm were completely preformed in the adult organism from which it had come. (Therefore the preformation theory was also called *emboîtement*: it was conceived on the analogy of a box-within-a-box, etc., *ad infinitum*). Thus, the possibility of individual variations from generation to generation, needed to account for transmutation, was denied by the preformationist theory: according to that theory each of the successive individuals had been implicitly created when the first male (for the spermists) or the first female (for the ovists) of that individual's species had been originally created.[68] When preformationism was abandoned, this obstacle to an acceptance of transmutation was cleared away.[69]

Ecology and Population Theory

A further scientific problem connected with the growth of evolutionary theory was to be found in the field of political economy, viz., the problem of population. In 1798 Malthus published his *Essay on Population*, and this work (as is well known) influenced both Darwin and Wallace in their independent formulations of the theory of the origin of species by natural selection.[70] However, it will be well to make clear why it was possible to make so easy a transition from the Malthusian doctrine to the problem of the extinction of species.

In order to make this clear we must first note that one of the major points discussed by both paleontologists and naturalists was the relation between plants and animals and their environments. That there was a close relation between them was a fact clearly attested by all of the evidence, and the problem that arose was the problem of explaining this relation. Among the transmutationists, for example, Buffon used the hypothesis of the direct action of the environment as an explanation, whereas Lamarck used the tendency of the animal to adapt itself to the environment as the key to the solution. Similarly, the creationists held either that God had successively created the various species, fitting them to the environments that then existed or that after the original creation of all living forms, geological catastrophes had occurred, rendering some of these species extinct and accounting for the particular localization of others.[71] In all of these theories the fittingness of the species to its environment had been stressed. The complexity of this fittingness had been stressed by Buffon in his pioneering work in geographical zoology, and it was one of the two major features of Alexander von Humboldt's studies in plant geography. As Humboldt pointed out in the preface to his *Personal Narrative* and in the prefaces to both the first and second editions of his *Aspects of Nature,* he was interested in conveying the feelings aroused by the grandeur of the unity of nature *and* he wanted to show "the concurrent forces and powers" that constituted this unity.[72] These forces were the ecological factors at work in nature. And it was widely recognized that among such factors were the interrelations of different species.[73]

Thus in 1833 the physiologist Bell, in his Bridgewater Treatise on *The Hand, Its Mechanism and Vital Endowment, as Evincing Design,* wrote as follows: "As in the present day every creature has its natural enemy; or is checked in production, sometimes by a limited supply of food, sometimes by diseases, or by the influence of seasons; and as in the whole a balance is preserved, we may reasonably apply the same principle in explanation of the condition of things as they existed in the earlier stages of the world's progress."[74] And in the same year Lyell published the second volume of his *Principles of Geology,* in which the eighth and ninth chapters were specifically devoted to the same problems. Thus it should occasion no surprise that, in entries for the subsequent year, Darwin's *Journal of Researches* show that he, too, was attempting to explain the extinction of species in ecological terms;[75] this was a problem common to all who engaged in natural history at the time. Recognizing this, and looking back upon Malthus's *Essay on Population,* one can readily see how later readers could have been struck by the application of the Malthusian doctrine to their problem: at the very outset of his work, after stating his fundamental thesis, Malthus himself immediately draws the analogy between ecological relations among plants and animals and the question of the checks on human population.[76] Thus, the problem of population, which was a problem of interest to political economists, social theorists, and historians,[77] contributed a share in the growth of evolutionary theory by virtue of Malthus's views.

In this case, then, as in others whose histories we have here hastily sketched, a scientific problem that arose independently of the growing philosophic interest in evolutionary modes of thought did in fact contribute to the theory of biological evolution. Furthermore, the fact that Darwin's *Origin of Species* presented a view of evolutionary development toward which all of these various scientific theories had tended to converge helps to explain why the scientific and religious implications of that work were instantly understood.

Notes

My interest in the history of nineteenth-century thought began in 1950 when I was asked to teach a course in that field at the University of Michigan. The present study, and the one that follows, were by-products of the research that eventually led, in 1971, to the publication of my book, History, Man, and Reason.

1. The best treatment of this topic is to be found in A. O. Lovejoy, *The Great Chain of Being* (Cambridge, Mass., 1936), especially ch. 8 and 9. For Professor Lovejoy's treatment of the more specifically biological problems, cf. his articles in *Popular Science Monthly*: "Some Eighteenth Century Evolutionists," 65:238ff. and 323ff.; "The Argument for Organic Evolution Before 'The Origin of Species'," 75:499ff. and 537ff.; "Kant and Evolution," 77:538ff. and 78:36ff.; "Buffon and the Problem of Species," 79:464ff. and 554ff.

2. *Principles of Geology* (1st ed.), 1:36. The close connection between questions of science and theology throughout the development of evolutionary thought is amply documented both in Edwin T. Brewster, *Creation: A History of Non-Evolution Theories* (Indianapolis, 1927) and in C. C. Gillispie, *Genesis and Geology* (Cambridge, Mass., 1951).

3. *Principles of Geology*, 1:67-69.

4. Ibid., 71-73.

5. Ibid., 72f.; Cuvier, *Essay on the Theory of the Earth* (trans. by Jameson), 2nd ed. (1815), pp. 50-51, 54.

6. Cf. E. Perrier, *La Philosophie zoölogique avant Darwin* (Paris, 1896), pp. 12-13.

7. Cf. ibid., ch. 5.

8. For both types of definition, cf. E. Guyenot, *Les Sciences de la vie aux XVIIe et XVIIIe siècles* (Paris, 1941), p. 362.

9. On the Linnaean system, cf. W. Whewell, *History of the Inductive Sciences* (3 vol., London, 1837), 2, bk. 16, ch. 4; Eric Nordenskiöld, *History of Biology* (New York and London, 1932), pp. 203-18; Perrier, pp. 34-38.

10. For example, Adanson, the French botanist, found Linnaeus's system of classification arbitrary, because it was merely based on the reproductive organs, and he attempted to substitute a classification that would take into account more of the parts of the plant and thus be less artificial.

11. "La nature . . . est dans un mouvement de flux continuel," apud Perrier, p. 64.

12. Ibid., p. 62. The problem of Buffon's view on species is a vexed one. In his early study of this subject A. O. Lovejoy defended the view that Buffon *did* believe in the objective reality of species (*Popular Science Monthly*, 79:464ff. and 554ff. Cf. Lovejoy, *Great Chain of Being*, pp. 229-330). On the same subject, cf. E. Radl: *Geschichte der biologischen Theorien in der Neuzeit* (2 vols., Leipzig, 1909-13), 1, ch. 11, no. 3.

13. Perrier, p. 67.

14. Ibid., p. 57.

15. On Lacépède and species, cf. Guyenot, p. 408ff.

16. Cf. Lyell, *Antiquity of Man* (2nd Amer. ed.), pp. 389-90. Cf. Packard's confirmation of Lyell's dating of this change in Lamarck (Packard, *Lamarck* London and New York, 1901, pp. 230-31).

Cf. also Charles C. Gillispie, "The Formation of Lamarck's Evolutionary Theory," *Archives Internationales d'Histoire des Sciences,* 37 (1956):323-38.

17. *Zoological Philosophy* (H. Elliot translation), p. 35.

18. Ibid., p. 56.

19. Ibid., p. 57.

20. From the opening lecture of his course (1803); Packard, p. 255.

21. *Système analytique des connaissances positives de l'homme* (1830), p. 84.

22. Cf. *Zoological Philosophy*, p. 363ff.

23. Packard, p. 230. It is also interesting to note that the contrast between the *usefulness* of abstract classifications and the *truth* to be obtained through natural classifications was paralleled in Condillac's contrast between the functions of abstract ideas and the principles of adequate explanation. Cf. "Traité des systèmes," in *Oeuvres philosophiques,* 1:122a45-b10. It is also of interest that Diderot attacked the Linnaean view of nature in Lockean terms (cf. Bréhier, *Histoire de la philosophie,* 2:437, 448).

24. Buckle, *Miscellaneous Works,* 1:152. This is Lamarck's heritage from Cabanis. Cf. his discussions of the latter in *Zoological Philosophy.*

25. A resume of his position on about all philosophical subjects is to be found in his *Système analytique.*

26. Cf. *Zoological Philosophy,* p. 183ff.

27. This distinction was also drawn by Buffon, who held that the ultimate particles of the inorganic and the organic were different in character, though both were material. Cf. Perrier, p. 69.

28. *Zoological Philosophy,* pp. 213 and 187-89.

29. *Système analytique,* p. 37f. Cf. *Hydrogéologie,* p. 67, cited in John J. Judd, *The Coming of Evolution* (Cambridge, 1910), p. 155.

30. *Zoological Philosophy,* pp. 183-84.

31. Perrier, p. 68.

32. *Zoological Philosophy,* p. 36.

33. Ibid., pp. 126-27.

34. Lyell was at first attracted to it, but then rejected it for reasons that we shall soon note. In spite of Lyell's lengthy treatment of Lamarck, Darwin viewed Lamarck's speculation with great distaste (Cf. letters written to Hooker in 1844, as given in *Life and Letters of Darwin,* 1:384 and 390, and in *More Letters of Darwin,* 1:41; also a letter to Lyell in 1863, as given in *Life and Letters of Darwin,* 2:198-99.)

35. *Theory of Earth,* 116.

36. *Règne animale,* 6, in Whewell, 2:492.

37. Cf. *Zoological Philosophy,* part 1, ch. 2 and pp. 56-57.

38. Cf. passage cited from Whewell above.

39. Whewell, 2:565.

40. This was also Lyell's conclusion in his *Principles of Geology* in 1832 (cf. his recapitulation at the end of the 4th chapter of vol. 2).

41. For the correspondence of Hooker relating to species in the years 1843-59, cf. J. Huxley, *Life and Letters of Sir J. D. Hooker,* 1, chs. 23-24. (Also, p. 83.) For Hooker's view regarding species in his *Flora Novae-Zelandiae,* cf. Turrill, *Pioneer Plant Geography: The Phytogeographical Researches of Sir Joseph Dalton Hooker* (The Hague, 1953), p. 143ff.

42. *Origin of Species* (1st ed.), p. 484; (Modern Library ed.), p. 371.

43. *Antiquity of Man,* p. 412. Cf. Haeckel's comment on his own *Generelle Morphologie* (1866) as the attempt to found "a natural system" of classsification on the basis of Darwin's theory. (Preface to the English edition of Haeckel, *The History of Creation.*)

44. What Linnaeus called genera were later called families, a term introduced in 1780 by Batsch: a family was wider than a genus, but narrower than an order (cf. Lyell, *Antiquity of Man,* p. 474, and Perrier, p. 38).

45. Cf. *Life and Letters of Charles Darwin,* 2:113f.

46. For a resume of this material, cf. Lyell, *Antiquity of Man,* pp. 473-94.

47. *Life, Letters, and Journals of Lyell,* 2:325.

48. Ibid., 2:365. Cf. also *Antiquity of Man,* p. 406. Two further points in this letter to Darwin are worthy of comment. 1. Lyell is correct in his interpretation of Lamarck's views as a naturalist, but Lamarck hesitated (inconsistently) to espouse these same views as a philosopher, believing that man had a special origin. (Cf. Perrier, p. 88.) 2. In this same letter Lyell quotes a student of Cuvier's as holding that even Cuvier did not believe that species were real, but only useful modes of classification. It is difficult to reconcile this with Cuvier's writings, but it is interesting to note that Cuvier, no less than Linnaeus and Lamarck, drew a distinction between natural and artificial classifications.

49. The second chapter in his work, p. 37ff. (American ed., 1851).

50. Cf. Lyell, *Antiquity of Man,* pp. 473-75.

51. First Amer. ed., 1837, p. 126f.

52. Gillispie, *Genesis and Geology,* p. 150. Cf. also the letter written by Sedgwick (who had been Darwin's teacher in geology) acknowledging the receipt of *The Origin of Species* (in *Life and Letters of Charles Darwin,* 2:42-45).

53. *Cosmos,* 1:359. (This reference is to the English translation that appeared in the same year as the original.)

54. Cf. *Descent of Man,* preface. Cf. his letter to Wallace (Dec. 22, 1857) in *Life and Letters of Darwin,* 2:467.

55. E.g., Cuvier, *Theory of the Earth,* pp. 127-47; Lyell, *Principles of Geology,* 2, ch. 16.

56. In *The Vestiges of Creation,* p. 149, Chambers takes the doctrine of recapitulation as an established fact, citing a number of biologists from Harvey to Tiedemann. This principle that "ontogeny recapitulates phylogeny," usually associated with the name of Haeckel, was actually much discussed prior to Darwin—e.g., it was criticized by Cuvier and by Rudolphi, and defended by Meckel. Cf. also Perrier, p. 98f.

57. *Antiquity of Man,* p. 406.

58. Cf. *Life and Letters of Darwin,* 2:200 and 198.

59. Cf. *The Life-work of Lord Avebury,* p. 70ff. (John Lubbock became Lord Avebury.)

60. Cf. *Life and Letters of Charles Darwin,* 2:193-204.

61. Cf. Prichard, *Researches into the Physical History of Mankind* (3rd ed., 1836), preface. This was also the opinion of Rudolphi, who is cited by Prichard. (On Rudolphi, cf. Nordenskiöld, p. 354.) The method by which this type of theory could be harmonized with Biblical authority was to claim, as did Bory de Saint-Vincent, that the account of the creation of Adam and Eve referred to only one species of man. (Cf. Wiseman, p. 112f., on Bory.)

62. On Virey, cf. Wiseman, p. 113 (where he cites the article "Homme" in the *Dictionnaire des sciences naturelles,* vol. 21) and Virey, *Histoire des moeurs et de l'instinct des animaux* (Paris, 1822), 1:21 et passim.

63. Prichard, pp. 3-6.

64. On his method cf. Prichard, pp. 9 and vi n.

65. Cf. Wallace's letter to Bates in 1847, in Wallace's *Letters and Reminiscences* (ed. by Marchant), 1:91; cf. *More Letters of Darwin,* 1:43-46 for the relations of Darwin's to Prichard's views.

66. Cf. Lyell's discussion of these points in *Antiquity of Man,* pp. 385-88.

67. For a brief summary of the controversies in embryology, cf. Guyenot, pp. 209-33.

68. Cf. ibid., p. 359.

69. It is worthy of note that, in general, the early transmutationists, such as Buffon and Lamarck, were hostile to the preformationist theory, though they were not in a position to substantiate epigenesis. (On Buffon, cf. Guyenot and Perrier; for Lamarck, cf. *Zoological Philosophy,* pp. 240-43 and *Système analytique,* pp. 117-20.) Furthermore, the doctrine of epigenesis suggested the comparison between embryonic development and the development of species. This comparison was not only made by Meckel, who translated Wolff's work on epigenesis, but was clearly formulated and developed by Serres, the pupil of Geoffroy de Saint-Hilaire. (On Meckel, cf. Nordenskiöld, pp. 355-59; on Serres, cf. Perrier, pp. 259-62.) It is perhaps not too much to say that the stress that the theory of epigenesis necessarily laid on the concept of *development* itself fostered—or, at the least, was allied with—the application of the concept of development in the

whole of nature. Thus Serres viewed the whole animal kingdom as if it were one developing individual, and Chambers in the *Vestiges of Creation,* relying on Serres's theory (pp. 149-52), makes the principle of development the key to what he claims to be "the first attempt to connect the natural sciences into a history of creation" (p. 278). (On the principle of development, cf. ibid., pp. 153-55.)

70. For Darwin's account of how he chanced to be reading Malthus, and of the influence of Malthus on the formulation of his theory, cf. *Life and Letters of Darwin,* 1:68, and *More Letters of Darwin,* 1:118. The two preliminary essays of 1842 and 1844 also contain explicit references to Malthus (*The Foundations of the Origin of Species,* ed. Francis Darwin, pp. 7, 88, 90; cf. pp. xv-xvi). For an account of how Wallace first struck upon the theory of natural selection and then recalled Malthus's work, which he had read twelve years earlier, cf. Alfred Russel Wallace, *Letters and Reminiscences,* 1:108.

71. The first of these views was typical of the Progressionists, such as Sedgwick and Hugh Miller; the second was typical of Cuvier, although his views have sometimes been equated with those of the Progressionists. For examples of the distinctness of his views from theirs, cf. his *Theory of the Earth,* pp. 125f., 171f., and the passage cited from his *Recherches sur les ossements fossiles* by Gillispie, p. 99f.

72. Cf. also *Cosmos,* 1:23, 24.

73. Lamarck often discussed this factor, e.g., *Zoological Philosophy,* pp. 54-55.

74. P. 38. Bell belonged to the group referred to as Progressionists (ibid., pp. 164-68), and rejected transmutation of species.

75. Darwin, *Journal of Researches,* pp. 178-80. In this passage he mentions Buffon, and at the time he of course knew Humboldt's *Personal Narrative,* and frequently referred to it. He had also previously received the second volume of Lyell's *Principles* (cf. Judd, *The Coming of Evolution,* p. 103), but his explicit reference to it in this passage was added between the original edition of 1840 and the revised edition of 1845.

76. Malthus (Everyman ed.), 1:5-6; cf. also p. 9 on relation between the whites and the American Indians, and p. 29 for natural selection as weeding out deformities among the American Indians.

77. The background of Malthus's own work is to be found in theories propounded by Godwin, Rousseau, and Robert Owen, but other facets of the problem were also debated by Rev. Robert Wallace and Hume. Cf. Hume's essay "On the Populousness of Ancient Nations," and E. Mossner's account of this debate in *The Forgotten Hume* (New York, 1943), pp. 111ff.

25

Darwin's Religious Views

The purpose of this study is to trace the changes in Darwin's religious views insofar as it is possible to do so on the basis of available materials. It would seem that such a study is justified on two counts. First, the general picture that emerges from the chapter devoted to this subject in *The Life and Letters of Charles Darwin,* edited by his son, Sir Francis Darwin, is not as detailed as one might wish.[1] Second, the enormous impact of Darwin's theory on the theological discussions of his contemporaries makes it of interest to see how Darwin himself faced the implications of his theory.

Early Orthodoxy

As is well known from the sketch of his life which he wrote for the benefit of his family,[2] in his early years Darwin was thoroughly orthodox in his religious beliefs. When he abandoned the idea of entering medicine, his father suggested that he become a clergyman. While Darwin at this time believed in "the strict and literal truth of every word in the Bible," he had some doubts as to certain dogmas of the Church of England, though he does not specify which dogmas he doubted.[3] His doubts, however, were laid at rest, and Darwin entered Cambridge with the intention of becoming a country clergyman. While at Cambridge his already strong interests in natural history grew, but it can scarcely be supposed that he felt any conflict between his scientific interests and his intended vocation. Not only do we fail to find any expression of such a conflict in his account of his beliefs, but we may note the extent to which clergymen of that period took an active scientific interest in all aspects of natural history.[4] That this should have been the case need occasion no surprise when it is recalled that there had for a long time been a close affiliation between science and theology: scientific problems were widely viewed in relation to the teachings of both revealed and natural theology.[5] Among the standard treatises that epitomized the intimate relations between the two fields were Paley's *Evidences of Christianity* and his *Natural Theology,* and these were works that were closely studied by Darwin as a student at Cambridge and that were greatly admired by

Reprinted by permission from the *Journal of the History of Ideas,* 19 (1958):363-78. Copyright © 1959 by the Journal of the History of Ideas, Inc.

him.[6] Thus, there is no reason to doubt that at the time he left Cambridge and joined the *Beagle* expedition, his orthodoxy was wholly unshaken. As he recalled in his autobiographical sketch, during the five years of that expedition (1831 to 1836), he was sometimes "heartily laughed at by several of the officers (though themselves orthodox) for quoting the Bible as unanswerable authority on some point of morality."[7]

Break with Orthodoxy

During the two years following his return from the *Beagle* expedition, that is, from late 1836 to 1839, Darwin "was led to think much about religion,"[8] and he tells us that he gradually came to see "that the Old Testament was no more to be trusted than the sacred books of the Hindoos."[9] At this time he discarded all belief in miracles and revelation. While he did not do so without a considerable struggle,[10] there is no evidence that he subsequently ever wavered with respect to this point.[11]

Unfortunately, Darwin's autobiographical sketch (which we have thus far followed) does not give us an explicit account of the reasons lying behind this change in his views. In the passages in question it would seem that "the higher criticism" of the period was not without its effect, but there is no evidence that this criticism was at the time known at first-hand by Darwin. It is perhaps not too speculative to suggest that what had first undermined his orthodoxy was his acceptance of Lyell's views in geology, which ran counter to the orthodox interpretation of the creation. It does not seem farfetched to assume that when Darwin became cognizant of this conflict between what had to his satisfaction been established by science and what was then accepted as the clear evidence of Scripture, a wholesale doubt of the orthodox interpretation of Christianity arose in his mind.

In addition to this factor, during the period immediately following the *Beagle* expedition, Darwin had started his notebooks on the evidence for the transmutation of species.[12] Now, the doctrine of transmutation was clearly in conflict with the orthodox interpretation of Scripture; yet Darwin believed that there was strong *"indirect"* evidence that it had taken place.[13] Therefore, his own beliefs on this point could scarcely help but make him suspicious of theological orthodoxy.

However, it is almost surely the case that it was not merely this general conflict that had led him during these three years to "think much about religion." The scientific problem that, as he tells us, caused him the greatest difficulty in advancing his theory was that of accounting for the wonderful adaptations in the organs of plants and animals.[14] Darwin held that the indirect evidence in favor of the transmutation of species was not sufficient to justify accepting that hypothesis until an adequate explanation could be found of the means by which adaptations had been brought about.[15] It is small wonder, therefore, that he was led to think much about religion during this time, because what he was attempting to do was to account for the adaptations of organisms, that is, to account for precisely those facts of natural history which Paley had made the basis of his natural theology. It was not until after 1838, when he had hit upon the principle of natural selection, that Paley's argument from design lost all of its force for him.[16] Combining the principle of natural selection with the greatly extended notion of geologic time which Lyell had introduced, Darwin argued in the 1844 draft of his theory that one no longer had to accept either the doctrine of special creations or Whewell's thesis that "the beginnings of all things are hidden from man."[17]

Compatibility of Theism and "The Origin of Species"

Although Darwin's views were heterodox in the period when he was working on the materials that subsequently became the *Origin of Species,* he had by no means given up theism as such. He tells us that the transition in his religious views was slow and that he "did not think much about the existence of a personal God until a considerably later period."[18] Furthermore, there is no reason to doubt the sincerity of his references to the Creator in the concluding paragraphs of the *Origin.*[19] To be sure, Darwin knew that his views were unorthodox and would be greeted as such; for example, he asked Lyell whether he should warn his publisher, Murray, of the fact. But, as he pointed out, "my book is not more *un-*orthodox than the subject makes inevitable . . . I do not discuss the origin of man . . . I do not bring in any discussion about Genesis, etc. . . . Had I better say *nothing* to Murray, and assume that he cannot object to this much unorthodoxy, which in fact is not more than any Geological Treatise which runs slap counter to Genesis."[20]

The reason why Darwin could at this time hold that his evolutionary theory was consistent with theism (though not with its orthodox forms) was that the realm of explanation with which he was dealing was that of "secondary causes."[21] What he insisted upon was that in scientific explanations it was not only needless, but positively false, to introduce the hypothesis of special acts of Divine Creation to explain the natural order of events. The whole of the evidence he had amassed in the *Origin of Species* was designed to prove that there were sufficiently subtle gradations in all types of organs to allow for the action of natural selection and thus to account for the origin of new species by the agency of that "secondary cause" alone. His problem was not to account for *ultimate origins,* but merely to account for the changes that had occurred among the organisms that naturalists could observe. As he wrote to Lyell, when the latter in examining the proof sheets had challenged some aspects of the *Origin*:

We must under present knowledge assume the creation of one or of a few forms in the same manner as philosophers assume the existence of a power of attrac-

tion without any explanation. But I entirely reject, as in my judgment quite unnecessary, any subsequent addition "of new powers and attributes and forces;"
. . . If I were convinced that I required such additions to the theory of natural
selection, I would reject it as rubbish, but I have firm faith in it, as I cannot believe, that if false, it would explain so many whole classes of facts, which, if I am
in my senses, it seems to explain.[22]

Bearing in mind this use of the illustration of gravitational attraction in
explaining his position, it is small wonder that Darwin should have been
delighted when, shortly thereafter, he discovered, through reading Brewster's biography of Newton, the Newtonian insistence on precisely the same
point: that it was the function of natural philosophy to explain phenomena
by secondary causes, and not in terms of ultimate metaphysical hypotheses.[23]

This distinction between explanations in terms of *secondary* (*intermediate*
or *natural*) causes and explanations in terms of *ultimate* causes was the common property of the age. It was, for example, drawn by Herschel and by
Lyell, as well as by Positivists.[24] However, it was a distinction that was
capable of being put to many uses. Positivism, of course, banned all explanations that attempted to transcend the sphere of secondary causes,
whereas (as we shall see) Herschel felt it necessary to supplement these
causes by a consideration of the Ultimate Cause, and Lyell along with Gray
merely argued for their compatibility. So far as Darwin himself was concerned, it seems safe to say that he only used the distinction as a means of
making clear that he was *not* attacking religion in general by advancing his
theory of the origin of species by natural selection. He could therefore
derive considerable satisfaction from the approval of his theory by the
author Charles Kingsley, who was also a clergyman and a botanist. Kingsley
wrote: "I have gradually learnt to see that it is just as noble a conception of
Deity, to believe that he created primal forms capable of self-development
into all forms needful *pro tempore* and *pro loco,* as to believe that he required
a fresh act of intervention to supply the *lacunas* which He himself had made.
I question whether the former be not the loftier thought."[25] Darwin was
pleased to include reference to this statement in later editions of the *Origin.*[26]

Rethinking His Religious Position

However, in the two years immediately following the publication of the
Origin of Species Darwin was gradually forced to rethink his own religious
position. In part, this was doubtless due to the general outcry that had
greeted his work. However, it was primarily through his correspondence
with Lyell and Gray, both of whom were much concerned with the religious
implications of his theory, that Darwin was led to reexamine his beliefs.

Originally, as we have seen, he was content to put forward his hypothesis
as a doctrine of the secondary causes at work in nature and leave questions
of ultimate explanations undisturbed. However, both in the *Origin of Species*

and subsequently, he felt obliged to defend his hypothesis by attacking its alternative: the doctrine of special creations. Now, the arguments he used in this attack were in some cases compatible with theism, but in other cases they raised real difficulties for that position. Among the arguments that were damaging to the special creationist doctrine as applied to species, but which were wholly compatible with theism in general, were the following. First, that the special creationist fails to make explicit just what he is holding, seeking to hide the vagueness of his hypothesis in the mystery of creation. In this connection Darwin says:

> Do they really believe that at innumerable periods in the earth's history certain elemental atoms have been commanded suddenly to flash into living tissues? Do they believe that at each supposed act of creation one individual or many were produced? Were all the infinitely numerous kinds of animals and plants created as eggs or seed, or as full grown?[27]

Second, Darwin points out in the same passage that even the special creationist will admit (as, for example, Cuvier and Whewell were forced to admit) that variations *within* one species can be explained by secondary causes: thus, the nontheological explanation that they are willing to acknowledge in some cases, they attempt to rule out in others. Darwin criticizes this on two grounds: (1) that it violates "Maupertuis' philosophical axiom of least action," explaining phenomena by more principles than are necessary, and (2) that because supposedly distinct species bear the marks of common origins, one would have to hold that these marks were deceptive.[28] Neither of these arguments would impugn a theistic interpretation of nature; they merely attack the doctrine of special creations of plant and animal forms.

However, there were at least three other arguments that Darwin employed to attack the doctrine of special creations, and each of these contains implications that tend to conflict with a theistic interpretation of natural law, though they do not flatly contradict it. The first of these arguments consists in the fact that Darwin insisted that because breeds as distinct as the breeds of pigeons have been formed by the artificial selection exercised by man, we need not assume any special creation where natural selection is at work.[29] On the surface this would seem to be wholly compatible with theism, yet implicitly it is not, for Darwin's theory assumed that variations upon which the principle of selection worked were *random* variations. Because he did not believe that it would be possible to suppose that the variations in pigeons were providentially arranged in order that man might breed new varieties, so he did not suppose that the variations in nature were providentially arranged.[30] To this extent, Darwin's hypothesis tended to undercut the theistic argument from design.

A further argument that Darwin put forward against the views of the special creationist also had hidden implications for the religious position of at least the liberal theologians of his day. In attacking that doctrine of special creation which was held by the Progressionists, he pointed out that they assumed that each species was created with a view to its relations to the then existing habitat in which it would live. However, if this had been so, one might expect that organisms would be so created as to provide for the welfare of other organisms in the same environment, that is, that the teleological principle would not be confined to producing what is merely beneficial to that particular type of organism itself. Darwin, however, denies that we ever find a structure in an animal which is so designed that it operates for the exclusive benefit of another species; it must always operate for the benefit of its bearer.[31] In Darwin's theory this is no accident; in a special creationist theory there would be no reason why this generalization should hold. While some theologians might have been willing (or even anxious) to accept the view that this state of affairs was compatible with providential design,[32] Darwin and other liberally oriented theologians could surely not help but be troubled by the view that Divine Providence operated through an unmitigated egoism.[33]

Finally, we may note that one of Darwin's arguments against special creationism and in favor of his own theory quite explicitly stands in opposition to a theistic interpretation of that theory. Darwin points out on more than one occasion that if we were to hold the view of the special creationist we would have to assume the existence of an arbitrary and capricious Creator, because animals and plants vary in all sorts of minute and apparently purposeless ways from one another.[34] And closely coupled with this argument was Darwin's longstanding feeling, expressed in both the 1842 and 1844 drafts of his theory, that it would be derogatory to our idea of the Creator to believe in the direct creation of parasites, and the like.[35] These considerations not only told against the doctrine of special creations, but were contrary to any interpretation of his theory which held that the origin of species by natural selection acting upon variability was a manifestation of a providential foresight and will.

Not having been primarily concerned with the theological implications of his theory, Darwin only slowly came to question his earlier confidence in the compatibility between his theory and theism. As he later recalled, during the time that he had been working on the *Origin of Species* he had felt that one must accept that form of the theistic argument which is based on the impossibility of conceiving of the wonders of nature and the capacities of man as having arisen as a result of "blind chance or necessity."[36] Because he felt when he published the *Origin* that his theory and theism were compatible, it came as a disturbing fact to learn that Herschel, whom he greatly admired, had spoken of that theory as "the law of higgledy-piggledy."[37] What Herschel meant became explicit when he criticized Darwin's view in the 1861 edition of his *Physical Geography* :[38]

We can no more accept the theory of casual and arbitrary variation and natural selection as a sufficient account, *per se,* of the past and present organic world, than we can receive the Laputan method of composing books (pushed à *outrance*) as a sufficient one of Shakespeare and the *Principia*. Equally in either case an intelligence, guided by a purpose, must be continually in action to bias the directions of the steps of change—to regulate their amount, to limit their divergence, and to continue them in a definite course. We do not believe that Mr. Darwin means to deny the necessity of such intelligent direction. But it does not, so far as we can see, enter into the formula of *this* law, and without it we are unable to conceive how far the law can have led to the results. On the other hand, we do not mean to deny that such intelligence may act according to a law (that is to say, on a preconceived and definite plan). Such law, stated in words, would be no other than the actual observed law of organic succession; or one more general, taking that form when applied to our own planet, and including all links of the chain which have disappeared. *But the one law is a necessary supplement to the other, and ought, in all logical propriety, to form a part of its enunciation.*

Lyell and Gray, with whom Darwin corresponded concerning these matters, did not go so far as Herschel. They did not insist that it was necessary to state explicitly the providential aspect of evolution in formulating the law of its secondary causes, but both did believe that unless the doctrine of natural selection was supplemented by this extrascientific hypothesis it would not be ultimately tenable.[39] Their views with respect to this point obviously troubled Darwin, and he repeatedly returned to the question of the relation between his theory and the theistic interpretation of the order and harmony of the natural world.

Darwin was troubled by the question of what evidence, if any, could be adduced in favor of an overall plan in nature once he had, as he believed, adequately accounted for the amazing adaptations in the organic world.[40] Furthermore, he had long felt that the existence of natural evil was a serious stumbling block for those who accepted theism.[41] In searching for an alternative to the views of Gray, he briefly proposed that one could "look at everything as resulting from designed laws, with the details, whether good or bad, left to the working out of what we may call chance."[42] This was an obvious attempt to allow for an overall plan in nature, to insist at the same time on the sufficiency of secondary causes, and to escape from the problem of natural evil. However, immediately after putting forward this suggestion, Darwin added: "Not that this notion *at all* satisfies me. I feel most deeply that the whole subject is too profound for the human intellect. A dog might as well speculate on the mind of Newton. Let each man hope and believe what he can."[43] This attitude of agnosticism—as it came to be called[44] —linked with a willingness that each person should believe as he saw fit, was characteristic of Darwin's religious position at the time.[45] As he later said in characterizing his views: "In my most extreme fluctuations I have never been an Atheist in the sense of denying the existence of a God. I think that generally (and more and more as I grow older), but not always, that an Agnostic would be the more correct description of my state of mind."[46] However, it would seem that the quality of his agnosticism changed over the years, and it is this point that I now wish to establish.

In 1860 Darwin wrote to Gray: "I grieve to say that I cannot honestly go as far as you do about Design. I am conscious that I am in an utterly hopeless muddle. I cannot think that the world, as we see it, is the result of chance; and yet I cannot look at each separate thing as the result of Design."[47] Six months later he wrote Gray concerning Herschel's views, which he found similar to Gray's, "I have been led to think more on this subject of late, and grieve to say that I come to differ more from you."[48] And six months thereafter, though still in a quandary, Darwin's further remarks to Gray suggest that his convictions were even more strongly opposed to those held by his friend and defender. He wrote:

> If anything is designed, certainly man must be: one's "inner consciousness" (though a false guide) tells one so; yet I cannot admit that man's rudimentary mammae . . . were designed. If I was to say I believed this, I should believe it in the same incredible manner as the orthodox believe the Trinity in Unity. You say that you are in a haze; I am in thick mud; the orthodox would say in fetid, abominable mud; yet I cannot keep out of the question. My dear Gray, I have written a deal of nonsense.[49]

Darwin's Agnosticism

In later years, Darwin continued to refer to the two arguments which lay at the foundation of his agnosticism in the period 1860-61, i.e., to the adequacy of natural selection in explaining the evidence of apparent design in nature and to the problem of evil.[50] Yet in his later years there was added a third general type of argument which fortified this agnosticism and made his position into one more critical of theism than it had previously been. This argument derived from his willingness to apply his theory of evolution to man's mind.

When Darwin wrote the *Origin of Species* he was convinced that his theory could be applied to man as well as to other animals, but he did not wish to jeopardize the acceptance of the theory by placing emphasis on this fact. However, in turning his attention to the problem of the evolution of man, and particularly of man's mind, he saw a further reason for agnosticism. As he said in 1876, "Can the mind of man, which has, as I fully believe, been developed from a mind as low as that possessed by the lowest animals, be trusted when it draws such grand conclusions [viz., concerning Theism]?"[51] And even later he said, "The horrid doubt always arises whether the convictions of man's mind, which has been developed from the mind of lower animals, are of any value or at all trustworthy."[52] This, of course, was said in connection with man's speculation concerning theological matters, and not with respect to man's power to grasp the order of nature through science. But with respect to theological problems, this scepticism of the mind's trustworthiness apparently played its part in undercutting the reliance that he was willing to place on inward convictions. In 1876 he explicitly stated that in so far as the conviction of the existence of God, and of immortality, rests on "feelings of wonder, admiration, and devotion," it is of no evidential value; and even when this conviction is connected with reason and rests on the argument that the universe and man could not be the result of "blind chance or necessity," doubt that man's mind (because of its origin) can be relied on in these matters is the final conclusion that he reaches.[53] Thus the fact of *belief,* which had formerly loomed large as an element capable of counteracting the doubts raised against theism by the argument from secondary causes and by the problem of evil, was no longer a potent force. In closing *The Variations of Animals and Plants under Domestication* (1868) he is arguing against Gray's view of an ultimate providential design, and he says: "*However much we may wish it,* we can hardly follow Professor Asa Gray . . ." [italics mine]. At this time, then, the evidential value of his earlier conviction seemed to be without worth. Because, however, man's mind was incapable of grasping a solution to this question, as it was also incapable of grasping a solution to the questions of free-will and predistination,[54] Darwin did not attempt to hold that Gray was positively mistaken. He was, as his son informs us,[55] always averse to expressing himself publicly on a question on which he had not thought sufficiently and especially on one which he considered a private matter for each individual. Yet there can be little doubt that the quality of his agnosticism had changed after 1860 and 1861. During that period, under the impetus of the views of Lyell and Gray, he had been (as he said) "bewildered"[56] and "in a maze."[57] The general theistic convictions he had when he wrote the *Origin of Species* had given way to doubts as he examined and criticized the views held by them. In the end his agnosticism was not one brought about by an equal balance of arguments too abstruse for the human mind;[58] it was an agnosticism based on an incapacity to deny what there was no good reason for affirming. Thus, those who, at the time, regarded agnosticism as merely an undogmatic form of atheism would, in my opinion, be correct in so characterizing Darwin's own personal position.

If this be doubted, let me briefly indicate further confirmatory evidence. First, as Darwin tells us, his own religious experiences had declined; and he also placed no reliance upon the evidential value of such experiences.[59] Second, he continued to reject any belief in revelation.[60] Third, the purposiveness of nature which he had implicitly assumed when he wrote the *Origin of Species* he now held was not in fact present in nature. It was this last point that was crucial, because Darwin had from the beginning placed most emphasis on purposiveness as evidence for a Creator.

To how great an extent Darwin had viewed "Nature" as acting for the benefit of species is clear in many passages in the *Origin of Species.* At the time he assumed that we should regard "every complex structure and instinct as the summing up of many contrivances, each useful to its possessor"[61]: nothing would be preserved were it not of positive use. Thus he was able to hold that "as natural selection works solely by and for the good of each being, all corporeal and mental endowments will tend to progress toward perfection."[62] The clearest theoretical statement of this view is given in Darwin's answer to one of Lyell's objections, when Lyell was examining the proof sheets of the *Origin of Species*. Darwin wrote: "Natural Selection acts exclusively by preserving successive slight, *useful* modifications. Hence Natural Selection cannot possibly make a useless or rudimentary organ. Such organs are solely due to inheritance . . . and plainly bespeak an ancestor having the organ in a useful condition."[63] Why, we may ask, should he have so insisted on the positive usefulness of every variation that was preserved?

There were two reasons for this. First, the analogy he had drawn between the artificial selection of breeders and natural selection had from the first tended to make him personify the power of natural selection. This is evident in his letter to Gray which, as read to the Linnean Society in 1858, served as the initial public report of his theory. There he says:

> Man, by this power of accumulating variations, adapts living beings to his wants — he *may be said* to make the wool of one sheep good for carpets, and another for cloth, etc.
>
> Now, suppose there was a being, who did not judge by mere external appearance, but could study the whole internal organization — who never was capricious — who should go on selecting for one end during millions of generations, who will say what he might not effect. . . .
>
> I think it can be shown that there is such an unerring power at work, or *Natural Selection* (the title of my book), which selects exclusively for the good of each organic being.[64]

It was Wallace who (in 1866) first pointed out to him how his use of the term *natural selection* and his comparison of natural selection with man's selection had led critics to believe that Darwin himself should have supplemented his law with statements concerning an ultimate conscious design in nature. Wallace wrote:

> The same objection viz. that thought and direction are essential to the action of natural selection has been made a score of times by your chief opponents. . . .
> I think this arises almost entirely from your choice of the term "Natural Selection" and so constantly comparing it in its effects to Man's Selection, and also your so frequently personifying nature as "selecting," as "preferring," as "seeking only the good of the species," etc. etc. To the few this is as clear as daylight, and beautifully suggestive, but to many it is evidently a stumbling block.[65]

The fact that this analogy between natural selection and man's selection constituted a stumbling block for many is easily comprehended when we recall the extent to which natural theology had emphasized the argument from design as proof of God's existence. As a matter of fact, in *The Descent of Man* (1871), Darwin himself acknowledged that this mode of argument was so thoroughly ingrained in his thought that it had led him to assume that all variations that were preserved must have been of positive use to the organism, and hence to the species. He wrote:

> I was not able to annul the influence of my former belief, then almost universal, that each species had been purposely created; and this led to my tacit assumption that every detail of structure, excepting rudiments, was of some special, though unrecognized, service.[66]

Thus it was the implicit teleology of the naturalists of his time, as well as his analogy between natural and human selection, that had led Darwin to view all variations that were preserved as marking an advance in adaptiveness and as thus being "progressive."[67] When this previous tendency in his thought was thus explicitly disavowed,[68] the break with Lyell and Gray must be considered complete: the tendency to view organs in terms of purposiveness was explicitly rejected, and the acceptance of useless variations (i.e., those which are neither beneficial or harmful) accords ill with the argument that the Divine Purpose acts uniformly through the secondary causes of variations and natural selection.[69] Thus it seems wholly accurate to say that all that prevented Darwin from denying the truth of theism was the antidogmatic cast of his own mind and his acceptance of the limitations of all human minds, considering their lowly origins. The theological struggles he had undergone were over.

Notes

1. This work will be cited as *LLD* in the following footnotes. Page references will refer to the two-volume edition (New York, 1888), followed by references in square brackets to the revised three volume edition (London, 1888).

Other abbreviations are as follows:

MLD: More Letters of Charles Darwin, ed. by Francis Darwin, 2 vol. (London, 1903).

FOS: The Foundations of the Origin of Species; Two essays written in 1842 and 1844, by Charles Darwin, ed. by Francis Darwin (Cambridge, 1909).

LCL: Life, Letters, and Journals of Sir Charles Lyell, ed. by his sister-in-law, Mrs. Lyell, 2 vols. (London, 1881).

HP: The Huxley Papers, preserved in The Muniments Library of the Imperial College of Science and Technology, London. The descriptive catalogue of this material, prepared by Warren R. Dawson, was published in 1946 by Macmillan and Co. for the Imperial College.

2. Cf. *LLD*, 1, ch. 2 [1, ch. 2].

3. *LLD*, 1:39 [1:45].

4. Cf. Darwin's account of his friendship with Professor Henslow, who introduced him to Leonard Jenyns, a clergyman (*LLD*, 1:44-46 [1:52-55]). Henslow himself later had a parish, and Jenyns was to a large extent a supporter of Darwin's evolutionary theory (cf. *LLD*, 2:87 [2:293]). Charles Kingsley was another example of a clergyman with active scientific interests, and one may note, scattered through Darwin's correspondence, the prevalence of letters to and from clergymen discussing points in natural history. Interest on the part of clergymen in scientific problems is also evident in Huxley's correspondence.

5. For an indication of some points at which science and religion came into contact, cf. my article "The Scientific Background of Evolutionary Theory in Biology," reprinted above (ch. 24).

6. *LLD*, 1:40f. [1:47]. Cf. 1:278 [1:809] and 2:15 [2:219].

7. *LLD*, 1:277 [1:307f.].

8. *LLD*, 1:277 [1:307].

9. *LLD*, 1:277 [1:308].

10. *LLD*, 1:278 [1:308f.].

11. The allegation that, on his deathbed, he was reconverted to orthodoxy appears to be absolutely without foundation. The allegation is to be found in *HP*, 13.136; 13.67 and 13.183 give the replies by Francis Darwin and Huxley.

12. Cf. *LLD*, 1:437 [2:78] and 1:453 [2:95].

13. Francis Darwin pointed out that his father believed in the transformation of species as early as 1832 (cf. *FOS*, intr.). This belief was greatly strengthened by his visit to the Galapagos Islands in 1835, and from that point on it continued to gather strength. However, the evidence was still "indirect," i.e., he had no hypothesis by means of which to explain how this transformation had taken place. This was only provided when, in reading Malthus in 1838, he hit upon the idea of natural selection as an explanatory principle.

14. *MLD*, 1:213. Cf. *LLD*, 1:478 [2:121].

15. *LLD*, 1:67 [1:82].

16. *LLD*, 1:278 [1:309].

17. *FOS*, p. 248. Cf. W. Whewell, *History of the Inductive Sciences* (London, 1837), 3:587f. According to Aveling's account (which was, to be sure, challenged by Francis Darwin), Darwin said that at the age of forty (i.e., in 1849) he gave up his belief in Christianity. Cf. E. B. Aveling, *The Religious Views of Charles Darwin* (London, 1883). In what follows it will be seen that Aveling's account is not so unreliable as Francis Darwin suggested (cf. *LLD*, 1:286n. [1:317n.]).

18. *LLD*, 1:278 [1:309]. His son's account is primarily concerned with this later period.

19. *LLD*, 1:282 [1:313].

20. *LLD*, 1:507 [2:152].

21. Statements to this effect are to be found in both the 1842 and 1844 Essays in *FOS*, pp. 51f., 251, 253f.

22. *LLD*, 2:6f. [2:210f.].

23. *LLD*, 2:83f. [2:289f.]. Cf. his introduction of this argument into the third edition of *Origin of Species* (1861), p. 514.

24. It is not possible to say how early Darwin knew of Comte's doctrine, but in 1861 he contrasted scientific and theological modes of explanation (*MLD*, 1:192). However, it is clear that he had not read Comte himself, and in 1869, after reading Huxley's attack on Comte, he lost interest in doing so (cf. *MLD*, 1:313). We may note that just prior to this attack Darwin was apparently unaware of the difference between Comte's Positivism and Huxley's position: Darwin had forwarded a Comtist writing to Huxley without being aware that it would give serious offense to him (cf. *HP*, 5.262 and 5.264).

25. *LLD*, 2:82 [2:288]. Kingsley, however, soon came to see that acceptance of Darwin's theory involved the consequence that "all natural theology must be rewritten" (*HP*, 19.205). He himself inclined toward a spiritualistic monadology (cf. *HP*, 19.221, 19.229, 19.235).

26. Cf. the second edition of the *Origin of Species* (1860), p. 481.

27. *Origin of Species* (first edition), p. 482f. [Modern Library edition, p. 369]. Darwin was forced to concede to two of his correspondents that this passage was somewhat unfair (*MLD*, 1:163 and 173), yet he kept the passage in later editions. As one can see from his remarks about Owen, the fundamental difficulty of the mysteriousness of the special creations remained (*MLD*, 1:178). Lyell felt a similar difficulty in Agassiz's views regarding special creationism applied to man (*LCL*, 2:331).

28. This passage was introduced into the third edition, published in 1861 (cf. p. 517f.). A comparable argument concerning Maupertuis' principle had been stated by Darwin in a letter to Lyell in 1860 (cf. *LLD*, 2:139 [2:290]).

29. Cf. *LLD*, 2:97 [2:303], and his remark on Jordan, *LLD*, 2:84 [2:290].

30. In 1861 he wrote to Lyell: "He who does not suppose that each variation in the pigeon was providentially caused, by accumulating which variations, man made a Fantail, cannot, I think, logically argue that the tail of the woodpecker was formed by variations providentially arranged." (*MLD*, 1:191). This example was a favorite one of his (cf. *LLD*, 1:283f. [1:314] and 2:146 [2:353f.]).

31. *Origin of Species* (first edition), p. 201 [Modern Library edition, p. 148].

32. Cf. the Calvinist acceptance of Darwinism as discussed by H. W. Schneider in "The Influence of Darwin and Spencer on American Philosophical Theology," *Journal of the History of Ideas*, 6 (1945):3-18.

33. Cf. Kingsley's position in *HP*, 19.162 et passim.

34. Cf. *LLD*, 2:139 [2:347] and 2:97 [2:303].

35. *FOS*, pp. 51 and 254.

36. *LLD*, 1:282 [1:312].

37. *LLD*, 2:37 [2:240].

38. Apud *MLD*, 1:191n.

39. For Gray's view cf. his *Darwiniana* (New York, 1876), especially pp. 144-59 and 176f. (This article was originally published in the *Atlantic Monthly* in October 1860.) Lyell's views were less consistently maintained; however, for the most part he shared Gray's position. Cf. his early letter to Herschel (*LCL*, 1:467ff.), his praise of Gray's view (*LCL*, 2:341), and his public association of his own views with those of Gray in his *Antiquity of Man* (London, 1863), pp. 502-6; also, his subsequent letters to Darwin (*LCL*, 2:384ff. and 441ff.). All of these passages are of a piece: none of them involves the assumption of special creations or of any interference in the realm of secondary causes, but only the assumption of a Divine Plan unfolding through natural law. However, in 1859, when he was considering Darwin's *Origin of Species*, he for a short time deemed it necessary to assume "continued intervention of creative power" and this he coupled to a "principle of improvement," thus apparently seeking to *supplement* Darwin's view, and not interpret it as being merely consistent with a Divine Plan. The exact nature of his position at this time is difficult to ascertain because three of his four letters to Darwin on these points have apparently not been preserved, and we only have Darwin's replies to them. However, it would seem that Lyell's position was essentially that of Herschel during this brief period. This inconsistency with his main position was doubtless due to the conflict that he continually felt between his "feelings and old sentiments" and his reasonings (cf. *LCL*, 2:362, 363). Gradually, once again, he took a more moderate position, but, like Gray, he always remained a Theist. He apparently shared the convictions of the Unitarians, but was averse to challenging the religious beliefs of others (cf. *HP*, 6.122).

40. Cf. letter to Lyell, *LLD*, 2:97 [2:303]. Also, *LLD*, 1:278ff. [1:309ff.] and three further letters written to Lyell in 1861 (*MLD*, 1:190-94).

41. Letter to Gray, *LLD*, 1:284 [1:314f.]. Cf. *LLD*, 1:283 [1:313].

42. *LLD*, 2:105 [2:312].

43. The whole of this passage is worth quoting:

With respect to the theological view of the question. This is always painful to me. I am bewildered. I had no intention to write atheistically. But I own that I cannot see as plainly as others do, and as I wish to do, evidence of design and beneficence on all sides of us. There seems to me too much misery in the world. I cannot persuade myself that a beneficent and omnipotent God would have designedly created the Ichneumonidae with the express intention of their feeding within the living bodies of Caterpillars, or that a cat should play with mice. Not believing this, I see no necessity in the belief that the eye was expressly designed. On the other hand, I cannot anyhow be contented to view this wonderful universe, and especially the nature of man, and to conclude that everything is the result of brute force. I am inclined to look at everything as resulting from designed laws, with the details, whether good or bad, left to the working out of what we may call chance. Not that this notion *at all* satisfies me. I feel that the whole subject is too profound for the human intellect.

A dog might as well speculate on the mind of Newton. Let each man hope and believe what he can. Certainly I agree with you that my views are not at all necessarily atheistical. The lightning kills a man, whether a good one or a bad one, owing to the excessively complex action of natural laws. A child (who may turn out an idiot) is born by the action of even more complex laws, and I can see no reason why a man, or other animal, may not have been aboriginally produced by other laws, and that all these laws may have been expressly designed by an omniscient Creator, who foresaw every future event and consequence. But the more I think the more bewildered I become; as indeed I probably have shown by this letter." (*LLD*, 2:105-6 [2:311f.]).

Darwin later refers back to this belief, and again acknowledges its unsatisfactoriness (*LLD*, 2:247 [3:64]).

44. The term was coined by Huxley, probably in 1869. On the controversies concerning the meaning of the term, and the date and circumstances of its coinage, cf. George W. Hallam: "Source of the Word 'Agnostic'," *Modern Language Notes*, 70 (1955):265-69. Huxley's essay entitled "Agnosticism" was not published until 1889. However, as he tells us, the term was given currency by the *Spectator.* This was apparently in January 1870 (cf. *Oxford English Dictionary*), and the term shortly came to have wide currency. Darwin himself used it to characterize his position at least as early as 1876, when he wrote the autobiographical sketch of his life (cf. *LLD*, 1:282 [1:313]).

45. Cf. also the postscript of a letter to Lyell, *LLD*, 1:98 [2:304], and a letter to Gray on design, *LLD*, 2:146 [2:353f.].

46. *LLD*, 1:274 [1:304].

47. *LLD*, 2:146 [2:353f.].

48. *LLD*, 2:165 [2:373].

49. *LLD*, 2:174f. [2:382].

50. On the first point, cf. the last paragraphs of *Variation of Animals and Plants,* which Darwin later said was an argument that no one had refuted (*LLD*, 1:279 [1:309]). On the second point, cf. *LLD*, 1:281 [1:311].

51. *LLD*, 1:282 [1:313]. This view was already foreshadowed in a passage quoted above (cf. note 43): "The whole subject is too profound for the human intellect. A dog might as well speculate on the mind of Newton." Yet, when expressed in this way, the argument seems to imply an acceptance of a Divine Mind, concerning which we must forever remain ignorant. If this is truly implied, then Darwin's views clearly did change in the direction of a more radically skeptical attitude toward the truth of Theism.

52. *LLD*, 1:285 [1:316].

53. *LLD*, 1:281-82 [1:311-13].

54. Cf. the concluding sentence of *Variation of Animals and Plants*; also, *LLD*, 2:98 [2:304].

55. Cf. his comments in chapter 8 of *LLD*, 1.

56. *LLD*, 2:105, 106 [2:311, 312].

57. *LLD*, 1:283 [1:313].

58. The last passage in which I have found Darwin confessing that his views are "in a muddle" is in an 1870 letter to Hooker, but even at that time his doubts seemed to be far stronger than his affirmations (cf. *MLD*, 1:321). Cf. his statement in 1873 in reply to a letter from a Dutch student (*LLD*, 1:276 [1:306f.]).

59. *LLD*, 1:281 [1:312].

60. *LLD*, 1:277 [1:307].

61. *Origin of Species* (first ed.), p. 485 [Modern Library ed., p. 371].

62. Ibid., p. 489 [Modern Library ed., p. 373].

63. *LLD*, 2:9 [2:213].

64. *LLD*, 1:480 [2:123].

65. Cf. *MLD*, 1:267f. Wallace suggested obviating the difficulty by substituting Spencer's term *survival of the fittest* for *natural selection.* In his reply, Darwin acknowledged that it would be helpful to work the term *survival of the fittest* into his text more frequently, but he was unwilling

to abandon the original term—which was by then familiar. Cf. Darwin's own recognition of this problem, *LLD*, 2:138ff. [2:346].

66. *Descent of Man* (Modern Library ed.), p. 442.

67. *MLD*, 1:142 and 164.

68. Cf. his remark to Alphonse de Candolle: "When I read your remarks on the word 'purpose' I vowed I would not use it again; but it is not easy to cure oneself of a vicious habit." This was written in 1881 (cf. *MLD*, 2:429; cf. the earlier letter to de Candolle, *MLD*, 1:369). For de Candolle's general philosophic position, and his criticism of Darwin's use of the concept of development and his use of the term *nature*, cf. *Darwin considéré au point de vue des causes de son succès* (1882), appendix A, and his *Histoire des sciences et des savants depuis deux siècles* (1873), p. 433.

69. On the causes of variations, a summary of Darwin's views is given in the concluding section of *Variation of Animals and Plants*. On useless variations as "inevitable consequences of modifications in other parts," cf. *MLD*, 1:286.

Name Index

All references to individuals discussed or cited are printed in roman type. Italic type is used when an individual is merely mentioned.

Ackerman, James, 118 n. 9
Adams, Henry, 194 n. 12
Adanson, Michel, 303 n. 10
Agassiz, Louis, 318 n. 27
Alexander, Samuel, 7
Allport, Gordon W., 270 n. 25
Ames, Adelbert, 118 n. 10
Anderson, Alan Ross, 211 n. 19
Anderson, Robert F., 258 n. 5
Aristotle, 120, *136,* 291, 300
Asch, Solomon E., 210 n. 13, 211 n. 16
Ast, Friedrich, 46
Augustine, Saint, 74
Austin, J. L., 34 n. 8, 35 n. 14
Austin, John, *260,* 276
Aveling, Edward B., 318 n. 17

Bagehot, Walter, 15, 19 n. 11
Bain, Alexander, 22 n. 32, 271 n. 40
Ballachey, E. L., 210 n. 13
Barber, Bernard, 233 n. 3
Barnes, J. A., 234 n. 10
Barth, Paul, 83 n. 4
Basson, A. H., 258 n. 5
Bateson, Gregory, 215-16, 218, 220, 221, 229
Batsch, August, 304 n. 44
Beard, Charles A., 38
Beck, Lewis W., 18 n
Bell, Charles, 302, 306 n. 74
Benedict, Ruth, 188, 216, 217, 218, 220, 237 n. 46
Bennett, Jonathan, 258 n. 5
Bentham, Jeremy, *129,* 260-64, *267, 272,* 276, 278
Berelson, Bernard, 209 n. 4
Bergmann, Gustav, 193 n. 9
Bergson, Henri, 56 n. 9

Berkeley, Bishop George, 31, 35 n. 12, 123, 124
Berlin, Isaiah, 84, 95 n. 4, *192,* 193 n. 4, 195
Bernheim, Ernst, 83 n. 4
Bidney, David, 211 n. 19
Black, Cyril E., 138-39, *141 n,* 144 n. 27
Blakey, Robert, 287 n. 41
Bloch, Marc, 134-35, 140, 144 n: 26
Blumenbach, Johann F., 297, 299
Blumenfeld, David, 19 n. 7
Blumenfeld, Jean B., 19 n. 7
Boas, Franz, 234 n. 15
Bory de Saint-Vincent, 305 n. 61
Boucher de Perthes, 299
Boyle, Robert, 289
Bradley, F. H., 56 n. 9
Brandt, R. B., 278, 284 n. 4, 287 n. 47
Braudel, Fernand, 141 n. 1
Bredemeier, Harry C., 233 n. 3
Brewster, David, 310
Brewster, Edwin T., 303 n. 2
Brinton, Crane, 136
Broad, C. D., vii, 56 n. 5, 65-66, 70 n. 3, 82, 122-23, 168 n. 6, *171*
Brodbeck, May, 193 nn. 2, 4, 9
Brown, J. F., 210 n. 13
Brown, Robert, 233 n. 2
Brucker, Jacob, 120
Brunswik, Egon, 170 n. 17
Buckle, Thomas, 294
Buffon, G.-L., Comte de, 118 n. 4, 292, 294, 302, 304 n. 27, 305 n. 69, 306 n. 75
Bulwer, E. L., 268 n. 7, 286 n. 21
Burckhardt, Jacob, 97, 98, 99, 100, 111 n. 3
Burlingame, L. J., 117 n. 4
Burnet, Thomas, 290
Butler, Bishop Joseph, *129,* 262

Cabanis, P.-J. G., 304 n. 24
Campbell, Donald T., 168 n. 1
Candolle, Alphonse de, 321 n. 68

Cantril, Hadley, 210 n. 12
Chambers, Robert, 290, 297, 298, 306 n. 69
Chisholm, Roderick, 176
Church, Ralph W., 258 n. 5
Cohen, Gerald A., 247-50
Cohen, Morris R., vii, 64, 70 n
Collingwood, R. G., 84
Comte, Auguste, 74, 106, 132, 134, 136, 142
    n. 3, 144 n. 28, 186, 190, 210 n. 11, 285 n. 15,
    318 n. 24
Condillac, Etienne Bonnot de, 304 n. 23
Croce, Benedetto, 84, 97, 106, 109
Crutchfield, Richard, 210 n. 13
Cutler, Preston, 209 n. 4
Cuvier, Georges, Baron, 290, 295, 297, 298,
    299, 305 n. 48, 306 n. 71, 311

Danto, Arthur, 95 n. 2, 102
Darwin, Charles, ix, 39, 40, 114, 214, 244, 247,
    248-50, 289-303 passim, 307-21
Darwin, Francis, 307, 318 nn. 11, 13, 17
Davidson, Donald, 57 n. 19
Davis, Kingsley, 233 n. 3
Delacroix, Eugène, 34 n. 6
della Volpe, G., 258 n. 5
Descartes, René, 3-6, 7, 8, 15-16, 16, 17, 20
    n. 20, 25, 35 n. 12, 121, 123, 124, 156, 258 n. 7
Dewey, John, 39-40, 41, 42, 210 n. 7
Diderot, Denis, 304 n. 23
Dilthey, Wilhelm, 46, 106
Diogenes Laërtius, 120
Donagan, Alan, 84, 88, 209 n. 3, 210 n. 14
Doney, Willis, 129 n
Dore, Ronald P., 233 n. 3
Dray, William, 84, 85-86, 88, 89, 90, 92-93, 94,
    95 n. 3, 96 n. 11, 230, 239 n. 62
Ducasse, C. J., vii
Duhem, Pierre, 33 n, 46, 55
Durkheim, Emile, 82, 135, 195, 211 n. 21, 216,
    223, 235 n. 23, 244

Edel, Abraham, 70 n. 1
Emmet, Dorothy, 233 n. 2, 239 n. 60
Ermarth, Michael, 111 n. 9

Falconer, Hugh, 299
Fechner, Gustav, 211 n. 15
Firth, Raymond, 215, 232 n, 235 n. 21, 243,
    244
Firth, Roderick, 183 n. 4
Flew, Anthony, 258 n. 5
Fortes, Meyer, 235 n. 21

Frazer, James G., 133, 215, 234 n. 17
Frye, Northrop, 104

Galileo, 114
Gallie, W. B., 96 n. 10, 102
Gardiner, Patrick, 84, 86, 95 n. 3
Gay, Peter, 141 n
Geiger, Moritz, viii
Gellner, E. A., 193 n. 4, 194 n. 21
Genovese, Eugene D., 143 n. 13
Gillispie, C. C., 117 n. 4, 290, 303 n. 2, 304
    n. 16, 305 n. 52, 306 n. 71
Ginsberg, Morris, 193 n. 4
Gluckman, Max, 239 n. 62
Godwin, William, 306 n. 77
Goldstein, Leon J., 193 nn. 4, 9, 234 n. 17
Gottschalk, Louis, 141 n. 2
Graebner, Fritz, 215
Gray, Asa, 310, 313, 314, 315, 316, 317
Green, T. H., 258 n. 5
Greene, John C., 118 n. 4
Guyenot, E., 303 n. 8

Haeckel, Ernst, 304 n. 43, 305 n. 56
Haines, George, IV, 56 n. 8
Hall, E. W., 284 n. 2
Hallam, George W., 320 n. 44
Hamilton, William, 261
Hanson, N. R., 47, 48, 58 n. 29, 119 n. 10
Harding, Thomas G., 142 n. 3
Hartley, David, 262
Harvey, William, 305 n. 56
Hayek, F. A., 96 n. 6, 184, 186, 193 n. 7, 195
Hegel, G.W.F., 7, 74, 97, 106, 109, 122, 129,
    186, 190
Helvétius, Claude, 269 n. 19
Hempel, Carl G., 70 n. 3, 84, 86-91, 93, 94,
    95 n. 3, 96 n. 14, 232 n, 232 n. 2, 233 n. 4,
    240 n. 63
Hendel, C. W., 258 n. 5
Henle, Paul, 70 n. 4
Henslow, John Stevens, 317 n. 4
Heracleitus, 120
Herard, H. B., 210 n. 13
Herder, J. G., 128, 129, 194 n. 16
Herschel, John, 310, 312, 313, 314
Herskovits, Melville J., 82, 211 n. 19
Hobart, R. E., 258 n. 3
Hobbes, Thomas, 6, 35 n. 12, 129
Hodge, M.J.S., 117 n. 4
Hofstader, Albert, 157 n. 4
Hogbin, H. L., 215, 219

Hollinger, David A., 118 n. 8
Homans, George C., 233 n. 3, 241-45
Hooke, Robert, 280
Hooker, Joseph D., 296, *304 n. 34*, 320 n. 58
Hull, Clark, 161, 169 nn. 9, 15, 209 n. 4
Humboldt, Alexander, 298, 302, 306 n. 75
Hume, David, viii, ix, 7-9, 10-11, 19 n. 9, 28, 31, 35 n. 13, 47, 123, 124, *129*, 253-57, 306 n. 77
Hutcheson, Francis, *129*
Huxley, T. H., 258 n. 5, 297, *317 n. 1*, 318 nn. 1, 24, 320 n. 44

James, William, 16, 18, 19 n. 13, 21 nn. 25, 30, 32, 33, *58 n. 25, 116*, 123, 210 n. 7
Jenyns, Leonard, 317 n. 4
Jones, E. E., 210 n. 13
Judd, John J., 304 n. 29, 306 n. 75

Kahn, Robert L., 210 n. 13, 211 n. 18
Kant, Immanuel, 16, 17, 120, *121, 122*, 123, *129*, 280
Kaplan, Abraham, 83 n. 8
Kaplan, David, 142 n. 3
Kardiner, Abraham, 82
Karpf, F. B., 210 n. 8
Katz, Daniel, 210 n. 13, 211 n. 18
Katz, David, 20 n. 15, 169 n. 14
Kellogg, L. A., 199
Kellogg, W. N., 199
Kepler, Johannes, 114
Kingsley, Charles, 310, 317 n. 4, 319 n. 33
Köhler, Wolfgang, viii, 62, 63 n, 116
Koffka, Kurt, 116, 159, 196
Krech, David, 210 n. 13
Kristeller, Paul O., 95 n. 2
Kroeber, Alfred, 82, 212 n. 26
Kuhn, T. S., 37, 48, 50-55, 58 n. 25, 112-17

Lacépède, B.G.E., Comte de, 292
Laing, B. M., 258 nn. 2, 5
Laird, John, 258 nn. 5, 7, 11
Lamarck, Chevalier de, 113, 118 n. 4, 249-50, 292, 292-95, 295, 297, 298, 299, 302, 305 n. 69, 306 n. 73
Lasswell, Harold, 83 n. 8
Lawrence, William, 299, 300
Leach, E. R., 235 n. 17
Leeuwenhoek, Anton van, 301
Leibniz, G. W., 35 n. 12, *121*, 123, 124
Leroy, A.-L., 258 n. 5
Levy, Marion J., 233 n. 3

Lewes, G. H., 70 n. 3, 271 n. 41
Lewis, C. I., *176*
Lindsay, A. D., 261, 269 n. 17
Linnaeus, C., 118 n. 4, 291, 292, 296, 297, 299
Locke, John, ix, 47, *121*, 123, 124, *294, 304 n. 23*
Lovejoy, A. O., 43, 56 n. 6, 64, 70 n. 6, 183 n. 5, 303 nn. 1, 12
Lowie, R. H., 234 n. 10, 236 n. 29
Lubbock, John, 299
Lyell, Charles, 280, 292, 296, 297, 298, 299, 300, 302, 304 nn. 34, 40, 306 n. 75, 308, 309, 310, 313, 315, 316, 317, 318 n. 27

Mabbott, J. D., 283 n. 1, 284 n. 6
McConnell, Donald W., 96 n. 8
McDougall, William, 159, 196-97, 197, 199, 210 n. 13, 223
McGilvary, E. B., 42-44, 56 n. 4
Mach, Ernst, 35 n. 13, 46, 55
Machlup, Fritz, 193 n. 5
MacNabb, D.G.C., 258 n. 5
Maier, Charles S., 144 n. 27
Maitland, F. W., 95 n. 4, 106
Malinowski, Bronislaw, 82, *174*, 194 n. 13, 214, 214-21, 222-23, 225, 227-29, 229-32, 233 n. 3, 236 n. 27, 237 n. 46
Malthus, Thomas, 114, 301, 302, 318 n. 13
Mannheim, Karl, 44, 105
Marquis, Donald G., 209 n. 4
Marx, Karl, 97, 106, 109, 132, 142 n. 3, 186, 188, 189, 247-50
Maund, C., 258 n. 5
Maupertuis, P.-L. M. de, 311
Mead, G. H., 44, 56 n. 9, 210 n. 14
Mead, Margaret, 236 n. 27
Meckel, Johann F., 301, 305 nn. 56, 69
Meinong, A., 258 n. 5
Merton, Robert K., 82, 232 n. 1, 233 n. 3
Metz, Rudolf, 258 n. 5
Michelangelo, B., *34 n. 6*
Michelet, Jules, 97, 98, 99, 100
Michotte, A. E., 258 n. 9
Mill, James, *20 n. 16*, 269 n. 11, 270 n. 23, 284 n. 7, *287 n. 45*
Mill, John Stuart, ix, 20 n. 16, 61, 63 n, 70 n. 3, 106, 259-71, 272-88
Miller, Hugh, 291, 297, 298, 306 n. 71
Miller, J. G., 209 n. 4
Mommsen, Wolfgang J., 57 n. 21
Mondrian, Piet, *34 n. 6*
Montaigne, Michel, 128
Moore, Barrington, 143 n. 10, 144 n. 25

Moore, G. E., 125, 272
Moore, Omar K., 211 n. 19
Morgan, Lewis H., 132
Morgenbesser, Sidney, 232 n. 2
Muenzinger, K. F., 170 n. 17
Murdock, George P., 142 n. 8, 190
Murphy, Arthur E., 39, 56 n. 4
Murphy, Murray, 22 n. 32
Murphy, Robert F., 142 n. 3
Murray, J., *309*

Nadel, S. F., 82
Nagel, Ernest, 70 n, 95 n. 4, 213, 232 n, 239
    n. 60, 240 n. 65
Needham, Rodney, 245 n. 1
Neisser, Ulric, 170 n. 19, 213
Newman, Cardinal J. H., 19 n. 11
Newton, Isaac, 128, 129, 289, *294,* 310
Niebuhr, B. G., 106
Niebuhr, Reinhold, 75, 81, 83 n. 1, 111 n. 4
Nietzsche, Friedrich, 97, 106, 109
Nordenskiöld, E., 303 n. 9
Nowell-Smith, Patrick, 84, 96 n. 9

Oakeshott, Michael, 84
Oppenheim, Paul, 70 n. 3
Owen, Richard, 297, 318 n. 27
Owen, Robert, 306 n. 77

Packard, Alpheus S., 303 n. 16
Paley, William, 307-8, 309
Palmer, Richard E., 57 n. 20
Palmer, Robert R., 135, 138, 144 n. 25
Parmenides, *120*
Parsons, Talcott, 82, 233 n. 3
Passmore, John, 95 n. 1, 96 n. 11, 258 n. 5
Peirce, C. S., 3, 21 n. 32
Pepper, Stephen, 104, 111 n. 8
Perrier, E., 303 n. 6
Perry, Ralph B., vii
Pitt, Jack, 96 n. 13
Planck, Max, 51
Plato, *120, 122*
Poincaré, Henri, 46, 55
Popkin, Richard, 258 n. 5
Popper, Karl, 84, 184, 186, *192,* 195
Postman, Leo, *170 n. 17*
Price, H. H., 18 n. 1, 19 n. 11, 258 n. 5
Prichard, James C., 299, 300
Pythagoras, *120*

Quine, W. V., 21 n. 31, 33 n, 46, 59 n. 47

Radcliffe-Brown, A. G., 82, 188, 214, 216, 221,
    221-29, 229-32, 233 n. 3, 234 nn. 13, 17, 235
    n. 17, 243-44
Radl, E., 303 n. 12
Randall, John H., Jr., 41-42, 56 n. 7, 57 n. 18
Ranke, Leopold von, 97, 98, 99, 100, 111 n. 3
Ratzel, Friedrich, 215
Rawls, John, 276, 285 nn. 10, 13
Ray, John, 290, 291
Reis, Lincoln, 95 n. 2
Renan, Joseph Ernest, 142 n. 7
Richards, Audrey, 235 nn. 17, 22
Rickert, Heinrich, 83 n, 106
Rivers, W.H.R., 215
Rorty, Richard, 37
Ross, E. A., 196, 197
Rousseau, J.-J., 128, 129, 306 n. 77
Rudolphi, Karl, 305 nn. 56, 61
Russell, Bertrand, vii
Rustow, Dankwart A., 144 n. 23
Ryle, Gilbert, viii, 150-57, *168*

Sahlins, Marshall D., 142 n. 3
Saint-Hilaire, Geoffroy de, 292, 298, *305 n. 69*
Schaefer, Alfred, 258 n. 5
Scheffler, Israel, 58 n. 22, 232 n. 2
Scheler, Max F., viii
Schleiermacher, F., 46
Schmidt, Wilhelm, 215
Schneider, David M., 241-45
Schneider, H. W., 319 n. 32
Schumpeter, Joseph, 184
Sedgwick, Adam, 263, 279, 298, *305 n. 52, 306*
    n. 71
Serres, Marcel Pierre, 305 n. 69
Service, Elmer R., 142 n. 3
Shand, Alexander, 223, 235 n. 21
Sheard, N. B., 169 n. 14
Sherif, C. W., 210 n. 13
Sherif, M., 210 n. 13
Sidgwick, Henry, *129,* 268 n. 4, 288 n. 47
Skinner, B. F., 161, *165,* 165-67
Smart, J.J.C., 283 n. 1
Smith, Adam, 261
Smith, G. Elliot, 215
Smith, N. K., 258 n. 5
Smith, Tony, 143 n. 13
Spencer, Herbert, 74, 106, 119 n. 10, 132, 134,
    142 n. 3, 144 n. 28, 320 n. 65
Spengler, Oswald, 74, 106, 136
Spinoza, Benedict, 6-7, 11, 19 n. 11, *122,* 124
Steward, Julian H., 142 n. 3

Stratton, George M., 119 n. 10
Sumner, W. G., 273
Swammerdam, Jan, 301

Tarde, Gabriel, 210 n. 7
Taylor, Helen, 269 n. 11
Theophrastus, 120
Tiedemann, Friedrich, 305 n. 56
Tilly, Charles, 139, 144 nn. 22, 27
Tilly, Louise, 139, 144 n. 27
Tilly, Richard, 139, 144 n. 27
Tocqueville, Alexis de, 97, 98, 99, 100
Tolman, E. C., 160, 162-63, 163-64, *164, 165*
Toynbee, Arnold, 74, 136, 194 n. 11
Troeltsch, Ernst, 106
Tyler, Ralph W., 209 n. 4
Tylor, E. B., 133, 190, 206, 214

Urmson, J. O., 268 nn. 3, 4, 272-74, 279, 285
    nn. 11, 12

Vico, G. B., 107
Viner, Jacob, 121
Virey, Julien-Joseph, 299

Wallace, Alfred Russel, 114, 301, 305 n. 65,
    306 n. 70, 316
Wallace, Rev. Robert, 306 n. 77
Walsh, W. H., 84, 92

Ward, Robert E., 144 n. 23
Ward, W. G., 284 n. 7
Warner, R. Stephen, 143 n. 16
Warnock, Mary, 269 n. 19
Watkins, J.W.N., 185, 195, 209 n. 3
Watson, J. B., 159-62, 163-64, *164, 165, 166*
Weber, Max, 137-38
Wellman, Carl, 284 n. 2
Wertheimer, Max, 116
Westermarck, Edward A., 133, 215
Whewell, William, 268 n. 7, 269 n. 10, 280,
    287 n. 40, 303 n. 9, 309, 311, 318 n. 17
Whiston, William, 290
White, Hayden, 97-110
Whitehead, Alfred N., 42
Whorf, Benjamin L., 37, 47, 48-50, 55
Wiesner, B. P., 169 n. 14
Wilbanks, J., 258 n. 5
Williams, Bernard, 4
Wilson, Margaret D., *129 n*
Winch, Peter, 211 n. 17
Wiseman, Nicholas, 298, *305 n. 62*
Wittgenstein, Ludwig, 3, 37, 47, *119 n. 10, 158,*
    164, 168, 200
Wolff, C. F., 301, *305 n. 69*
Woodward, C. Vann, 144 n. 29
Woodward, John, 290

Zabeeh, F., 258 n. 5
Zilsel, Edgar, 193 n. 9